ALSO BY JOHN ASHBERY

POETRY

Turandot and Other Poems

Some Trees

The Tennis Court Oath

Rivers and Mountains

The Double Dream of Spring

Three Poems

The Vermont Notebook

Self-Portrait in a Convex Mirror

Houseboat Days

As We Know

Shadow Train

A Wave

Selected Poems

April Galleons

Flow Chart

Hotel Lautréamont

And the Stars Were Shining

Can You Hear, Bird

Wakefulness

The Mooring of Starting Out: The First Five Books of Poetry

Girls on the Run

Your Name Here

As Umbrellas Follow Rain

Chinese Whispers

Where Shall I Wander

A Worldly Country

Notes from the Air: Selected Later Poems

Collected Poems, 1956–1987 (edited by Mark Ford)

Planisphere

Quick Question

FICTION

A Nest of Ninnies (with James Schuyler)

PLAYS

Three Plays

ESSAYS AND TRANSLATIONS

Reported Sightings: Art Chronicles, 1957–1987

Other Traditions (The Charles Eliot Norton Lectures)

Selected Prose

Pierre Martory, *The Landscapist: Selected Poems*

Arthur Rimbaud, *Illuminations*

Collected French Translations: Poetry (edited by Rosanne Wasserman and Eugene Richie)

COLLECTED FRENCH TRANSLATIONS

Prose

JOHN ASHBERY

COLLECTED FRENCH TRANSLATIONS

Prose

EDITED BY ROSANNE WASSERMAN

AND EUGENE RICHIE

FARRAR, STRAUS AND GIROUX   NEW YORK

Farrar, Straus and Giroux
18 West 18th Street, New York 10011

Owing to limitations of space, all acknowledgments for permission to reprint previously
published and unpublished material can be found on pages 397–398.

Library of Congress Cataloging-in-Publication Data
Collected French Translations : Prose / [translated by] John Ashbery ; edited by
Rosanne Wasserman and Eugene Richie. — First edition.
    pages   cm
Includes bibliographical references.
ISBN 978-0-374-25803-0 (hardcover)
    1. French prose literature—Translations into English.   I. Ashbery, John, 1927–
translator.   II. Wasserman, Rosanne, 1952– editor of compilation.   III. Richie, Eugene,
editor of compilation.

PQ1278 .C65 2014
844—dc23

2013033017

Designed by Jonathan D. Lippincott

www.fsgbooks.com
www.twitter.com/fsgbooks • www.facebook.com/fsgbooks

1   3   5   7   9   10   8   6   4   2

Jacket art: Details of collages by John Ashbery: *Moon Glow*, 2008 (16 × 16 ¼ in.);
Chutes and Ladders III (For David Kermani), 2008 (18 ½ × 18 ⅜ in.); *Mannerist Concerns*,
2008 (16 ⅜ × 16 ½ in.). Courtesy of Tibor de Nagy Gallery, New York.

For Anne Dunn

CONTENTS

"CURIOUS RESEMBLANCES": JOHN ASHBERY TRANSLATES FRENCH PROSE

Introduction by Rosanne Wasserman and Eugene Richie

John Ashbery's *Collected French Translations* are gathered into two volumes. This volume presents a selection of English translations of twenty-eight prose pieces composed by seventeen writers: not only masters of fiction, but also poets, playwrights, artists, musicians, and critics. The other volume is a bilingual collection of 171 poems written by twenty-four poets. Both volumes offer published translations long unavailable, as well as some previously unpublished works. As we identified, located, and edited these selections, Ashbery has guided our choices and helped us find materials. Each volume offers unique opportunities for insight into the wide and varied scope of French cultural influence on Ashbery's work, over the decades of his productive and resonant career. This influence appears not only in his own poetry, but also in his responses to visual art, music, and cinema. Encountering these translations will open, for interested readers and scholars alike, windows into Ashbery's relationship with many well-known French writers, artists, and cultural figures. Both volumes will also introduce several unfamiliar voices from the vast canon of French literature, writers who have been given special attention here by one of our most distinguished American poets.

We have included here all of the fiction that Ashbery has translated and published before, but we have selected the essays, choosing, for example, among pieces from a large group of articles originally published in *Art and Literature* and *ARTnews*. In addition, some of Ashbery's translations of Raymond Roussel remain in manuscript in the Ashbery Resource Center archives of the Flow Chart Foundation; these pieces are currently being prepared for publication by Ava Lehrer. And, most recently, Ashbery has translated the prose piece by Pierre Martory included here—the introduction to a 1954 French translation of Henry James's *Washington Square*.

The French originals that Ashbery used for these translations came from libraries, bookstores, his own and his friends' collections, and manuscripts; also, some pieces were given or assigned to him when he was asked to translate works. Due to considerations of length, this volume is not bilingual. However, many of the original French prose works are currently quite easily available, if a reader wishes to explore further. The Appendix offers a chronology of the first publication dates of every translation in the two volumes, as an aid to scholars who might want to compare Ashbery's translation work with the publication dates of his own poetry and prose. In addition, full bibliographical information about the English translations and any reprints appears at the end of each author's selection. We have consistently used for this book only the latest of Ashbery's available drafts of any published or unpublished translation.[1]

Ashbery and French

Ashbery's engagement with the French language and its literature spans nearly eighty years.[2] As a child in upstate New York, Ashbery read French fairy tales in English, including the masterworks of Charles Perrault, and among his earliest encounters with French itself were entries in a children's encyclopedia, the 1923 edition of *The Book of Knowledge*. He had a glimpse into the lives of Europeanized Americans through his grandfather Henry Lawrence's cousins, Paul and Lillian Holling. These siblings lived for decades in France and England, sending letters to the Ashbery household and fascinating gifts to the little boy. They had returned to the United States briefly in 1929, then repatriated to the family hometown in Pultneyville, New York, in advance of World War II.[3] The

---

1. For information about the published translations, we have relied primarily on David Kermani's annotated bibliography of the poet's early work: David K. Kermani, *John Ashbery: A Comprehensive Bibliography* (New York: Garland Publishing, 1976). We have also used the annotated searchable catalogue of the Ashbery Resource Center archive (www.flowchartfoundation.org/arc/home/catalogue/).

2. The introduction that follows is in part abridged from the introduction in *Collected French Translations, Volume 1: Poetry*, but also offers other insights, particularly into Ashbery's encounters with French prose. For a more detailed chronological discussion of his life and work within the French language and its literature, please see the poetry volume.

3. Thanks to John Ashbery, David Kermani, and Karin Roffman for these and following details, from private conversations, January 1 and 2, 2012.

worlds that these stories, books, and associations invoked stayed with him throughout his life, creating a sense of French literature as "a place of romance and pageantry, and all the things one wants"[4]—an enraptured description of his choices in these volumes, spanning centuries from Marie-Catherine d'Aulnoy's magical story "The White Cat" to the synchronic, cinematic poetries of Pascalle Monnier.

Even in his teens, Ashbery's French-language skills were impressive. His cousin Paul Holling's sometimes off-color French books were not too advanced for the precocious adolescent. At fifteen, he writes in his diary, on May 15, 1943, after spending an evening at a neighbor's house, which had belonged to the Hollings and which still housed some of Paul's European possessions: "I was over there tonight . . . reading Chansons de Bilitis in the French. Nana said, 'Wouldn't the Hollings be pleased if they knew you could read French Novels!' I felt like answering: 'Not if they knew the ones I pick out to read.' "[5] He also resorted to recording his more private experiences in French, which his mother, Helen, who was apt to look at his correspondence and diary, could not read; sometimes, to disguise cognates, he abbreviated French words or used puns to throw her even further off track. Clearly, the older generation never found him out: He duly records in his diary on July 28, 1943, that for his sixteenth birthday, his parents gave him a French dictionary.

Ashbery studied French as soon as he could, rapidly excelling in classes and exams at his upstate New York high school. In 1945, his first year at Harvard, he again took classes in French, as well as a course in elementary Italian; Harvard's Houghton Library houses his notes, in French, for these classes. Later, during the summer of 1948, between his junior and senior years, he began to read Marcel Proust in translation, in preparation for a September course with Harry Levin: "Proust, Joyce, and Mann."[6]

As an undergraduate at Harvard, he never abandoned his childhood program of learning on his own, choosing what he loved and what most interested him from whatever venues were available,[7] building an eccentric and personal canon. The movies of Jean Cocteau were among

---

4. Ashbery, "John Ashbery," *Bookworm*, KCRW, interview by Michael Silverblatt, May 21, 2009, www.kcrw.com/etc/programs/bw/bw090521john_ashbery.

5. Ashbery, unpublished diaries, transcribed by Karin Roffman, e-mail of January 3, 2012.

6. Roffman, conversation; Ashbery, "John Ashbery," *Bookworm*; Ashbery, conversation.

7. For details on Ashbery's self-education as recorded in his childhood diaries, see Karin Roffman, "The Art of Self-Education in John Ashbery's Childhood Diaries," *Raritan: A Quarterly Review* 30, no. 4 (Spring 2011), 94–116.

his favorites, and he returned to movie theaters repeatedly to watch the 1950 film *Orpheus*, enchanted with the car radio that broadcasts surreal poetry by Cégeste in Hades, and with Jean Marais's portrayal of Orpheus. As he told a student journalist at Bard College,

> I've often been struck by a line from the Cocteau movie *Orpheus*. He was being examined by these three sinister judges, and one of them says, "What do you do," and [Orpheus] says, "I am a poet," and the judge says, "What does that mean?" to which Orpheus replies, "It's to write and not be a writer."[8]

During his college and graduate school years, he began also to read writers whom he has called "fringe" Surrealists, such as Pierre Reverdy,[9] Guillaume Apollinaire, Max Jacob, and Raymond Roussel.[10] "We all 'grew up Surrealist,'" Ashbery has claimed.[11] Even as a child, he immediately identified with the Surrealist paintings that he saw in a *Life* magazine article reviewing the Museum of Modern Art's 1936 blockbuster "Fantastic Art, Dada and Surrealism" show;[12] and he wondered "why there couldn't be something like that in poetry."[13] At the same time, he was taking art classes at the Memorial Art Gallery in Rochester. This interface of art and poetry continued throughout his creative and working life: Certainly, Ashbery's "derivation of a painterly poetics from a French tradition"[14] owes a deep debt to his years (1960–1965) of writing art criticism in Paris for the *International Herald-Tribune*.

As a Fulbright scholar from 1955 to 1957, Ashbery lived first for a month in Paris, then took classes in Montpellier, and finally worked as a teaching fellow in Rennes, escaping to Paris as often as he could. Continuing to live in Paris after his Fulbright, he began writing as an art

8. John Englert, "John Ashbery: Bard's 'Literalist of the Imagination,'" *The Bard Observer*, May 17, 1991, 7, inside.bard.edu/campus/publications/archive/pdfs/OB91_05_17.pdf.

9. Ashbery, "Obituary for Pierre Martory," *Selected Prose*, ed. Eugene Richie (Ann Arbor: University of Michigan Press, 2004; Manchester, U.K.: Carcanet, 2004), 270.

10. Ashbery, "Appearing on Belgische Radio en Televisie, Brussels (date unknown)," interview, *Pennsound*, accessed December 2, 2011, writing.upenn.edu/pennsound/x/Ashbery.php.

11. Ashbery, "Growing Up Surreal," *ARTnews* 67, no. 3, May 1968, 41.

12. "I think that it was at that moment I realized I wanted to be a Surrealist, or rather that I already was one," as Ashbery says in his 1995 "Robert Frost Medal Address," *Selected Prose*, 246.

13. Ashbery, "John Ashbery," *Bookworm*.

14. David LeHardy Sweet, *Savage Sight/Constructed Noise: Poetic Adaptations of Painterly Techniques in the French and American Avant-Gardes*, North Carolina Studies in the Romance Languages and Literatures, no. 276 (Chapel Hill: University of North Carolina Press, 2003), 231.

critic for the *International Herald-Tribune* in 1960. This journalism, as Jed Perl notes, discussing *Reported Sightings*, gave the poet a chance to inscribe his visions not only of artworks but of Paris itself:

> Introducing a Toulouse-Lautrec show, he remarks, "The crowd waiting in the rain outside the Petit Palais museum in Paris rivaled the one queueing up for the latest Alain Delon movie on the Champs-Élysées." The Petit Palais, the movie theater on the Champs-Élysées, the long lines of people, the dark-haired movie star, and the dwarfish fin de siècle painter somehow come together to paint a little portrait of Paris in 1964—and the portrait has a staying power.[15]

At the same time, he undertook editorships of important art and literature journals, all of which kept him focused on translations, not only of poetry and fiction, but also of articles about artists. As coeditor of the journals *Locus Solus* and *Art and Literature*, he was able to cast a wider net. Since he was responsible for getting issues together and to the printer, some of these translations were done primarily to fill up the pages of an issue. But these years were particularly productive in his canon-building. In *Art and Literature*, he published translations from the poetry and prose of Jacob, Antonin Artaud, Georges Bataille, Michel Leiris, and Marcelin Pleynet; as well as pieces by artists Odilon Redon, Giorgio de Chirico, and Jean Hélion, and by the composer Iannis Xenakis. While Ashbery's engagement with Roussel is widely familiar, it may be a surprise to readers of this volume to find the tour-de-force of Reverdy's *Haunted House*, reprinted here in its entirety,[16] or passages from the Surrealist painter de Chirico's novel *Hebdomeros*, which, as Ashbery has told us, he was reading for the first time while on the SS *France* en route to Le Havre in 1964. "It was so amazing," he says; "I had never read anything like it before."

Like Arthur Rimbaud's writing, the idiosyncratic prose and poetry of the then-little-known author Raymond Roussel attracted the young American poet, in particular because of what Ashbery calls "the very striking absence of the author from his work."[17] Once Kenneth Koch had

---

15. Jed Perl, "A Magically Alive Aesthetic," *Conjunctions* 49 (2007), "John Ashbery Tribute," ed. Peter Gizzi and Bradford Morrow, 366.

16. Pierre Reverdy, *Haunted House*, trans. Ashbery (Brooklyn, N.Y.: Black Square Editions and the Brooklyn Rail, 2007).

17. Ashbery, "Appearing on Belgische Radio."

brought Roussel's work to his attention, Ashbery researched it through-out France in the late 1950s, hunting down Rousselian materials for a possible doctoral dissertation in French literature at New York Univer-sity.[18] In fact, David Lehman describes how, in a 1956 letter to Koch, Ashbery joked about his enthusiasm for Roussel at the expense of other French writers:

> One of the funniest moments in Ashbery's Paris correspondence with Kenneth Koch occurs in an undated letter from 1956 whose salutation is "Dear Montcalm." "I hate all modern French poetry, except for Raymond Roussel," Ashbery proclaims. "Molière, Ra-cine, and La Fontaine are the only truly modern French poets. I do like my own wildly inaccurate translations of some of the twentieth-century ones, but not the originals."[19]

Ashbery is characteristically modest here about the success of his own hard work, while revealing the excitement he feels about the possibilities of translation. His claiming of three seventeenth-century writers as mod-erns clearly demonstrates how thoroughly grounded he felt in the French tradition, as well as the extent to which he recognized Roussel's work as growing essentially from that same ground.

Another source for prose-poetry style was de Chirico's writing; as the poet David Shapiro describes,

> Ashbery was admittedly moved by the interminable digressions and flourishes of de Chirico, whose prose tends to burst out in terribly long sentences that go on for pages, and whose novels have but one character. The skena may change several times in de Chirico's sentences, as in Ashbery's, and the course of this sen-tence is as a cinematic flow.[20]

Ashbery's later translations included many longer works, such as the won-derful fairy tale "The White Cat" by d'Aulnoy, which opens the prose collection here. During his Paris decade, 1955–1965, Ashbery met the

---

18. See, e.g., Ashbery, "Introduction to Raymond Roussel's 'In Havana,'" *Selected Prose*, 54.

19. David Lehman, *The Last Avant-Garde: The Making of the New York School of Poets* (New York: Dou-bleday, 1998), 126, 219n.

20. David Shapiro, *John Ashbery: An Introduction to the Poetry* (New York: Columbia University Press, 1979), 29.

editors of the journal *Tel Quel* and the members of its circle, with their interest in Lautréamont, Bataille, and Artaud. He also translated prose works by Artaud and Bataille, and sections of de Chirico's *Hebdomeros*. Among other prose pieces that drew his interest are writings by Henri Michaux and Alfred Jarry, as well as pieces by Roussel, Salvador Dalí, Pleynet, and Raymond Mason, which he would translate and publish in *ARTnews*.

In his preface to *Selected Prose*, Ashbery says that his many critical articles and reviews collected there and elsewhere are the "results of an activity that has always been something more than a hobby, if less than a calling."[21] But who can doubt that something was calling him, over and over, in French? The sheer quantity of Ashbery's translated texts, and the particularity of his choices, as reflected in this collection, permit Anglophone Ashberians to share his delight in the French authors whom he was called to translate, and reveal his dedication to a literature that he loves. The canon that Ashbery has built for over a half century, as he worked to develop a set of reference points, of tools to enhance the development of his own work and that of his friends, has opened American poetry and the arts to new methods and inspirations. Indeed, he has received significant honor as a French cultural ambassador, having been named by the French Ministry of Education and Culture a Chevalier de l'ordre des arts et des lettres in 1993, followed by induction in 2002 as Officier into the French Légion d'honneur. In 2011, he received the Medal of Honor from New York University's Center for French Civilization and Culture. Ashbery's commitment to French literature clearly deserves such recognition. His translations move American writers and readers closer to Wallace Stevens's concept that "French and English constitute a single language."[22] And, for those readers whose experience of French may be limited, he is a guide with exceptional taste and fresh perspective. As Micah Towery has asked, "Why do we want to read Ashbery's translations of Rimbaud? I see two motivations: The first is to read Rimbaud without learning French; the second is to read Ashbery reading Rimbaud."[23]

---

21. Ashbery, Preface to *Selected Prose*, v.

22. Wallace Stevens, "From *Adagia*," *Wallace Stevens: Collected Poetry and Prose*, ed. Frank Kermode and Joan Richardson (New York: Library of America, 1996), 914.

23. Micah Towery, "Google Translates Poetry," *THEthe poetry* (blog), December 5, 2011, www.thethepoetry .com/2011/12/google-translates-poetry/.

Ashbery and French Prose

As with his art criticism and many of the essays and reviews in his *Selected Prose*, Ashbery was often given pieces to translate through his work assignments, although he preferred to choose pieces because he liked someone's work and wanted to call attention to it. Nevertheless, not all of his translations were his own choices. As a paid professional in the early 1960s, he translated a scholarly study of Herman Melville by the Sorbonne professor Jean-Jacques Mayoux; unfortunately, the book had many uncited quotations from Melville translated into French, for which Ashbery had to locate the originals, forcing him to purchase many English-language works by Melville. He also put into English an essay on the modernist Swiss sculptor Alberto Giacometti by Jacques Dupin, the French poet and art critic, which is included in this collection. In fact, Ashbery relates that he once met Giacometti on a train from Basel, Switzerland, to Paris; a while after the artist had been seated across from him, Ashbery noticed that he was looking in his direction and sketching with his finger on the arm of his seat. Eventually, Ashbery spoke to him, and the two discussed Roussel, whom Giacometti greatly admired (after this brief conversation, however, the artist no longer sketched him).[24] The delights of Dupin's essay include quotations from Giacometti's evocative, poetic journals.

Furthermore, not all of Ashbery's paid translation work was literary: Dell once hired him to translate two pulp detective novels. He worked under a translator's pseudonym, Jonas Berry, which he used since its sound approximated the way the French pronounced his name. Of these books, *Champagne obligatoire* by Nöel Vexin (titled by Dell as *Murder in Montmartre*) and *La Biche* by Geneviève Manceron (*The Deadlier Sex*),[25] Ashbery says that he "was obliged" by the demands of Dell's American detective novel market "to add some soft-core sexy passages."[26] The poet had, not long before this job, just written his own detective-story spoof, his play *The Philosopher*.

---

24. Ashbery, private conversation.
25. Lehman has other details in *Last Avant-Garde*, 147.
26. Ashbery, "Contributor's Statement," special issue on "Poetry and Translation: Interchanges," *Mantis* 2 (2001): 45.

Ashbery and Translation

Asked by his interviewer Guy Bennett, "How would you define the re-
lationship between your own writing and the work you translate?" Ash-
bery answers, "Sometimes I see curious resemblances."[27] Locating lines
with clear influences and determining subtler forms of those resem-
blances in the vast body of Ashbery's work will be a task to keep his
readers occupied for many years.[28] Ashbery himself gives few precise
pointers; in interviews, in fact, he often denies having been influenced,
then offers a clue or two a moment later. He muses on this response
himself, in conversation with his friend the novelist and Oulipian Harry
Mathews:

> JA: People always ask me what influence my years in France had
> on my work. Of course I'm incapable of answering, but I've often
> felt that there really wasn't much influence, except that it's very
> nice to live in a beautiful, cultured city with very good food—
> surely this played an important part in it. But I never felt that
> French poetry, with a few exceptions—Roussel, Rimbaud, Lau-
> tréamont, etc. . . .
> HM: Reverdy, no?
> JA: Reverdy, yes, of course—were very influential. In fact, I'm not
> sure how influential any of them were. I admire them; they are
> very great writers. But except for a few fortuitious resemblances
> to Reverdy or Roussel, they don't seem to have influenced me
> directly.[29]

The word "directly" is, clearly, the crux of the matter. For example, in
response to a more direct question from Bennett—"Has your work as
a translator influenced the way you write poetry?"—Ashbery replies,
"Once in a while, but in ways I often don't notice right away and am un-
able to pinpoint." He does, however, reveal in this 2002 interview that, at

---

27. Guy Bennett and Béatrice Mousli, eds., *Charting the Here of There: French and American Poetry in Translation in Literary Magazines, 1850–2002* (New York: New York Public Library/Granary Books, in association), the Book Office of the Cultural Service of the French Embassy in the United States, 2002), 114.
28. Shapiro's *John Ashbery: An Introduction to the Poetry* is a good place to start.
29. "John Ashbery Interviewing Harry Mathews," *The Review of Contemporary Fiction* 7, no. 3 (Fall 1987), 44.

that time, he considered his most successful translations to be de Chirico's "Monsieur Dudron's Adventure" and Roussel's *Documents to Serve as an Outline.* Then he notes something about the Roussel work that sounds like an echo of one of his own poetic techniques: "The Roussel [translation] presented difficulties since he tried to express complicated things in as few words as possible, and pushed this method to extremes."[30] Ashbery's own poems supply copious examples of this technique, from the early poem "America" in *The Tennis Court Oath,* with its gaps in narrative—

> a hand put up
> lips—a house
> A minute the music stops.[31]

—to, years later, associative disjunctions like those in "Notes from the Air" from *Hotel Lautréamont:*

> A yak is a prehistoric cabbage: of that, at least, we may be sure.
> But tell us, sages of the solarium, why is that light
> still hidden back there, among house-plants and rubber sponges?[32]

Roussel is, says Ashbery, "one of the writers I enjoy reading most."[33] His many years of translating, introducing, and publishing the works of Roussel were especially rewarding, although any influence was often subtle. Douglas Crase points out that the 1962 poem "Into the Dusk-Charged Air," "with its Rousselian list of every river in the encyclopedia, was published in the same summer as his translation of the first chapter from Roussel's *Impressions of Africa.*"[34] Mark Ford asks him in 2003, "Do you think your Roussel research affected your own poetry? Were your experiments with words in this period a response to his *procédé?*" Ashbery replies,

> I don't know. I've often thought about that, and thought that there
> must be some influence—otherwise, why was I so passionately

30. Bennett, 114.
31. Ashbery, *Collected Poems 1956–1987,* ed. Mark Ford (New York: The Library of America, 2008), 48.
32. Ashbery, *Notes from the Air: Selected Later Poems* (New York: Ecco, 2007), 67.
33. Ashbery, "Appearing on Belgische Radio."
34. Douglas Crase, "The Prophetic Ashbery," in *John Ashbery,* Modern Critical Views, ed. Harold Bloom (New York: Chelsea House, 1985), 142.

interested in him? But I don't see much evidence of it—except in the digressions of *Nouvelles Impressions d'Afrique*, which in a much less visible way I use regularly.[35]

Moreover, Roussel's work touched chords in Ashbery that reflect his earliest encounters with studying the French language. Ford continues, referring to the artwork that accompanies Roussel's cantos, "How about the relationship between the banality of the illustrations by Zo in that book, and the difficulties the cantos themselves present? I often feel your work spans exactly those sorts of polarities," to which Ashbery answers, "Yes, I think that was what attracted me to Roussel even before I knew how to read him. These illustrations were exactly like the ones I had in a French reader when I was in high school, and the elaborate punctuation was like an exercise in a textbook."[36]

There are many other subtle examples of the French language's influence on Ashbery's work. In 1980, David Remnick asked Ashbery directly about the effects on his poetry from the process of translating: "You've translated from the French several authors like Breton and Roussel. Does translation affect your work in any way?"[37] Ashbery at first, as usual, questions any such influence, but then goes on to recall his experiences with de Chirico's *Hebdomeros*, "in which translation did work in an influential way":

> I found that the very curious style of this work got into my own work and would keep recurring long after I had done this translation. It was 1964, I think. When I go back and reread that book, I am aware that there are echoes of it even today in my poetry but I was never aware of those echoes while I was writing my poem.

Remnick pursues the question, saying, "Is it a particular tone or syntax in de Chirico?" Ashbery's response offers hints about his own work: "It's a slightly ironical, rhetorical tone. A very expansive tone. His sentences go on for pages in the novel and, in the course of them, very unexpected things will happen. Sudden shifts and inversions." Shapiro recognizes a

---

35. John Ashbery and Mark Ford, *John Ashbery in Conversation with Mark Ford* (London: Between the Lines, 2003), 45.
36. Ashbery and Ford, 45.
37. Ashbery, "John Ashbery: An Interview," interview by David Remnick, *Bennington Review* 8 (September 1980), 16.

direct influence from de Chirico in Ashbery's "The System," "felt most acutely in the long sentences with their interminable hyphenations and parentheses, leading only to *cul-de-sacs*."[38] Ashbery may also reference here the familiar sense of surprise and irony in his work, where a poem may contain reversals, inversions, or paradoxes, as in "April Galleons":

> Just being under them
> Sometimes makes you wonder how much you know
> And then you wake up and you know, but not
> How much.[39]

An early paradox reads, "*It had been raining but / It had not been raining*" (Ashbery's italics, from "A Boy," in *Some Trees*).[40] Similarly, he may finish a poem with an unexpected question, as in the lines "Why do I tell you these things? / You are not even here," from "This Room" in *Your Name Here*.[41]

One wonders at times whether these "curious resemblances" are simply what those with similar sensibilities naturally share, as they individually create lasting works of art and literature in a timeless, borderless dialogue with each other. Certainly, Ashbery has always had high expectations of the benefits a poet might gain by putting in the hard work of Englishing French texts. Reviewing Marianne Moore's book *Tell Me, Tell Me* in 1966, Ashbery finds a "new, tough simplicity" in her work that "might be a result of the discipline imposed by her La Fontaine translations": "Forced to avoid digressions and to keep syntax and verbal texture severely uncluttered, Miss Moore created a style whose tense, electric clarity is unlike anything in poetry except perhaps La Fontaine, and even this is debatable." [42] The miraculous result of this labor for Moore, and indeed for Ashbery, is another lovely oxymoron: Not only does translation transform a poet's original work, but also the poet can offer us

---

38. Shapiro, 154.

39. Ashbery, *Collected Poems*, 884.

40. Ashbery, *Collected Poems*, 9. Ashbery offers, with this kind of self-contradictory statement, a version of the philosophical puzzle known as G. E. Moore's paradox, a problem of logic considered by Ludwig Wittgenstein; see Ben Hickman, *John Ashbery and English Poetry* (Edinburgh: Edinburgh University Press, 2012), 27–53.

41. Ashbery, *Notes from the Air*, 249.

42. "Jerboas, Pelicans, and Peewee Reese: Marianne Moore," review of *Tell Me, Tell Me: Granite Steel, and Other Topics* (New York: Viking Press, 1964), from *Book Week* 4, no. 8 (October 20, 1966), in Ashbery, *Selected Prose*, 86.

translations "closer to the originals than the originals themselves," [43] as the intuitive, interpretive alchemy of translation enhances and deepens our sense of a text, bringing out the best of its original. One such example of the poet's instinct in action appears here in the translation of d'Aulnoy's seventeenth-century fairy tale "The White Cat." As Marina Warner notes, "John Ashbery's only liberty with the text" has been, when choosing a name for a magical parrot, to substitute "Sinbad" for "Perroquet." "As *The Arabian Nights* were soon to appear in Antoine Galland's influential translation (1704–17), Sinbad seems an apt anticipation." [44] A poet's liberties with a text should at best give it apt but fabulous wings.

"I don't think," Mathews stated in 1993, "John's intermittent career as translator has attracted the attention it deserves; it would, as they say, reward careful study, not just for the practice of translation itself but for the kind of literature translated, some of it unknown in English before." [45] We hope that attention to the canon circumscribed in his *Collected French Translations* will not only go a long way toward correcting that lacuna in Ashbery studies, but, on a much greater scale, will also help to balance what some observers have perceived as a parochialism in American letters. Such an attitude might be responsible for the statement of the permanent secretary of the Swedish Academy, Horace Engdahl, who reportedly once claimed, "The U.S. is too isolated, too insular. They don't translate enough and don't really participate in the big dialogue of literature." [46] No one who now reads these translations, which document a lifetime's participation in French literature, could ever mistake how fully Ashbery's American voice has resounded in that big dialogue. We hope that readers who visit and stay awhile here will enjoy these translations, finding many answers and asking fruitful new questions as they read Ashbery reading others.

---

43. Ashbery, *Selected Prose*, 86.

44. Marina Warner, Glossary, *Wonder Tales: Six French Stories of Enchantment* (New York: Farrar, Straus and Giroux, 1996), pp. 231–32.

45. Harry Mathews, "Introduction to a Reading by John Ashbery and Pierre Martory," Dia Center for the Arts, New York, October 5, 1993, unpublished typescript, Flow Chart Foundation, Hudson, N.Y.

46. Alison Flood, "Nobel Judge Attacks 'Ignorant' US Literature," *The Guardian* (October 1, 2008), www .guardian.co.uk/books/2008/oct/01/us.literature.insular.nobel.

COLLECTED FRENCH TRANSLATIONS

Prose

MARIE-CATHERINE D'AULNOY

(1650–1705)

THE WHITE CAT

There was once a king who had three sons, stout and courageous lads; he feared that the desire to reign might seize hold of them before his death; there were even rumors that they were seeking to acquire vassals, so as to deprive him of his kingdom. The king felt his age, yet he was still sound of mind and body, and by no means inclined to surrender a position he filled with much dignity; therefore he concluded that the best way to live in peace was to tease them with promises which he would always be able to avoid fulfilling.

He summoned them to his chamber, and after having spoken to them in a most kindly manner, he added: You will no doubt agree with me, dear children, that my advanced age no longer allows me to pursue affairs of state with the zeal of times gone by; I am afraid that my subjects may suffer because of this, and wish to place my crown on the head of one or another of you; but it is only right that, in view of such a prize, you seek various ways of pleasing me, even as I prepare my plans for retiring to go and live in the country. It seems to me that a little dog, one that is faithful, clever, and pretty, would keep me company very well; hence without choosing my eldest son, neither my youngest, I declare to you that whichever of you three brings me the most beautiful little dog will at once become my heir. The princes were surprised by their father's inclination to have a little dog, but the two younger ones might turn it to their advantage, and accepted with pleasure the commission to go look for one; the eldest was too timid or too respectful to argue his rights. They took leave of the king; he gave them money and jewels, stipulating that they return without fail in a year, on the same day and at the same hour, to bring him their little dogs.

Before setting out they traveled to a castle at only a league's distance from the city. They brought their closest confidants with them, and, amid much feasting, each brother swore eternal loyalty to the other two, that they would proceed to act without jealousy or bitterness, and that the most fortunate would always share his fortune with the others; finally they went away, promising that on their return they would foregather in the same castle before going together to meet their father; they wanted no one to accompany them, and changed their names so as not to be recognized.

Each journeyed by a different route: The two eldest had many adventures; but I am concerned only with those of the youngest. He was gracious, with a merry and witty temperament and a handsome mien; his body was nobly proportioned, his features regular, he had beautiful teeth, and much skill in all the activities that befit a prince. He sang agreeably; he plucked the lute and the theorbo with a delicate touch that people found charming. He knew how to paint; in a word, he was highly accomplished; and as for his valor, it verged on fearlessness.

Hardly a day passed without his buying dogs, big ones, little ones, greyhounds, mastiffs, bloodhounds, hunting dogs, spaniels, barbets, lapdogs; no sooner had he found a handsome one than he found one handsomer still, and parted with the first so as to keep the other; for it would have been impossible for him to travel with thirty or forty thousand dogs, and he wanted neither gentlemen-in-waiting, nor menservants, nor pages in his retinue. He kept pushing forward, with no idea of where he was going; suddenly he was overtaken by darkness, thunder, and rain, in a forest whose paths he could no longer distinguish.

He took the first road he came to, and after walking for a long time he spied a dim light, which convinced him that there must be a house nearby where he might take shelter until the morrow. Guided by the light, he arrived at the gate of a castle, the most magnificent one that could ever be imagined. The gate was made of gold, studded with carbuncles, whose pure and vivid glow illuminated the whole countryside. It was the one the prince had glimpsed from far away; the castle walls were of translucent porcelain in which various colors were mingled, and on which was depicted the history of all the fairies, from the creation of the world down to the present: The famous adventures of Peau d'Âne, of Finessa, of the Orange Tree, of Graciosa, of the Sleeping Beauty, of the Great Green Worm, and of a hundred others, were not omitted. He was delighted to recognize the Goblin Prince, for the latter was his first cousin once removed. The rain and the stormy weather prevented him from tarrying further while getting drenched to the bone, besides which he could see nothing at all in places where the light of the carbuncles didn't penetrate.

He returned to the golden gate; he saw a deer's hoof fastened to a chain made entirely of diamonds; he wondered at the negligence of those who lived in the castle; for, he said to himself, what is there to prevent thieves from coming to cut away the chain and rip out the carbuncles? They would be rich forever.

He pulled on the deer's hoof, and at once heard the tinkling of a bell, which must have been gold or silver judging from the tone; after a moment the door opened, but he saw naught but a dozen hands that floated in the air, each holding a torch. He was so astonished that he paused at the threshold, and then felt other hands pushing him from behind with some violence. He went forward in trepidation, and, as a precaution, placed his hand on the hilt of his sword; but on entering a vestibule all encrusted with porphyry and lapis, he heard two ravishing voices singing these words:

> Fear not these hands in the air,
> And in this dwelling place
> Fear naught but a lovely face
> If your heart would flee love's snare.

He could hardly believe that such a gracious invitation would bring him harm; and feeling himself pushed toward an enormous gate of coral, which opened as soon as he approached, he entered a salon paneled with mother-of-pearl, and then several chambers variously decorated, and so rich with paintings and precious stones, that he experienced a kind of enchantment. Thousands of lights attached to the walls, from the vaulted ceiling down to the floor, lit up parts of the other apartments, which were themselves filled with chandeliers, girandoles, and tiers of candles; in sum, the magnificence was such that he could scarcely believe his eyes, even as he looked at it.

After he had passed through sixty chambers, the hands ceased to guide him; he saw a large easy chair, which moved all by itself close to the hearth. At the same moment the fire lit itself, and the hands, which seemed to him very beautiful, white, small, plump, and well proportioned, undressed him, for he was drenched as I have already said, and feared he might catch cold. He was given, without his seeing anybody, a shirt splendid enough to wear on one's wedding day, and a dressing gown made of cloth-of-gold, embroidered with tiny emeralds which formed numbers. The disembodied hands brought him a table on which his toilet articles were laid out. Nothing could have been more elegant; they combed his hair with a deft and light touch which pleased him mightily. Then they clothed him anew, but not with his own clothes; much richer ones had been provided. He silently admired everything that was happening around him, and sometimes he succumbed to shudders of fear that he was not quite able to suppress.

After he had been powdered, curled, perfumed, decked out, tidied up, and rendered more handsome than Adonis, the hands led him into a salon that was superbly gilded and furnished. All round the room one saw the histories of the most famous Cats: Rodillardus[1] hanged by his paws at the council of rats; Puss-in-Boots of the Marquis de Carabas; the scrivener Cat; the Cat who turned into a woman, witches turned into cats, the witches' sabbath and all its ceremonies; in a word, nothing was more remarkable than these pictures.

The table had been laid; there were two places, each set with a golden casket which held the knives, forks, and spoons; the buffet astonished him with its abundance of rock-crystal vases and a thousand rare gems. The prince was wondering for whom these two places were laid, when he saw cats taking their place in a small orchestra set up just for the occasion; one held up a score covered with the most extraordinary notes in the world; another a scroll of paper which he used to beat time; the others had small guitars. Suddenly each one began to miaow in a different key, and to scratch the guitar strings with their claws; it was the strangest music ever heard. The prince would have thought himself in hell, had he not found the palace too wonderful to admit of such an unlikely circumstance; but he stopped his ears and laughed uncontrollably as he watched the various posturings and grimaces of these newfangled musicians.

He was reflecting on the queer things that had already happened to him in this castle, when he saw a tiny figure scarcely a cubit in height entering the room. This puppet was draped in a long veil of black crepe. Two cats attended her; they were dressed in mourning, wearing cloaks, with swords at their sides; a large cortege of cats followed; some carried rat traps filled with rats, others brought mice in cages.

The prince was struck dumb with amazement; he knew not what to think. The black figurine approached, lifting its veil, and he perceived the most beautiful White Cat that ever was or ever will be. She appeared to be very young and very sad; she began to miaow so gently and sweetly that it went straight to his heart; she spoke to the prince: Welcome, O king's son; my miaowing majesty is pleased with the sight of you. Madam Cat, said the prince, you are most generous to receive me with so much hospitality, but you seem to be no ordinary beastie; your gift of speech and the superb castle you own are evident proofs of this. King's son, replied the White Cat, I pray you, pay me no more compliments; I am simple in speech and my manners, but my heart is kind. Come, she continued, let dinner be served, and let the musicians cease, for the prince doesn't understand what they are saying. And are they saying something, Madam? he inquired. I am sure they are, she continued; we have poets here gifted with infinite powers of wit, and if you rest awhile among us, you will have cause to be convinced. I have only to listen to you to believe it, said the prince gallantly; but then, Madam, I consider you a rare Cat indeed.

Supper was brought in; the hands whose bodies were invisible served it. First, two bisques were placed on the table, one of pigeon, the other of well-fattened mice. The sight of one prevented the prince from tasting the other, for he supposed that the same cook had prepared them both; but the little Cat, who guessed what his thoughts were from the face he made, assured him that his meal was cooked separately, and that he could eat what was served him, in the certitude that there would be neither rats nor mice in it.

The prince didn't have to be asked twice, sure in his belief that the pretty little Cat had no intention of deceiving him. He noticed a tiny portrait painted on metal that she wore at her wrist, which surprised him. He begged her to show it to him, imagining that it must be a portrait of Master Minagrobis,[2] the king of the Cats. What was his astonishment to find it that of a young man so handsome that it seemed scarcely possible that nature might have formed another like him, yet who resembled him so strongly that one couldn't have portrayed him better.

She sighed, and becoming more melancholy, kept a profound silence. The prince realized that there was something extraordinary in all this; however, he dared not inquire what it was, for fear of displeasing the Cat, or distressing her. He chatted with her, telling her all the news he knew, and found her well versed in the different interests of princes, and of other things that were going on in the world.

After supper, the White Cat invited her guest into a salon where there was a stage, on which twelve cats and twelve monkeys were dancing a ballet. The former were in Moorish costume, the latter in Chinese. It is easy to imagine the sort of leaps and capers they executed, while from time to time clawing at one another; it was thus that the evening came to an end. White Cat bade good night to her guest; the hands that had guided him thus far took over again and led him to an apartment that was the exact opposite of the one he had seen. It was not so much magnificent as elegant; the whole was papered with butterfly wings, whose diverse colors formed a thousand different flowers. There were also feathers of extremely rare birds, which perhaps had never been seen except in that place. The bed was draped with gauze, attached by thousands of knotted ribbons. There were huge mirrors extending from the ceiling to the parquet, and their borders of chased gold depicted an immense crowd of little cupids.

The prince lay down without saying a word, for there was no way of making conversation with the hands that waited on him; he slept little, and was awakened by an indistinct noise. The hands immediately drew him from his bed and dressed him in a hunter's habit. He looked out into the courtyard of the castle and saw five hundred cats, some of whom had greyhounds on a leash, while others were sounding the horn; it was a great celebration. White Cat was going hunting; she wanted the prince to come with her. The officious hands presented him with a wooden horse which galloped and cantered marvelously; he was somewhat reluctant to mount it, saying that he was far from being a knight-errant like Don Quixote; but his resistance was useless, and they placed him on the wooden horse. It had a cloth and a saddle made of gold-lace embroidery and diamonds. White Cat mounted a monkey, the handsomest and most superb ever seen; she had removed her long veil and wore a dragon's hood, which lent her an air so resolute that all the mice in the region were afraid. Never was a hunting party more agreeable; the cats ran faster than the rabbits and hares, so that when they caught one, White Cat had the spoils divided up before her, and a thousand amusing tricks of dexterity were performed; the birds for their part weren't too secure, for the kittens climbed the trees, and the chief monkey bore White Cat up as far as the eagles' nests, so that she might dispose of the little eagle highnesses according to her whim.

Once the hunt was over, she picked up a horn the length of a finger, but which gave out such a high, clear sound that it was easily audible ten leagues hence; no sooner had she sounded two or three fanfares than she was surrounded by all the cats in the land; some traveled by air, ensconced in chariots; others by water in barques; in a word, so many cats had never been seen before. Almost all were dressed in different costumes; she returned to the castle in pomp with this cortège, and invited the prince to come too. He was willing, even though all this cat business smacked a bit of sorcery and the witches' sabbath, and the talking cat astonished him more than anything else.

As soon as they were back at the castle, her great black veil was placed over her head; she supped with the prince, who was hungry; liqueurs were brought which he drank with pleasure, and instantly they blotted out the memory of the little dog which he was to bring back to the king. He no longer thought of anything but miaowing with White Cat, that is, of being her good and faithful companion; he spent the days in agreeable pastimes: Sometimes he went fishing or hunting; or ballets and chariot races would be staged, and a thousand other diversions to his liking; often the beautiful Cat would even compose verses and ditties in a style so passionate that one might have thought her in love, that one couldn't speak as she did without being in love; but her secretary, an old cat, wrote so illegibly that, even though these works have been preserved, it is impossible to read them.

The prince had even forgotten his country. The hands of which I have spoken continued to serve him. Sometimes he was sorry not to be a cat, so as to spend his life in such delightful company. Alas! he said to White Cat, how sorrowful I shall be when I leave you; I love you so dearly. Either become a girl, or turn me into a cat. She found his request most amusing, and gave only obscure answers, of which he understood almost nothing.

A year passes quickly when one has no cares or worries, when one is happy and in good health. White Cat knew the date when he must return, and as he no longer thought about it, she reminded him. Do you know, she said, that you have but three days to find the little dog that the king your father wants, and that your brothers have found very handsome ones? The prince came to his senses, amazed at his own negligence: By what secret charm, he exclaimed, have I forgotten the thing in the world that matters most to me? My kingdom and my glory depend on it; where will I find a dog that will win me a kingdom, and a horse swift enough to travel such a long way? He began to worry, and was sore aggrieved.

White Cat told him, in gentler tones: King's son, cease lamenting,

I am on your side; you may stay another day here, and, although your country is five hundred leagues distant, the trusty wooden horse will bear you there in less than twelve hours. I thank you, lovely Cat, said the prince; but it isn't enough for me to return to my father's house; I must also bring him a little dog. Ha! replied White Cat, here is an acorn inside which you'll find one more beautiful than the dog star itself. Oh, said the prince, Madam Cat, your majesty is making fun of me. Put the acorn next to your ear, she continued, and you'll hear him yap. He obeyed: At once the tiny dog began to yip and yap; the prince was transported with joy, since a dog that can be contained in an acorn must be tiny indeed. He wished to open it, but White Cat told him the dog might catch cold during the trip: It would be better to wait until he was in the presence of his father, the king. He thanked her a thousand times, and bade her a most tender adieu; I assure you, he said, that the days with you have seemed so short that I quite regret leaving you behind, and though you be the sovereign here, and all the cats who attend to you are much wittier and more gallant than our courtiers, I cannot resist inviting you to come with me. The Cat replied to this suggestion with nothing more than a profound sigh.

They took leave of each other; the prince arrived first at the castle where the meeting with his brothers was to take place. They arrived soon after, and were astonished to find a wooden horse in the courtyard who pranced better than any of those in the riding academies.

The prince came out to greet them. They embraced each other several times and recounted their various travels; but our prince took care not to tell the true story of his adventures, and showed them an ugly cur that was used for turning a spit, saying he had found it so pretty that he had decided to bring it to the king. Despite the affection that united them, the two brothers felt a secret joy at their brother's ill-advised choice; they were at table and trod on each other's feet, as though to tell each other they had nothing to fear from that quarter.

The next day they left together in the same coach. The two elder sons of the king had little dogs in baskets, so beautiful and so delicate that one would scarcely have dared to touch them. The youngest brought his poor turnspit, so filthy that no one could stand him. Once they were inside the palace, everyone gathered around to welcome them; they entered the king's apartment. He couldn't decide which of them to favor, for the little dogs that the two eldest proffered him were almost of equal beauty, and already they were arguing over which of them would inherit the crown, when the youngest settled their dispute by drawing from his pocket the acorn that White Cat had given him. He opened it at once, and everyone saw a tiny dog lying on a bed of cotton wool. He stepped through a finger ring without touching it. The prince set him on the floor, and at once he began to dance the saraband with castanets, as deftly as the most renowned Spanish dancer. His coat was of a thousand different colors; his fur and his tail trailed along the ground. The king was profoundly abashed, for it was impossible to find anything to criticize in this beautiful doggie.

And yet he had no wish to part with his crown. Its least rosette was dearer to him than all the dogs in the universe. So he told his sons that he was satisfied with their efforts, but that they had succeeded so well in the first task he had set them that he wanted to test their cleverness further before keeping his word; and so he was giving them a year to search by land and sea for a piece of cloth so fine that it would pass through the eye of a Venetian lacemaker's needle. All three were sorely distressed at being obliged to set out on a new quest. The two princes, whose dogs were less handsome than their younger brother's, gave their assent. Each went off in a different direction, with fewer friendly effusions than the first time, as the turnspit had somewhat cooled their affections.

Our prince set off on his wooden horse, and without caring to seek other help than that he could expect from the White Cat's friendship, returned to the castle where she had so cordially received him. He found all the doors open; the windows, the roofs, the towers, and the walls were lit by a hundred thousand lamps, which produced a marvelous effect. The hands that had served him so well before came to meet him, took the bridle of the excellent wooden horse and led him to the stable, while the prince entered the chamber of the White Cat.

She was lying in a little basket, on a mattress of spotless white satin. Her nightcap was somewhat askew, and she seemed dejected; but when she noticed the prince she did a thousand leaps and as many capers, to show him how happy she was. Whatever cause I might have had, she told him, to hope for your return, I admit, king's son, that I dared not flatter myself that you would; and I am usually so unlucky when I long for something, that this event surprises me. The grateful prince lavished a thousand caresses on her; he told her of the success of his trip, of which she knew more perhaps than he, and that the king wanted a piece of cloth that could pass through the eye of a needle; that in truth he thought such a thing impossible, but that he had determined to attempt it, placing all his faith in her friendship and help. White Cat assumed a solemn air, telling him that it was indeed something to ponder seriously, that fortunately there were cats in the castle who were excellent weavers, and that she herself would put her claw to the task and help to further his quest; thus he could set his mind at rest and not think of seeking elsewhere what he would find more easily in her domain than anywhere else in the world.

The hands appeared, bearing torches; and the prince followed them along with White Cat; they entered a magnificent gallery that bordered a great river, over which an immense and astounding display of fireworks was set off. Four cats were to be burned, whose trial had been in due accordance with the law. They were accused of having devoured the roast intended for White Cat's supper, her cheese, her milk; of having gone so far as to conspire against her person with Martafax[3] and Lhermite,[4] two famous rats of the region, and named as such by La Fontaine, a most reputable author: But with all that, it was known that there had been a great deal of intrigue in the affair, and that most of the witnesses had been tampered with. However that may be, the prince obtained their pardon. The fireworks harmed no one, and such beautiful skyrockets have still to be seen again.

A dainty midnight supper was served, which pleased the prince more than the fireworks, for he was very hungry, and his wooden horse had brought him more quickly than any coach could have traveled. The days that followed were like those that had gone before, with a thousand different celebrations that White Cat devised to amuse her guest. He was perhaps the first mortal to be so well entertained by cats, without any other company.

It is true that White Cat had a pleasant, good-natured, and almost omniscient mind. She was more learned than a cat is permitted to be. This surprised the prince sometimes. No, he told her, it's not natural, all the marvelous qualities I behold in you: If you love me, charming puss, tell me by what marvel you think and speak so accurately, that you could easily be received in the most learned academies? Enough of your questions, king's son, she would say; I am not allowed to answer, and you may push your conjectures as far as you like, without my preventing you; let it be enough that for you I shall always keep my claws drawn in, and that I interest myself tenderly in everything that concerns you.

Imperceptibly this second year flowed by like the first; the prince had scarcely to wish for something when the diligent hands would bring it to him then and there, whether it were books, jewels, paintings, antique medals; in fact he had but to say, I want such and such a jewel, that is in the treasury of the Great Mogul or the king of Persia, such and such a statue from Corinth or Greece, for whatever he desired to materialize before him, without his knowing who had brought it nor whence it had come. Such distractions are scarcely wearisome; and when one is in the mood for amusements one is sometimes more than pleased to find oneself master of the most beautiful treasures on Earth.

White Cat, who always kept an eye on the prince's interests, advised him that the time for his departure was approaching, that he need not concern himself over the piece of cloth he wished for, and that she had made him a marvelous one; she added that she wished this time to provide him with a retinue worthy of his rank, and, without waiting for his reply, she bade him look down into the great courtyard of the castle. There stood an open barouche made of flame-colored enameled gold, with a thousand emblematic figures which pleased the mind as much as the eye. Twelve snow-white horses, four abreast, hauled it, fitted with flame-colored velvet harnesses embroidered with diamonds and embellished with gold plaques. The barouche was similarly upholstered inside, and a hundred coaches with eight horses, crowded with noblemen of superb mien, magnificently clad, followed the barouche. It was further accompanied by a thousand foot soldiers whose uniforms were so densely embroidered that the cloth could not be seen underneath. What was singular was that wherever one looked, one saw the portrait of White Cat, whether in the emblems of the barouche or on the foot soldiers' uniforms, or attached with a ribbon to the jerkins of those who completed the procession, like a new order of merit that had just been bestowed on them.

Go, she told the prince, go and make your appearance at the court of the king your father, in a manner so sumptuous that your lordly air will sway him, so that he may no longer refuse you the crown you deserve. Here is a walnut; make sure you break it only when you are in his presence; you'll find therein the piece of cloth you asked me for. Adorable Blanchette, he said to her, I confess that I am so saturated with your kindnesses, that if you cared to consent, I would prefer spending my life with you to all the grandeurs that I have reason to anticipate elsewhere. King's son, she replied, I am persuaded of your goodness of heart, it is a rare piece of merchandise among princes, they want to be loved by everyone and to love nothing; but you are proof that the general rule has its exception. I take note of the attachment you display for a little White Cat, who is by nature good for nothing but catching mice. The prince kissed her paw, and left.

One could scarcely believe the speed at which he traveled, did we not already know how the wooden horse had borne him in less than two days more than five hundred leagues from the castle; the same power that animated the horse urged the others on so relentlessly that they took but twenty-four hours to make the journey; they made no halt until they reached the king's domain, where the prince's two elder brothers had already arrived; they, noting that the young prince still hadn't appeared, congratulated themselves on his negligence and muttered to each other: Here is good news; he's dead or sick, and won't be our rival in the important matter we have come to settle. Thereupon they unfolded their cloths, which in truth were so fine that they passed through the eye of a large needle, but not through that of a small one; and the king, greatly relieved by this pretext for a squabble, showed them the needle he had proposed, and which the magistrates, following his orders, had brought from the city treasury where it had been carefully locked up.

There was much murmuring over this dispute. The princes' friends, and especially those of the elder, for his cloth was the more beautiful, argued that this was a piece of outright chicanery, into which much pettifoggery and hair-splitting had entered. The king's supporters maintained that he was scarcely obliged to hold to conditions which he hadn't proposed; finally, to settle all their bickering, a charming sound of trumpets, oboes, and kettledrums was heard; it was our prince arriving in pomp with all his retinue. The king and his two sons were all equally amazed by such splendor.

After he had respectfully greeted his father and embraced his brothers, he withdrew the walnut from a ruby-encrusted casket and cracked it open; he supposed he would find the much vaunted piece of cloth within, but instead there was a hazelnut. He cracked again and was amazed to find a cherry stone. Everyone exchanged glances, the king was laughing quietly and thought his son a ninny for having the naivety to think that he could transport a piece of cloth in a walnut, yet why wouldn't he think so, since he had already brought him a little dog that fitted inside an acorn? Accordingly he cracked the cherry stone, which had a solid kernel; at that an uproar broke out in the chamber, everyone was saying that the prince had been duped in his adventure. He replied nothing to the courtiers' malicious pleasantries; he opened the kernel and found a grain of wheat and inside that a millet seed. Ha! Now it was his turn to be suspicious, and he muttered between his teeth: White Cat, White Cat, you have tricked me. At that moment he felt a cat's claw on his hand, which scratched him so forcefully that his hand bled. He couldn't decide whether this scratch was meant to encourage him or make him lose heart. Nevertheless he pried open the millet seed, and great was the astonishment of all when he withdrew from it a piece of linen four hundred ells long, of such extraordinary stitchery that all the birds, animals, and fish were depicted on it, along with the plants of the Earth, its rocky peaks, the curiosities and shellfish of the sea, the sun, the moon, the stars, the heavenly bodies and planets of the heavens; as well as the portraits of the kings and other sovereigns who reigned on Earth at that time; those of their wives, their mistresses, their children, and all their subjects, down to the last street urchin. Each one according to his condition was portrayed with the character that suited him, and was dressed according to the fashion of his native land. When the king saw the piece of linen he grew as pale as the prince had blushed red while he was searching so long for it. The needle was presented, and the cloth was passed and repassed through it six times. The king and the two princes maintained a gloomy silence, even though the beauty and rarity of the piece of linen forced them to acknowledge from time to time that everything else in the universe was inferior to it.

The king heaved a deep sigh, and, turning toward his sons, said: Nothing can console me in my old age as much as the spectacle of your deference to my wishes; therefore I wish to put you to one more test. Go once more on a yearlong journey, and whoever returns at the end of the year with the most beautiful maiden shall wed her and be crowned king on his marriage; it is of course imperative that my successor have a wife. I swear and promise that I shall no longer postpone the recompense I have offered.

The injustice of all this stunned our prince. The little dog and the linen cloth were worth ten kingdoms rather than one; but he was so well bred that he in no way wished to oppose his father's will, and, without hesitation, climbed back into his barouche; all his retinue followed, and he returned to his beloved White Cat; she knew the day and the moment he would arrive; the road was strewn with flowers, and a thousand incense-burners were smoking on every side, and especially within the castle. She was seated on a Persian carpet, beneath a tent made of cloth-of-gold, in a loggia from which she could see him approaching. He was received by the hands which had always served him. All the cats climbed up to the eaves, so as to congratulate him with a desperate caterwauling.

How now, king's son, she said to him, so you have returned without a crown? Madam, he replied, your favors would indeed have gained it for me; but I am persuaded that the king's distress at parting with it would be greater than my pleasure in possessing it. No matter, she said, you must neglect nothing to deserve it; I will serve you on this occasion; and since you must lead a beautiful maiden back to your father's court, I'll look for one who will win you the prize. Meanwhile, let's rejoice; I have ordained a naval battle between my cats and the terrible rats that infest the region. My cats will be at a disadvantage, perhaps, for they are afraid of the water; but otherwise their superiority would be too great, and one must, insofar as possible, let equality reign in all things. The prince admired the probity of Madam Kitty. He sang her praises, and accompanied her onto a terrace which looked toward the sea.

The cats' vessels consisted of large chunks of cork, on which they sailed along quite easily. The rats had joined together several eggshells, and these were their warships. The combat was cruelly unsparing; the rats dived into the water, and swam much better than the cats, so that the latter were twenty times victors and vanquished; but Minagrobis, admiral of the feline fleet, pursued the rattish hordes to their ultimate débâcle. He devoured the general of their navy with his sharp teeth; it was an old, battle-scarred rat who had gone thrice around the world in stout vessels, wherein he was neither captain nor sailor, but merely an uninvited scrounger.

White Cat did not desire the total destruction of these unfortunates. Well versed in politics, she understood that if there were neither rats nor mice in the land, her subjects would lapse into a state of idleness that might be detrimental to their well-being. The prince spent this year doing what he had done in the preceding ones, that is to say in hunting, fishing, and gaming, for White Cat was an excellent chess player. From time to time he couldn't resist plying her with new questions, so as to know by what miracle she was able to speak. He asked her if she was a fairy, or whether someone had transformed her into a cat; but as she never said anything but what she wished to say, neither did she answer anything but what she wished to answer, which were random words signifying nothing, so that he had no trouble concluding that she didn't choose to share her secret with him.

Nothing flows faster than days that pass without care and without chagrin, and if the Cat hadn't been so careful to remember the time for his return to the court, it is certain that the prince would have forgotten it absolutely. She advised him on the eve that it was only up to him to carry away one of the most beautiful princesses in the world, that the hour to destroy the fairies' fatal handiwork had at last arrived, and that he must resolve to cut off her head and tail and throw them immediately into the fire. Me! he exclaimed. Blanchette! My love! Me, a barbarian who would slay you! Ah, no doubt you wish to put my heart to the test, but rest assured that it is incapable of lacking in the love and gratitude it owes you. No, king's son, she continued, I suspect you of no ingratitude; I know your worth; neither you nor I may control our destiny in this affair. Do as I wish and we shall each of us begin to know happiness, and you will understand, on my honor as a cat, that I am truly your friend.

Tears came two or three times to the eyes of the young prince, at the mere thought that he must cut off the head of his little pussycat who was so graceful and pretty. Again he said everything he could think of to dissuade her; she replied obstinately that she wished to die at his hand; and that it was the only way to prevent his brothers from assuming the crown; in a word she urged him with such ardor, that trembling, he drew his sword and with an unsteady hand cut off the head and tail of his good friend the Cat; at the same moment he witnessed the most charming metamorphosis imaginable. White Cat's body grew tall, and suddenly changed into a girl. It would be impossible to describe how perfect she was in every detail, how superior to all other maidens. Her eyes delighted all hearts, and her sweetness gave them pause: Her form was regal, her manner noble and modest, her nature affectionate, her manners engaging; in a word, she towered above all that was most lovable in the world.

Seeing her, the prince was overcome with surprise, a surprise so delightful that he thought he must be under a spell. He was unable to speak; his eyes weren't big enough to look at her; he was too tongue-tied to explain his amazement, but even this paled when he saw an enormous crowd of ladies and lords enter the room, each with their cat's skin slung over their shoulders: They knelt before the queen and expressed their joy at seeing her again in her natural state. She received them with tokens of kindness which bore ample witness to the goodness of her heart. And after holding court for a few moments, she ordered that she be left alone with the prince, and addressed him thus: Do not imagine, my lord, that I was always a Cat, nor that my condition among men was a lowly one. My father was the ruler of six kingdoms. He loved my mother tenderly, and gave her absolute freedom to do as she wished. Her chief passion was for travel, and so it came about that while she was carrying me she undertook to go and see a certain mountain, of which she had heard tell surprising things. As she was on her way there, she was told that close to the place she was passing through was a fairy's ancient castle, the most beautiful in the world, or at any rate so it was supposed to be, according to legend, for since no one ever entered there, no one could be sure; but what was known with certainty was that in their garden those fairies had the finest fruits, the tastiest and most delicate that ever were eaten.

Immediately my mother the queen had such a violent urge to taste them that she made straight for the castle. She arrived at the gate of that magnificent edifice, which glittered with gold and lapis on all sides, but she knocked to no avail; no one at all appeared; it seemed that everyone inside was dead. Her appetite whetted by frustration, she called for ladders to be brought so that she might climb over the walls into the garden; and this would have happened, but the walls grew taller before their very eyes, even though nobody was seen at work on them; ladders were joined together; they collapsed under the weight of those ordered to climb them, who were injured or killed.

The queen was in despair. She saw great trees laden with fruits which she imagined to be delicious, she would eat of them or die; thus she had gorgeous tents pitched before the castle, and remained there six weeks with all her court. She neither ate nor slept, but sighed unceasingly; she spoke of naught but the fruits of the inaccessible garden; at last she fell dangerously ill, without anyone's being able to supply her with the slightest remedy, for the inexorable fairies hadn't even made an appearance since she installed herself near their castle. Her officers were all deeply distressed: One heard nothing but sobs and sighs, while the dying queen demanded fruits of those who served her, but would have only those that were denied her.

One night when she had dozed off a bit, she saw on waking a little old woman, ugly and decrepit, seated in an armchair by her bedside. She was surprised that her ladies-in-waiting would have let a stranger come so close, when the woman said: We find your majesty most importunate, to wish so obstinately to eat of our fruits; but since your precious life hangs in the balance, my sisters and I have consented to give you as much as you can carry with you, and for as long as you stay here, provided you make us a gift. Ah! good mother, speak, I'll give you my kingdoms, my heart, my soul, if only I may have fruits; I couldn't buy them too dear! We wish, she said, that your majesty give us the daughter you are carrying in your womb; as soon as she is born, we shall come to fetch her; she will be well cared for with us, there are no virtues, no beauties, no sciences with which we shan't endow her: In a word, she will be our child, we shall make her happy; but note that your majesty will not see her again until she be wed. If this proposal suits you I shall cure you straightaway, and lead you to our orchards; in spite of the night you will see clear enough to choose what you like. If what I tell you displeases you, good evening, your highness the queen, I am going to sleep. However harsh the law you impose upon me, replied the queen, I accept it rather than perish; for it is certain that I haven't a day left to live, thus I shall lose my child in losing myself. Heal me, wise fairy, she went on, and let me not wait a moment before savoring the privilege you have just granted me.

The fairy touched her with a little gold wand, saying: May your majesty be free of all the ills which bind you to this bed. At once it seemed to her that a harsh and heavy cloak that had been crushing her was lifted from her shoulders, and that there were places where she felt it still. It was apparently these places where the evil was the most severe. She had her ladies summoned, and gaily told them how well she felt, that she was going to rise from her bed, and that at last the fairies' palace gates, so strongly bolted and barricaded, were to be opened for her to eat the lovely fruits, and take away as many as she pleased.

All of her ladies-in-waiting supposed that the queen was raving, and that at this moment she was dreaming of the fruits she had so longed for; so that instead of replying they began to weep, and had the physicians awakened so they could see the state she was in. This delay drove the queen to despair; she at once demanded her robes; they were refused her; she grew angry, her face reddened. They said it was because of the fever; but now the doctors arrived and, after they had taken her pulse and performed their usual rigmarole, were obliged to admit that she was in perfect health. Her ladies, realizing the error their zeal had caused them to commit, sought to repair it and lost no time in dressing her. Each begged her pardon, the matter was settled, and she hastened to follow the old fairy who was still awaiting her.

She entered the palace, where nothing could have been added to make it the most beautiful place in the world; you will believe it easily, my lord, added Queen White Cat, when I tell you that it's the very one in which we are at this moment; two other fairies a little less aged than the one who led my mother met them at the gate, and welcomed her most kindly. She beseeched them to lead her directly to the garden, and toward the espaliers where the finest fruits were to be found. All were equally good, they replied, and if it weren't for your wanting to have the pleasure of plucking them yourself, we should have only to call out for them to arrive here. I beg you, ladies, to let me have the satisfaction of seeing such an extraordinary sight. The oldest stuck her fingers in her mouth and whistled three times; then called out: Apricots, peaches, clingstones, nectarines, cherries, plums, white cherries, melons, pears, muscats, apples, oranges, lemons, currants, strawberries, raspberries, come when I call! But, said the queen, all those you have just called for ripen in different seasons. That is not the case with our orchards, they told her; we have all the fruits that exist on Earth, always ripe, always good, and they never spoil.

And at that very moment they arrived, rolling, creeping, pell-mell, without getting bruised or dirty; in such wise that the queen, anxious to slake her craving, flung herself on them, seized the first that came to her hands, and devoured rather than ate them.

Feeling a little sated now, she begged the fairies to let her go and see the espaliers, so as to have the pleasure of inspecting them before making her choice. We are happy to let you, said the three fairies, but remember the promise you gave us; you will no longer be allowed to retract it. I am persuaded, she replied, that life here with you is so agreeable, and this palace seems so fine to me, that were it not for the love I bear my husband the king, I would offer to remain here; for this reason you must never believe that I would take back my word. The fairies, delighted, opened all their gardens and enclosures to her; she stayed for three days and three nights without wishing to leave, so delicious did she find everything. She gathered fruits for her provision, and since they never spoil, she had four thousand mules brought to her and laden with them. The fairies added gold baskets of exquisite workmanship to hold them, and several rarities whose price was excessive; they promised to raise me as a princess, to make me perfect, and to choose me a husband; that she would be notified of the wedding and that they sincerely hoped she would attend.

The king was delighted by the queen's return; the whole court bore witness to his joy; there were balls, masquerades, tilting at the ring,[5] and feasts at which the queen's fruits were served as a sumptuous treat. The king ate them in preference to everything that was served him. He knew nothing of the bargain she had struck with the fairies, and often asked her in what country she had found such delicacies; she replied that they came from an almost inaccessible mountain; another time she said they came from valleys, and then from a garden in the depths of a vast forest. The king was surprised by so many contradictions. He questioned those who accompanied her, but she had so sternly forbidden them to tell anyone of her adventure, that they dared not speak of it. Finally, disturbed by what she had promised the fairies, and sensing the time of her confinement fast approaching, she sank into a frightful state of despondency, so that even her appearance was altered. The king was distressed, and urged the queen to tell him the cause of her sadness, and after much shedding of tears, she told him everything that had happened between herself and the fairies, and how she had promised them the child she was expecting. What! cried the king, we have no offspring, you know how much I long for a child, and for a matter of two or three apples you are capable of giving yours away? Obviously you love me not at all. Thereupon he overwhelmed her with a thousand reproaches, causing my poor mother to feel she would die of grief, but not content with this, he had her shut up in a tower with guards on all sides to prevent her from having commerce with anyone in the outside world, save the officers who waited on her, and even so he removed those who had been with her to the fairies' castle.

The bad blood between the king and queen plunged the court into deep consternation. Everyone doffed their rich robes to dress in a manner more suited to the general sorrow. The king, for his part, appeared inexorable; he no longer saw his wife, and as soon as I was born he had me brought to his palace to be nursed, while she remained a prisoner and crushed by misery. The fairies were ignorant of nothing that had happened; they grew irritated, they wanted me, they considered me their property and that they had been robbed of it. Before mapping a vengeance which would be proportionate to the crime, they sent an illustrious embassy to the king, warning him to release the queen and restore her to favor, and to beg him also to hand me over to their ambassadors so that I might be raised and educated by them. The ambassadors were so stunted and deformed, for they were in fact hideous dwarfs, that they were in no way able to persuade the king to do their bidding. He refused them rudely, and if they hadn't left posthaste they might have met with a worse fate.

When the fairies learned of my father's actions, their indignation knew no bounds; and after dispatching into his six kingdoms all the ills that could render them desolate, they unleashed a horrendous dragon who scattered venom wherever he passed, devoured grown men and children, and with his breath caused trees and plants to die.

The king was sunk in the deepest despair; he consulted all the sages in his realm to learn what he should do to protect his subjects from the misfortunes in which he saw them engulfed. They advised him to seek throughout the world for the finest doctors and the surest remedies, and, on the other hand, to release criminals condemned to die so that they might combat the dragon. Quite satisfied with this opinion, the king acted on it but received no consolation, for the death toll continued to grow, and no one could approach the dragon without being devoured, so that at last he had recourse to a fairy who had protected him from his earliest childhood. She was very old, and scarcely ever left her bed anymore; he betook himself to her dwelling and reproached her a thousand times for having let destiny persecute him without coming to his aid. What do you want me to do, she said, you have annoyed my sisters; they have as much power as I, and it is very rarely that we act against each other. Think of appeasing them by giving them your daughter, that little princess belongs to them. You have shut up the queen in a prison cell: What has that lovable woman done to you for you to treat her thus? Decide then to keep the word she gave, and I guarantee that you will be showered with blessings.

The king my father loved me dearly, but seeing no other way to save his kingdoms and be rid of the fatal dragon, he told his old friend that he had resolved to believe her, that he would agree to hand me over to the fairies, since she assured him I would be cherished and raised as a princess of my rank; that he would also send for the queen, and that the old fairy had only to tell him to whom he should deliver me to have me brought to the fairies' castle. She replied that I must be carried in my cradle to the top of the mountain of flowers; you may even stay in the region, she said, to be a spectator of the celebration that will be held there. The king told her he would go there in a week's time with the queen, and that she should notify her sister fairies, so that they might do whatever might seem fitting to them.

No sooner had he returned to the palace when he had the queen summoned with a tenderness and pomp equal to the wrath and fury with which he had her made prisoner. She was so changed and dejected that he could scarcely recognize her, had not his heart assured him that this was the same person he had loved so much. With tears in his eyes he begged her to forget the grief he had caused her, assuring her that it would be the last she would ever suffer on his account. She replied that she had brought it on herself through the imprudence of promising her child to the fairies; and if anything could plead in her behalf, it was the state she was in; at last he informed her that he would place me in their hands. The queen in turn fought against this proposal; it seemed that some fatality must have been in all this, and that I would always be an object of discord between my father and my mother. After she had wept and moaned for a long time, without his granting her wish (for the king saw only too well the tragic consequences, and that his subjects would continue to die, as though it were they who had brought misfortune on the family), she agreed to everything he wanted, and preparations for the ceremony began.

I was placed in a cradle made of mother-of-pearl, ornamented with as much elegance as art can summon. Garlands of flowers and festoons hung round it, and the flowers were precious stones of different colors which flashed so brightly when the sun struck them that one had to look away. The magnificence of my costume surpassed, if it were possible, that of the cradle. My swaddling bands were fashioned from enormous pearls; twenty-four princesses of the blood carried me on a sort of finely wrought litter; their robes were unmatched, but they were allowed to wear no other color but white, in keeping with my innocence. The whole court accompanied me, each according to his rank.

As we all started up the mountain, a melodious orchestra was heard approaching; at last the fairies appeared, thirty-six in all; they had invited their closest lady-friends to accompany them; each was seated in a shell of pearl, larger than the one on which Venus emerged from the sea; seahorses, which travel with difficulty on land, drew them in their chariots; they acted more pompous than the greatest queens in the universe, but were in fact exceeding old and ugly. They brought an olive branch, to show the king that his submission found favor with them; and when they held me, they caressed me so fondly that it seemed they no longer wished to live with any goal but that of making me happy.

The dragon they had employed to avenge themselves on my father followed behind them, bound with diamond chains; they held me in their arms, bestowed a thousand caresses on me, and endowed me with numerous advantages; then began the fairies' dance. It was a sprightly one indeed; and it was amazing to see these old ladies hop and gambol. Thereupon the dragon who had devoured so many people approached. The three fairies to whom my mother had promised me perched on him with my cradle between them; he spread his enormous scaly wings, finer than crêpe and shot through with a thousand bizarre colors, and thus we traveled back to the castle. My mother, seeing me in the air, exposed on the back of that furious dragon, couldn't prevent herself from uttering several piercing cries. The king consoled her, reminding her of the promise his friend had given that no harm would befall me and that they would take as good care of me as I would receive in his own palace. She calmed herself, even though it was most painful for her to contemplate losing me for so long, and to be the only cause of it; for if she hadn't desired to eat the fruits in that garden, I would have remained in the kingdom of the king my father, and would not have had to endure all the sorrows that I have still to recount to you.

Know then, king's son, that my guardians had had a tower built expressly for me, in which there were a thousand handsome apartments for all the seasons of the year, magnificent furniture, delightful books, but no door: One could enter only through the windows, which were prodigiously high. There was a lovely garden on top of the tower, decked with flowers, fountains, and nooks of greenery which protected one from the heat of the most scorching dog days. It was here that the fairies brought me up with attentions that surpassed all that they had promised the queen. My clothes were of the latest fashion, and so magnificent that, seeing me, one would have thought it were my wedding day. They taught me everything suitable to my age and rank; I gave them very little trouble, for I learned almost everything with great facility; they found my gentle temperament most agreeable, and since I had never seen anyone but them, I might have stayed quietly in this situation for the rest of my life.

They always came to visit me astride the furious dragon of whom I have already told; they never spoke to me of the king or the queen; they called me their daughter, and I thought I was. Not a soul lived with me in the tower, except for a parrot and a little dog that they gave me for my playmates, for they had the gift of reason and were marvelously well spoken.

One side of the tower was built alongside a sunken road, so encumbered with trees and ruts that I had never seen anyone on it since they had confined me there. But one day, as I was at the window chatting with my parrot and my dog, I heard a noise. Looking around I perceived a young knight who had stopped to listen to our conversation; I had never before seen a man except in pictures. I was by no means vexed that a chance encounter provided me with this opportunity, so that, not fearing in the least the danger that comes with the satisfaction of seeing an amiable object, I drew closer to look at him, and the more I looked at him, the more pleasure I experienced. He made me a deep bow and fixed his gaze on me, seeming at a loss how to converse with me, for my window was so high up that he feared being overheard, and he well knew that I was in the fairies' castle.

Suddenly, night fell; or rather, it arrived without our noticing; he blew two or three times on his horn, and delighted me with several fanfares, then he left without my being able to discern even the direction he took, so thick was the darkness. I remained plunged in a waking dream; I no longer experienced the same pleasure in chatting with my parrot and my dog. They recounted me the most delightful things imaginable, for fairy animals become very witty, but my thoughts were elsewhere, and I hadn't learned the art of controlling myself. Sinbad the parrot noticed this, for he was clever, and didn't mention what was on his mind.[6]

I didn't fail to arise at daybreak. I ran to my window, and was agreeably surprised to find the young knight at the foot of the tower. He was sumptuously clad, and I flattered myself that I was partly the cause, nor was I mistaken. He spoke to me through a kind of trumpet which carried his voice up to me, and by this means he told me that, having been indifferent until now to all the beautiful women he had seen, he suddenly felt so powerfully stricken with me that he couldn't live unless he were to see me every day of his life. I was highly pleased by this compliment, and most disturbed that I was unable to respond to it, for I should have had to shout at the top of my voice, and put myself in danger of being heard better by the fairies than by him. I was holding a few flowers which I threw down to him; he caught them as though they were a distinguished favor, kissed them several times and tendered me his thanks. Then he asked me if I thought it wise that he come every day at the same time and stand beneath my windows, and that if I did so, to throw him an object of some kind. I had a turquoise ring which I quickly removed from my finger and threw down to him in haste, signaling him to go away as fast as possible, for I had just heard the fairy Violenta on the other side of the tower, who had mounted her dragon to bring me my breakfast.

The first thing she said on entering was: I smell a man's voice here: Dragon, look for him. Ah! I had guessed right! I was terrified that the beast might fly through the other window and follow the knight, in whose fortunes I already took a lively interest. Truly, good mother, I said (for the fairy wished that I address her thus), you are making sport of me. Does a voice smell of something? And if it did, is there a mortal bold enough to venture to climb this tower? You speak truly, child, she replied, and I am delighted to see you reason so prettily; I suppose it must be the hatred I have for all men that sometimes persuades me they can't be far off. She gave me my breakfast and my distaff. When you have eaten you must get back to your spinning, she told me, for you did nothing yesterday, and my sisters will be angry. In truth, I had been so preoccupied with the stranger that it had been impossible for me to spin.

As soon as she left I threw down the distaff with a mutinous little gesture, and climbed up to my terrace to gaze as far off into the country-side as I could. I had an excellent telescope; nothing blocked my view, I peered about on all sides, and discovered my knight at the top of a mountain. He was resting under an opulent tent made of cloth-of-gold, and was attended by a large retinue. I had no doubt that he was the son of some king of the region of the fairies' castle. Since I feared that if he returned to the tower he might be discovered by the terrible dragon, I picked up my parrot and told him to fly as far as the mountain, that he would find the stranger who had spoken to me there, and to beg him on my behalf not to come back again, for I dreaded the vigilance of my guardians, and feared lest they cause him harm.

The parrot fulfilled his assignment with his inborn cleverness. Every-one was surprised to see him fly straight to his destination and perch on the prince's shoulder so as to whisper in his ear. The prince experienced the joy and pain of this embassy. The precautions I had taken for him flattered his heart; but the obstacles that prevented him from speaking with me crushed him, without being able to dissuade him from carrying out the plan he had devised for pleasing me. He asked Sinbad a thousand questions, and Sinbad for his part asked him a hundred others, for he was by nature inquisitive. The prince gave him a ring for me in exchange for my turquoise; it too was a turquoise, but much more beautiful than mine; it was carved into a heart shape and set with diamonds. It is only right for me to treat you as an ambassador, he added: Here is my portrait; take it and show it only to your lovely mistress. He fastened the portrait under Sinbad's wing and placed the ring in his beak.

I awaited the return of my little green messenger with an impatience I had never felt before. He told me that he to whom I had dispatched him was a great king, that he had received him as hospitably as could be, that I could be sure he no longer wished to live except for my sake, and that despite the great peril of coming to the foot of the tower, he was determined to undertake anything rather than renounce seeing me again. This news intrigued me very much, and I started to cry. Sinbad and Fido consoled me as best they could, for they loved me tenderly; then Sinbad presented me with the prince's ring, and showed me the portrait. I confess I had never been so delighted as I was at being able to contemplate close up him whom I had hitherto perceived only from a distance. He seemed even more attractive than before; a hundred thoughts flooded my mind, some agreeable, others sad, giving me an appearance of extreme restlessness. The fairies who came to see me noticed this. They told each other that doubtless I was growing bored, and that it was time to think of finding me a husband of the race of fairies. They mentioned several, and settled on little King Migonnet, whose kingdom lay five hundred thousand leagues from their palace, but that was of scant importance. Sinbad listened to this learned council and came to tell me of it, saying: Ah! how I pity you, dear mistress, if you become Queen Migonnet! He's a frightful-looking scarecrow, I regret to tell you; in truth the king who loves you wouldn't have him as his flunkey. Then you've seen him, Sinbad! I should say I have, he continued; I was brought up on a branch alongside him. What, on a branch? I continued. Yes, he replied, for he has the claws of an eagle.

Such a tale afflicted me strangely; I gazed on the charming portrait of the young king, I esteemed that he had given it to Sinbad only so that I might find a way to see him; and when I compared his face with Migonnet, I no longer hoped for anything from life, and resolved to die rather than marry him.

I slept not a wink all night. Sinbad and Fido chatted with me; toward morning I dozed off a little; and, since my dog had a keen nose, he sensed that the prince was at the front of the tower. He woke Sinbad: I'll wager, he said, that the king is down there. Be still, chatterbox; since you almost always have your eyes open and your ears cocked, you're annoyed when others sleep. But let's wager, brave Fido insisted, I know that he's there.

And as for me, I know he's not; haven't I forbidden him to come here on behalf of our noble mistress? Ah, this is too much, you're getting on my nerves with your excuses, cried my dog; a man of passion consults only his heart; and thereupon he began to tug so hard at Sinbad's wings that the parrot grew furious. Their quarreling awoke me; they told me its cause; I ran or rather flew to the window; I saw the king stretching out his arms to me, telling me with his trumpet that he could no longer live without me, beseeching me to find a way to leave my tower or to let him enter it, that he called on all the gods and the elements to witness that he would marry me at once, and that I would be one of the greatest queens in the universe.

I ordered Sinbad to go and tell him that what he wished seemed all but impossible; that nonetheless, in view of the promise he had given me and the oaths he had tendered, I would work diligently to help him realize his wishes; that I begged him not to come every day, lest he be finally spied by someone, and that the fairies were pitiless.

He withdrew overcome with joy, thanks to the flattering hopes I held out to him while I found myself in the worst predicament I had ever known, when I reflected on what I had just promised. How could I leave this tower, which had no doors? And with only the help of Sinbad and Fido? And I so young, so inexperienced, so fearful? I therefore resolved not to undertake anything which had no hope of success, and I sent Sinbad to tell the king. He was ready to kill himself before Sinbad's very eyes, but finally he ordered him to persuade me either to come and watch him die, or to comfort him. Sire, cried the winged ambassador, my mistress is sufficiently convinced, she lacks only power.

When he came to tell me all that had happened, I was more afflicted than before. Fairy Violenta arrived; seeing how my eyes were red and swollen, she said that I had wept, and that if I didn't tell her why she would burn me, for all her threats were always terrible. I answered, trembling, that I was tired of spinning, and that I longed to have nets to catch the little birds who came to peck at the fruits in my garden. What you desire shall cost you no more tears, my daughter; I shall bring you all the cords you need; and in fact I received them that very evening; but she cautioned me to think less of work and more about making myself beautiful, since King Migonnet would soon be arriving. I shuddered at this disturbing news, and answered nothing.

As soon as she left I began to work on two or three bits of netting, but my real endeavor was to fashion a rope ladder which would be skillfully made, even though I had never seen one. It is true that the fairy never supplied me with as much cord as I needed, and she kept repeating: But daughter, your weaving is like Penelope's, it never progresses, and you are continually asking me for more supplies. O! Good mother, I said, it's easy enough for you to talk! Can't you see that I'm inexperienced, and that I keep spoiling my work and throwing it into the fire? Are you afraid of my impoverishing you with my string? My simple airs delighted her, even though she had a most disagreeable and cruel nature.

I dispatched Sinbad to tell the king to come one evening beneath the tower windows, that he would find a ladder there, and that he would find out the rest when he came. As a matter of fact I anchored it firmly, resolved to flee with him; but when he saw it he climbed it in haste, without waiting for me to come down, and burst into my chamber while I was preparing everything for my flight.

The sight of him so filled me with joy that I forgot the peril both of us were in. He renewed his gallant vows, and beseeched me to delay no longer in accepting him as my husband; we enlisted Sinbad and Fido as witnesses of our marriage; never was a wedding between persons of such high rank celebrated with less noise and festivity, and never were hearts happier than ours.

Day had not yet come when the king left me: I told him the fairies' frightful plan of marrying me to little Migonnet; I described his face, which horrified him as much as me. Hardly had he left when the hours began to seem like days; I ran to the window and followed him with my gaze despite the darkness; but what was my amazement on seeing in the distance a chariot of fire drawn by winged salamanders, traveling with such speed that the eye could scarcely follow it! The chariot was escorted by a quantity of guards mounted on ostriches. I had barely time enough to glance at the ugly sprite who was traveling through the air in this fashion; but I concluded at once that it was a fairy or an enchanter.

Soon after, fairy Violenta entered my chamber: I bring you good news, she said; your lover arrived a few hours ago; prepare to receive him; here are some jewels and finery. What! I cried out. And who told you I wished to be wed? It's not my intention at all; send King Migonnet back where he came from; I won't add so much as a pin to my dress; let him find me beautiful or ugly, it's all the same to me. Ah, ah, replied the fairy, such a little rebel, such a harebrain! I'm in no mood for jokes, and I'm going to . . . You'll do what to me? I retorted, blushing at the names she had called me. Can one be more dismally treated than I, shut up in a tower with a parrot and a dog, having to look several times a day at the frightful face of a dragon? Ha! Ungrateful wretch, said the fairy, and what did you do to deserve so much care and trouble on the part of others? I've said it all too often to my sisters, that we shall have but a sad recompense. She went to find them and tell them of our quarrel, and all were equally shocked.

Sinbad and Fido pleaded desperately with me, saying that if I continued in my refractory ways, they foresaw that harsh treatment would be visited on me. I felt so proud at possessing the heart of a great king that I scorned the fairies and the advice of my little friends. I refused to don my finery, and purposely coiffed my hair awry, so that Migonnet might find me displeasing. Our interview took place on the terrace. He arrived in his chariot of fire. Never since there were dwarfs was such a tiny one to be seen. He walked on his eagle's claws and his knees at the same time, for there were no bones in his legs, so that he was obliged to support himself on two diamond crutches. His royal robe was only half an ell long, and a third of it trailed on the ground. His head was as big as a bushel basket, and his nose so large that a dozen birds perched on it, whose chirping delighted him; he had such an enormous beard that canaries had made their nests in it, and his ears overtopped his head by a cubit, but this was scarcely noticeable thanks to the high pointed crown that he wore so as to appear taller. The flame of his chariot roasted the fruits, withered the flowers, and dried up the fountains of my garden. He approached me with open arms to embrace me; I stood up straight, and his first equerry was obliged to lift him; but as soon as he drew near I fled into my chamber and slammed shut the door and the windows, so that Migonnet returned to the fairies' abode extremely vexed with me.

They asked him a thousand pardons for my brusqueness, and to calm him, for he was very powerful, they resolved to lead him into my chamber at night while I was asleep, to bind my hands and feet and put me with him in the burning chariot, so that he might carry me away. Once this plan was agreed upon, they hardly even scolded me for my insolent behavior. All they said was that I should think about making amends. Sinbad and Fido were surprised at such mildness. You know, mistress, said my dog, my heart tells me no good can come of this. My ladies the fairies are strange personages, especially Violenta. I made fun of his warnings, and awaited my beloved husband with wild impatience.

He himself was too impatient to put off seeing me again; I threw down the rope ladder, fully resolved to run off with him; he climbed it nimbly and proffered me such tender words that I still dare not summon them to memory.

While we were speaking together with the same tranquility we would have had in his palace, the windows of my chamber were suddenly battered in. In came the fairies on their terrible dragon, followed by Migonnet in his fiery chariot and all his guards on their ostriches. The king, fearless, put his hand to his sword, thinking only of saving me from the most horrible misadventure that ever was, for, would you believe it, my lord? those barbarous creatures unleashed their dragon on him; he was eaten up before my very eyes.

In desperation at his fate and mine, I threw myself into the jaws of that hideous monster, hoping he would swallow me, as he had swallowed all that I loved in the world. He would have liked to, but the fairies, even more cruel than he, wouldn't let him. She must be kept for more lingering torments, they screamed; a speedy death is too gentle for this shameless creature! They laid hands on me; at once I saw myself turn into the White Cat; they brought me to this magnificent palace of my father and metamorphosed all the lords and ladies of the kingdom into cats; they spared those whose hands alone would remain visible, and reduced me to the deplorable state in which you found me, informing me of my birth, of the death of my father and of my mother, and that I would never be released from my feline condition, save by a prince who would perfectly resemble the husband they had torn from me. 'Tis you, my lord, who possess that resemblance, she continued: the same features, same aspect, even the same voice; I was struck by it the moment I saw you; I was informed of everything that would happen, and I know as well what will happen: My torment will end. And my own, lovely queen, said the prince, throwing himself at her feet, will it be of long duration? Already I love you more than life itself, my lord, said the queen. We must go to see your father; we shall judge of his feelings for me, and learn if he will consent to what you desire.

She went out; the prince gave her his hand, she mounted into a chariot with him; it was far more magnificent than those he had had before. The rest of the cortège matched it to such a degree that all the horseshoes were made of emeralds, and their nails were diamonds. Perhaps it was a sight never seen before or since. I pass over the agreeable conversations that the queen and the prince were having; if she was matchless in beauty, she was not less so for her mind, and the young prince was as perfect as she, so that they thought only of charming things.

When they were near the castle where the brothers were to meet, the queen entered a rock crystal whose facets were adorned with gold and rubies. Its interior was curtained so that none could see her, and it was borne by beautifully formed and superbly clad youths. The prince remained in the chariot, from which he saw his brothers strolling with princesses of extraordinary beauty. As soon as they recognized him they asked him if he had brought a fiancée; he told them that he had been so unlucky that throughout his travels he had encountered only ugly women, and that the only thing of rarity he could find to bring was a little White Cat. They began to laugh at his innocence. A cat, they said, are you afraid the mice will eat our palace? The prince replied that in effect it wasn't wise to offer such a present to his father; thereupon they set out on the road to the city.

The elder princes rode with their princesses in barouches made of gold and lapis lazuli; their horses' heads were adorned with plumes and aigrettes; in short, nothing on Earth could surpass this brilliant cavalcade. Our young prince followed behind, then came the rock crystal, which everyone stared at admiringly.

The courtiers hastened to tell the king that the three princes were arriving. Have they brought beautiful ladies with them? he retorted. It would be impossible to find anything that could outshine them. This reply seemed to annoy him. The king greeted them cordially, and couldn't decide on whom to bestow the prize; he looked at the youngest and said: So, this time you have come alone? Your majesty will find inside this rock crystal a little White Cat, who miaows so sweetly, and draws in her claws so nicely, that your majesty will surely approve of her. The king smiled, and was about to open the crystal himself, but no sooner had he approached it than the queen, using a spring, caused the whole thing to fall in shards, and appeared like the sun after it has been for some time veiled in clouds; her blond hair cascaded over her shoulders and fell in thick ringlets down to her feet; her head was wreathed in flowers, her fragile white gown was lined with pink taffeta; she arose and made a deep curtsey before the king, who, overcome with admiration, couldn't prevent himself from crying out: Here is the incomparable one, and it is she who deserves the crown.

Your highness, she replied, I haven't come here to deprive you of a throne which you occupy with so much dignity; I was born with six kingdoms; allow me to offer you one of them, and one to both of your sons. All I ask for in recompense is your friendship, and this young prince for my husband. We shall still be well provided for with three kingdoms. The king and all the court uttered long shouts of joy and astonishment. The marriage was celebrated at once, and those of the two princes as well, in such wise that the whole court spent several months in pleasures and diversions. Each then left to govern his realm; the lovely White Cat was immortalized, as much for her kindness and generosity as for her rare merit and her beauty.

> This young prince was lucky indeed
> To find in a cat's guise an august princess
> Whom he would later marry, and accede
> To three thrones and a world of tenderness.
> When two enchanting eyes are inclined
> To inspire love, they seldom find resistance,
> Especially when a wise and ardent mind
> Moves them to inspire lasting allegiance.

> I'll speak no more of the unworthy mother
> Who caused the White Cat so many sorrows
> By coveting the accursed fruits of another,
> Thus ceding her daughter to the fairies' powers.
> Mothers, who have children full of charm,
> Despise her conduct, and keep them from all harm.

1. Rodillardus: Bacon-gnawer, the name of a cat borrowed by La Fontaine from Rabelais; see "The Rat's Council," Fables II, 11. (Warner)
2. Minagrobis: An echo of La Fontaine's Raminagrobis in "The Rat Leagues," Uncollected Fables, which were only published posthumously in 1696, i.e., not long before Mme d'Aulnoy wrote her tale. Grobis: Old French word for a haughty cat. (Warner)
3. Martafax: Another echo of La Fontaine, "The Battle of the Rats and the Weasels," in which the doughty warrior rats are called Artarpax, Psicarpax, and Meridarpax. Fables IV, 6. (Warner)
4. Lhermite: Another nod in the master fabulist's direction, cf. "The Rat Who Retired from the World," Fables VII, 3. (Warner)

5. Tilting at the ring: In this chivalrous variation on the tourney, the contestants do not drive at each other with lances lowered, but at a hoop or ring (often beribboned). (Warner)

6. Sinbad: John Ashbery's only "liberty" with the text, which has "Perroquet" for the parrot's name. As *The Arabian Nights* were soon to appear in Antoine Galland's influential translation (1704–17), Sinbad seemed an apt anticipation. (Warner)

Wonder Tales: Six French Stories of Enchantment, ed. Marina Warner (London: Chatto and Windus, 1994; New York: Farrar, Straus and Giroux, 1996; New York: Vintage, 1996).

ODILON REDON

(1840–1916)

FROM *TO ONESELF*

1869, Paris, April 12—Nature, through an admirable law, intends us to profit from everything, even from our mistakes and vices; it is an unending life, a continual labor whose sap is inexhaustible. A single glance at ourselves proves life and shows us the step taken. What then are an old man's reflections on the past and all the faith he draws from them?

There are those who ask the meaning of the word "spiritualism." They are the same ones who obey only their instincts and who take the highest revelations of poetry for madness. The ideal is a chimera; the luster of truth, the certitudes of the conscience have as their sole cause the nature of our earliest education and the environment in which we lived.

The word "spiritualism" will always be understood as expressing the opposite of the word "materialism." To define it is impossible.

The beautiful and the good are in heaven. Science is on Earth; it crawls. The material hope of the immediate future gives great energy in action. To act against every hope is to act by virtue.

The law of man will replace Scripture only when it has become the sincere expression of the universal conscience.

When society desires good sufficiently to incorporate into its laws the spirit of morality and good which presides over individual effort, that day will be the definitive reign of liberty and of obedience to the divine word.

In the beginning the ideal touched a few men in particular: These were the prophets. Their empire was legitimate and the divine pressure they exerted on the others was fertile and necessary. But the days come when the unanimity of desires will turn law into a docile expression of the great human conscience and consequently the only incitement to liberty.

•

There is something in the heart which dries up when one reads pages written too close to human nature. The fault of certain writing is to have stripped it naked, made it cynical and abject; it would have been better to reveal it in what it possesses of grandeur and consolation.

To write and to publish is the noblest, most delicate work a man can do, for it involves others: To act on another's mind, what a task, what a responsibility before the truth and before oneself! Writing is the greatest art. It traverses time and space, is manifestly superior to the others such as music, whose language also becomes transformed and leaves its work of the past in the night of time.

Your evil lies in the aristocracy. At the very hour of liberty, you flung yourselves on the goods of the earth, and the vices followed you. Self-ishness, concupiscence, despotism, sensuality, complete forgetting of the general welfare. You haven't a shadow of the republican virtue which in spite of everything animated the bold revolutionaries, your generous liberators. Are you guilty of all these evils? Who will reply? Liberty in your hands could never shine with supreme luster. The evil is the fault of the nobility who deviated first; in days of weakness and doubt, one calls on the absent faith; one forgets that liberty implies force and weakness, and that this very abandon proves it.

The fault, the failing, that perpetual obstacle to the realization of good, comprise the cost of our efforts.

When I am alone, I love the open highways; I talk with myself alone. I walk along freely and my body leaves my mind unchained; it argues, reasons, presses me with questions.

But with God, and as a friend of nature, I prefer paths encumbered by the obstacles of a wild way which no human labor has touched. My foot moves freely through the damp grass and I am inspired by the contact of the branch that my face grazes; the stones, the bushes, though filled with thorns, stop me only to converse with me and speak to me; and even in a dark, black wood, I love the storm, the abundant rain, the cold, the ice and the snow; all that winter that men complain of has for me an eloquent language and attracts me, charms me, has always given me deep delight.

Plastic art expires at the breath of the infinite.

Happy are the sages whose life is reasonable and whose strength balances their desire. They dominate us, whatever the mediocrity and inferiority of their intelligence; they judge and dominate us because they do not struggle. A calm life is a merited life. The nobility have it; let us not be jealous. By their high assurance in living off leisure, off their fortunes, they shocked only well-born souls; they are honest, dignified, even kind; their manners are exempt from petty bourgeois preoccupations. This is not their wrong. They are guilty only in their selfish error of supposing the people incapable of the same feelings they have; and also for having given throughout history that fatal example of luxury, superfluity, and personal encroachment, of which the taste for well-being, a characteristic of our time, is the consequence. The people could imitate only what they had seen; hence their torment, for they do not yet have their own tradition. Leisure, repose, reflection, the beneficial occupation of reading had not yet put a little of the ideal into their lives. The preoccupations of thought have not yet made the dignity and nobility of life felt in their souls. Could it be otherwise? They would have had to be angels in order to live through the first days of liberty.

There is a stupid laughter which reveals the heart and lays bare the hidden depths of the soul. There is another kind which reveals celestial joys.

A man of action is not ironic.

The end of a full day gives the mind infinite compensations. The supreme leisure of the souls of the elect is wholly in those exquisite hours which follow painful and fertile effort. There is an age in which the equilibrium of forces allows us to lay hold of these celestial and suave joys, the most beautiful ones in life, and the only ones as well which give us the right to say we have lived.

•

What distinguishes the artist from the dilettante is merely the suffering that the former experiences. The dilettante seeks only his pleasure in art.

There is suffering to be claimed from those we love. The spirit of justice takes precedence over kindness, and yet there are moments, hours of love and grace, in which one would gladly be unjust in order to give, to love. I have never been able to read in myself which is better, he who gives or he who justifies? There is much cause for reflection in this.

Shall we ever arrive at the certainty, at the consciousness of having done all, given all? One walks continually in doubt mingled with confidence, and these dispositions hold alternately the thread of our lives.

And the world, and most of those who are close to us, see in the exercise of art only a work of relaxation and repose!

The taste for art is nothing beside the preoccupations of the heart. And each artist is a man, a being who must also be watched over and cultivated. The man is perhaps merely a simple procedure for the work of the artist. Art is powerless to render the nuances of these situations and all the delicacy of their influences.

The artist must not think that a divine right has placed him above the others. The sense of creation is indeed something, but it is not everything. Some thoroughly mediocre man, or even one totally incapable of appreciating beauty, can show lofty and noble traits of conscience. Certainly we must bless heaven for letting us live in a world in which Beethoven and the God of art have diffused life; above all we must be proud to understand it; but I find deeply self-centered and mediocre the wholly personal suffering of those who would on this account place themselves above others.

The world is peopled by intrepid talkers and blasphemers; they harm themselves alone. The real damage, the true torture is for me only in the spectacle of a false authority which imposes itself. I am vexed only with those who, through their credit, their position, or the authority of a word irregularly acquired, open naive souls to the first joys of goodness and beauty. I blame also those who beneath the vaults of our temples vent an unhealthy clamor about goodness; those who martyrize genius; those, finally, who in their conscience falsify and pervert the natural meaning of the truth. These are the real culprits. This is the evil to be exorcised.

The positivists do not love modern beauty. They are cut off from its music, unless it be lively, dramatic music.

I have known some who were noble-hearted, simple, and touching in their good nature. They have kindness, quietude, something which resembles the feeling of duty accomplished. They have a part of the truth, but they do not have the truth.

The law which directs us toward what we do not have is a fecund and necessary one; we love what completes us. Art, morality, and justice proceed toward nobler ends. The error is to search for the poet's set form of words. Nature is too diverse in her infinite activity for it to be possible for us to penetrate her action and understand its procedures. The heart—love in its shrewd docility—is still the best and the only guide; perhaps it is only through the heart that truth reveals itself; it has the tact, the certainty, the affirmation.

If a vague and perpetual regret mingles with all the hours of your life, if it persists, obstinately forcing its way into your thoughts, your actions, your leisures, then your will is only a lost force, your duty is not fully accomplished.

We behave proudly in the very first moment of intimacy with the things of the mind; those who have seen the ostentation and the external trappings of beauty, everything that has no inner beauty, love these more than her. They speak emphatically, they enter the church to be adored by it. This preoccupation with their person is a sign of their inferiority.

What *remains*, and what must be known of the *great centuries*, are the masterpieces. They are its complete, single, and real expression. At other times, what is essential and characteristic in the works of the human spirit is better written down in the secondary, inferior documents, and nearer to the people, that true artisan of all things.

Every conduct which lets others believe something other than our thought is a lie. Every act whose motive is concealed is a lie. Even silence in certain circumstances can give rise to misunderstanding. Where then is loyalty, sincerity?

The common error of worldly folk is to believe that the world ends with them. A single misplaced word, a gesture, clothing suffice to hide one. They see only the skin of the people.

•

"The heart has its reasons," it has them, pursues them, deliberates in us according to infinitely mysterious secret laws, so that on the occasion of a meeting, a chance meeting with a woman, it takes possession of the whole person, is a domination and invasion, an obscure moment of weakness, in which one can no longer make out very clearly what conduct is; in which the notion of good and evil no longer exists, or is no longer necessary, because what belongs to the heart in that divine moment is something of eternity.

•

1876, May. —Without belonging or wanting to belong to any sect or school, especially where art is concerned, one cannot deny a loyalty of mind which must applaud the beautiful wherever it is found, and which imposes on the one who understands it the desire to communicate and explain it.

I am not *intransigeant*; I shall never acclaim a school which, though good faith is evident, nevertheless limits itself to pure reality, without taking the past into account. To see and to see well will always be the first precept of the art of painting—that is a truth which has always been true. But it is important also to know the nature of the eye that looks, to seek the cause of the feelings experienced by the artist and communicated to the dilettante, and indeed to determine whether there are any; to see, in a word, whether the gift he has offered is of the right sort and sound in fabric. And it is only after this work of analysis and criticism has been completed that it is important to set the finished work in its place in the temple to beauty which we build in our minds.

In the crowd, we take away with us the obstinacy of our fate.

•

Common sense is the talent for good judgment, even without culture, and in a commonplace order of truth. This talent is of supreme use to men who have to do only with the realities of the immediate, the nearest life. It is indispensable to those who create art; also, its absence can sterilize the precious gifts of the finest intellects.

And yet, one may totally and absurdly lack all practical sense and still have genius. So be it!

But the painter always has an eye, an eye that sees.

1876—Photography, used solely for reproducing drawings or bas-reliefs, seems in its proper role in relation to art, which it seconds and aids without leading it astray.

Imagine museums reproduced in this way. The mind balks at calculating the importance which painting would suddenly assume if placed on the same level as literary power (power of multiplication), with its new security assured in time.

•

I am repelled by those who pronounce the word "nature" with greedy mouths, and nothing in their hearts.

I see those who, at the summit of their years and talent, have only their *manner*, an impotent set of theories, a sterile idiosyncrasy, baseness, vain desire to appear clever. They neglect the studies of Corot, which are masterpieces of awkwardness: There the eye and the mind have absolute control; the hand is slave to observation. Corot is the ingenious and sincere imitator of the practice of the art of painting as we find it in the studies of the old masters. Landscape made in this way interests me and attracts me like a delectation. And to think that industry is taking over the studio model: The shops sell photographic life studies, all kinds of nudes, limbs and so on: a truly deadly result. They are as hideous to see as a plaster cast made from life.

The same cynicism prevails for landscape: trees, forests, streams, plains, skies, clouds. One could go no further toward falsifying the view, corrupting students, destroying the seeds of art in young minds.

Rembrandt, despite his masculine energy, kept the sensibility which leads into the paths of the heart. He ransacked its innermost recesses.

Engraving is a completely different agent from faithful photography. It does not render inferior the work which it retraces or re-creates; it is not superior to it; its aim is different; it is something else.

Every document of emotion and passion, of sensibility or even of thought left on marble, on canvas, or in a book, is sacred. This is our true patrimony, the most precious one. And with what nobility it clothes us, poor and precarious creators that we are: The least chronicle, the most precise date of a simple human event—will they ever say what the marvels of a cathedral proclaim, or the tiniest shard of stone from its walls! Touched by mankind, it is impregnated with the spirit of the times. Each era has left a spiritual era in this way. It is through art that the moral and thinking life of humanity can be recaptured and reexperienced.

If it were given us to be able to collect and suddenly call into being the immense chain of materials on which man has left the stamp of his sorrow or the joy of his passion, all palpitating with life, what a sublime reading it would be!

If I had to speak of Michelangelo on the occasion of his centenary, I would have spoken of his soul. I would have said that what it is vital to see in a great man is, more than anything, nature, the force of soul which animates him. When the soul is powerful, the work is too. Michelangelo passed long periods of time without producing. It was then that he wrote his sonnets. His life is beautiful.

There is in Amsterdam a picture which is still in the house where Rembrandt saw it and placed it. The nail from which it hangs is still the same one that the master drove into the wall, in the place and the light that he chose. In France we are incapable of thus conserving works of art, so long and in the same place.

Music is a nocturnal art, the art of the dream; it reigns in winter, in the hour when the soul confines itself.

Music fashions our soul in our youth, and we remain faithful, later on, to the first emotions; music renews them like a kind of resurrection.

Redon's journal, 1867–1915; *À Soi-même: Notes sur la vie, l'art et les artistes* (Paris: Henri Fleury, 1922). *Art and Literature* 6 (Autumn 1965).

ALFRED JARRY

(1873–1907)

FEAR VISITS LOVE

FEAR: Your clock has three hands. Why?

LOVE: It's the custom here.

FEAR: Oh dear, why those three hands? I'm so upset . . .

LOVE: Nothing could be more simple, more natural. Calm yourself. The first marks the hour, the second draws along the minutes, and the third, always motionless, eternalizes my indifference.

FEAR: You're joking. I can't believe that you would dare to presume . . . No, *you* wouldn't dare . . .

LOVE: To lock and load my heart?

FEAR: I don't understand a word of what you're saying.

LOVE: And when I stop talking?

FEAR: Oh! I understand much better.

LOVE: That's precisely the explanation.

FEAR: What explanation?

LOVE: The one I don't wish to give you.

FEAR: I ought to have suspected before I came here that everything would be singular . . .

LOVE: Except for the plurality of my existence. Not content with being double, I am often triple.

FEAR: On my way to your house I crossed a boulevard, deserted as far as infinity, and I walked along beside a great wall, a wall so high and so long that I could barely see a few treetops over it, like clowns' pompoms. I am sure that behind that wall is a cemetery.

LOVE: There is always a cemetery behind a wall.

FEAR: You shouldn't joke about things you don't know about.

LOVE: I am not in the habit of joking about things which are known to be in the public interest. The only thing I find very funny is *fear*. When you tremble I feel like laughing.

FEAR: You're not very lovable.

LOVE: I am loved. That's enough for me.

FEAR: In this very high, very long wall, I finally found an extremely narrow little door, apparently without a lock.

LOVE: I consider that my door should be sexless. It's more chaste.

FEAR: However, by groping in the dark I finally managed to open it.

LOVE: Excellent . . . breach, Madame. In the night all doors are gray, open . . .

FEAR: I entered a blackness, a dark alley which flowed like a torrent at the bottom of a gorge, and I lifted up my head to seek God.

LOVE: Another breach, since you don't believe in God.

FEAR: It's true, I don't believe . . . But when I'm afraid, it comforts me . . .

LOVE: Absurd. Absurd. Absolute. Absolute.

FEAR: I arrived home by way of the absurd or the absolute, which doesn't matter since I arrived. But I'm beginning to feel like a wanderer in a bad dream. Your house doesn't exist, and you yourself are a figment of my imagination.

LOVE: Nothing here is imaginary. You may touch what belongs to me. You may touch it, on condition that you don't take it with you, for, in all probability, it doesn't belong to you.

FEAR: I sought God, yes, and very high up, in the sky or the ceiling of that alley which flowed like the torrent in a gorge, I found something like transparent water. So there were two torrents to cross, one with my feet, the other with my head. And the inexplicable *wall*, that high cemetery wall continued, forming an angle . . .

LOVE: The angle of eternity.

FEAR: You don't seem to be aware of what goes on in your house. So listen seriously to me.

LOVE: I pay very little attention to the details[1] of my door.

FEAR: You're wrong. It's frightening.

LOVE: Then go on wasting your time. My own is fixed from now on by the third hand of the clock.

FEAR: Over my head the limpidity of the water diminished, and at my feet the mud increased. I walked in slime with a stale odor of musk. In the night witches come and empty their slop pails under the windows of young men. Witches whose bloody hands crush muskrat brains for soap. Vile porridge. Suddenly the water of the sky flowed away between two rooftops and disappeared, taking the stars with it, all the stars. There was no more freedom, my feet took root in the ground. You know of course that freedom ends when the stars fall?

LOVE: . . . Starfall.[2] Of course.

FEAR: I stood before another door, even more hermetically shut than the first. *Two steps, of which the first was missing* . . .

LOVE: Of which the first . . . And what held up the second, Madame?

FEAR: Nothing. You knew there had been a first step because there was a gap. Yet the second led you to a threshold! Perhaps the hole of the first step was a cellar window, an air shaft . . .

LOVE: *The* shaft,[3] if I understand correctly.

FEAR: At first I didn't believe that. You only believe the things that give you pleasure. After an hour and a half I placed my toe on the second step and felt it was firm.

LOVE: Nothing is firm except the things held up by emptiness. The globe, for instance.

FEAR: I climbed the chimerical staircase which one never comes down again.

LOVE: You climbed the ladder of the spheres like an astrologer's compasses. It's not new, but you did it without realizing it, because it's a little too logical for you.

FEAR: I climbed . . . *like an astrologer's compasses?* You're not going to tell me my legs are skinny, I hope! Let me get on with the story.

LOVE: Uh . . . do go on, Madame. As for me, I'm going to rest a bit until you've finished, as I'm very lazy. Good night.

FEAR: It was in your corridor of misfortune that I had a foretaste of death! Once the hermetically sealed door was open (this one had no lock, only a copper knocker, and it opened as though it were melting under the repeated blows), I entered, contracting my lips and nostrils so as not to breathe the air of an accursed house. A dog went in with me. I don't know what dog. He was more frightened than his master (I was his master since he had followed me blindly this far), he clung to my skirts, he licked my hands and wet them with the anguish of his tongue which was almost cold. I had an urge to kill him or hug him affectionately so that he wouldn't leave me. He was a good dog, he didn't growl, at the same time he sniffed the doubtful things in that house. He should have growled. The cry of an animal would certainly have brought me back to my natural feelings. And one can only give in to one's supernatural feelings, since they are outside one. I was well aware that the fidelity

of a dog can't counterbalance the sweetness of the wings of the un-
known, which are membranous. Don't tell me that there are human eyes
in the darkness, and that infinity is a pupil; don't tell me that the net-
work of human nerves ends in eyes which are black birds, that network
which is a tree splattering the night with its electric tendrils, and whose
dead mirror would be a fragment of fulgurite. I am, at present, in a
country where the dogs tremble without daring to bark. At the end of
the corridor gyrates a pale staircase. The steps balk at the light. It must
be a staircase that bites. It's going to snap shut under my feet, grab my
feet. I won't climb it. And I climb! The dog deserts me, I realize that he
is backing away from the mortuary teeth of the staircase. I turn as I
climb, but it's not me that turns, it's the pale spiral. It has the slow and
vertiginous movement of a huge ship rolled by the sea. At each step my
heart leaves me and I find my heart again as soon as I have my back to it.
I must be moving around my heart. There is some sort of gas lamp in
the center of the well of the pale staircase. It makes that light I don't see.
Another door. Oh, this one is pretty. It's completely transparent, a pale,
pinkish violet amethyst. It's perhaps a simple stained-glass window. It's
sealed with lead, like a coffin. Behind it the bodies of reptiles are slither-
ing in soft laziness. Two white snakes. When they lean against the glass
there is a swelling which breaks into bubbles of lilac air. These white
snakes have suckers. They have feet. Long sinewy feet. This glass dis-
torts the objects behind it, and the new door—which opens—reveals
two arms, just arms . . .

LOVE: Mine.

FEAR: Here I am in an amazing room.

LOVE: Quite so. There is only one bed.

FEAR: And it's not yours.

LOVE: At any rate it's the one I sleep in when you are here.

FEAR: It's carved out of yew.

LOVE: The turtledoves coo at their ease in the branches of the yew.

FEAR: But the roots of the yew pierce the bellies of the dead.

LOVE: In that case yews are called cypresses. You go too far!

FEAR: My goodness, how you insist on the honorary titles of trees! I sup-
pose *you* never get carried away.

LOVE: It is certain that I don't know you.

FEAR: Do you know yourself?

LOVE: With pleasure. I admit it . . . according to the temple of Apollo,
at Delphi.

FEAR: We shouldn't speak lightly in this room, it's so dark you can hear the spiders spinning in its brain.

LOVE: Since you began to talk seriously they have spun all the canvas for the sails of the boat that is carrying me far from you.

FEAR: It has two windows, this room, two windows facing north . . .

LOVE: Only in the evening . . .

FEAR: Daylight never penetrates here, does it?

LOVE: Yes, it does, when I change my shirt.

FEAR: And what is that screen of mirrors?

LOVE: It's the cage I keep the daylight in . . . I mean . . .

FEAR: No, don't joke about it! This bedroom is sacred.

LOVE: Consecrated, Madame.

FEAR: Don't overdo it. It's not cold in here, though.

LOVE: The tropics, or almost . . . especially since you're magnetized by the North.

FEAR: I want to look out the window.

LOVE: Choose: There is one casement for seeing who's coming, and another for seeing who's going. At the first is fastened a *spy*[4] of smoky silver, almost black. At the second blooms a pot of basil whose yellow flowers have the violent perfume of cat's breath. I never open that one because I don't like flowers . . . and I like even less the musky breath of cats, vile rat-snatchers.

FEAR: Oh, this wall, this wall which reaches to the sky and blocks up space!

LOVE: Behind it is an army which is awaiting orders to proclaim me king . . . or shoot me. I had it built so as not to be disturbed by the perspective.

FEAR: You can hear the sound of the ocean.

LOVE: It's the wind in the alley, together with the passing of the *transatlantic trolleys*.

FEAR: The *spy* reflects the clouds which you can't see because the sky is walled up. It's like a black dreaming of white forms. I am terrified of that *spy*.

LOVE: Wait! With a little spit and my handkerchief, I'm going to brighten it for you.

FEAR: Don't. We would see words written on it. Quickly—back into the room. Someone is coming. I heard the whole sea rising . . . and the transatlantic trolleys too.

LOVE: Then look again, now.

FEAR: I see a woman, a very pale woman, with eyes of green water, who is leaning from the same window we are. I see that she is centuries old, because she is standing against a twenty-year-old tree whose two branches are garlands. It is the *Sea*[5] and *Love*. She is leaning against a maypole whose whiteness is that of the Eucharist, a maypole with the body of a supple man, and, members with members, waves with waves, shivers with shivers, the *Sea* is trying to invade *Love*, and *Love* is trying to resist the *Sea*. (Perhaps it is only a *mother* and her *son*, a most natural offshoot.) I also see clouds galloping in squadrons of white rumps. I see . . . also that I see nothing more. I tried to lean out and almost lost my balance. Let's go back in.

LOVE: You really are dizzy this time.

FEAR: Yes, I was afraid to recognize myself in that eternally treacherous woman: the rising *Sea*!

LOVE: Come on, look me in the eye and stop divagating[6] with your pointless waves and shivers! What else do you see?

FEAR: I barely see your real face, but above it I see the white dial of your strange clock where there are three hands.

LOVE: The first marks the hour, the second drags the minutes, and the third, always motionless, eternalizes my indifference.

FEAR: Ah! You don't love me anymore!

LOVE: That was the one thing to fear, Madame.

1. The French is *bagatelles*; *bagatelle*, besides meaning "trifle," is also a slang word for the vagina. (Trans.)

2. *Toile tombe*, "planting falls," a pun on Fear's previous words, *étoiles tombent*, "stars fall." (Trans.)

3. A play of *jour de cave*, "cellar window," and *jour*, "understood," *de souffrance*, "day of suffering." (Trans.)

4. *Espion* means both "spy" and "window mirror," a device enabling one to see visitors outside from within. (Trans.)

5. Throughout this speech and Fear's next one there is punning on the words *mer*, "sea," and *mère*, "mother." (Trans.)

6. There is a play here on the words *divaguer*, "to divagate, wander from the point," and *vagues*, "waves." (Trans.)

"La Peur chez l'Amour," from *L'Amour en visites* (Paris: P. Fort, 1898). *Fiction* 2, no. 1 (1973).

RAYMOND ROUSSEL

(1877–1933)

AN UNPUBLISHED NOTE

Tuesday

Dear Sir

Agreed for tomorrow Wednesday at seven.

Thank you for your astounding sonnet. So many rhymes for "Roussel"! It is a tour de force and *"lis braire"*[1] is terrific. It reminds me of this couplet of twelve-syllable lines:

> *Dans ces meubles laqués, rideaux et dais moroses*
> *Danse, aime, bleu laquais, rit d'oser des mots roses.*[2]

fondly,
    Raymond Roussel

---

1. "Read to bray," a pun on *libraire*, "bookseller." (Trans.)
2. "Amid this lacquered furniture, these gloomy curtains and canopies, / Dance, make love, blue lackey, laugh to venture blushing words."

    The two lines are almost identical phonetically. By an odd coincidence, Breton, who couldn't possibly have known of this letter, quotes this same couplet in his preface to Jean Ferry's "Essay on Raymond Roussel," attributing it to Charles Cros and citing it as a precedent for Roussel's linguistic experiments. Breton however gives *ris*, the familiar imperative of the verb *rire*, to laugh, rather than Roussel's *rit*, the third-person singular, which here makes no sense grammatically. The lines were published in an article by Charles Cros in his *Revue du monde nouveau* (April 2, 1874), but according to the editors of the Pléiade edition of his works, are "undoubtedly not by him." They formed the first and fourth lines of a quatrain;

the two inner lines are similarly constructed "totally rhyming" verses. The article satirizes the formal strictures of the Parnassian poets. (Trans.)

Probably written by Roussel to Pierre Frondaie. *Atlas Anthology* 4 (1987). Reprinted in *Selected Prose*, by John Ashbery, ed. Eugene Richie (Ann Arbor: University of Michigan Press, 2004; Manchester, U.K.: Carcanet Press, 2004).

FROM *IMPRESSIONS OF AFRICA*

Chapter One

About four o'clock that afternoon of June 25, everything seemed ready for the coronation of Talou VII, Emperor of Ponukele and King of Drelchkaff.

Although the sun had passed the zenith, the heat remained oppressive in that region of equatorial Africa, and each of us remained acutely conscious of the sultry, threatening weather, untempered by the slightest breeze.

In front of me extended the vast Square of Trophies situated at the very heart of Ejur, the imposing capital formed of innumerable huts and lapped by the Atlantic Ocean, whose distant roar I could hear on my left.

The perfect square of the esplanade was outlined on all sides by a border of venerable sycamores; weapons deeply imbedded in the bark of each trunk served as supports for various heads, banners, and all kinds of decorations placed there by Talou VII or by his ancestors on their return from many a triumphant expedition.

On my right, in front of the central point of the line of trees, stood a red theater resembling a huge Punch-and-Judy, on whose pediment the words "Club of the Incomparables" in silver letters on three lines were surrounded by dazzling golden rays radiating in all directions like sunbeams.

On the stage, which was presently visible, a table and chair seemed to await a lecturer. Several unframed portraits pinned to the backdrop were underlined by an explanatory label which read "Electors of Brandenburg."

Closer to me, on a line with the red theater, stood a broad wooden pedestal on which Nair, a Negro youth of barely twenty, was standing and leaning forward, engaged in an absorbing task. On his right, two stakes planted respectively at two corners of the pedestal were attached at the top by a long, supple cord, sagging under the weight of three objects hanging in a row and distinctly visible, like the prizes in a lottery. The first object was none other than a bowler hat on whose crown the word "PINCHED" was inscribed in whitish capital letters; then came a dark gray suede glove whose palm, facing me, was ornamented with a letter "C" lightly traced in chalk; finally, a fragile sheet of parchment dangled from the cord: Covered with curious hieroglyphics, it bore at the top a rather crude drawing representing five people, obviously meant to appear ridiculous through their general aspect and the exaggeration of their features.

A prisoner on his pedestal, Nair had his right foot caught in a veritable snare tightly fastened to the solid platform; like a living statue he was making slow and punctual gestures, while murmuring groups of words learned by heart. On a specially designed support in front of him, a fragile pyramid, made of three panels of bark joined together but noticeably raised, served him as a loom; on an extension of the support, within easy reach, was a supply of fruit pods, whose outsides were covered with a grayish vegetable substance resembling the cocoon of a larva just before it turns into a chrysalis. Pinching with two fingers a fragment of these delicate envelopes and drawing his hand slowly toward him, the youth created a tensile bond resembling the gossamer threads that drift through the woods in spring; with these imperceptible filaments he was weaving a marvelously subtle and complex web, moving his hands with amazing agility, crossing, tying, interlacing in every possible way the dreamlike ligaments, which formed a gracious amalgam. The phrases he murmured to himself served to regulate his perilous, precise manipulations; the slightest error and the whole work would have been spoiled, and, without the automatic aid to his memory furnished by a certain memorized formula, Nair would never have been able to accomplish his task.

On his right, other pyramids placed along the edge of the pedestal with their summits pointing backward allowed one to appreciate the appearance of his work after its completion: The base, upright and in plain view, was faintly indicated by an almost invisible fabric, more tenuous than a cobweb. Fastened by its stem deep inside each pyramid, a red flower led the eye straight through the imperceptible veil formed by the aerial web. Not far from the stage of the Incomparables, to the actor's right, two poles four or five feet apart supported an apparatus in motion; the nearest pole held a long spindle around which a strip of yellowish parchment fitted tightly; solidly nailed to the farther post, a square board horizontally placed served as a base for a vertical cylinder which was being slowly turned by clockwork.

The yellowish band, unfolding uninterruptedly over the whole distance of the interval, embraced the cylinder, which, in turning, drew it continually back to itself, to the detriment of the distant pivot forcibly involved in its gyratory motion.

On the parchment, groups of boldly drawn savage warriors succeeded each other in diverse attitudes; one column, running at breakneck speed, seemed to pursue a fleeing enemy; another, lying in ambush behind an embankment, seemed to await patiently an opportunity to show itself; here, two phalanxes equal in number were engaged in fierce hand-to-hand battle; there, fresh troops struck out with fierce gestures to fling themselves bravely into a distant melee. The unfurling parchment constantly offered new strategic surprises thanks to the infinite multiplicity of the effects obtained.

Facing me, at the other extremity of the esplanade, stood a kind of altar preceded by several steps covered with a thick carpet; a coat of white paint veined with bluish lines gave the ensemble, seen from a distance, the appearance of marble.

On the sacred table, represented by a long board fastened halfway up the structure and covered with a cloth, could be seen a rectangle of parchment speckled with hieroglyphics and standing erect next to a heavy cruet filled with oil. Next to it, a larger sheet of luxurious heavy paper bore this title carefully traced in gothic letters: "Reigning House of Ponukele-Drelchkaff"; under this heading, a round portrait—a kind of delicately tinted miniature—depicted two Spanish girls of thirteen or fourteen wearing the national mantilla—twin sisters, judging from the exact resemblance of their faces; at first sight, the picture seemed to be part of the document, but on closer examination one discovered a narrow band of transparent muslin which, adhering both to the circumference of the painted disk and the heavy vellum, rendered as perfect as possible the juncture of the two objects, in reality independent of each other; to the left of the double effigy the name "SOUANN" was printed in heavy capitals; beneath it the rest of the sheet was filled by a genealogical tree comporting two distinct branches, issuing parallel from the two gracious Iberians who formed its topmost point; one of these lines terminated with the word "Extinction," whose letters, almost as large as those of the title, aimed brutally at a sensational effect; the other, which did not extend quite so far down as its neighbor, seemed on the contrary to defy the future by the absence of any terminal bar.

Near the altar, toward the right, stood a gigantic palm tree, whose magnificent foliage attested to great age; a placard attached to its trunk bore the commemorative inscription: "Restoration of the Emperor Talou VII to the Throne of His Forefathers." Sheltered by the palm leaves, a stake planted in the ground supported a soft-boiled egg on the square platform furnished by its summit.

On the left, equidistant from the altar, a tall plant, old and decrepit, offered a sad pendant to the luxuriant palm; it was a rubber tree whose sap had dried up and which had fallen almost into decay. A litter of woven twigs, placed in its shade, bore the horizontal cadaver of the Negro king, Yaour IX, dressed in the classic costume of Gretchen in *Faust*, with a pink woolen dress, small alms-purse, and thick blond wig, whose long braids, drawn over his shoulders, reached halfway down his legs.

On my left, facing the red theater and with its back to the row of sycamores, a stone-colored building suggested a miniature version of the Paris Bourse.

Between this edifice and the northwest corner of the esplanade was a row of several life-size statues.

The first depicted a man mortally wounded by a weapon thrust into his heart. Instinctively his two hands clutched at the wound, while his legs bent under the weight of his body, which was about to topple over backward. The statue was black and seemed, at first glance, to be made in one solid piece, but as one looked at it one slowly became aware of a multitude of grooves running in all directions and generally forming numerous parallel groups. Actually the work was composed solely of countless whalebone corset stays cut and molded according to the necessities of the modeling. Flat-headed nails, their points no doubt bent on the inside, fastened these supple strips together; they were juxtaposed so artfully as not to leave the slightest interstice. The face itself, with the details of its agonized expression, was made of nothing but carefully fitted-together stays which reproduced faithfully the form of the nose, the lips, the eyebrow ridges, and the eyeballs. The handle of the weapon that pierced the dying man's heart suggested that a great technical difficulty had been overcome, on account of the elegance of the hilt, in which could be perceived the traces of two or three whalebones cut in short fragments and curved to form rings. The muscular body, the clenched arms, the sinewy legs about to give way—everything seemed to palpitate or suffer, as a result of the striking and perfect contours imparted to the invariable dark-colored strips.

The feet of the statue rested on an extremely simple vehicle, whose low platform and four wheels were fabricated with other ingeniously combined black whalebone fragments. Two narrow rails, made of a raw, reddish, and gelatinous substance, which was nothing other than calves' lights, were aligned on a blackened wood surface, and gave because of their relief if not their color the exact illusion of a segment of railroad; the four immobile wheels fitted them without crushing them.

The wooden railbed formed the top of a wooden pedestal, entirely black, whose front displayed a white inscription which read: "The Death of the Helot Saridakis." Underneath, in the same snowy lettering, could be seen the following diagram, half in Greek and half in French, and accompanied by a slender bracket:

$$\text{DUEL} \quad \begin{cases} \bar{\eta}\sigma\tau\text{ov} \\ \acute{\eta}\sigma\tau\eta\nu \end{cases}$$

Next to the helot a bust of a thinker with knitted brows wore an expression of intense and fecund meditation. On the pedestal one could read the name:

IMMANUEL KANT

Next came a sculptural group representing a touching scene. A horseman with the ferocious face of a myrmidon seemed to question a nun standing with her back to the gate of her convent. In the background, which ended in a bas-relief, other armed men mounted on restless steeds awaited their chief's command. On the base the following title engraved in concave letters, *The Lie of the Nun Perpetua*, was followed by the interrogative sentence: "Is this where the fugitives are hiding?"

Farther on, a curious evocation, accompanied by the explanatory words "The Regent Bowing before Louis XV," showed Philip of Orleans respectfully bending low before the child-king, aged about ten, whose pose was full of natural and unconscious majesty.

Unlike the helot, the bust and the two groups had the appearance of terra-cotta.

Norbert Montalescot, calm and vigilant, was walking about near his works, surveying in particular the helot, whose fragility rendered the careless contact of a passerby even more to be dreaded.

Beyond the last statue stood a tiny cell without a door, whose four walls, of equal width, were made of heavy black canvas which no doubt blocked the sun's rays. The roof, slightly inclined along a single plane, was made of strange pages from a book, yellow with age and cut in the form of tiles; the text, in English and printed in large type, had faded and in some places completely disappeared, but certain pages whose top was visible bore the title *The Fair Maid of Perth* still legibly printed. In the center of the roof was a tightly shut trapdoor, which, instead of glass panes, was fitted with the same pages tinted by age and wear. The whole of the fragile covering must have created inside a diffuse, yellowish light, soft and full of repose.

A kind of chord like that of brass instruments, but much fainter, escaped at regular intervals from inside the cell, and created the exact impression of musical breathing.

Just opposite Nair, a tombstone, on a line with the Bourse, served as a support for the various parts of a Zouave's uniform. A rifle and some cartridge pouches had been added to this cast-off military clothing, obviously destined to perpetuate piously the memory of the entombed man.

Erect behind the funeral slab, a panel covered with black cloth offered to the gaze a series of twelve watercolors, arranged by threes in four equal rows symmetrically placed one above the other. The resemblances between the people in the pictures gave one to suppose that the series was linked to some dramatic narrative. A few words by way of a title had been traced with a brush above each picture.

In the first painting a noncommissioned officer and a flashily dressed blond woman were ensconced in a luxurious Victoria; the words "Flore and Sergeant Major Lécurou" summarily designated the couple.

Next came "The Performance of *Daedalus*," represented by a wide stage on which a tenor in Greek robes seemed to sing with all his voice; in the first row of the stage box could be seen the sergeant major seated next to Flore, who was peering through her lorgnette in the direction of the singer.

In "The Consultation," an old woman in a voluminous cloak was drawing Flore's attention to a celestial planisphere pinned to a wall, and knowingly extending her forefinger toward the constellation Cancer.

"The Secret Correspondence," which began a second row of pictures, showed the woman with the cloak offering Flore one of those special stencils necessary for decoding certain cryptograms and which consist of a simple sheet of cardboard bizarrely pierced with holes.

The décor of "The Signal" was the terrace of an almost deserted café, in front of which a dark-complexioned Zouave seated alone at a table was pointing out to the waiter a large moving bell at the top of a nearby steeple; underneath one could read this dialogue: "Waiter, why is the bell ringing?" "For the evening service." "Then bring me an *arlequin*."

"The Sergeant Major's Jealousy" depicted the courtyard of a barracks where Lécurou, raising four fingers of his right hand, seemed to address a furious reprimand at the Zouave already seen in the previous picture; the scene was brutally accompanied by this phrase of military slang: "Four days' C.B.!"

At the beginning of the third row, "The *Bravo*'s Rebellion" introduced a very blond Zouave who, refusing to execute an order of Lécurou, answered with the single word "No!" inscribed underneath the watercolor.

"The Culprit's Death," underlined by the command "Aim!" showed a firing squad aiming, under the sergeant major's orders, at the heart of the golden-haired Zouave.

In "The Usurious Loan," the woman in the cloak reappeared holding out several banknotes to Flore, who, seated at a desk, seemed to be signing an acknowledgment of a debt.

The final row began with "The Police in the Gambling Den." Here a wide balcony from which Flore was leaping into space allowed one to see through a certain open window a large gaming table surrounded by punters terrified by the inopportune arrival of several personages dressed in black.

The next-to-last picture, entitled "The Morgue," showed, head-on, the corpse of a woman lying on a slab behind a glass partition; behind, a silver chatelaine hung in a conspicuous place was weighted down by a precious watch.

Finally, "The Fatal Affront" ended the series with a nocturnal landscape; in the shadows one could see the dark Zouave administering a slap to Sergeant Major Lécurou while, in the distance, standing out against a forest of masts, a kind of placard illuminated by a powerful streetlamp displayed three words: "Port of Bougie." Behind me, forming a pendant to the altar, a dark rectangular shed of very small dimensions had as a façade a light grating of slender wooden bars painted black; four native prisoners, two men and two women, paced silently inside this exiguous prison; above the grating the word "Depot" was inscribed in reddish letters.

Beside me a large group of passengers from the *Lynceus* stood awaiting the appearance of the promised parade.

How I Wrote Certain of My Books and Other Writings, ed. Trevor Winkfield (Cambridge, Mass.: Exact Change, 1995). First published in *Portfolio and ARTnews Annual* 6 (Autumn 1962).

DOCUMENTS TO SERVE
AS AN OUTLINE

Note by John Ashbery

In an essay published in 1962 in the French review *L'Arc*, reprinted below, I discussed the opening chapter "In Havana" which had been suppressed, at Roussel's request, from the posthumous printed version of *Documents to Serve as an Outline*, and my reasons for overriding Roussel's wishes in this regard. I wrote among other things that "it appears obvious that it was not doubts about the quality of the work that prompted Roussel to write the note quoted above, but a simple desire for symmetry: Shorn of their introduction, the six 'documents' form an easily publishable whole."

Today, thirty years later, I am not so sure. It is impossible to know what Roussel would have understood by terms such as "quality" and "symmetry," and I should have realized this. The fact that he considered two early efforts, the poem *L'Âme de Victor Hugo* (originally entitled *Mon Âme*) and the novel in verse *La Doublure* as the apogee of his work, after which it was all downhill, is proof enough either of his own unreliable judgment vis-à-vis his own writing or of the impossibility of fathoming what his aesthetic criteria were. Most readers of Roussel would, I think, consider them minor if not downright tedious efforts, especially *L'Âme de Victor Hugo*, and agree that his writing career begins immediately afterward, with the long poem *La Vue*. Thus any aesthetic judgment of his work ought to come with the warning that it probably contradicts or at least has no bearing on the author's intentions.

Another problem I have in assessing the *Documents* is precisely their title, which was assigned to them by Roussel in his note to the printer regarding posthumous publication, and might well have been different, of course, if he had lived to complete the book. But why "documents" and why "outline"? "In Havana" apprises us that the documents were to be assembled as evidence by the thirty members of a club whose raison d'être was to prove the superiority of Europe over America (only six of the planned thirty were printed). Yet it is difficult to see in what way they fulfill their purpose, or any purpose. They are merely tales within tales, from which a didactic lesson seems totally absent. There is no mention of North America or Americans (except for the brief appearance of the Arctic explorer T . . . in "In Havana," who has nothing to do with the club's stated goal). It is true that most of the tales have a European setting, though some do not. Some take place in imaginary countries ("Eisnark" or "Belotina") while almost all of the fourth document is nominally set in Honduras and is chiefly concerned with narrating the plot of a drama by the great (and fictitious) Honduran poet Angelo Essermos—surely an example of *Central* American superiority, one would have thought; elsewhere a Mexican novel plays an important role. Could this seeming discrepancy between the *Documents*' stated theme and their actual content have been cause for Roussel's decision to excise the first chapter? Doubtless we'll never know (though it will be interesting to see if the recently discovered hoard of Roussel's papers presently being catalogued at the Bibliothèque Nationale includes any which have a bearing on the *Documents*).

As for *canevas*, which I have *faute de mieux* translated as "outline," it too seems a misleading if not mystifying appellation. Harrap's dictionary gives other possible translations: "groundwork, sketch, skeleton (of drawing, novel, etc.)." The original meaning is canvas in the sense of an embroidery canvas—something to be finished. Harrap's cites the phrase "*broder le canevas*, to embroider the story, to add artistic verisimilitude to a bald and unconvincing narrative." Yet the *Documents* in no way resemble sketches; they are in fact the most drastic examples of Roussel's constant urge to pare his writing down to its barest essentials (brevity being his chief, if not only, aesthetic criterion)—something hardly possible in a first or early draft. In *Roussel l'ingénu* Michel Leiris writes: "As for style, the only qualities Roussel seems to have sought for, beyond the strictest grammatical correctness, are the maximum of exactitude and concision. I remember causing him a lively pleasure by chance, in praising the extraordinary brevity (to the point where, spoken on stage, the text was very difficult to follow) of each of the anecdotes whose linkage constitutes *L'Étoile au front*: 'I forced myself to write each story with the fewest possible words' was Roussel's approximate reply."

Perhaps, however, there were other ways in which the *Documents*, despite their radical bouillon-cube condensation (and this is perhaps as good a place as any to apologize for inevitable shortcomings in my translation, which doubtless employs more words than Roussel would have liked in some cases and in others makes his succinctness sound more eccentric than it is in the original). One possibility is suggested by Leiris in a 1987 addendum to his earlier essay "Autour des Nouvelles Impressions d'Afrique." He speaks of an earlier version of Chant 1 of *Nouvelles Impressions d'Afrique* deposited with Leiris's father (Roussel's business manager) on March 6, 1917, which began and ended "exactly like the version printed in the book, but comprising a quite limited number of insertions, so that the reader doesn't find himself entangled in a labyrinth. This text, in flawless alexandrines, presents itself not as a simple first draft but as a considerably shorter though seemingly finished version of the definitive text, making the latter seem the extraordinarily dense result of a kind of phenomenal padding whose aim is above all to demonstrate the power of an imagination." Thus, what appears to us as the stylistic perfection of the *Documents* (from Roussel's point of view, at least) may be misleading: Quantity could have been as important as quality, and the relatively brief tales may have been meant to be "padded" to staggering proportions, resulting in a tome of enormous length, since the book if completed on the scale of the *Documents* as they were published would already have been some three hundred pages long. Perhaps that's what was haunting Roussel during his apparently last encounter with Leiris, in Mme Dufrène's apartment at the beginning of 1933, when Leiris found him looking "slumped, and as though speaking from a great distance." On Leiris's asking him whether he was still writing, Roussel replied: *"C'est tellement difficile!"*

The difficulty may well have been increased for him by the fact that he was intentionally forging a vast cryptogram. In the manuscript of the *Documents*, which I examined at the home of some relatives of Roussel, all dates are left blank, and proper names are indicated only by a first initial. This is also the case with the galley proof of "In Havana." In his note concerning the eventual publication of the *Documents*, Roussel requests that someone at the publishing firm fill in the dates and proper names; Michel Leiris tells us that he customarily asked this of his publisher, but invariably changed the names himself. A recently discovered manuscript of *Locus Solus*, sold at auction last year, contains many such changes; for instance, the name of the principal character, Martial Canterel, was arrived at only after eight or nine other names (with different initials) had been rejected. These however were normal French names; many of those in the *Documents* are sheer invention. It seems unlikely that an employee at Lemerre would have arrived at names like Ornigec, Tercus de Lal, Bahol de Jic, Dramieuse, Dess, and Gléoc. Fanciful names abound in *Impressions d'Afrique*; there, of course, they can be accounted for by the "exotic" locale; moreover, the European characters have conventional names. In the *Documents*, even French characters have outlandish names, suggesting that Roussel himself supplied them, for purposes of his own. Some of the characters however are actual historical figures: Jesus and Mary Magdalene appear twice, and personages from French history such as Barras, Carrier, Desaix, and even Napoleon have cameo roles in narratives that are of course dependent to some extent on historical circumstance. (Unfortunately I can't remember whether or not these names were also left blank in the manuscript I saw.)

Thus we are obliged to read these Chinese-box tales with the understanding that we are not being told all; that behind their polished surface an encrypted secret probably exists. I am reminded of the metaphor Henry James used in *The Golden Bowl* for the hidden relationship between the Prince and Charlotte as it appeared to Maggie Verver: that of an elaborate pagoda with no visible entrance. In Roussel's case this persistent feeling of not knowing precisely what he is up to paradoxically adds to the potent spell of the writing. The stories are intriguing in themselves, the strangely crystallized language a joy to savor, and at the same time a kind of "stereo" effect enhances the experience. We are following him on one level and almost but not entirely missing him on another, a place where secrets remain secret—the "Republic of Dreams" of which Louis Aragon declared him president.

Introduction to "In Havana,"* by John Ashbery

The text which follows is apparently the first unpublished work of Raymond Roussel to be discovered up to now.[1] It was intended to be the first chapter of Roussel's last, unfinished novel, which was published minus this opening chapter in his posthumous collection, *How I Wrote Certain*

---

*This article was published in the French review *L'Arc* in 1962. I wrote it in English and it was translated into French by a friend, the late Michel Thurlotte. My original text seems to have disappeared, so that for the purposes of this publication I have had to translate it from French back into English.

of My Books, under the title *Documents to Serve as an Outline*. In addition to its purely literary attractiveness, the fragment presents a number of peculiarities.

The first is that it survived at all. The published *Documents* were preceded by a note from Roussel dated January 15, 1932:

> If I die before having completed this work and in case someone wishes to publish it even in its unfinished state, I desire that the beginning be suppressed, and that it begin with the First Document, which follows, and that the initials be replaced by names which will fill in the blanks, and that it be given a general title: *Documents to Serve as an Outline*.

Nonetheless the publisher Lemerre had begun by printing the beginning Roussel later wanted to suppress: The proofs for most of it are extant, and for the last few lines, a handwritten note which has turned up among papers of Roussel discovered since his death. The fact that at the time he wrote the note in January 1932 he had finished only six of the thirty Documents which were to make up the novel leads one to believe that at his death in July 1933 he had still not made a definitive decision to keep or suppress the first chapter: Perhaps he had it printed so early on in order to give himself time to reflect on the matter.

For several reasons I have decided not to observe Roussel's stated desire that the chapter not be published. First and most important, it seems to me that any text by Roussel deserves to be known. In addition it appears obvious that it was not doubts about the quality of the work that prompted Roussel to write the note quoted above, but a simple desire for symmetry: Shorn of their introduction, the six "documents" form an easily publishable whole.

The personality of the writer furnishes an additional justification: It is well known that he was haunted by the idea of posthumous glory. "This glory will shine on all my works without exception; it will reflect on all the events of my life; people will look up the details of my childhood and admire the way I played prisoner's base," he confided to Dr. Pierre Janet, who treated him. Since the glory to come was the great consolation of his unhappy life, we might conclude that the publication of this text would not have displeased him.

The first chapter sheds new light on the *Documents* it was meant to precede and which are, in my opinion, one of Roussel's most remarkable works.[2] We now see that the novel was to take place in Cuba, but that it was interrupted almost at the beginning by a series of digressions (as in *Impressions of Africa* and *Locus Solus*). Each of the chapters is made up in turn of dozens of very short narratives, adroitly dovetailed, which form the actual fabric of the novel. Each document, we can now see, is an illustration of the superiority of Europe over America and is the result of patient research by a member of the club of which M . . . is the female president.

However, the mysterious aspects of the work, those surrounding the coded meanings in which it seems so rich, those resulting from Roussel's method of composition and the very nature of his writing (of which he left only a brief explanation in his essay "How I Wrote Some of My Books"), cannot be explained merely by his known techniques of composition. On the single galley proof which comprises the text, proper names are left blank and replaced by initials, while dates are omitted.[3] No doubt this will provide those who believe Roussel's work to be one vast and theoretically decipherable riddle with a persuasive argument. The presence of the initials and the absence of any name or date strongly suggest the use of a code. This hypothesis is all the more plausible given Roussel's well-known passion for mystery and mystifications, cryptograms, ciphers, and other tools of secrecy.

Thus, to start with commonplace phrases, deform them, obtain phrases that are very close phonetically and use the latter as elements of a narrative, is to use a code. Moreover, references to ciphers and clues abound in his work: The *"grille"* or cipher stencil that figures in the story of the Zouave in *Impressions of Africa* reappears in the Fifth Document, where the soldier Armand Vage inherits from a wealthy sister "a piece of cardboard pierced with two holes, which could only be a stencil meant to lead to the discovery of a treasure." (More of him later.)

As regards style, the text has the same radical concision and peculiar transparency of the *Documents*. After the acrobatics of *New Impressions of Africa*, with its interlaced parenthetical passages inserted willy-nilly in the procrustean bed of the alexandrine, Roussel's prose reaffirms its rigor, even more marked here than in *Locus Solus*. He submits his sentences to processes of condensation that result in amazing verbal crystallizations. Furthermore he imposes a new discipline on himself by forcing each of the episodes of his book to fulfill a narrative function: A . . .'s "measure of authority" serves the same story-spinning purpose in this preparatory chapter as does the superiority of Europe in the Documents themselves. Incidentally the procedure recalls the "lists of examples" in *New Impressions of Africa.*

In the course of these few pages we come upon a number of motifs and words dear to Roussel. Among the former are the passionate friendship of two siblings (recalling Séil-Kor and Nina in *Impressions of Africa,* Fermoir and Tige in "The Coils of the Great Serpent," and perhaps Roussel's deep affection for his own sister when they were children); the theme of twins (the "Espagnolettes" of *Impressions of Africa*) of unequal growth (the rubber tree and the palm in the same book); the *catin* (harlot, strumpet) who appears in *New Impressions* and throughout Roussel's work) with a past described as *houleux* (turbulent, checkered): Jean Ferry correctly cites the latter as one of Roussel's favorite adjectives. Moreover the setting of the book, *Havana, Cuba,* hints at a coarse play on words. Concerning the scatological element in *New Impressions,* Ferry wrote in his book-length essay on the poem: "I shall limit myself to pointing out Roussel's extraordinary prudery with regard to this sort of subject matter in his earlier works. I should very much like to know, once others have studied and resolved the problem, what sluices burst in him on this occasion, causing these malodorous streams to run together." But it seems to me that these references had already appeared, in hidden form, in previous works. Among the objects ornamenting the Square of Trophies in *Impressions of Africa* is a small privylike building whose gently sloping roof is made of *feuillets* ("leaves" but also "sheets of toilet paper") taken from the book *The Fair Maid of Perth* (the French pronunciation of Perth is the same as that of *pertes,* a type of vaginal discharge); several portraits of the Electors of Brandenbourg ("Brandebourg," the localized version of the place-name, might be a pun on *bran de bourg*: "shit of the town"); and a watercolor depicting the "immoral" Flore training her lorgnette (the phrase is *"braquer sa lorgnette,"* transformable into a spoonerism, *lorgner sa braguette*: "ogle his codpiece") on an actor performing on a stage. One could cite other examples that seem to suggest that the solemn façade of Roussel's prose style is in fact riddled with puns, spoonerisms, and other *jeux de mots* which are often of an obscene nature.[4]

But "Cuba"; the "Club" with its thirty members, each charged with the mission of "providing the handsomest stone for the edifice"; as well as the fact that, of a total of thirty Documents, only six were completed, bring us once again to that "cube" that occurs throughout Roussel's work, and whose possible meaning is suggested by André Breton in his preface to Ferry's "Essay on Raymond Roussel." "The cube . . . represents one of

Roussel's chief preoccupations and one of the main clues in his play [*The Dust of Suns*], and is also one of the capital stages in the production of the philosopher's stone . . . Fulcanelli, in his work on alchemy, reproduces the image of a cubical stone secured by ropes that is part of a bas-relief decoration of the St. Martin fountain, a few steps from the theater where *The Dust of Suns* was performed." And a similar stone makes a striking appearance in the Fifth Document: "On his twenty-first try, struck by the words 'cube' and 'mesmerize' [*méduser*], perfectly framed by the two holes in the stencil, Armand Vage abstained from further meditative reading: '*A cube would mesmerize him.*' Having lifted a remarkably cubical mossy stone at the edge of a brook that ran through his sister's garden, he discovered a substantial hoard."[5]

One hesitates before a number of possible interpretations. The puns suggested by this "Cuba" where the novel is situated make one wonder whether Roussel hasn't proceeded "alchemically" on several levels: that of the psychological unconscious (sublimation of *shameful* material by the work of the artist); that of language—Cuba for *cul bas* (posterior), *Havane* (the French word for a shade of tan like that of a cigar) for the color of excrement; and finally that of alchemy itself in Breton's sense.

The text presents a further singularity. At the end of the chapter, M . . . , looking for a costume befitting her role as president of a club founded to publicize the glory of Europe, has a sudden inspiration. "Among some Dresden porcelains displayed from time immemorial in a vitrine in her parlor was one that depicted the Abduction of Europa.[6] A graceful garment, closely modeled after that of the statuette—and completed by a flesh-colored leotard—became her presidential uniform." Curiously, a Dresden figurine representing the Abduction of Europa figured in the important art collection of Mme Roussel, the writer's mother. A photograph of it is reproduced in the lavish catalogue printed for the sale of the collection, which was organized by Roussel and his sister in 1912, shortly after their mother's death. This porcelain was then an object that Roussel himself had seen "from time immemorial" in his mother's salon (it is perhaps worth pointing out that her name, Marguerite, begins with an M), and is not a figment of his imagination. Yet we know that Roussel made it a rule to exclude all reality from his work; Janet writes: "Martial [Roussel] has a very interesting conception of beauty in literature: The work of art must contain nothing real, no observation of the real or spiritual world, only totally imaginary arrangements." For a reason we cannot know, Roussel here uses an existing object, a porcelain statuette sold at auction twenty years earlier. One could hardly deduce the presence of an autobiographical element in his work from the circumstance, but it is nonetheless interesting since it suggests that the relationship between the life and work of this most secretive of French writers may be less disjunct than was previously supposed. The details we possess concerning that life are, unfortunately, minimal, but it is always possible that new facts will be revealed which will shed further light on an oeuvre so carefully concealed behind enigmas of all kinds.

Will the cipher be decoded? Will the secret—philosopher's stone or "hoard"—which those familiar with the work (Leiris, Breton, Ferry) agree that it conceals, ever be discovered? It's unlikely, despite the new clues that "In Havana" seems to contain. Doubtless the attraction of a work like this is directly linked to the obscurity of its author's intentions; its charm is partly that of some antique mechanism constructed for a use that escapes us today. Perhaps the message Roussel wanted to leave with us comes down to this: the impossibility of knowing all; the possibility of a superior knowledge to which we will not attain.

1. 1962.
2. Not everyone agrees: Rayner Heppenstall, in his *Raymond Roussel: A Critical Study*, sees in them signs of "deterioration of mind."
3. This was not a new practice for him: The names of characters were also left blank in the published version of "The Place of the Red Buttons," one of the *Texts of Early Youth*. In the manuscript of the *Documents*, which I saw once at the home of some distant cousins of Roussel, dates were left blank and names indicated by an initial and a blank. But since the proofs have apparently not survived, it is impossible to know whether the names and dates were eventually supplied by Roussel or (as he had requested in his note) by another hand. The names *sound* Rousselian.

   Speaking of proofs, when I was beginning research on Roussel in about 1959 I went to the offices of Lemerre, which was then moribund but still extant, asking to see any papers they might have relating to Roussel. I was told that there were indeed files but that I would need the permission of a member of the family in order to examine them. I received this permission from Michel Ney, Roussel's nephew and heir, who accompanied me to the Lemerre offices, whereupon the same official I had spoken to previously told us that they had no Roussel papers! A few months later Lemerre shut down for good and its archives were, I believe, destroyed.

4. I am indebted to Pierre Martory for suggesting these possible plays on words, and also for discovering a copy of the catalogue of Mme Roussel's art collection (see note 6) at a Paris flea market, at a time when no one knew of its existence.

5. Strangely, Palermo, the city that Roussel seems to have chosen as his place of death, numbers among its monuments a cubical castle of the Norman period known as "La Cuba."

6. The French phrase "L'Enlèvement d'Europe" could mean both "The Abduction of Europa" and "Europe's Carrying Off the Prize."

Mme Roussel owned more than eighty Dresden figurines (as well as paintings by Gainsborough, Lawrence, Fragonard, Nattier, Greuze, Corot, and others), including, in addition to "Europa," two allegorical figures representing America and Africa.* In my copy of the sale catalogue, someone jotted down both the estimates and the actual prices attained by the various lots at the auction: There, at least, America seems to have triumphed with a price of 12,500 francs, as against 1,500 fetched by "The Abduction of Europa."

In Havana

In Havana in the year   lived a pair of orphans, the fourteen-year-old A . . . L . . . and his twin sister M . . .

Born to a Spanish colonial family, the two children grew up under the affectionate guardianship of their spinster great-aunt S . . . , a capable, unpretentious person, well-versed in managing her own affairs.

As is usual, the two twins had grown unevenly in the maternal womb: M . . . had absorbed many a vital essence, to the detriment of A . . . , who, incurably fragile, had only by a miracle reached adolescence.

Between A . . . and M . . . reigned the fanatic tenderness typical of twins. Moreover A . . . , who was extremely gifted, was able to exert a beneficial ascendancy on his entourage, to which his sister wholeheartedly submitted. In school he dominated the class, and, drawing additional prestige from the title of *veteran*, the result of a serious illness which had forced him to stay in a form a second year, counseled some, sustained others, or settled the quarrels of others with but a word or two.

Two examples will show the scope of his authority.

---

*For pictures of these three Dresden figurines, see "Introduction to Raymond Roussel's *Documents to Serve as an Outline*," *Selected Prose*, by John Ashbery, ed. Eugene Richie (Ann Arbor: University of Michigan Press, 2004; Manchester, U.K.: Carcanet Press, 2004), 51–52. (Eds.)

Among his friends he counted the son of N . . . O . . . , a parvenu well known throughout the land—and that of R . . . V . . . , whose name called to mind a mysterious scandal.

A humble servant to a planter, N . . . O . . . had, with the aid of a lottery ticket, been able while still very young to lay the foundations of a fortune which, thanks to his talents and miserliness, had become considerable.

But his origins had gained him nothing but the contempt of Cuban high society, from which he suffered and which he attempted to conquer through the purchase of a title.

He left for Rome—and returned a papal count.

But the fashionable Cubans, not in the least impressed, saw this as a provocation and took umbrage. Not only were the advances of the new nobleman rebuffed, but it was agreed that he would be sent a syntax whose luxurious binding was decorated with the ornate crest of a count. It was a way of neatly twitting the pretensions of the unlettered former flunkey.

Count d'O . . . understood—and kept his peace.

Besides, other cares would soon preoccupy him.

Havana at the time was fêting an Italian operatic company whose star was the beautiful and amoral A . . . , known as the "queen of the vocalise."

As the vocal repertory offered nothing sufficiently difficult to show off fully her astounding virtuosity, A . . . had had arranged for voice, using lyrics suggested by the title, the "Spinning Song" for piano by D . . . , whose perilous chromatic runs, aiming at subtle imitative effects and forbidden to lesser talents, followed one another relentlessly. And the execution of the work, already a tour de force for the fingers, became for the vocal cords a miraculous exploit.

A . . . accomplished this feat effortlessly, attaining, while always singing pianissimo, an extreme velocity in which the phrasing of the separate notes that stretched out each syllable was never compromised.

At the end of each last act, urgent curtain calls forced A . . . to sing her "Spinning Song," resulting each time in a triumph.

The first time d'O . . . saw A . . . appear on stage, her dazzling beauty produced a delightful agitation in him which immediately doubled at the sound of her voice. His desire, increasing with each act of the opera, burst all bounds at the end when the customary "Spinning Song," adding the crowning touch to her prestige, caused her to surpass herself as a lyric artist and then radiate in a final apotheosis.

When after an easy conquest the totally ecstatic d'O . . . heard talk of the troupe's departure, his anguish revealed the depth of his passion. He made A . . . alluring offers in an attempt to persuade her to abandon her career and stay with him, whereupon she ascertained her strength and, deciding to exploit the situation to the hilt, refused him all save marriage and held out until he yielded.

The irruption into his existence of a wife with a checkered past only aggravated the ostracism from which d'O . . . suffered—and against which he decided to struggle yet another time.

It was on horse racing, a popular sport in Cuba, that he built his hopes. A racing stable would bring with it a certificate of smartness—and acquaintances in the brilliant society of the racing world.

He acquired a stable and, in A . . .'s honor, chose as his colors the green, white, and red of the Italian flag, alert for every chance to support her with visible tributes against the disfavor of prudes.

But, if the couple had a few sporting successes in the hippodrome, these met with nothing but further snubs, and d'O . . . , chagrined, soon parted with all his horses.

This disappointment was followed by a joy: the birth of a son.

Now it was this son, S . . . d'O . . . , thirteen years old at the time of the story, who was a friend of A . . . L . . .'s.

A classmate having called S . . . , during a whispered argument at school, "son of a lackey and a strumpet," the youth had retorted with a challenge.

At the first sign of fisticuffs during recess, A . . . had intervened—then made inquiries.

Given the odious nature of the insult, he insisted that S . . . receive public apologies—and as usual, was deferentially obeyed.

As for V . . .'s son, he had unjustly suffered the consequences of certain suspicions that hung over his father.

Orphaned at an early age, the latter had, on reaching his majority, rapidly dissipated a modest inheritance and, of comely aspect, had then sought . . . and found an heiress.

A few years of high living melted the dowry away, and the irritated parents-in-law subsidized only meagerly the couple—henceforth beset by difficulties which the birth of a son only augmented. Now, scarcely had V . . .'s wife risen from childbed when her father and mother died mysteriously within the same hour.

The autopsy furnished proof of a double poisoning.

An investigation of foodstuffs having led to naught, it became neces-sary to look elsewhere. Suspicion finally settled on the glue of a supply of stamps of touching origin.

Two years previously the American T . . . had attempted, on his vessel the *B* . . . , an audacious polar exploration.

When the anticipated time of his return had been largely exceeded, a public subscription to finance a search party was initiated.

Notably a stamp was created which, showing the *B* . . . lost amid floes, accompanied the franking stamp on many an envelope.

More than one hand was forced by the ploy of sending out an unso-licited sheet of a hundred stamps—for which a canvasser soon appeared, to request either the return of the sheet or a contribution.

Now a sheet of this type had reached the home of V . . .'s parents-in-law and been utilized at once, the canvasser having been welcomed on his arrival.

It was two weeks afterward that they died.

Six stamps remained—and analysis proved the presence of poisoned glue.

Since no envelope could be found, the investigation came up short—and foundered. But suspicions concerning the too-fortunate V . . . were bruited about—without touching his wife, who enjoyed universal esteem.

Since then, however, gossip had never ceased.

Now, stirred by resemblances in their vulnerability, young V . . . had applauded when public apologies were made to S . . . d'O . . . .

Embittered, the insulter sought a vengeance which, anonymous this time, would be sure not to earn him a new punishment.

At an opportune moment he crept into the deserted dormitory and, budding draughtsman that he was, made in charcoal on the wall behind young V . . .'s bed a sketch wherein, under the title "Papa's Double Blow," two hearses were seen, one behind the other, near a framed corner vi-gnette filled by a large stamp illustrating a polar catastrophe.

He began to hate his own handiwork when he saw its discovery pro-voke a general malaise—and the tears of the concerned party.

Informed of the event, A . . . gathered all together—and doubly stigmatized a cowardly anonymous insult which struck at the son in the person of the father.

Then he painted such a radiant picture of redemption through con-fession that the miscreant,[1] weeping in turn, came and bowed before the victim, avowing his guilt and beseeching forgiveness.

One can imagine the effect on a sister—and a twin sister at that—of a force already so dominant over mere comrades.

Each of A . . .'s words was an article of faith for M . . . , and she would gladly have braved any peril for the triumph of a cause championed by him.

And indeed, together with his inclination toward acts of goodness, the precocious adolescent did occasionally cherish great humanitarian dreams—which he boldly planned to realize someday.

Deeply attached as he was to his natal island, he would in particular have liked to see come into being there a more refined civilization, born out of intensive imitation of Europe.

Ardently he admired Europe—to which his Spanish blood in fact allied him: the homeland of great memories, of solid traditions, of master-pieces of art, of sublime intelligences—while on the contrary setting little store by the vulgar industrialism of upstart America.

And often, when confiding his thoughts to M . . . , he would frame passionate plans for distant future projects which this special patriotism suggested.

Alas, he was not to see that future; death which from his cradle had never ceased to hover over him took him at twenty, wasted by a malady of the lungs—under the haggard eye of M . . . , henceforth inconsolable.

Nonetheless, the sentiment of a sacred mission to be fulfilled sustained her in her sorrow.

A . . . , on his deathbed, had solemnly appointed her to realize in his stead his patriotic dream—and, with outstretched arm, she had sworn obedience.

A year later her great-aunt died full of years, leaving M . . . a fortune which would allow her to take up the cudgels at once.

Sensing first of all how little she would be able to accomplish alone, she had printed and circulated gratis a brochure containing an explicit call for aid. Here A . . .'s desideratum was fully laid out—along with the project of founding, together with those who shared her ideas, a club for both sexes whose members would meet at M . . .'s home.

Approvingly understanding, numerous intellectuals pledged their membership with patriotic zeal.[2]

Every club must be governed; a vote was taken, and, on the first ballot, M . . . was unanimously elected president.

Thereupon she was urged to invent for herself some insignia, the wearing of which during meetings would attest to her authority.

Prodded thus, she began to reflect seriously and, after a period of dissatisfaction, by force of elimination finally adopted a bold idea—at first rejected as overshooting the mark.

In fact it was a matter not of a simple ornamental accessory, but of an entire costume.

Among a group of Dresden porcelains displayed from time immemorial in a vitrine in her parlor was one depicting the Abduction of Europa. A graceful garment closely modeled after that of the statuette—and completed by a flesh-colored leotard—became her presidential uniform.

The meeting at which she first wore it took on a character of inaugural solemnity. A new activity reigned in the search for policies to be adopted. And finally each member was given the assignment of providing appropriate testimony to Europe's superiority.

With emulation helping, it became for the intellectual elite who made up the club a race to see who would furnish the handsomest stone for the edifice.

And several weeks passed, during which M . . . received a sheaf of arguments for her cause: the thirty documents which follow.

1. Considering that Roussel has supplied names, or at any rate initials, for characters who barely make an appearance in his narrative, he seems here to be going out of his way to avoid naming the "miscreant" who plays such a pivotal role. (Trans.)
2. This sentence replaces on the corrected proofs the following incomplete sentence from the original version: "Numerous idlers, counting on many joyous parties purchased with little effort . . ." (Trans.)

First Document

Around 1435 the Lord de Courty, dreaded for his tyranny and hardness of heart, was living on his lands in Burgundy.

Did a pretty peasant lass dare to spurn him? . . . Her plot of land confiscated, she and her dear ones were reduced to beggary.

Thus it came about that a beautiful blond orphan girl, Eda Bercin, was forced, the very day of her act of disobedience, to leave the thatched cottage in a field which she shared with her frail grandmother.

It was winter. The two unfortunates, snubbed by their frightened betters, trudged through falling snow to the forest of Vigelal, where Porvioux cave afforded them a shelter.

There, collapsed on the frozen ground, the fragile grandmother shuddered and breathed her last.

Henceforth Eda, too proud to beg, having fashioned herself a bow and arrows, lived as a cave dweller from the spoils of the hunt.

The arrival of spring found her wandering one day along a flowery path, where she was tempted by some fresh-blown bluebells that seemed to need naught but a breeze so as to herald the springtide with a joyful ding-a-ling.

She made a nosegay of them—then, attracted by the new green grass, lay down on the ground—where sleep overtook her at the very moment a young vagabond, Romé Daigle, appeared at a bend in the road.

Abruptly Romé stopped short, dazzled by her beauty. And a strange fear seized him at the thought of seeing her eyelids part: What if her eyes, which he imagined celestial, were to disappoint him!

He picked up three bluebells that had escaped from Eda's hand . . . then, with a hair gathered from her shoulder, wound their stems in a golden spiral.

Then he fled.

Henceforth Romé, an incorrigible night owl, led a confused existence, in austere and frugal solitude.

What was to become of him? . . . Never again could he desire another girl than Eda, whom the fear of a special disillusion prevented him from seeking out.

The order of the *Gray Crosses* had recently been founded, inspired by this deed mentioned by Saint-Priacet:

Shortly after the Crucifixion, as she was passing the stall of the fence Zacri, the Magdalen recognized a trove of tinseled finery, scarves and sashes embroidered in gold or silver, which had once been stolen from her.

Now, immediately upon her conversion she had adopted a modest garb—and burned her handsome adornments.

For a trifling sum she took possession of the accursed rags so as to burn them too—thanks, obviously, to Jesus, who desired that she be enabled to annihilate the final traces of her past.

The presence of the finger of God became undeniable when the heap of ashes that Mary Magdalen had publicly created before her door was given the shape of a cross by a strangely capricious breeze; the populace knelt around it in a circle, having understood that if the Redeemer, who had transformed a sinner into a saint, had just changed ashes of impure origin into a sacred symbol, it was to further affirm the accessibility of the kingdom of heaven.

Wishing to indicate her recognition of divine intervention, the Magdalen cried:

"I thank thee, Lord, for deigning to *cross* out my past."

And the phrase became celebrated.

Into the order of the *Gray Crosses* entered anyone, man or woman, who, disowning a turbulent past, made a vow to change direction. The members sported a long black hooded gown bearing on its chest a meaningful ash-gray cross. Living ascetically on alms, they wandered from town to town, forcing their way into places of debauchery to recruit adepts while preaching on the theme *Cross out your past*, the while distributing a sacred picture wherein, from a cross of ashes that a kneeling crowd surrounded, one saw these words formed by the meanders of a slender thread of smoke: "Fenced frippery."

Romé became a Gray Cross—and sallied forth.

One evening, having been able to interrupt a drinking bout in a brothel so as to be heard, he was soon forced to leave accompanied by boos.

But after a few steps he heard these words:

"Fircine Démil is now one of yours."

One of the brothel girls had followed him—and confessed her sins.

A matron, Mémelle Partar,[1] notorious as a procuress of adolescent girls, had enrolled her, while still little more than a child, in her troop—whose doyenne she had become at the age of fifteen.

To call attention to the rapidity, striking at the time, of her rate of growth, Mémelle was fond of repeating the phrase "The doyenne grows taller," finding in the antithesis supplied by these words a useful reminder of the immaturity of her brood.

An ingenious businesswoman, Mémelle had been able to increase her revenue thanks to the universal human foible of gambling.

One could, if one chose, pay only half price—then lose the sum or be served as one desired, according to the decision of fate, consulted, given the special nature of the case, by means of an object reeking of love.

Mémelle in her youth had received a pledge of sincere passion: a heart cut from a plaque of gold. The name Gorlodo, engraved on one of its two sides, indicated whose heart was in question—a heart made from inexhaustible treasures of love, as the chosen metal additionally testified.

It was this heart, furnished on one side with the name, which, tossed high in the air and spinning as it came down, favored the customer or not in falling heads or tails—while the young heroine of the moment, selected in advance, followed it with impassive eyes.

Often had the heart been wagered for Fircine, who, scrupulous, believed that having been shamefully *played* rendered her unworthy of redemption.

So that she might detest less the image of chance as arbiter, Romé told her about Cacitaine.

Cacitaine, a young Galilean woman of good family, having been abandoned in an advanced state of pregnancy by her secret lover, was unable to hide her condition for long.

After a furious "Get out!" her father had added mockingly, pointing to the beast that would carry her away:

"—I'll forgive you when that donkey ambles home!"

An hour later, Cacitaine reached a shady grove where Jesus and his disciples had just finished their midday meal—and was obliged to reply to the questions prompted by her tears.

The others looked at the Master. Which would he choose, for a guilty woman redeemed by a trial: clemency or rigor?

Choosing to resort to the impartiality of chance, Jesus caused the water contained in an amphora to be thrown on the embers of the culinary hearth, saying to Cacitaine:

"The fire's victory shall mark thine own."

After a moment of uncertainty, the fire took.

Soon only a black spot remained at the center of the invading red flames; its disappearance caused Jesus to point toward Cacitaine—and then toward the place whence she had come.

And Cacitaine felt her mount turn of its own accord and, ambling now, return to the fold—where her father, realizing the miracle that had occurred, welcomed her with open arms.

Fircine's serenity was restored.

And soon after, two Gray Crosses were seen setting off together: Romé and Fircine, bound by the purest sibling tenderness.

Passing one day through Murleau, they wished to meet the renowned and reverend hermit Danecteur.

Extremely feeble, the wise Danecteur could tolerate a visit only when exposed to the invigorating stimulus of fresh air and sunshine.

Those who wished recourse to his sanctifying words knew that entry into his tiny garden was allowed only when a rainbow was visible in the spray of its fountain.

One fine morning, the rainbow being present, Romé and Fircine ventured in.

At the sound of their footsteps, Danecteur came out of his cottage, showed them to a semicircular bench—and proceeded to recount the *Relapse of Bahol de Jic.*

Young and rich, Bahol de Jic was descended from an illustrious family—indeed from its *iron branch*, which owed its name to the rigidity of its members' morals.

One beautiful day, during a clement autumn when the leaves had barely turned yellow, Bahol overheard a chorus of youthful voices in the wood. Soon a group of maidens appeared, who, without interrupting their song, invited him civilly to join them.

Bahol took the arm of Farvette—and succeeded in dropping behind the others.

Pleasant hours ensued.

Already night was getting on and, since Farvette was fearful of tarrying too long:

—"Let's go and find out what time it is by the stars," said Bahol.

And Farvette added:

—"We'll see if Clarcée hasn't slipped away again."

There was much talk at the time of the star Clarcée, which had abruptly reappeared after an absence of half a century—a few hours after the death of old Colas, who had once become fabulously rich—in a curious manner.

At twenty, having sold all but his shirt for love of wine, Colas had cried: "Now I have nothing left but to sell my soul to the devil."

That very day, walking beside a field, he saw a brilliant solar glint in a freshly made furrow—and understood that Satan had accepted the bargain.

In courteous terms he confirmed to him the abandonment of his soul, fearing that, for want of this precaution, the glimpsed treasure might vanish at his touch.

It was indeed a treasure—which Colas jealously covered up again, after having taken what was sufficient to buy the field in cash.

The next night Clarcée was missing from the celestial sphere, Satan having succeeded in stealing it from God as a hostage lest *his* soul be disputed him.

Rich, the drunkard Colas had fifty years of opulent debauchery and, dying unrepentant, went straight to Satan's dwelling, and the latter was thus enabled to return Clarcée to its place.

Having reached a clearing, Bahol and Farvette gazed at Clarcée, whose position indicated an hour already late—and allowed their lips to join in a farewell.

The next day Bahol was summoned before his father, who, having had wind of the escapade, warned him that as a member of the iron branch he would be punished with death in the event of a relapse.

Often Bahol would go to visit his nurse and foster sister in their hut, accepting some humble courtesy from the two women, who, eager to entertain him, heaped the table with fruits and delicacies from the dairy.

—I would like a *dear story*, nurse, Bahol would say, purposely using an expression familiar to his lips from childhood.

And an old tale heard in days gone by would again charm his hearing.

One day—a fatal day—the door was opened to him by a terrified Nine, who gestured toward her mother, deathly pale on her bed where since morning death had been at work.

Bahol was forced to control himself, for the dying woman had raised her eyelids.

—Do you want a *dear story*?

—Yes, nurse.

—Well, then! Trillat was pining away ever since his fiancée drowned while bathing; her body had never been found. He had a tiny skiff made so that after his death his heart could be placed in it—and consigned to the current of the murderous river. He well knew that there where his beloved lay, his heart would plunge of its own accord to rejoin her forever. Finally he passed away—and was obeyed. Rudderless and faced with a thousand dangers, the heart, reclining in its skiff, drifted away. Now, Princess Dramieuse was traveling through the country then. Such was her beauty that, wherever she stopped, a working day officially became a holiday in order that all eyes might be favored. She sang with a voice so pure that, begged by all to do so, she expressed herself with gestures in order to spare her voice. Enamored of the unexpected, she would at the beginning of each stage of the journey open the cage of a trained bird which, having alighted on a distant perch and thus shown the direction to be taken, voluntarily returned to its prison, and the journey would continue. One morning, troubled by the bird's unaccustomed celerity, Dramieuse, followed by her retinue, hastened her horse's gait. While fording a stream she stopped suddenly at the sight of a heart ensconced in a skiff moving directly toward her on the current. At that, Dramieuse . . .

These words were the last.

Nine closed the dead woman's eyes—then fell into Bahol's outstretched arms.

Now, from their long sibling embrace a sudden vertigo was born . . . and their lips joined of themselves.

Bahol, coming to his senses, cried out: "The relapse!"—then anticipated paternal justice by stabbing himself.

Danecteur having risen to his feet, Romé and Fircine thanked him and took their leave.

They realized that the perspicacious hermit had chosen a tale designed to put them on guard against any deviation of their sibling intimacy.

Soon afterward Romé was struck dead by a crazed avenger who had been deprived of his lover by Romé's preaching, which had converted her.

Alone henceforth, Fircine journeyed onward in a single direction so as to fulfill a mission that the dying Romé had time to confide to her.

Arriving at Vigelal, she was able to find Eda and return to her, along with revelations concerning her, the famous bluebells whose stems were bound with a hair.

When news of this had spread, Lord de Courty was ashamed on comparing his own reactions with Romé's in regard to the beauty of Eda—who regained her abode.

Second Document

In 1880 the poet Pérot, known as Pérou,[2] the acclaimed bard of sailors and the sea, was still living in Saint-Nazaire.

Having straddled Pegasus at the age of twenty, Pérot had replaced the *t* in his name with its alphabetical successor, finding the pseudonym Pérou gratifyingly suggestive of a richness of ideas and veins of golden rhyme.

Sixteen lustra passed without bowing him.

At his hundredth birthday party he danced the hornpipe—and during the following days chiseled a witty *Proud Sonnet* relating his prowess.

One morning he did not awake.

The sonnet still lacked its final line.

A statue was erected in his memory and placed facing the sea, depicting him shading his eyes with one hand and gazing adoringly at his booming muse. His *Proud Sonnet*, engraved on the pedestal, assumed due to its lack of a final line the touching prestige of a swan song.

Now, the *thirteen-line statue* came to be considered unlucky—and passersby made horns at it.

Ten years afterward the shipowner Boulien dismissed a servant for theft; furious, the latter, arming himself with a paperweight, broke a mirror from a distance while shouting before running away: "Misfortune on your house!"

Quicksilver flowed, revealing the corner of a piece of paper—on which Boulien recognized his father's handwriting.

Intrigued, he augmented the damage—and read:

"Lean back against the thirteen lines and look at Friday."

Out in the ocean off Saint-Nazaire can be seen two profiles formed by two cliffs on Hurga—an uninhabited island where no one sets foot—called Robinson and Friday.

Friday, the more thick-lipped of the two, brings misfortune due to its name, and the rash viewer who glances at it accidentally must make horns.

Boulien obeyed—then, having reached the islet of Kirdrec, withdrew from a certain tumulus that his line of sight had grazed during the operation, a casket filled with gold coins that made him understand everything.

An emancipated thinker and highly militant member of the *Anti-Superstition League,* his father had wished to combat the fear produced by the breaking of a mirror, the number thirteen, and Friday, by causing a treasure to be revealed by them.

Informed by Boulien, the league published the event to advance the good cause—and Claude Migrel, the son of Annette Migrel, saw it one morning in his newspaper.

At twenty, already mother of a bastard son, Annette Migrel, a shepherdess with miraculous vocal gifts, caused pedestrians to gather round when, guarding her sheep, she would sing near a highway.

Discovered and launched, she became a great star and, ambitiously prodigal mother that she was, provided her son with the finest teachers.

Forced, after a hundred vain efforts, to recognize himself a cipher, he withdrew timidly into his shell, allowed the nuptial season to pass, and, when his mother died, remained alone contemplating his misanthropy, until the day when a letter from home informed him of the death of a widowed cousin, father of a three-year-old child destined for an orphanage.

He adopted the orphan—but, remembering his own distress, decided to make of his atavistic counterpart a peaceful illiterate.

Carefully he chose as governess a silly girl on whose ignorance he could rely.

And Jacques, under Eveline's guidance, grew up far from the alphabet.

One summer found all three at Verca, a pretty Piedmontese resort whose proximity to Marengo naturally suggests a visit to the battlefield and the famous Bossenelle tower, last vestige of a fortified castle.

It has been said that at 5 p.m. on June 14, 1800, as the French defeat was drawing to a close, Time, suddenly grown torpid in its flight, fell through the ruined roof into the Bossenelle tower and was overcome by sleep, stopping the course of events until Desaix arrived to change it.[3]

Later, amused at the thought of having imprisoned not only the pope and kings but Time itself, the emperor commissioned the great sculptor Varly to immortalize the event *in situ*.

Around 1778, after having tasted the carefree happiness of childhood and first youth, Varly, impoverished, attempted with difficulty to inaugurate a career, while François Varly, his rich younger half brother on the mother's side, was unable to overcome his pride in order to help him.

One of Varly's neighbors was a working girl with an invalid mother.

During periods of unemployment, frequent alas, Lucette would come to pose for the *Dryad Coaxing a Faun*—adorned with a sylvan crown from which a leaf, at the end of the first sitting, had slipped inside a book.

Now, the sight of the *Dryad* overwhelmed François—who married the model soon after.

Fifteen years later he died childless, dividing his estate between his widow and his brother.

Varly at last declared his sentiments.

—I knew it all along, said Lucette. One day, arriving early for the sitting, I was idly flipping through your books, found the leaf, and understood. I loved you too—and sacrificed myself to pamper my mother's declining years.

And Varly, after so much suffering in silence, tasted for long years the joys of a husband and father—until the day when the sudden death of his only son deprived his wife of her reason.

Having grown old amid grief, Varly, inspired by the contrast offered by the various phases of his life, caused wide bands of pink and black marble to alternate in the drapery of his *Time*—meanwhile scattering raised dots of the contrasting color throughout, so as to dispel the idea of the absolute and demonstrate that two moods could complement each other, as was demonstrated by the keenness of his memory with regard to the slight cares that beset his happy moments and the rare felicities of his somber periods: sisterly attentions of Lucette; smiles of the poor mad creature prompted by the sight of him.

And this bicolored raiment of time caught Napoleon's fancy.

One morning soon after Migrel's return, as Jacques, the eternal fainéant, having just studied the engraved illustrations in a book, was placing the bookmark between the last page of the preface and the first page of the text, and noticed, vexed at being unable to read them, here a word in roman characters contrasting strongly with one in italics, there an italic word contrasting with a roman one—he remembered, thanks to this reciprocal highlighting, what the guide had said concerning certain pink and black dots as they stood contemplating the drowsy reclining statue of *Time* in the Bossenelle tower.

That evening, as they looked at the two pages, he explained his parallel to Migrel, who, alarmed, henceforth kept him away from even picturebooks.

Forced to nurture himself elsewhere, Jacques fell back on the photographs accompanying the text of the newspaper Eveline read, demanding her commentaries.

Sensational news items quickly became his preference—and the *Crime of the rue Barel* fascinated him.

The empirical Sableux and the down-at-heels actress and singer Doumuse, one cuckolded, the other beaten, lived abjectly in the rue Barel.

A doctor without diploma destined for handcuffs, Sableux owed a sort of reputation to a stroke of luck.

One stormy morning toward the end of July in the Avenue Fortas, Prince Norius, a conspirator exiled by his brother the king of Ixtan, was working at his open window, a partial map of Asia before him. Clinging to the idea of seizing the crown and full of plans for his future reign, he was that day examining a sort of fissure in the coast of Ixtan which he dreamed of widening so as to make an anchorage of it.

Sableux was passing along the Avenue Fortas at that moment, on his way to a certain scientifico-medical club founded by a philanthropist, which he had succeeded in joining by dint of intrigue. He knew that at noon, at the close of the meeting, each member, after drawing lots, would be given a reconnoitering trail to follow, baited with an interesting prize.

Soon the expected storm erupted. A gust of wind drew Prince Norius to the window where his map had just been blown away upward, forcing him to raise his eyes—which a powerful flash of lightning suddenly blinded, wrenching a cry from him.

The passersby, including Sableux, stopped, and the news soon spread.

Now, Sableux, continuing on his way, recalled a certain day when, plugging his ears so as to be less bothered by Doumuse, who was practicing vocal exercises in the background, he was perusing a passage from *Racelon* by Pragé, that precursor whose books, despite meager first printings, have survived so many others—a passage concerning the purely nervous prolongation of certain sudden passing seizures of blindness and the possibility of curing the ill with a counterirritation by causing a sudden intense emotion in the patient.

One month later, informed by the newspapers of numerous unsuccessful attempts at treatment, he contrived a meeting with Klédi, the prince's chief confidant, and, thanks to the potentially useful passage from Pragé, obtained certain revelations from him.

The prince had had by a French mistress an idolized twelve-year-old son, Harbert, a talented lycée student who had just been awarded *Enrico Vivarès*, a novel with a Mexican setting, as a prize for an honorable mention.

Enrico Vivarès wants to enroll in the Farquita, that famous league that strives in vain to regulate Mexico.

Set loose alone in a labyrinth, bravely confronting anxiety, he walks for a long time toward the unknown, directed at every crossing of the ways by an arrow.

Finally he emerges on the stage of a crowded auditorium, where one of the leaders slaps him publicly, not without the utterance of a polite phrase which turns his gesture into the simple emblem of a momentous hierarchical elevation.

Then he receives a noose of gold thread mounted on a pin which is fastened to his lapel—the league's insignia, intended to remind the wearer continually of this diabolically draconian article: *Of whosoever betrays one of our secrets an ironic funeral eulogy shall be printed whose delivery will announce his prompt and certain death by hanging.*

Hero of a thousand adventures, Enrico Vivarès henceforth serves the league with zeal, risking mortal danger while repressing brigands and contending with the opposing clans.

One evening while on leave in Mexico City, he ends up, drawn by their then-considerable renown, at the home of the Gordias family (four brothers and their four sisters), who, at specified hours daily, surrounded by a paying crowd eager to learn, play while explaining it the "sertino," a game of their invention which has recently been launched with success.

The sertino requires many players—and eight decks, each of whose cards bears the picture of one of the eight planets, with its name printed beneath.

Hence an infinity of combinations which, rendering it one of the most demanding of games, bestows a kind of royalty on the sertino.

As Enrico enters, Carcetta, one of the players, is recounting to the public the subtle reasons for which she has just flung a *Uranus-club* on the table.

Hearing the new arrival's footsteps, she looks up and their glances cross, welding them together forever.

During the engagement a secret confided by Enrico to Carcetta, and soon made indiscreet through flightiness, has grave repercussions.

The postman delivers to Enrico a letter which he reads without flinching: his ironic funeral eulogy. Instead of awaiting his certain capture he gives himself up—and is hanged, attended by a priest.

And a tailpiece under the words THE END shows a funereal angel with black wings carrying his soul away.

There follow several pages under the naive title "Emergency Epilogue," which, for sensitive readers, depict a pardoned Enrico whom Carcetta marries.

Now, Harbert doted on the adventures of Enrico Vivarès and several times had talked of running off by himself to Mexico to enroll in the Farquita.

At the instigation of Sableux, Klédi had him write a farewell letter to his father, announcing, along with a tender request for pardon, the accomplishment of his project.

Simulating terrible consternation, Klédi rushed to tell the prince that the boy had disappeared—and began to read him the letter . . .

But at the first words Norius seized hold of it, and, in his panic not even noticing his sudden recovery, read it and turned ghastly pale.

Then, immediately undeceived, he had but to taste the joys of the miraculously healed.

Thanks to a generous recompense, Sableux and Doumuse lived for a while in the lap of luxury.

Doumuse took advantage of it by trying to attract attention with flattering press notices and sumptuous stage costumes.

At the time she was singing in a suburban theater the leading role in *A Chatelaine during the Reign of Terror.*

The Marquise d'Ernange lives almost as a prisoner in her château near Nantes, where the tyrant Carrier reigns supreme.

And she fancies she has found a way to embark for England.

In 1788 the city of Nantes, for the celebration of the four-hundredth anniversary of the exploit of one of its sons, the navigator Discoul, who in 1388 was the first to cross the *line*, issued a commemorative local coin—a silver crown with a complete geographical map, a kind of flattened globe whose equator is purposefully made of gold.

The revolutionary upheaval having prevented its being put into circulation, Carrier controls the supply—and transforms each crown—which in fact returns to him after being utilized—into an emblematic permit of embarkation.

Extremely venal—and armed with the threat of execution by drowning—he delivers a life-saving crown only in exchange for a substantial sum.

Lest his good humor appear suspicious, he requires each payer to provide a convincing written explanation of the reasons for his wish to depart, interspersing his tale with contemptibly flattering political formulas.

The marquise has just sold her jewels when an occasion for direct negotiation handily presents itself.

It is Christmas eve. The stage is divided in half, showing the chapel in the château where a small group is attending mass—and a salon made ready for the midnight feast. Suddenly a chorus of revolutionaries is heard in the wings—followed by a peek through a shutter chink accompanied by commentaries, and the breaking-in of a door. Carrier and his trustiest henchmen appear and, smashing everything on the altar to smithereens, demand an immediate palinode from the pious assembly.

Once the storm has passed, the Marquise takes Carrier aside and bargains successfully; he will receive her the next day following his *welding*, a nap much practiced at the time, which *welded* morning to afternoon, and which we now call *siesta*.

Arriving at the agreed-on hour with the money and the written text, the marquise receives one of the coveted crowns—and sets sail.

Now, the rich costumes and adulatory newspaper items had their effect, and Doumuse performed in a theater then much in vogue—where she was noticed by Lucien Brelmet, young scion of a wealthy family who in a few years had recently squandered a handsome fortune and a famous stamp collection.

A single stamp—in truth a treasure in its own right—still remained in his possession: that of the Republic of Eisnark.

In 1884 there had been much talk of the poet Ole, a native of the Swedish island of Eisnark, which, perched in the middle of the Arctic Ocean, has the form of a trapeze.

Popular and ambitious, Ole had, one fine day, declared his natal island a republic and himself its president—and the Swedish rulers had smiled and looked the other way rather than send warships so far to so little purpose.

Then a stamp was created—polychrome and of course cut in the shape of a trapeze—the very one of which Brelmet owned a specimen.

One sees on the left Ole declaiming before a crowd under the gaze of his muse—the latter a creature of dreams immune to cold, her filmy attire (in the style of yesteryear) contrasting with the heavy winter coats of the others. To suggest the high latitude, the words exhaled by Ole's lips fall as snow before him. There follow, from left to right, depictions of Ole's most famous poems: *The Man in the Pink Cloak*, whose hero is a sixteenth-century Venetian libertine; *Where Love of Lucre Can Lead*, a ringing cry of horror against a beggar woman, delighted that her child's cough stimulates public generosity through commiseration; *The Winner Rejoices*, which hinges on the euphoria of a young hopscotch player whose victory is near and assured; *The Morning Chain*, wherein the dreams of a young girl fly away hand in hand as she gradually regains consciousness; *The Gentle Warning*, which analyzes the ecstasy of a future mother on feeling the first quivering in her loins; and *The Last Flower*, where the terrestrial globe is shown, after a thousand millennia, killed by the cold.

Ole died prematurely, and the Eisnarkians, not knowing where to turn, became Swedes again on condition of a promise of general amnesty.

The famous stamp, used for only a short time by a small group, became one of the rarest and costliest of its kind.

Brelmet sold his specimen—and treated himself to the love of Doumuse.

Now the jealous Sableux, who until now contented himself with beating the servilely wanton Doumuse, saw red when he discovered a patrician rival.

Having heard tell of an approaching Friday the thirteenth, he decided to act on that day, which seemed to him doubly auspicious for the lethal work he envisioned.

A feigned absence on the destined day drew the couple to his lodgings—which his key allowed him to enter and thereby to create two bullet-riddled cadavers.

The whole story, revealed in court, reached Jacques through the medium of the press and Eveline; profoundly shaken, the lad was at once seized by a violent spasm of fear—with immediate pathological consequences—of the number thirteen and of Friday.

Knowing that the uneducated are particularly defenseless against psychic sufferings with such absurd origins, Claude Migrel, faced with the greater of two evils, began to reproach his line of conduct when the Anti-Superstition League's article came to culminate his conversion by making him wish that Jacques himself might be able to read and reread until sated.

And the young laggard was finally given tutors.

Third Document

There exists in a small chapel at Lourdes a reliquary containing two manuscripts dictated by the unlettered Bernadette, each authenticated by a cross traced in her own hand, above the signatures of witnesses.

At each pilgrimage a meticulously chosen maiden, deemed worthy of touching them thanks to her purity, reads them aloud to the crowd:

"One day a lady with a haughty mien and strange discourse appeared to me.

"It was the fairy Fussive; one of her peers had just died well past the age of three thousand years—and I was to replace her.

"With a wave of her hand she caused a very blue river to appear, and a small boat ferried us away, so opulent that its sails had lace inserts, though the wind filled them nonetheless.

"Once we had reached the realm of the fairies, I was given a bow and arrows so as to shoot at a map of the heavens—my godmother was to be a star chosen by fate.

"My fourth arrow pierced the map—near the star Cérenée, whose name became mine.

"Then I was ushered into a chamber where the old queen of the fairies, still very beautiful, was loudly scolding, indeed almost castigating, a young fairy entrusted with regilding the sun's spots, who, without apology, had put off her task and was still carrying the intact scroll of gold leaf meant for this purpose.

"Once this scene was over I was presented to the queen, who whisked me off to my apartments.

"First we crossed the *Chamber of Obsolete Magic Formulas*, whose walls were papered with printed pages faded by time.

"The next room was populated by those on whom the fairies had showered their gifts—statues purposely made of steel, an infinitely durable metal well-suited to emblematize their immortality!

"To show me that she had deliberately raised her voice just now and had cause to fear the abuse of power, the queen passed on to me what she said was her favorite mental refrain—a text she read me while contemplating the pedestal of the statue of Cratus.

"It was *The Flimsy Red Colossus*, a satire in which Cratus contrasts the ineffectuality of an imaginary Caesar with the omnipotence conferred by his purple robe, and wherein he takes aim at the *reddish-purple fraud* as he depicts the people suffering under the tyrant's thrall.

"The statue nearest that one showed an adolescent in a schoolboy's uniform. And when I expressed surprise at seeing so much youth joined to so much glory:

"'—It's Hector Prangel,' the queen told me. 'His father, Léon Prangel, having, as a humble militiaman, so amply demonstrated a heroism which has remained unsung, the fairies made amends for this injustice by consecrating his much-vaunted paternal love. Having suddenly become thanks to them an enlightened man of letters, Hector at the age of fifteen wrote a remarkable tragedy, *King Oedipus V*, whose hero is heir to an imaginary dynasty founded by Jocasta's husband. In a kind of preamble, Oedipus V, confessing his reluctance to do so, speaks of his shady origins which render him ill-suited to rule—and swears to compensate for them with virtuous deeds. He keeps his word—and answers every question with a profound precept-couplet.'

"Then the queen drew me into another chamber, whose walls were covered with bookshelves crammed with books.

" '—There are only fairy tales here,' she said, 'and here is the only known copy of Escieur's *Short History of the Fairies*.' And she showed me a volume honorifically placed in the center of the room on a stand half-surrounded by gold trelliswork adorned with foliage.

"Not far from us an extremely ugly woman was holding a fresh pile of pink books[4] under her arm and had just finished making a place on a shelf for the new additions. On the queen's saying to her, 'Come, Kristule,' she quickly put her books away and drew near.

"Fussive had spoken to me of Kristule, endowed with great influence through the friendship of the queen, glad that a striking ugliness served as a foil to the remains of her own beauty.

"Soon I continued onward consigned to Kristule's care by the queen—who turned back.

"On leaving the library I found myself in a corridor, and then, having crossed the threshold of the first door on the right, in the *Bedroom of Sweet Transference*, reserved for the new fairies still intoxicated with their changed condition, and wherein—Kristule told me—an invisible curbing hand punished with a wound any step in the direction of exaggerated pride.

"Left alone by Kristule, I had the vision—which made me recoil in terror—of my own silhouette, whose emaciated state evoked prolonged fasting.

"I understood that, guilty of demonry, I had just been enlightened by heaven concerning the path to my redemption.

"I waited until the middle of the night to make my escape—and found once more the skiff, in which, thanks to a favorable shift in the wind, I reached my point of departure.

"And I gave myself over to severe purifying fasts."

While this dictation, apparently done at leisure, charms by its correctness, the other, entirely written in a cursive hand with multiple abbreviations, betokens haste—an exquisite *Cradle Song for Jesus* that sprang, one Christmas, from the lips of the suddenly inspired Bernadette.

Having finished reading her two texts, the maiden, raising a small gold trapdoor at the back of the chapel, reveals a bone and a branch studded with diamonds, the gifts of zealots.

Then, pointing to the bone, she speaks of Ovide Torchu. Passing one day close to a group of conscripts seated at table in front of a tavern, Bernadette stopped short. One of them, Ovide Torchu, a journeyman of ill repute, had just sliced off the thumb of his right hand, shouting, "Down with the drill!"

She picked up the thumb and the mutilated hand—which, thanks to her, instantly became whole and normal.

At the same moment Ovide Torchu was transfigured. He became a good soldier and then an honest man—and after his death his thumb, through a clause in his will, was cut off anew to become a relic.

Displaying the branch next, the girl proceeds to tell of Luc Neytral.

Passing Luc Neytral, who was on his way to the mountains, on a local road one morning during a harsh winter, Bernadette cried out: "The frozen water will deceive you, cross only in front of the yew."

Toward noon, Luc Neytral was walking along a frozen river on a high plateau, when he spotted on the opposite bank an anfractuosity seemingly made to afford shelter for his meal—and, farther on, a yew.

Impressed, he was careful to cross in front of the yew.

Having reached the anfractuosity, out of curiosity he tossed a stone in the right direction, which disappeared after breaking the ice—very thin at that place due to a subterranean hot spring whose discovery the event occasioned.

And having refreshed himself wrapt in thought, Luc Neytral piously plucked a branch of the yew.

Fourth Document

In February 1886 the Honduran minister to Paris, His Excellency Remo Corcitès, was recalled, owing to the intrigues of one of his rivals for the favors of a reigning belle—the Breton deputy Mérédic, who had in fact just rendered himself even more governmental through an altered nuance with a clever pretext.

And under the headline *The True Reason for a Transformation*, a reactionary newspaper had portrayed a jealous Mérédic, shamelessly athirst for influence.

Corcitès, a widower, had a son of thirteen, Guldo, consumed by nostalgia for his homeland, the sunny backdrop of his early childhood—a humble country which he had honorifically daubed with gold on a planisphere in his classroom.

Since appointment to a prestigious domestic post, which accompanied the recall, stipulated "neither demotion nor further exile in prospect," the homesick youngster's joy was complete, and he read his father *The Worst of Fates*, which he had long adored in secret, wherein Angelo Essermos, a much revered poet from their country, Honduran to the core, bemoans in six-syllable verses the lot of the diplomat enrolled in foreign service.

Repatriated in time to make his way to Angelo Essermos's tomb in the midst of a procession in celebration of the twentieth anniversary of his death, Guldo spied, in a glass-enclosed recess in the mausoleum, a pair of dice placed on a sheet of paper on which the handwriting of two individuals intersected—objects whose history was recounted by the leader of the pilgrims.

At a time when he was still unknown, seated one day at an empty table in the Café Sylvius, whose beautiful proprietress and his eternal creditor, the widow Soneda, he happened to be courting, Essermos, while inveighing against a new tax on alcohol in whose name he had just been refused any further extension of credit, noticed the arrival of a regular customer, the journalist Cactero, whom he challenged to a game of dice with his watch as forfeit.

Destiny smiled on him, and Soneda, having recovered her outlay, honored him with a handsome receipt carefully traced on ruled paper, while a flask of *To Be Drunk on One's Knees*—a liquor of the region said to justify its vainglorious name—was uncorked and served to toast both the winner and the loser.

And soon the tipsy Essermos, in lines of verse perpendicular to those already written, elaborated this theme on the receipt: "Soneda, as our two hands are here, may our two hearts one day be joined."

Now these lines, beautiful ones indeed, captivated Cactero, who was able to popularize them easily by publishing a facsimile of the receipt in his newspaper.

Suddenly haloed in glory, Essermos was able to stage his *Gerta*, a medieval verse-drama whose première successfully launched his career.

The young queen-regent of Carmedia, Gerta, widow of Granor VI and mother of little Granor VII, finds consolation with the royal treasurer Hukloude.

They have within the palace what they call their "gilded nest," a rich chamber for caresses whose wall can part in two places to produce the suspect orifice of a secret corridor.

Gerta is in somber spirits, and the people are in despair. In times gone by a sorcerer predicted that the ruling family would be extinguished by *one* tragic death. Three times already periods called *false fear* had been experienced, born out of the momentary lack in the royal house of an heir, even a collateral one. And now the child-king Granor VII, with no eventual successor, is fatally at risk.

A moving scene takes place in the gilded nest, in which Hukloude annotates a certain *List of Salaries* while awaiting Gerta, who soon joins him.

A frown darkens the queen's forehead.

Every seven years, so that the invincibility of the power of the monarchy may be symbolically affirmed in public, the leaders of the ten noblest families of the realm seize the extremity of a long pole whose other end is held solely by the king, who, triumphant over simulated adverse efforts, forces them back.

Now, the seven-year due date is near. The king is only twelve—and the very spirit of the trial requires that he be sequestered. If, among the *ten*, some ambitious deadly conspiracy . . .

Hukloude reassures her. He is of the same mind—and has consulted an astrologer, whose calculations concerning the ordeal have produced the word *Norm*. And, laughing, he adjures the queen to deal with her misgivings by using a certain arbitrary privilege of ostracism that is within her power.

Next, one sees in the course of a series of scenes:

1. A playful Granor VII, frolicking unceremoniously with peasants of his age—whom he arranges in two rows so as to lecture them in pompous imitation of his tutor—not forgetting to puncture here and there with a pun the farcical severity of the latter's stilted language.

2. The queen leading Granor VII before the statue of Gic, whose story she tells him.

Gic, a humble rope-maker's apprentice, and Clotta, whose prosperous father would not hear of a poor son-in-law, loved one another without hope.

For their secret meetings they had chosen, within an abandoned close, a stone bench surrounded by a spinney.

One evening a stranger brings Gic a rope, offering him a sackful of gold if he will make it invisibly breakable at one point—thus saving the life of the traitor Sarnilas.

All at once inebriated by visions of a forthcoming marriage, Gic said "Yes"—and succeeded.

The next day at dawn a procession was leading Sarnilas to his execution along the river Closeris just by Siouf bridge, so rickety that no one ever ventured on it, even prudently taking note of this warning carved in its threshold: "Pass on, having prayed, swift runner."

Suddenly, having broken with a single effort the rope binding his wrists, Sarnilas, raining blows around him, escaped—and crossed, soon to disappear, the dangerous bridge where none dared pursue him.

Toward evening, Gic, armed with his gold, sat gloating on the stone bench, his mind filled with delightful dreams. As the warm autumn waned, the migratory birds, still not contemplating their exodus, sang gaily in every register.

Clotta joined him, learned everything—and stung the traitor's accomplice with an eternal adieu.

Aspiring henceforth to nothing higher than a life of penitence, Gic entered the order of Bassorian monks after having affirmed, according to the rule, his renunciation by hideously scarring his face, and placing on his ring finger, as a recompense for his heroic mutilation, a lapis destined to elicit pious kisses, like the ecclesiastical amethyst.

Gifted with natural eloquence, he won renown for a multitude of homilies which after his death—not without first soliciting help from here and there to make up for his lack of instruction—a well-born Bassorian, Tercus de Lal, published in series of ten.

And at the place on the bench where, out of disappointment, his holy vocation had been born, a statue was erected to his memory whose finger bore a real lapis endowed with great power of protection for whoever kissed it.

And Granor VII gladdens his fearful mother by placing his lips against the blue stone.

3. The queen paying a visit to the rich Tinophir, known as *The Insular.*

Proprietor of the island of Dièsne in the river Nadur, Tinophir tirelessly plays the role of the government's Dutch uncle.

An eccentricity has made of him an inveterate thief, who never fails to give back to his victims much more than the value of his pilferings.

Far from blushing at his essentially harmless failing, he draws attention to it, and, as a kind of profession of faith, has caused to be engraved on a stone panel in the great hall of his palace the famous *Chain of Attila* cited by Crôle—a cynical succession of arguments through which the haughty chieftain, exacting approval from those around him, liked to arrive publicly at a pact with his conscience concerning the legitimacy of his depredations.

The queen came as a supplicant.

Each time that a crown prince of Carmedia was born, the twelve months, figured by twelve symbolically costumed maidens, would come to perform a dance around his cradle awhile—a fervent company—praying aloud that Time might smile uninterruptedly upon him, his natal month serving as monitor.

Born in January,[5] Granor VII had a totally white monitress clad in a snowy gown embellished with a large icicle diamond, which Tinophir had stolen—and more than compensated for next day by canceling a large debt owed him by the crown.

Gerta asks for and receives the loan of this jewel which, paramount in the dance around the cradle, seems to her well suited to protect Granor VII during the dreaded ordeal.

In a voice weakened by emotion she thanks Tinophir, apologizing for thus abusing his generosity.

4. The queen and Granor VII in the garden of the proverbially credulous Viaz, known as the *holy stutterer*. Good fortune is guaranteed anyone who can make him *swallow* a story that will momentarily suppress his stutter through surprise.

Instructed in advance, Granor VII addresses him thus:

The wealthy Ablasson adores redheads—and jealously cloisters a bevy of them in his palace.

One of them, Margealia, known for her goddesslike bearing, is fast maturing and dreads abasement.

Ablasson loves to carouse with his redheads but, jealous, will allow no man at his table, save his amusing crony Tric, whose incomparable verve is combined with a reassuring ugliness.

Sequestered with only her rivals for company, Margealia confides her fears to Tric, who, shrewdly obliging parasite that he is, vows to help her.

Shortly thereafter Tric, who knows that Ablasson loves to read and values his own opinions, begins matters by tossing out a laudatory phrase concerning Varocourt's *Nature's Shillyshallying*.

The next day he brings the book itself, interspersed with glosses designed to emphasize the main argument.

Varocourt shows how different, depending on the individual, the rate of aging can be—for example, how much faster a countrywoman declines than a lady of the town. He studies the female form from age to age, and maintains that the *third physique*—which he locates at the age Margealia has reached—often marks the apogee.

Ablasson reads—and, influenced, bestows his favors on Margealia.

Tric does not stop there.

He goes to the Galati, an Eden so dense that its origins are considered prehistoric. A famous echo exists there; whoever succeeds in rendering it sevenfold by shouting loud enough will, it is said, feel a salutary inspiration fulgurate within him.

Victor at the third shout, Tric, on an impulse, goes to pluck a full-blown lily—then thrusts his hand through the single hole in the hollow trunk of a decaying tree. And the lily, in more than full bloom, strikingly regains its vibrancy thanks to the contrast offered by the ambient darkness.

Tric understands—and succeeds in having Ablasson recruit several women older than Margealia, who enhance her charms.

But he goes further still.

Ablasson, blatantly debauched, proclaims himself moreover a skeptic and unbeliever, cynically insists on immortalizing himself just as he is—by means of a strange tomb now under construction.

Tric asks Margealia for her portrait—and with certain ends in view presents it to the mortuary artist.

Soon afterward Ablasson, convoked, goes to see his finished tomb, accompanied by Tric.

His instructions have been closely heeded.

Reclining on the funerary stone, a polychrome statue of a woman: red hair, short horns, cloven feet, coral lips with a lubricous smile. Forming a half circle around the chevet, a wall whereon are cited honorifically in letters of gold illustrious felonies crowned with definitive success. In front of the wall and behind the tombstone, a round stele whose horizontal summit bears a finely engraved reproduction of Créno's famous painting, *The Death of St. Ardelle*, a work inspired by this text of Exian: "St. Ardelle, when Death came to bestow his fatal accolade, received from an angel who had suddenly appeared an offer of postponement—and refused, saying: '*What more beautiful than death to the heart of a believer?*'" But the fiercely impious Créno had derisively given St. Ardelle a pose that contradicted her utterance, having her struggle, terrified, in the embrace of the scythe-wielding skeleton. From the summit to the base of the stele, Méroci's *Plea against Rigor* is engraved spirally.

Now the artist, supplied with the portrait, had given his she-devil the face of Margealia, who succeeds in deriving additional favor from this eternal distinction of rank.

Tric noticed that a little space remained at the bottom of the gold-lettered wall—and through Margealia, he acquaints Ablasson with the *Beneficial Fib of the Sage Octul*:

"A castaway clinging to a spar, Octul is washed ashore on the savage island of Nactade, whose natives force him to perform the vilest tasks. But his learning serves him well. Certain stars regularly disappear for a time—the result, some say, of their occultation by some dark sphere that gravitates around each. Recalling that, in the neck and withers of Pegasus, an absence of this sort is about to end, Octul, on the proper night, points his finger in the right direction and makes a thousand public grimaces from which the phenomenon seems to issue. And the natives, dazzled by so much power, crown him their king."

Ablasson applauds—and Margealia reigns more supreme than ever, while the funerary wall is further enriched.

Surprise has dictated several interruptions to Viaz, whose stuttering has diminished—then disappeared, to Gerta's great joy.

5. Granor VII listens to his mother, near a statue of Jortier.

Shortly before a certain Varnio-Carmedian war, Jortier, renowned for his exceptionally acute vision, boasted of being able to defeat all comers with regard to the minute deciphering of any object approaching from a distance.

Three daredevils accepted the challenge—and, on commission, an artist executes behind closed doors a medium-size painting designed for subtle decoding, which, advancing slowly on the day of the contest, he himself tenders toward the three contestants in turn (each strictly positioned in a narrow circle), and stops, docile, at the first cry of *Halt!*, scraping the ground with his heel, while an explanatory bulletin is drawn up and delivered to the judges. Jortier closes the tournament and, sure of himself, boldly posts himself far behind the circle so as to magnify his victory. Now, *his* heel mark is the most distant, and his bulletin the best. He alone was able to make out in the painting, entitled *Love's Message*, the painter's profound concept: the proof, supplied by the *habitus*, of incipient decline in an artfully made-up coquette who laughs as she reads some smoldering love letter.

War breaks out and, thanks to the opportune utilization of Jortier's special gift, unsuspected and very faint diurnal signal lights used by the enemy engender victory.

And later on a statue is erected to Jortier the warrior, projecting from afar his powerful decoding gaze, and a superstition soon accrues to it: To whomever places himself, as he climbs a certain knoll on an overcast day, in the axis of the imperious stone gaze, Jortier will predict the future by rendering the weather fine or foul.

Granor VII ascends the knoll at a sign from the queen—who is soon enraptured by a ray of sunlight piercing a dreary tent of clouds.

6. Hukloude talking with the queen before the tomb of Erroi, who, somewhat renowned for his burlesque poem, *The Skinflint's Siesta*, tried to stave off oblivion by pledging on his deathbed to bestow from the beyond a salutary piece of advice on whoever would come to read his masterwork to his remains.

And in a resounding voice, Gerta reads *The Skinflint's Siesta*:

The Jew Irny, a pawnbroker, falls asleep after his noonday repast—and this is his dream. The very noble and very rich Duke Fanéon IX of Siar has a first-class servant-mistress, Nicette, an early-rising manageress with an exhaustive account book in which even the barnyard hens are registered. An indefatigably militant champion of her lover, she is forever proudly recounting the *Miracle of Urou*—then hastily adding that the brotherhood of the Paléreux commemorates it annually with a sacred pantomime: "Two centuries ago, the woodcutter Flac, forced by poverty to work even at night, was returning home late beneath a calm and entirely overcast sky, when through a sudden rent the full moon revealed itself, lighting up a thicket in which his wife was embracing a lover—whom he felled with a single blow of his axe. It was the lecherous Duke Fanéon II of Siar, a recluse whose death elevated in illustrious wise—given the clearly miraculous nature of the rent, produced in calm weather exactly where and when it was needed—a head of the collateral branch, direct ancestor of Fanéon IX." Nicette dies prematurely, and Duke Fanéon IX, after excusing himself in a prayer for being unable to endure life after so much heartbreak, tries, valorous in the extreme, to get himself killed in battle—but in vain. Henceforth, seeking oblivion, he madly squanders exorbitant sums, sucking up the finest wines through a golden tube and sponsoring a renowned buffoon, expert at erudite teasing. And the day comes when Irny makes him a loan which, too usurious, results in a trial. Condemned to temporary exile, Irny wants to demonstrate the capacity of a certain clause added to the contract to annul the verdict—and argues so long-windedly that, little by little, sleep decimates his audience . . .

It is here that the anticipated illumination transfigures the queen: A narcotic, carefully dosed and surreptitiously administered, will, at the propitious hour, turn those she fears into innocuous dozing bundles of rags.

7. The queen visits the alchemist Suleil who desires, before preparing the desired narcotic, to consult a skeleton, that of Hulda, whose inspirational virtues he praises.

Hulda, a noble Norwegian, dwelt in her castle of Chriven, taking advantage of the frequent absences of her husband, Aag, a renowned hunter, to seek romance on the heath of Blège, where it was her custom to sing—in a voice so beautiful that invisible elves greeted each couplet with a salvo of applause—until the arrival of a passerby to her taste, whom she would then lure into a nearby wood.

Apprised, Aag decided to punish Hulda in a manner befitting her cynicism.

Would she go so far as to prostitute herself on Good Friday—which was fast approaching?

Leaving on a feigned pilgrimage he came, on the appointed day, to the heath of Blège, in a monk's hooded habit.

Hulda was there, singing to the applause of the invisible elves, verses concerning Tius, the great navigator: "Tius, as a child, had caught from his nurse a violent fear of the werewolf, which his father used when necessary to combat his bouts of laziness. One day, seized with fright, having finished his schoolwork early and not wishing to take recreation too soon, he drew an imaginary map of certain unexplored northern countries which already fascinated him—and which, later in life, he would go on to reconnoiter. And a square was cut from a sail of his ship of discovery, on which a hyperborean landscape in dull sunlight was painted, and which was glued to the corner of his schoolboy's fantastical drawing, that a strange divinatory accuracy had destined for fame."

Hulda, encountering Aag at this moment, ogled his silhouette in a flattering manner—then tackled new verses: "The Lord of Ruge loved Caditte, the chaste leading lady of *Mysteries*, who demanded in exchange for her hand that he, like her, would convert to Klormisme, a dissident religion then in fashion. Accusing her jokingly of pilfering his heart, Ruge obeyed—and, like every Klormist neophyte, was required, as a sign of zeal, to write with his blood the gospel of the Dishonored City: *In those days Jesus was traveling through the lustful city of Gouffar, when suddenly he saw its famous motto outrageously displayed in letters of solid gold on the façade of a public building*: Fornication depreciates once it becomes marital. *And Jesus having pointed at the gold, it formed in place of the motto an anathema in enormous letters*: Gouffar, Disgraced City. *Terrified, the Gouffarians fled—and mended their ways. So successfully that a year later, as Jesus was walking beside a field, he saw a working woman approaching him—a former Gouffarian jade, who proudly showed him her calloused hands.* And the Lord of Ruge became a happy husband.

Another meeting . . . and Hulda slipped into the famous wood followed by Aag, who, having pushed back his cowl, killed her on the spot and left her there to the mercy of the ravens, who quickly transformed her into a skeleton—soon to be gathered up by Suleil, who, keeping in mind the applauding elves, endowed her with supernatural virtues.

Having placed his ear between the jaws of the skeleton in search of counsels, Suleil composes a mixture which he gives to Gerta.

8. The famous *Ordeal of the Perch*. Granor VII's sham adversaries were secretly drugged—effectually or not? there is nothing to indicate which—and the king, adorned with the icicle diamond lent as a good-luck charm by Tinophir, won a normal victory.

Here the leader of the pilgrims fell silent—and the pious procession left the tomb of Angelo Essermos.

Fifth Document

In 1905, the newly promoted colonel of the 56th Infantry regiment decided to revive a certain anniversary which had unjustly fallen into neglect.

For as long as anyone could remember, each senior officer of the regiment had honorifically kept in his possession a medal depicting St. George, the patron saint of soldiers.

One of these, Armand Vage, acting on an anonymous tip, had one day discovered his wife in flagrante delicto—and had performed so well with a truncheon that a serious wound, the result of a sound thrashing, had made him a widower, easily acquitted by the court.

Vage's only relative was an older sister, an avaricious spinster from whom he inherited among other things a piece of cardboard pierced with two holes, which could only have been a cipher-stencil for locating a buried treasure.

The deceased, a great reader, had selected pages with the aid of scissors, glue, and sheets of cardboard, the latter of the same dimensions as the stencil, indicating that one should look there.

Disregarding the instances in which the two holes encircled nothing of interest, Vage, seeking illumination, meditated on these gists of pages:

1. The conspiracy of the Ardecists—who have gathered together at a banquet to choose a ringleader, either Balu or Dircet. On the menu is chicken with a new sauce that needs naming. *"Poulet à la Flourdas,"* proposes Balu, who goes on to laud the antique virtues of his hero:

Flourdas discovers that his father is the leader of a band of forgers who, to cover their traces, operate on an island. Inflexible, Flourdas's conscience turns him informer, resulting in the setting up of a police trap leading to mass arrests—and the suicide of his father, who has time to leap from a window.

Dircet, as a rival, raises captious objections concerning the case: Is one to admire Flourdas for his strength or condemn him as a parricide?

"Poulet à la Flourdas," shout the assembled conspirators, who, realizing the worth of an energetic man, choose Balu as their leader.[6]

2. Lodet's fable of the *Two Neighbors*. Sangal, an enthusiastic gourmet who likes only rich dishes, boasts that he can recite a thousand notable menus. His neighbor Dess, a model of sobriety, takes pleasure only in the constant embellishment of his garden. As a result of his excesses, Sangal dies prematurely after long suffering. Dess, on the contrary, serenely attains an age so advanced that he is able to observe the superannuation of certain tulips whose hybridization he had witnessed.

3. The confiteor of Crude, who covets at the same time as Barnille the hand of the hesitant Enice. Crude dreams of utilizing a certain neurotic fear of storms that afflicts his rival, so as to eliminate him. On the eve of an excursion planned by the trio, Crude ascends to the sky to find Orni-

gec, who is specially charged with determining the length of lightning flashes—and pays him to dispense them in good measure at the appointed hour. Next day, during their promenade, Ornigec outdoes himself, and Barnille exhibits such cowardice that the disgusted Enice becomes affianced to Crude. Later, the happily married Crude experiences remorse for his tactic, which leads him to confess.

4. The prediction of Nadéac. A fervent yachtsman, the haughty Count of Festol receives visitors only in audience because he is descended from a certain bastard son of a king of Neustria. The wall of his yacht's cabin is adorned with a grayish map of old Europe, in which Neustria stands out in bright red. At the moment of undertaking a long crossing, he gives audience to the renowned wizard Gourtane, who, as is his custom, appears costumed as Caliban—and soon predicts a shipwreck for him while examining the figures traced on a sheet of white paper in black dust which he scatters from a phial held over it. Furious and deeply disturbed, Festol has Gourtane seized by his servants and succeeds in extracting from him a comforting confession of charlatanism: Instead of drumming up business through a reputation as an invariably *superior* prophet, Gourtane, in order to tinge his alleged supernaturality with an appearance of truth, sometimes purposely imitates Cassandra by pretending to rebel in vain against evil powers—such as Caliban, whose costume he has assumed to that end.

5. The punishable rhymes of Soge, a popular author of irreverent ballads. It is a question of a poster emblazoned, in verse and music of Soge, with a pseudo-letter from King Mostar to his sister, concerning an extra zero added purely in her favor to a sum taken from public funds for the restoration of a lacustrian village ill-used by a waterspout. Now, rumors of incest have circulated with regard to the brother and sister. And the lampooner, to add to the incriminating exaggeration of intimacy contained in the cynicism of the confession, has throughout caused the word "we" to be printed in red instead of black.

6. The fine didactic role of Anne de Greux, a young widow of the age of Louis XIV, whose hand is sought by a country neighbor, her vassal Gaston de Sessine. Now Anne is a *précieuse*, and Gaston, orphaned early in life, is, though well-born, unlettered and unpolished. Gaston is not repugnant to Anne, who tames and instructs him, using as a goad when

necessary a certain fear that haunts him of being abandoned by his guardian angel, whom, she tells him one day when his English translation is execrable, she will go so far as to exile by a hundred wing-flaps if he fails again.

7. The hesitations of another young widow of the same era, Solange de Briveneuc, also a *précieuse*, whom two suitors, d'Arcel and d'Hourcuff, amorously deluge with their poems—and one fine day call upon to choose between them. Solange enjoins each, promising herself to him who best succeeds, to compose some verses about a painting by Querbois showing a giantess, the Plague, with a basket on her back into which she is stuffing heaps of *her* corpses—and utilizes, on the appointed day, a backsliding *ex aequo*. Promptly badgered, the procrastinatrix finally resorts to a wager concerning the weather, the winner of which she swears to accept. After a glance at an opaline December sunset, d'Arcel, gainsaid by d'Hourcuff, predicts an impending frost—and, triumphant, soon brings the *précieuse* a lyre of ice just removed from a mould hastily fabricated in advance. But Solange, eluding her oath, becomes affianced to d'Hourcuff, whom the unexpected death of a brother the very day before has made an heir to great nobility and wealth.

8. The megalomania of Estal, a metaphysician with a twin brother, rebuked by his father when, as a naive greenhorn already sufficiently full of himself to see, paranoid, imaginary enemies desperate to extinguish his self-styled budding genius, he had hidden phials everywhere while launching a series of experiments in immunization in the style of Mithridates. Later Estal had to share an inheritance with his brother—and gave him a hefty supplement in order to reestablish a balance necessitated, in his view, by the extraordinary gifts heaven had lavished on him. In reality Estal left behind nothing but a worthless philosophical tome, *The Surprising Republic*, of which he made Merlin the puppet-president and wherein he attempts in vain to set up striking contrasts between the enchanter's magical omnipotence and his complete political ossification.

9. The austere sacred quadrille of the members of the Siliciah, an English religious sect that combats pauperism—a quadrille during which Caudley manages to murmur the words "Solace with a key" to Laura Plyde, his mistress with a jealous husband. After the sacred dance, each member receives, in the form of a tract signed by Caudley, a comforting dis-

course to be joined to their alms. Warned, Laura examines her copy—and discovers there a phrase with a double meaning canceling a forthcoming rendezvous which was to have been turned into a scandal by a treacherous orchestral serenade directed at the culpable windows.

10. The futility introduced into the conspiracy of Calogne by the accomplice Félistu, who, something of an ogre, was once kept so long at table by his enormous appetite that it was still being cleared—he having arrived late—at the end of an important council held that day by the affiliates.

11. The nervousness of the young prince Egelar who, one October evening, as his tutor had just ended his lesson by explicating Bréou's *Game-Board of Civility*—a sort of checkerboard school portfolio with illustrated squares, the last of which deals with the disesteem caused by pouring liquor down one's gullet without touching the flask to one's lips—felt himself overcome by *autumnal blackness*, the name he gave to a special melancholy occasioned by the curtailment of the days. As a remedy he resorted to one of his favorite distractions, summoning his two buffoons, Badre and Sinel, whom he incited to taunt each other by appraising them in two columns—with the aim of drawing up two reckonings to be paid in cash.

12. The solemn nightlong celebration under a beautiful starry sky filled with favorable auguries wherein the century-old tiff between the Proys and the Galiches was finally terminated. Charles and François de Proy, two close-knit twin brothers, had at the age of twenty (the house of Galiche being at that time reduced to an orphaned daughter, Berthe) affectionately resolved the difficulty created by their equal rights to the title of head of a great family: Through methodical permutations each became in turn the elder and the younger brother—until the day when Berthe, having attained her majority, enamored Charles and, totally free to choose a husband, promised herself to him. Fearful of preparing the way for bloody cousinships if he too were to marry, François, leaving his own desires completely out of consideration, retired to a monastery.

13. The public soliloquy of the patriot Korko against the conqueror Mirissu III, king of Ormada, who, proud of having enlarged his realm on its four cardinal borders, possessed, in addition to that of his ancestors, four

golden crowns with symbolic names. As he preached revolt to his oppressed compatriots, Korko shook an effigial gilded crown bearing the word "East"—their region. And such was its intentional fragility that the entire gilt finish fell off little by little. Bolstered by the spectacle of this fall from grace, Korko's incendiary discourse took hold so successfully that an insurrection soon broke out in that precinct, leading to the recovery of independence.

14. The sacrilege condoned by Jacqueline de Faublas, younger sister of the famous libertine who, far from protecting her as an elder brother should, shamelessly paid court to her. Jacqueline had in addition two obstinate suitors between whom a dialogue revealed by a door left ajar terrified her. Loyally, one of them, the next morning at five o'clock in the forest of Lul, was to surrender his place entirely to the other through a duel which death alone would decide. Believing that nothing less than a definitive inspiration of unheard-of horror could avert the terrible tragedy, Jacqueline at the calculated moment led her delighted brother into the forest of Lul, on arriving whither the two adversaries were paralyzed by the incestuous spectacle—after which she entered the Carmelite order.

15. The cynical pride of the rich *misdeal-marquis* of Bérouce, a country squire, who, when his hand appeared unpromising, would not shrink from inventing a pretext to deal the cards again. In his château, the painted dome of a circular room depicted a ballet danced by the neighboring households of petty squires—and himself, placed symbolically at the zenith. The sight of peasants at work caused him to descend from his coach, spouting odious raillery concerning the rage that the toil they undertook for his profit must inspire in them. One day when he came to amuse himself in this fashion at the expense of a sower, his principal toady dared allude to possibilities of vengeance, whereupon he annulled the writ concerning his promotion.

16. The argumentative use made by the egalitarian Geordot of the conjugal felicity of the brothers Arthur and Bertrand d'Oclode, who, as descendants of Marcel d'Oclode *the Zealous*, had each a curious mark on his forehead. Five centuries before, the heroic and triumphant defense of a city gate had left Marcel d'Oclode with, among many other scars, a star-shaped one on his forehead[7] produced by several sword thrusts at the

same spot. So that this trait so glorious for their house might never be eclipsed, all the newborn sons of the d'Oclodes received on their foreheads an astral abrasion generating an indelible commemorative scar. Now, visibly noble among all but exempt from prejudice, Arthur and Bertrand, following their hearts, had simultaneously married two exquisite peasant girls—and had a year later come to a draw, by each attaining the pinnacle, with regard to a bet whose winner was to be the brother with the happiest lot.

17. An inspiration felt one glacial *nivôse*[8] evening by Barras, surrounded at home by his cronies, some of whom took advantage of the fact that one *breathed* freely at last to proclaim their belief in the existence of the soul—denied by the others. Noncommittal at first, Barras suddenly stood up, moved, he said, by the spirit of Marthe Fabian, a long-mourned mistress who was eager to settle the question. As though transformed into an automaton, Barras went to get one of his favorite books, the *Novel of the Peninsula* by Bias de Priène, one of the seven sages of Greece, set on an imaginary peninsula which the author, encapsulating certain truths involving prominent contemporaries, peoples with an independent society of upright citizens with an ideal government. From this book Barras removed a dried daisy given him by Marthe Fabian and plucked its petals one by one while murmuring *freeze, thaw*, ending with the latter word. The next day a sudden rise in temperature rendered the believers' side victorious.

18. An amorous defeat suffered by the Duc d'Aumale in the wings of the Comédie Française, where Claude Bonnal's *Conquest of Algeria* was being performed. The duke had come to see himself on the stage taking a relaxing horseback ride on the eve of a battle while reciting his favorite poem, the famous *Playful Pastoral* by Charles d'Orléans; then, at the junction of two roads, dispatching several ambushed Arabs and nonchalantly continuing to recite his verses the while, his stage mount unfazed by the crackling gunfire; and finally espying the arrival of a young native girl amazed at her own tranquil bravura, whom he would go on to seduce—a splendid but virtuous actress, a true Mohammedan whose French diction was flawless. Enchanted, the duke had between the acts expressed to Nourdah his desire to see her pass, insofar as regarded him, from the level of fiction to reality. Impregnable, Nourdah, so as to gild the pill of her refusal in a flattering manner, had recited in Levantine

lingua franca—then translated—a passage from the Koran that speaks of corollaries to be deduced from the fact that one can list thirteen plants which, unlike the heliotrope, turn timidly away from the sun.

19. An example of wise mansuetude provided by the portraitist Crustal. At the age of thirty, as one of a numerous houseful of guests, Crustal was living in the château of the Comte de Bervé, where it was the custom for everyone to assemble each morning for breakfast. One day a ravishing girl of ten entered the dining room uttering a "Good morning, Philippe" which intersected the "Good morning, Philippine" from a boy her own age. Who had spoken first, Fred or Alice? With the anticipated prize at stake[9] the other children deliberated—and their vote gave rise to a verdict which, favorable to Fred, transformed Alice into such a pretty little weeping thing that Crustal dashed off a sketch of her on the spur of the moment. Later, having matured into a marvelous young maiden, Alice, at his ardent request, and dazzled by his success, married the talented and still handsome Crustal—and several years of happiness ensued. One August evening, having discerned his wife and a young male friend silhouetted in a tender embrace against a gleam of nocturnal light that persisted in the west, he went back indoors, mad with rage, to get a revolver—and stopped, riveted to the spot by the sight of the famous childhood sketch, which never left his possession. Induced by a sudden realization of their disproportionate ages to see in himself a Géronte[10] playing a juvenile role, he vowed to shut his eyes to the circumstance— and kept his word.

20. The appellation "*haloed native*" given by Prouglot in his "Proverbs Belied" to the sixteenth-century astrologer Bulias, a prophet in his own country. Luckily launched in his natal city by the timely realization of a prediction, made for the subsequent solstice, of the favorable outcome of a scandalous trial, Bulias, venal by nature, seized on the windfall to enrich himself by charging exorbitant prices for his horoscopes.

At the twenty-first attempt, immediately struck by the words "cube" and "mesmerize,"[11] perfectly framed in the two holes of the stencil, Armand Vage abstained from further meditative reading: *A cube would mesmerize him*. Having raised a remarkably cubical mossy stone at the edge of a stream that flowed through his sister's garden, he discovered a substantial hoard, which, having no family, he bequeathed to his regiment, where his death, which followed soon after, was for a time commemorated annually by a ceremony, the very same which the new colonel at the post, indignant at its having fallen into disuse, revived.

Sixth Document

In 1877,[12] revolution broke out in Belotina. The fleeing king was replaced by an extremely *red* oligarchy, named, since its members were seven and reciprocally responsible, the *Pleiade of Solidary Tribunes*. A sort of egalitarian patriotism was the order of the day, and, in a spirit of emulation, the *Star of Civism* was created, which anyone who had distinguished himself in appropriate fashion might receive in the form of a scar made on the right temple with a branding iron. A war erupted which, ill-starred, led to the siege of the capital. From adversity was born a tempering of ideals—followed by a total reaction. The *reds* kept their peace, the churches were filled to overflowing—and the pleiade was ousted in favor of a dictator, Ferlo, branded with the Star of Civism, who, heroic defender, was killed in a sortie at the height of his popularity at the very moment the urgency of creating an obsidional coinage began to be felt. Despite a treacherous allusion to the word "twaddle" (employed by him during the red period to characterize the religious preparations for Advent), his profile was used as effigy, underscored with the venerated date of his death, and framed by two weeping women, that on the right being given the features of his mistress, Digette Ralet.

A new dictator risen from the masses, Matthias Noc, delighted all the newspapers with his manifesto—notably *The Cudgel*, a specialist in the *scurvy* genre, which did not fail to play him a minor dirty trick in the form of a lampoon with three subjects in the purposely chosen ultra-strict form of triolets which, by their marmoreal quality alone, twitted the still-vulgar speech of the ex-plebian. The first related a quarrel that, provoked in a brothel by a disputed throw of the dice, had caused Noc to spout insults in argot; next came a proof of superstition—no small matter in the mood of religious reaction then rampant—furnished by the constant wearing under his shirt of a slender chain-necklace from which depended a locket containing a four-leaf clover; the final anecdote concerned a habit of obsequious fawning acquired when he had worked as a youth in a shooting gallery, vis-à-vis the former king, whom he had showered with outrageous compliments regarding a tricky miniature target hit by the still-inexperienced king, on which figured, symbol of speed, a sledge drawn by high-spirited steeds, the heart of the iemskik[13] figuring as bull's-eye, as in a hijacking plotted by brigands.

As these triolets merely gibed at him without attacking his rectitude, Noc thought them over, like a wise man eager to mend his ways. He got rid of the clover, learned to mistrust his natural pliability—and, so as to become more polished, had recourse to the counsels of Lord de Buc, a patrician highly versed in the art of good manners thanks to his illustrious origins, honorifically indicated by the title *The Lovely Turncoat* applied to Mary Magdalen, his ancestress, in one of the special prayers at Candlemas. In her first youth the Magdalen had been the *ray of sunlight* (in his phrase) of a rich elderly admirer closeted by his infirmities, Ségenal, whom she cuckolded with the handsome Buc, founder of the line. One evening, instead of greeting her with his customary tender metaphor, Ségenal asked her for an alibi, believing he had spied her, from his aged, nearsighted invalid's cushions, involved in a gallant pastoral escapade with Buc—and received merely a cynical confession leading to a parting of the ways.

And Noc soon polished his uncouth deportment thanks to his relations with Lord de Buc—whose coat-of-arms made allusion to the Ségenal incident—and flaunted his new learning by intentionally leaving a map lying about that he himself had expertly drawn, representing a prehistoric Asia with a bizarre, scientifically exact shape.

Knowing that in order to *stay the course* he must above all attend to the morale of the besieged population, Noc hired the comic singer Furdet to amuse the crowd gratis each evening.

A specialist in the daredevil genre, the aptly chosen Furdet boasted of knowing by heart a whole *cartload* of patter songs on various subjects:

Godable, forced by penury to emigrate, bids a final farewell to his mistress Krune. Seeing her fearing for him the dangers of the sea voyage, he reassures her with a legend told of his ship, "equipped with masts so perfectly conditioned for dealing with tempests that their builder is believed to be a relative of Lucifer." There follows a racy mutual oath: At appointed days and hours, each, thinking of the other and gazing at the *Coma Berenices* in the heavens, will commit a voluptuous solitary sin. Arriving at his destination deep in the tropics, Godable, unable to find a position, becomes the lover of a priestess of Ros, a deity much revered since the power of bringing cool weather is attributed to her—and heaps perjury on perjury.

As soon as he becomes master of Syracuse, Marcellus, in order to establish himself as absolute ruler controlling all lives, organizes his *impartial massacres*. His physician Parnolo, a Neapolitan charlatan, concocts for him a certain drug, lethal in tiny doses, which each day dispatches ten passersby of both sexes stopped at random. So as to reinforce the *impartial* aspect, Marcellus spares whoever divines the last (and most difficult) in a series of graded riddles—and bestows on him, as an eternal shield against a new beginning of the ordeal, a cockade on which is painted, thanks to a chauvinist whim of Parnolo's, the incomparable Bay of Naples. For a pretty woman, there are no riddles: Marcellus grants her the cockade solely in exchange for her favors. One day a comic-heroic scene breaks out. Two twin sisters, Guria and Forine, gray-haired virgins deeply devoted to each other, make up part of the *ten*. After Guria, who has just emerged victorious, Forine enters the interrogation room . . . and falls silent halfway through; having recrossed the sill, and forgetting her age, she offers herself, terrified, to the rescuing embraces of Marcellus—who, laughing uncontrollably, designates her to the poisoner. Magnificent, Guria then discards her cockade—and drinks with her sister.

In the course of a chaconne danced before Louis XV enthroned in a seat of honor on a dais, the Marquise de Pranier gives vent to a fit of sulks that signifies a breach with her lover, the fashionable poet Sance. The latter resigns himself—but swears that a scandal will avenge him. He knows himself replaced by the Baron d'Etulle—whom he has never seen—and, having posted himself, cunningly armed, in the latter's path disguised as a beggar, profits from the momentary distraction of the charitable pocket-explorer to interrupt, by stabbing him, a good-natured fragmentary sermon concerning the laziness of certain sturdy young men capable of working for a living. A love criminal soon released, Sance continues to write brilliantly. Later on, as a declining hack repelled by the word "*unharness*," he is sent a book whose plot, as a professional, he appreciates—the work of an author keenly athirst for logic, still too young to attract a public. Stirred by the scruple-smothering prospect of a prolongation of heyday, he executes a clever plagiarism—which he camouflages by making his setting the bottom of a lake and his characters water sprites. And from its fame success is born—whose cynical illegitimacy is discovered by the marquise, who, with all her forces, trumpets it like the old grudge-bearer she is.

King Dinoh, whose finances are in shambles, goes, after the obligatory payment of heavy alms, to consult in her temple the goddess Biuse, whose statue speaks—thanks, according to spiteful tongues, to an invisible flesh-and-blood female accomplice and a lucky acoustical phenomenon. Kneeling before the statue on a downy cushion, the monarch summons the goddess with a silver note struck with a hammer on a bell—and at once hears tell—along with precise auxiliary indications of its location—of an island where the discovery of a treasure, buried at the foot of a large cliff whose shape from a distance suggests the fleur de lys, will enable him to multiply his riches a hundredfold. Dinoh sets sail, searches in vain for the island, returns incensed—and goes to resume, in surly tones, his conversation with the *goddess*, who, forewarned, accuses his crew of ineptitude, which doesn't prevent her collection of *ex-votos* from being enriched soon afterward by the addition of a large marble plaque inscribed with a ferocious diatribe.

Clossida, split by two factions, has just installed a democratic government in place of its reigning prince, Iknar II, at the same moment that two books triumph: Kolour's *The Hundred Lessons of Analysis of the Kabbalah* and Plassas's *Sensual Pleasure in Plants*—read one day on a park bench by two idlers whose characters, retrograde in one, scientific in the other, cause them to quarrel. A small group of blind people clasping one another's hands passes by, guided by a single pair of good eyes as they leave an asylum founded by the fallen ruler, a circumstance which leads them to side with the reader of Koulour and to inflict on his antagonist, whom they call "Good-for-nothing egalitarian," a sound trouncing with their fists. Their hero—*noblesse oblige*—intervenes effectively, and the other, whose outing has cost him a drubbing, regains his home.

Marfo, a philosopher with independent doctrines, lives as an ascetic in the forest of Nède, pitying the lot—abject in his view since necessarily tinged with a servility summoning suppression—of any member of a society. With him lives a she-wolf, adopted when young, whom he calls his Egeria, admiring the fact that, while recognizing him, she has kept all the fierce instincts of her race. One autumn evening, while he drinks in with emotion the poetic spectacle offered by the yellow leafless forest, his gaze is suddenly struck by a flaw in the décor: a beehive, detestable emblem of discipline.

Harmony seems to reign in the court of the Russian nobleman Tisof, even while his "right-hand man" Uvrou, a meritorious aide issued from humble origins, is envied, behind smooth-spoken appearances, by a former companion in misery, Diar, who however owes him everything. Bribed by Diar, the pamphleteer Pressy produces a book wherein, in short paragraphs followed by an asterisk, he accuses Uvrou of fishing in troubled waters behind an appearance of disinterest. Diar sends the book to Tisof with a brief message in a counterfeit hand pointing out that the number of asterisks exceeds a thousand, and containing the description, with venomous comparisons, of a certain outergarment full of holes that Uvrou, now immensely rich, wore in his youth. But the nobleman, in disgust, throws book and message into the fire.

One morning in November 1683, the Comte de Lédu, a man of spirit, awakens at dawn full of sad thoughts; of a choleric nature, he had the night before offered an affront to one of the principal statesmen of the moment, resulting in the order to leave at once for his country estate. Then he seizes on an idea which had long slumbered in his mind: to enter the Nicolas Flamel[14] Academy—a great name well chosen as a banner, whose members enjoy special favor which might reestablish him. That same day he succeeds in obtaining a delay and, knowing that any application for candidature must be accompanied by an unpublished work, eagerly gets down to business. Purposely choosing a subject designed to enhance him in terms of heraldic antiquity, he sings the exploits of the Iberian Arco, from whom he is descended on his mother's side. Before each expedition, Arco always used to consult the witch Daca—who one day made herself his Cassandra in recounting him a fatal dream wherein he played the leading role. And Arco was killed during the first engagement. . . . Now, each reader on the committee is captivated from the exordium onward. So Lédu enters the Flamel Academy, receives its badge—a tiny king of hearts in diamonds and rubies, reminder of the favorite pastime of the alchemist, whom the invention of playing cards had enraptured—and returns to grace.

In the days of Louis XV, during a harsh winter, the Marquis de Grante, a member of parliament who has in the third estate an impudent foe, Pierre Ligot, always ready to pick a quarrel with him, goes in search of the charlatan Ruetti, a renowned maker of talismans, of whose shrewdness he has heard praises sung. Ruetti decides to try out a method of getting rid of the pest which he believes certain. He goes to look for two traps in the nearby forest: two incomplete rings of ice smeared with suet, each housing a doubly pointed spring designed to expand, lethally perforative, in the quarry's warm stomach. He carves the name of Pierre Ligot on a wooden statuette that he places in his garden at the center of one of the traps while hanging the other just above. According to him, Pierre Ligot cannot survive the symbolic placing of his image between two engines of death. But the destructive thaw arrives without causing suffering to Pierre Ligot.

Rogelle, a young and beautiful queen with absolute power, is afflicted with an unbridled sadism which sows terror around her. She owns a dossier wherein in the form of lists figure the names of the most expert among those she euphemistically calls "cajolers." The writer and traveler Bertol, who, in addition to his creative talent, has a pretty voice and sings accompanying himself on a sort of guitar, loves her silently from afar. To attract her attention and to give himself a chance to *have* her, he composes during an expedition, without denying himself the direst deceptions, an ultrasmutty book which causes a scandal. After reading it, the queen has him summoned on the pretext of hearing him sing. During the recital she ceaselessly directs *pairs* of winks in his direction. This very parity is a clear invitation, to which, after terminating on an old-fashioned chord, he responds ecstatically.

The pious Mélanie Rustier, always austerely dressed in iron gray, has a son, Périnot, who leads a hard life at sea, enrolled in the crew of Captain Mourck. Ambitious and eager to school himself so as to advance, he asks the ship's Aesculapius to lend him books—which include works on astronomy, a science at that time highly regarded in naval circles. One day he reads in Tycho Brahe the passage concerning the god Plutus, who, having heard tell of the existence of a rich gold mine on the moon, betakes himself there to exploit it—but, extremely ill-received with the cry of "Out!" by the Selenites, eager to keep their prize, returns, soundly pummeled by them. Henceforth, Périnot's mind is split: At times he is normal; at others, laughing and crazed, he imagines himself dipping both hands in the gold mine on the moon. In despair, Mélanie Rustier believes him possessed and does everything possible to have him exorcised.

In a country bordering on the Black Sea reigns Keran, nicknamed King "In a Minute" because of numerous fine promises that he always shrinks from fulfilling. At his court glitters the beautiful Discrine, who, though virtuous, lives on a grand scale with no visible resources. Keran, titillated, would like her for his favorite, but the slyboots refuses, holding out for a marriage proposal. Near the capital there is an Eden where, in a cave, an emblematic statue of Pomona in ripe maturity occupies a place of honor, coiffed with a golden rose and clad in an actual red tunic. The cave is sealed by a stone disk that rolls naturally, accessible to the frailest. Deeply revered, the statue, oracular at certain times fixed in advance, replies to questions as though with an echo. Keran, who is considering marrying Discrine, goes disguised as a sage on one of the appointed days to consult Pomona, who replies with only these words: "*Spy's Stitchery.*" From then on, Keran has Discrine put under surveillance and discovers her to be a spy who, esteeming her eventual royalty *in a minute* too problematical to abstain from running with the hare and hunting with the hounds, exchanges with a certain Pritane, a female spy in the service of a neighboring king, papers for which the red tunic, ceaselessly stitched and restitched, serves as repository. One day Keran confounds Discrine by showing her a complete project for a surprise war taken from the hiding place, as well as a treaty that takes victory for granted, one of whose clauses favors her personally—and contents himself with exiling her.

Penniless, Maciton bursts with a natural comic verve which he uses to make a living as jester to King Baoge; but in reality he is a scholar and an innovator who has founded a philosophical system with enthusiastic disciples, set forth in a folio entitled *God = Zero*. Baoge has an unacknowledged mistress: Kercia de Nize, who, posing as a strict and pious woman, detests the unbeliever Maciton and seeks to have him disgraced. One day, due to a beginning pregnancy, Baoge hastily marries off Kercia to the Baron de Fô in order to save appearances. One year later at a masked ball, Maciton, disguised as Harlequin, loudly congratulates Kercia for having been able to remain white as snow by having more or less the three proper trimesters between her marriage and her childbed.

But Kercia has recognized him by his voice and tells all to Baoge, who, annoyed and with a view to a general muzzling of the population, seizes on Maciton's militant impiety as a pretext to banish him from his territory. Transplanted, Maciton solicits the post of jester with King Nopal—and obtains it by publishing a wildly comic theorem, impossible to read without guffawing at every line.

The young Scandinavian writer Frug seeks his way in vain and, feeling himself full of potential, chafes at being a nonentity. Now he reads in an abridged version of Sédoual's *Universal Method* a phrase simultaneously calculated to summon the *Spirits of Vesper* so as to consult them and to banish the slightest cloud from the sky, absolutely clear weather being a condition necessary to their celestial descent. One almost perfect day, a rare event in his misty homeland, he pronounces the phrase in a loud voice. By chance, the last clouds dissipate after a few hours. Hallucinating, he thinks he sees around him the *Spirits of Vesper*, who counsel him to marry the *Beautiful* with the *Trivial*. After meditating a long time on their suggestion, he at last discovers the path so long desired and, bard of the people, writes his masterwork, in which vulgarities in no way diminish the splendor of the style.

The young Englishman Robert Cross has a twin sister, Mabel. Often they entertain the obscure poet Oakburn, who, though feeble and of ripe age, loves Mabel. At each occasion, his place is set with an evocatively labeled bottle of his tonic, the celebrated *Vin du Horse Guard*. Oakburn rhymes an amorous dialogue between an old oak and a tiny flower avid for loving protection. He purposely sends it to Mabel, writing PROLOGUE, a word pregnant with things to come, below the title. The clarity of the illusion causes Robert and Mabel to burst out laughing, and they agree to ridicule the grotesque suitor publicly. Before a large roomful of guests who find it wildly funny, Robert, without the least suspicion of danger, swears to Oakburn that he will give him his twin sister on the day when—mad supposition—each line of his verse will fetch the price of a hectare of land. Oakburn knows the vain and extremely rich Draham who, among his other possessions, owns immense farmlands which the invasion of a microbe has rendered forever useless. He addresses him a poem padded with praises, in which he requests the dreamed-of price—which he obtains thanks to the noxious microbe and to intoxicating prospects of publication in a major newspaper. Badgered forthwith,

Robert steals away at the sight of his sister in tears. Armed with his witnessed oath, Oakburn subpoenas Robert, who, resorting to a play on words, claims that he had promised Oakburn nothing more than his pair of opera glasses.[15] In view of his age and appearance, the judge decides against Oakburn, who, furious, calls him *sotto voce* a hireling.

Versed in the knowledge of arms, the haughty king Badir III of the Ukraine, who, ostentatious, never issues forth without an escort of twelve pages, has founded a strong army to subdue the neighboring peoples and establish an empire. Afflicted with a mortal malady, he survives thanks to a miracle which roots deep within him the faith in his destiny of conqueror. Spurred on by frustrated hopes, the neighboring kings, possible future vassals, deliberate—and decide to profit from the fact that he needs pastimes during his remission by sending him a reader, the noble and beautiful anti-Ukrainian Nellague, a person adulated among all others who cannot fail to bewitch him. They take legal cognizance of an oath given them by Nellague—flattered by their choice—to murder the menacing megalomaniac at the first propitious moment. Dazzled, the illustrious invalid hires her on the spot—but, handsome himself and cloaked in prestige, he makes her heart beat faster. One evening her reading puts him to sleep—and she, always in possession of a concealed dagger, feels the unclenching of an inner struggle between her love and her oath, which the vaunted rectitude of her ancestors reinforces. Finally, faithful to her vow, she kills him—and immediately gives herself up.

The tenor Gléoc, pained by the ugliness from which he suffers, succeeds admirably thanks to a magnificent high B, which he loses during a chill caught by him and his wife—who dies of it, not without his craftily giving out that he is quitting the boards from sorrow and that his B remains at his disposal. The torment caused by his hideousness, augmented by the desire for fallen obstacles with regard to possible good fortune, incites him to consult the sorcerer Brouce, whom marvelous procedures of all kinds have rendered illustrious. Brouce sells him at a high price a necklace from which depends a platinum lozenge that cannot fail to bestow on his two eyes the property of *flooring* any woman. Henceforth Gléoc, an irresistible seducer, has only to eliminate—without fearing that she will suffer consequences from it—whichever of his ardent admirers wearies him.

The patter songs of Furdet had the desired adjuvant effect. The besieged held out—and the enemy, one fine day, withdrew empty-handed.

1. Possibly a spoonerism for *mamelles par terre*: "breasts on the ground," i.e., pendulous breasts. (Trans.)

2. Pérou is the French name for Peru. (Trans.)

3. The French—*jusqu'à ce que vînt le changer Desaix*—may be another of Roussel's hidden puns; *changer Desaix* is phonetically identical to *changer de sexe*, "to change one's sex." Desaix was a general of Napoleon killed during a charge which determined the French victory at Marengo. (Trans.)

4. No doubt volumes from the Bibliothèque Rose, a popular nineteenth-century series of children's books which Roussel had certainly read as a child. (Trans.)

5. As was Roussel. (Trans.)

6. *Poulet* means both "chicken" and, in argot, "policeman." (Trans.)

7. An allusion, perhaps, to Roussel's play *L'Étoile au front*, "The Star on the Forehead." (Trans.)

8. The fourth month of the French Revolutionary calendar (December–January). (Trans.)

9. A French custom dictates that when someone opens an almond and finds two kernels instead of one, he or she must give one of them to a person of the opposite sex; the two then become "Philippe" and "Philippine," and when they afterward meet, whoever says "Bonjour" first wins a prize. Apparently Fred and Alice had already shared a double almond kernel. (Trans.)

10. An elderly character in Molière's *Les Fourberies de Scapin*. (Trans.)

11. *Méduser*: to turn to stone. (Trans.)

12. The year of Roussel's birth. (Trans.)

13. I am unable to identify the word "iemskik." Perhaps it is a kind of steed (a reindeer?) that leads the others. (Trans.)

14. Flamel (1330–1418), a jurist, was reputedly an alchemist. (Trans.)

15. The word in question is *jumelle(s)*, which can mean both "twin sister" and "opera glasses." (Trans.)

These versions of Ashbery's Note and Introduction, as well as the text of *Documents to Serve as an Outline*, are from *How I Wrote Certain of My Books and Other Writings* by Raymond Roussel, ed. Trevor Winkfield (Cambridge, Mass.: Exact Change, 1995).

"Note by John Ashbery" first appeared in *Atlas Anthology* 7 (1991), as Ashbery's "Introduction" to his translation of Roussel's *Documents pour servir de canevas*. Ashbery wrote this "Note" in English; we reprint it here to accompany his translation of *Documents to Serve as an Outline*. This version of "Note" was also reprinted as "Introduction to Raymond Roussel's *Documents to Serve as an Outline*," in Ashbery's *Selected Prose* (Ann Arbor: University of Michigan Press, 2004; Manchester, U.K.: Carcanet Press, 2004).

"Introduction to 'In Havana' by John Ashbery" first appeared in French, in *L'Arc* 19 (Summer 1962), as a preface to "Un inédit de Raymond Roussel," the first publication in French of Roussel's "À la Havane." It was translated from Ashbery's English into French for *L'Arc* by Michel Thurlotte. Ashbery then translated it back into English, as "Introduction to Raymond Roussel's 'In Havana,'" to accompany the first appearance of his translation of "À la Havane" in *Atlas Anthology* 4 (1987). The Introduction was also reprinted in Ashbery's *Selected Prose* (Ann Arbor: University of Michigan Press, 2004; Manchester, U.K.: Carcanet Press, 2004). The translation of "In Havana" was also reprinted in *Atlas Anthology* 7 (1991), as part of Ashbery's first complete translation of *Documents to Serve as an Outline*.

GIORGIO DE CHIRICO

(1888–1978)

ON SILENCE

Before man appeared on Earth the god Silence reigned everywhere, invisible and present. Black, flabby things, a species of fish-cliff, emerged slowly like submarines on maneuvers, then dragged themselves painfully onto the beach like disabled veterans deprived of their motorized wheelchairs. Vast epochs of silence on Earth, everything was steaming! Columns of steam arose from the seething pools, from between the tragic cliffs and the center of the forests. Nature, nature without noise! Uninhabited, silent shores; in the distance, on the milky and disturbingly calm seas, a red sun, disk of drama, solitary disk, sank slowly into the vapor on the horizon. From time to time a monstrous animal, a kind of small island with the neck of a swan and the head of a parrot, left the water to go inland, into the mysterious forest and the depths of the humid valleys. The shores were littered with strange shells: stars, tendrils, broken spirals; some of them moved a little, advancing by sudden starts, then would collapse as though exhausted by the effort and remain motionless again.

Evenings of battle on the edge of the ocean! O evening of Quiberon! In sublime poses of lassitude and sleep the warriors are stretched out now in their final rest, while, beyond the black cliffs with their gothic apostles' profiles, a moon of boreal pallor is rising in the great silence; softly its rays light up the faces of the dead and waken a veiled reflection in the metal of their arms.

Silence also reigns before battles; during the vigils of the chiefs, of the generals from whose authority there is no appeal, who, in their tents placed well apart from enemy action, ponder their strategic plans until dawn and try to remember what their predecessors did in the same situation. Silence is necessary, even indispensable to their meditation, for on this silence depends the quality of their strategic thoughts and consequently the fate of those warriors who are sleeping now, their arms within easy reach, and who, tomorrow, when the clarion will have sounded the alarm, when the scattered squadrons on the plain will suddenly swoop down more promptly than the eaglet, could know the intoxication of victory or the gall of defeat; they might experience triumph, the sublime joy of entering conquered cities as victors, of traversing empty streets between a double hedge of houses with solemn balconies and hermetically sealed shutters, whose occupants, not knowing how to show their resentment at hearing the rhythmic step of enemy phalanxes echoing under their windows, have found nothing better to do than shut themselves up in their bedrooms, their parlors, and their dining rooms, blinds lowered and doors shut: to sulk, in a word! But these same warriors could, alas, experience defeat, the shame of being dragged as prisoners through an enemy country, of passing through a howling and booing mob under a hail of rotten eggs and wads of dirty paper thrown by ferocious and grimacing urchins. This is why, in front of the tents of chieftains and generals on the eve of battles, it is essential that next to the indispensable sentry stands the younger brother of sleep: Silence.

God created the world in silence; afterward, when he had unleashed the elements and the animals onto the spheres which turn (or don't turn) in space, noise began. All creation is accomplished in silence; afterward its occult forces cause noise, or rather noises, to spring up throughout the vast world. First, in their chambers above the porticos, the philosophers meditate. Their double-glazed windows, while allowing them to enjoy the view of the hills, the harbors, the vast and beautiful squares ornamented with well-sculpted statues placed on low pedestals, prevent outside noises from entering and troubling their work of metaphysicizing thinkers. In the room no noise disturbs their meditation; occasionally little noises which strictly speaking aren't noises at all can be heard: the scratching of a mouse who, encouraged by the silence and the immobility of the sleeping dog, makes long forays across the library as though through a fantastic landscape of sheer cliffs and precipitous rocks, or else like a pilgrim, a traveler at the feet of the Sphinx, he halts beneath the plaster casts, the Belisariuses, the Socrateses, the Hippocrateses, the Minervas, and the Alexander the Greats, who, helmeted or bareheaded, bald or hirsute, gaze into space, tranquil, indifferent. Sometimes too, but barely perceptible and as though heard in a dream, the singing of the servant girl arrives at the philosopher's ear, as she washes the dishes or prepares the evening meal (the most propitious hours for meditation are those of afternoon); some of these songs are of a poignant sadness, for they tell of the sorrow which sometimes permeates the lives of weak and humble people:

> The leave, my captain,*
> You must grant my leave,
> When I left her she was sick
> . . . .
> Bearer who bears the coffin,
> Halt for a moment.
> I who never kissed her living,
> Now that she is dead,
> I want to place my lips
> On her forehead.

And the tick-tock of the clock on the mantel; glass globe on which Time is leaning, a tall withered old man with a flowing beard, thoughtful and sad between his scythe and his clepsydra. —But all this isn't really noise, and to the ear of the philosopher absorbed in his profound thoughts and lofty metaphysical speculations it penetrates like a hum, and, due allowance being made, like that harmonious vibration which, according to Pythagoras, the planets and the suns make as they evolve in space.

In this atmosphere from which all true, actual noise is carefully banished the thoughts of the philosophers ripen; they pass onto paper and then form volumes of printed writing. And thus they travel abroad through the world; they cross oceans, infiltrate all the races, become the bedside book of the rich man who suffers and the poor man who hates, and then revolts and revolutions arise as the storm arises in the sultry sky of a summer afternoon. Gangs of fierce and resolute men led by a kind of Colossus with the beard of an ancient god grab timbers from construction sites and thrust them like catapults against the doors of the grand hotels, the luxurious palaces, the sumptuous residences where millionaires have amassed their riches and the most precious works of art, for they never believed in the danger and always listened to the reassuring

---

*Army captain. (de Chirico)

speeches, read the soothing articles which began with the eternal refrain: *Our people have too much sense,* etc., etc.

•

Thus one could say that all true creation must be initiated in silence.

There is nothing more disturbing than people who talk while one is looking at a monument, a beautiful spectacle of nature, a statue, an objet d'art, or who loudly express their opinions in the theater or during the projection of a film. As for painting, one must contemplate it in silence; today, unfortunately, that breed of art lover, of connoisseur, who spends a long time in front of a picture, standing or seated, gazing at it without speaking and even, if the dimensions of the painting permit, taking it in hand so as to examine it minutely as one examines a jewel, a piece of cloth, or a bit of precious wood, etc., no longer exists.

People today start to speak the moment they are confronted by a picture, without focusing their gaze at the center of the canvas, without exploring it as they look, but pushing their line of vision toward the corners of the picture and even beyond; they are more concerned with acting smart and *appearing intelligent,* whether through exaggerated admiration in the presence of the eternals—It's magnificent! It's incredible! It's amazing—etc., or else with feigning skepticism, than with understanding and appreciating the true worth of the painting that is before them. In such cases we prefer the atmosphere of schools, of those severe classrooms with whitewashed walls where young people bend over their books and copybooks, thinking and studying in solemn silence, while all around them, in beautifully colored pictures fastened to the partitions, the aspects of the Earth, of plants and animals and human history, unfurl in silence; there are geography maps, sometimes gray, sometimes pink, but always blue where lakes open out and vast seas stretch away; there are polar bears splashing amid ice floes, and ostriches, yes, the unfortunate ostriches fleeing desperately before the Arab horseman hugging the flank of his steed spurred to a quadruple gallop; and then again History: Caesar, surrounded by his legions in the conquered valley; Pericles dying of the plague, amid his tearful family and friends; and then soldiers in uniforms whose shape and color changes from age to age; and monarchs, pot-bellied ministers, their chests a mosaic of ribbons and decorations, who gaze into each other's eyes and clasp hands in a historic gesture.

May God protect you from evil silence, my beloved friends! For there is also evil silence; a silence which engenders no work of the mind and no creation. The silence of the desert where death and desolation reign, where any seed that is sown will rot or become fossilized instead of bearing fruit, where the aridity slowly consumes everything by fire and the caravans pass noiselessly, for no man . . . for no man desires to sing, no ass has the strength to bray.

May God protect you as well, dear friends, from those heavy and painful silences that fall with unimaginable implacability and fatality, smack in the middle of a social event or a soirée when a tactless, uninformed, or malicious person lets fall one of those phrases which suddenly render all mouths speechless and in a split second transform a party of lighthearted folk, come together to enjoy each other's company and have a good time, into a gathering of preoccupied and taciturn individuals; that happens, for instance, when, in a salon frequented by puritanical persons, a blunderer incapable of sizing up the situation in the place where he happens to be, begins to speak of the problems of prostitution and homosexuality, or explains with a plethora of details the methods used in certain cases by obstetricians and midwives. You must also guard against those silences in nature when all the thousand things that make all sorts of noises in the fields, in the forests, in the valleys, and on the seacoasts suddenly fall silent, for they vaguely sense that somewhere over there, beyond the distant horizons, in the depths of the sky, behind the tall mountains, tempests and hurricanes are slowly forming, to burst forth with the roar of thunder and livid lightning flashes. We all know these moments, so highly exciting and dramatic. In villas hidden in the depths of parks the servants have left the windows open because it has been hot, relentlessly hot since the early morning hours; but suddenly the gusts of wind form terrible drafts; the magazines and illustrated journals left out on the metal chairs and wicker armchairs in the garden go swooping upward as high as the rooftops, while windowpanes are shattered and objects are overturned in the bedrooms; and then the storm erupts; the lightning plays mysterious and macabre tricks; cooks, master chefs, lie stretched out on the tiles of the kitchen floor, stripped of all their clothing, holding in their right hand a spit that has skewered the half-roasted body of a chicken [. . .]

•

The gentlemen-poets shut up in their rooms for days on end seated at their worktable smoking a pipe and covering their white pages of official foolscap with platonic sonnets look up to contemplate the spectacle, for they love that; they love nature's violence; they love seeing the trees of the garden convulsed under the tempest like the souls of the damned under the blows of eternal chastisement; they love to hear thunder, artillery salvos that awaken all the echoes at the four corners of the horizon; but often, as they watch the cataclysm cozily ensconced in their armchair, in the center of their room where their pipe has formed a fog which the smoker finds sweet and agreeable but which can be cut with a knife, as they witness the ravages of the storm snugly sheltered from the rain and the wind and are beginning to feel the perverse and unwholesome joy of the spectator watching the perilous trapeze act of a group of acrobats from a safe bench and who fears no vertigo and no fall, or of the sports enthusiast who, sheltered from the blows in his ringside seat, watches the two heavyweights in the ring flailing each other with all the force of their muscular arms, delivering tremendous uppercuts to the tip of the chin and straight rights to the stomach, a violent gust of wind blows open the window and an irresistible tornado scatters sheets of paper everywhere, thus introducing confusion and disorder into the midst of their work; then they forget everything and start chasing the white sheets of paper, catching them in flight with the charming gestures and movements of rhythmic dancing girls and chaste maidens pursuing playful butterflies through a lovely spring meadow strewn with flowers.

Beware, friends, of the silence that precedes such events.

Hebdomeros: With Monsieur Dudron's Adventure and Other Metaphysical Writing (Cambridge, Mass.: Exact Change, 1992). First published in *Big Sky* 9 (August 1975).

COURBET

For us who grew up and matured in this first quarter of the twentieth century, the name of the painter-poet of Ornans is rich in touching memories and a very gentle nostalgia. When we were born, he was already gone, exiled to the shores of a lake between his land and ours, in an ancient fishermen's inn on whose crumbling walls one could still read the symbolic words *Safe Harbor*, words which convey an indefinable impression of consolation and melancholy, like the final hymn of Pandolfo Colenuccio. And yet, all that past is near us, so near that we almost feel its warmth. That word, "yesterday," envelops us in nostalgic echoes, as when we awaken with our sense of time and logic still confused, and the memory of a happy hour lived the day before reverberates in our minds. Sometimes we think of Courbet and his work as we think of our father's youth.

He was a worker and a poet. Poetic inspiration was a necessary complement to his painting. His first activity was the worker's. Like those engineers of nineteenth-century Europe, bearded and powerful; like the industrialists, the colonizers, like all that generation of indefatigable constructors, sons of a continent already old, at the threshold of a new aspect of the life that inventions of all kinds had revealed (for already fleets of ships were plowing the seas, joining the continents more rapidly, and railroads were penetrating the darkness of tunnels and striating the plains), like these men, Courbet was a son of his time.

One imagines him, powerfully chested, tall, bearded, affable and melancholy, in the Baudelairean atmosphere of his Paris studio or in the smoke and noise of the Café de Madrid in the company of the ardent Gambetta and the romantic Jules Vallès, or again leaning on his long alpenstock, his shoulders laden like those of a Zouave in a colonial battalion, roaming the mountains, valleys, and forests of France in search of beautiful landscapes; emotional and curious, like an impassioned hunter in quest of game. And always he appears to us in the atmosphere of his time: a *Romantic*.

Romantic! A strange word, pregnant with meanings that seem to come to us from afar. A word that gives rise to suspicions and ambiguities. But for us, it means not only an emotive and moving art, an art firmly established on the solid pavement of reality, but also an art which lets us experience only that small portion of the great mystery of infinity that pierces the gap in flying clouds on a moonlit night.

There have been epochs, peoples, periods of art in the world that were absolutely devoid of romantic meaning. Egypt, for example. Against all that this word can evoke of construction, architecture, sculpture, painting, one sees the great inexorable vault of a silent, cloudless summer night; this image has for us something disagreeably mute, empty, and alarming; the complete absence of all happiness and hope. *It is not romantic.* But when, on a moonlit night, we look up to the sky in which great white clouds sail like icebergs adrift in the northern seas and when we discover in the archipelago of clouds, like the shreds of a suspended sea, the sky, nocturnal, somber, and profound, then a joyous, happy emotion seizes our minds and our hearts; a breath of presentiment, of adventure and nostalgia envelops us, and with this breath a name resounds in us, powerful: Homer!

Homer was a Romantic.

We are not aesthetes, still less are we fanatics, and we thus take little pleasure in dreaming. We have an inveterate habit of meditating deeply on each of our emotions and each of our feelings.

The fact that the night sky seems more beautiful to us seen through clouds has a reason that is precise and definite as a geometrical design. The cloud in the night sky represents reality; the lunar light defines, accentuates, and solidifies its volume as it illuminates it; thus it is an actual ceiling we see above us, so that when we glimpse the night's darkness through a crack in this ceiling, the emotion we experience is happy, and it is an emotion belonging to art. In the Iliad, the Homeric hero and the Homeric god always stand solidly on the planks of reality.

The Olympic gods who preside over the destinies of Priam's city are solid and real as the besieging Achaeans on the beach and the besieged Trojans assembled on the walls and towers to defend their city.

In the Odyssey, under the feet of wandering Ulysses there is always the solid surface of four tarred planks, the planks of his ship.

The sense of reality is always linked to a work of art. The deeper it is, the more poetic and romantic the work will be. Mysterious laws and reasons of perspective govern such facts. Who can contradict the disturbing relation that exists between perspective and metaphysics?

Courbet, who experienced the sense of reality more deeply than Delacroix, is thus more poetic and romantic than he, despite the opinion of critics of his time and ours. The error of considering Delacroix at first sight as the preeminently romantic painter is easy to commit; but all his art is only an aspect of movement, something oblique and swirling like banners twisted by a gale, horses and men bent beneath a tempest.

It is an aspect that is more literary than purely poetic. Courbet's romanticism is much more pathetic and solitary. Baudelaire himself is mistaken, and in his best things he is much closer to Courbet than to Delacroix.

Courbet places the reality of a face or an object in the foreground, in that hot summer evening light that he expressed with so much pathos. And it was a fruit or a face, a nude or a tree, a cliff or the whitecapped waves of a stormy sea. But behind the fruit and the twisted leaves, one perceives the sky in the distance and the clouds in flight; behind the reclining woman is the perforation of the window, dividing the trees and planes of the park below into rectangles; and behind the cliff polished by the waves rises the horizon lit up by the setting sun, and the great storm clouds fly away, low over the sea. The beautiful Baudelairean verses resound:

"Free man, you shall ever desire the sea! The sea is your mirror, there you contemplate your soul. In the infinite unrolling of its wave."

In each of his paintings, from the simplest still life to his vast compositions, you always hear the refrain of a romantic song, a song which was then not only French but European, which passed from country to country, from race to race. It was an evening music, most gentle. It was the lamentation of the *barbatouli* of the nineteenth century; it was their consolation. It was the repose of the weary engineer. There is something of this bizarre poetic sense in a phrase from this passage which Baudelaire dedicated to Franz Liszt: *"Through the mist, beyond the rivers, above the cities where the pianos chant your glory . . ."*

Courbet is a storyteller: *The Demoiselles of the Seine, The Wrestlers,*

The Picnic, The Kill are narrations, passages from a novel in which the characters don't appear under their present-day aspect (verism) but under their poetic and spectral aspect (realism). In the latter guise, even a portrait can disturb us and give us that ineffable emotion we experience in the presence of works of high poetic fantasy. His numerous self-portraits, the portrait of the art patron Bruyas, and that of the writer Jules Vallès, the romantic journalist, have that same spectral, pathetic, and touching quality we find in the first daguerreotypes and which lasts down to the moment when aestheticism and perfected machines and photographic methods inspired in us the horror of modern *artistic photography*, opaque, dirty-brown, confused, and idiotic.

In fact, in photography one sees very well the difference that exists between realism and verism. Modern photography, rapid, perfected, and aestheticizing, only shows us the wan, tiresome, present-day aspect of people and things. With the help of an old photograph one can even make a painting that is not lacking in poetry. Thus Manet did his portrait of Maximilian's execution from a photograph. Today, photography offers us assistance in the form of characteristic examples of Tito and Sartorio.

Nulla sine narratione ars. By the word "narration" we do not mean the recounting of a scene or a historical event. It is something very different indeed. The work of art must narrate something beyond the limits of its volume. The object or the figure represented must also narrate poetically what is far from it, and also what its very volume conceals materially. A certain dog depicted by Courbet is like a poetic and romantic tale of a hunt.

Since he was a poet, he was very fond of painting. In the museums of France, Flanders, and Germany, he studied the painters of the past. The supple and the solid tempted and disturbed him; the hard and the fragmented annoyed him. The more the painter is a poet, the more he feels the magic of his craft in his work, which is the most magical of all and also the most painful. Consequently, only the good painter, inspired by a lyrical élan, can find the right *modus operandi*.

After the first scenes and portraits, still stiff and heavy, and weak in atmosphere, like the portrait of his sister as a young girl, Courbet, guided by his poet's instinct, went on to perfect himself further and acquired a craftsmanship always more aerated and more profound. Like all great artists, he followed a continually ascending line. The misfortunes of his last years neither wearied nor discouraged him. Abandoned by his friends, in the solitary life he led near the lakes and mountains of his hospitable Switzerland, he idealized and spectralized poetically the landscapes that rose before him.

Perhaps the old castle of Chillon with its robust towers, situated down on the sunny shores of the lake, appeared more beautiful than the cliffs of Etretat and the wild landscapes of his birthplace to the ever happier enthusiasm of this *pictor poeta*, and perhaps while he worked at his last paintings, before lying down to rest at last in the arms of his good death, the last words of the aged Corot rose from his heart to his lips: "What beautiful landscapes! I have never seen such beautiful ones!"

Hebdomeros: With Monsieur Dudron's Adventure and Other Metaphysical Writing (Cambridge, Mass.: Exact Change, 1992). First published in *Art and Literature* 11 (Winter 1967).

THE ENGINEER'S SON

Strolling one evening
In the puritan city
We'll go seeking . . .
Beyond life the dark fountain
Where the child sleeps.
There the bitter brooks of faded illusions
Will dry up.
In the day without decline in love
Without complaint
We shall live again.
—Emile Bronnaire, *Poésies*

All the way along that shadowy avenue bordered with pepper trees, I imagined the drama of the Passion as paintings and engravings show it: Roman soldiers, helmeted and plumed, raising their heads to peer at Christ, and olive-skinned rabbis arguing with the gestures of Neapolitan *camorristi*. It was in autumn and the memory always returned at that time of year. The pepper trees were numerous and bushy, planted close together so that the avenue was quite dark in places; from the ground which had become sticky and slippery, for the red pellets of those gnarled, piperaceous trees completely covered it, arose a strong, sweetish odor; often, one of the rare promenaders would lose his balance as he walked along and, like a novice skater, would fan the air with outstretched arms so as to regain his stability. It was, in short, a kind of tropical forest through which the stubborn traveler hacks his way with axe and torch, under the constant menace of the poisonous insect whose sting is fatal and of the rhinoceros with ironclad flanks like a monitor, against which the armored bullets from Colt revolvers and grooved rifles flattened out lamentably. It was thus that I used to advance along the avenue of pepper trees in the days of my distant childhood. What about clearings, you will ask. Yes, there were some, but not many; one in particular dominated the others; it rose gently toward the palace of King Otto. A vast building decked out with a truly regal balcony, this palace had something both solemn and dreary about it; in another respect it disturbed one with certain ideas that it evoked: nocturnal fêtes ending a day of coronation or the marriage of a foreign princess, and also dark nights of revolution. Then the balcony would fill with a seething mass of gesticulating conspirators, and while all the windows shone like enormous rectangular lanterns, something small and black, a kind of dislocated dummy, would be tossed from the balcony onto the front steps and lie there without anyone's paying any attention to it, doubled up in the classic pose of assassinated rulers in historical paintings. What a delight then to take refuge in shadows and slink into the night, at the far end of the royal park, behind the palace, with one hand on the grip of the pistol, the other on the hilt of the dagger, with all one's passports and identity papers in order, and one's pockets crammed with useful objects: phials of tincture of iodine, Pyramidon pills, fountain pens, etc., and protected from the bite of vipers by high boots of unrivaled strength, reinforced with double, triple, and even quadruple soles. Ah! How good it was then to be in the shadows! Between the trunks of century-old cypresses and prophetic oaks one could *see without being seen.*

The nocturnal fête in the palace; night of revolt; the armed guard had crossed the river by torchlight singing the famous anthem "Watch Over the King." But for the attentive spectator these events were not so unexpected as they seemed. Already in the late afternoon when evening began gently to darken the mountains east of the city, and the rocks of the citadel were dyed a grayish mauve, one felt that *something was in the air,* in the words of the nursemaids who sat gossiping on the benches of the municipal square. Warning signs which could not elude a watchful observer had already authorized all those bizarre incidents and dangerous disturbances at the heart of a sober and thoughtful populace. Of these signs the most characteristic in my opinion was that the shepherds had already fled into the mountains and, although night had not yet descended completely on the countryside, one could now see their bonfires burning from peak to peak, which reminded certain folk of the means used by prehistoric tribes to communicate news across vast deserts untrodden by human feet, wherein lions, as though harnessed to invisible chariots, wandered in perfectly symmetrical couples hunting the antelope with gentle eyes.

And then one likes also to take refuge at noon (a clear, cool Sunday noon in winter) at the moment when the military band starts to play sublime and piercing tunes. For these are moments when the light is *everywhere*; the square is full of people, one rubs elbows with one's fellows at every step; the women are pretty and kind, already informed by their husbands of your brilliant career, aware that you are no upstart, secretly flattered by your attentions; the men have a reassuring manner and are dressed in the English style. At such moments suicide becomes something possible, and, I might even say, agreeable; if it had been a question, there in broad daylight and in the midst of the crowd, of throwing himself into the water of the ornamental lake and disappearing, he would not have hesitated an instant; I can assure you that it would have been a joy for him to dive into the clear water of the lake. But on this horrible winter night, with the owls hooting and the rusty arms clanking against the decrepit walls, in this ramshackle castle howling its terror through all the flues of its chimneys, on this storm-tossed night, in the middle of this bed with damp sheets, in this bed vast as a mountain and funereal as a catafalque, while the unpleasant memories and disgraces of his tumultuous life danced an obscene and infernal round before the alcove, on this night of insomnia and anguish—fire a pistol into one's brain? No! A thousand times no! He would never have done it. Not that he lacked courage; usually he was brave; twice he had volunteered for service in a cholera hospital in the Orient, and only recently on the waterfront, near the pier, he had intervened between two brawling sailors armed with Finnish knives. But tonight . . . No, it was unthinkable.

And yet he remembered so many odd things. A train with an old-fashioned locomotive puffing along the edge of a cliff above the sea. When the cars passed close to the wild quince trees he would divert himself by grabbing at the branches and pulling off the leaves; sometimes too, using an old revolver loaded with cartridges with projecting primers, and boasting neither a butt nor a cylinder, he would fire at the zinc-plated cones that crowned the turrets of certain villas of Helvetic appearance, half-hidden in the foliage.

For all these absurd and incoherent acts he had more than once incurred the criticism of the train personnel; once they had gone so far as to tell him an endless story about train cars that had had to be put away in sheds along the old waterfront, so riddled with holes they were, for irascible peasants would discharge their rifles at the passing trains to take revenge on certain equivocal individuals who would amuse themselves, when the trains passed close to the straggling villages, by gesturing obscenely at the peasant women leaning at the windowsills. There was scarcely any need to recount such a tale, and everything would have happened for the best if they had had the decency to take him more often in the afternoons into the cool and shadowy house surrounded by lemon trees, whose walls were ornamented with magnificent still lifes. A waste of time! The train still advanced and one sensed that the sea would soon disappear behind that irregular backdrop of trees and rocks. It was here that one of the most beautiful events in his life took place; he was so stunned by it that at first he was afraid he had been the victim of one of those hallucinations caused by some half-forgotten childhood memory, like the time that enormous mask appeared on the ceiling of his nursery one night when he couldn't sleep; but this time he was indeed obliged to yield to reality and his soul felt a very sweet and consoling emotion and, what was even better, a greater confidence than before in the gods' benevolence and the destiny of *superior men*: It was thus that he habitually spoke of Prometheus and Christ. Mercury* in person was helping the eagle of Jupiter to transport the injured man (Prometheus was hurt quite seriously on his right side). The rash plunderer was forcefully grasping in his fists the claws of the great winged creature, which moved onward in laborious flight. Sometimes its great wings woven of feathers as hard as iron flayed in passing the forearms of Prometheus, who grimaced in pain; but despite all this, and despite his wound which continued to bleed, he was fundamentally happy, and he had reason to be, for after all it was flight, liberation, and anyone in his place would have been as happy as he. Mercury, acting the part of the god who knows how to get out of scrapes and is never surprised at anything, held him up under the knees like those painted personages in the "Entombment": He gripped the straps of his petasus firmly in his teeth lest the wind blow it away. This trio advanced with difficulty, but it advanced

---

*This scene is an exact description of an engraving by Max Klinger, on whom de Chirico wrote an admiring essay in 1920. (Trans.)

nevertheless; sometimes the *group* flew so low that it almost grazed the foaming crests of the waves; the sea at this moment was of a green verging on gray, for it was the beginning of afternoon. In the distance a steamship of the Goudi Brothers Line seemed motionless despite the fact that its red-girdled smokestack disgorged with perfect regularity a dark brown smoke whose contours were carefully modeled like those clouds spaced out near alpine summits that you find in certain scientific tomes. As for Mercury, the god Mercury if you will, it was *he*, always the same; the Mercury of moving vans, and suburban villas burglarized at high noon; the Mercury of seaports; the Mercury of big navigation lines; the Mercury who soars in gliding flight above the stock exchange at the moment when all the roarers blacken the steps of the temple; the Mercury with the vague, disturbing gaze; the Mercury of tollhouses at the gates of cities; the Mercury of cities, European and transatlantic; the Mercury of Hamburg and San Francisco; the Mercury of *political rallies* held in white, geometrically ordered cities on the edge of the Pacific; the modern Mercury of the Berlin stadium; the Mercury of horse-drawn trolleys moving along tracks in front of the synagogue and the Protestant church in the clear, gentle September afternoon.

As a matter of fact it was in Germany that he had first met him. Won over early by his ideas of domination he would go so far as to get up at eight in the morning (he who usually slept till noon) to follow him in long walks outside the city. In those vacant lots the wind brought an odor of burning rubbish and from time to time the notes of a bugle practicing in a distant barracks; it was incredibly sad! And then that mania of always wanting to walk near a treacherous bog, perpetually soaked by the rain, even by a rain of two months ago, in which the wheels of the cart transporting the drainage conduits regularly got mired; each time several of them would be *caught* and then, confronted with the spectacle of the shouting driver and the beasts of burden exhausting themselves in vain efforts, he would repeat each morning the same sorrowful phrase: "My spirit is like the wagon wheels": *Wie die Räder des Wagens*. Finally, weary of not being able to make him change either his ideas or his humor, he decided to leave him; he had a box of chocolates from a well-known firm sent to his wife and that very evening he brought him to the station and pushed him into the first train leaving for Berlin, begging as he did so two gentlemen already seated in the compartment to keep an eye on him, as he had already shown signs of mental disturbance. He believed this to be the shortest cut to getting rid of him, but he was mistaken, for the painter lodged near the station in a modest apartment on the sixth floor; he lived there in two rooms that he had papered from floor to ceiling with the most bizarre and disconcerting drawings which made certain highly esteemed critics repeat for the thousandth time the famous refrain: *It's literature.* At the close of a discussion whose subject was a recent vernissage, the same critics had in fact laid down the law that *painting must be painting and not literature*, but he seemed to attach very little importance to all that, either because he understood nothing of it, or because he understood it all too well and therefore pretended not to understand. And he would always come back to his favorite theme: Nicholas the cook, Nicholas the chef of a thousand and one expedients who, in leisure moments, would assume the role of governess and take the colonel's children out walking near a large open terrain where, at certain times of year, the artillerymen engaged in rifle practice; sometimes too they would execute soldiers condemned to death. But it was rather the mountain that attracted him, the great dark mountain over there at the end of the plain, the great mountain swollen with mystery and adventure. He detested the plain with all his heart: "Perfidious plain," he used to say sometimes as though speaking in a dream, "Bleak and perfidious plain, there is no salvation in thee. The hare cannot escape the lean hound launched on its trail; the madly fleeing horseman cannot escape his enemy who follows him closely on a courser at full gallop; the tender and trembling turtledove cannot flee the implacable yellow-eyed vulture who contemplates her sideways without turning his head; perfidious plain, I detest thee."

And all his nostalgia, all his love went toward the mountain. Paths twisting along the edge of the abyss; from below rose a cool, damp smell together with the roaring of torrents and cascades. Sometimes the noise of something that flees and hides in the bushes. When day is at an end, the shadow of the mountain brings a premature night and then around the table dressed in white the evening meal was cheerless indeed.

When they talked of pregnancy and childbearing the mistress of the house always said in tones of resignation: "These are trials through which all we women have to pass." "Except those," interjected an aged boarder who until now had taken no part in the conversation, "except those who never become pregnant because of some physiological defect, or because they avoid pregnancy by artificial means." It was fundamentally logical, but these last words uttered in a sepulchral voice amid a silence of the tomb always produced a certain embarrassment and cast a chill over the company, and later, along toward the midnight hours, the conversation, already scarcely brilliant, languished even more and finally died out completely like a fire that no one bothers to stoke.

Hebdomeros: With Monsieur Dudron's Adventure and Other Metaphysical Writing (Cambridge, Mass.: Exact Change, 1992). First published in *Art and Literature* 11 (Winter 1967).

THE SURVIVOR OF NAVARINO

Prudent shadows of society
Cannot harm this first and belated . . .
My first and belated felicity.
                    —Giovanni Papini, *Poesia*

Will you follow me as far as the Sargasso Sea? The Sargasso Sea! I am sure he meant it ironically, for one could scarcely give the name Sargasso Sea to that part of the harbor which the blocks of the breakwater protected from the winds of the open and nearby sea. It was the right side of the breakwater for someone with his back turned to the town; on the left the sea foamed at noon, in a most harmless way, actually, and thus between the calm and agitation of these two expanses of water which were like a symbol of human life, the breakwater stretched away, an artificial promontory *built by the hand of man*, as Professor Alfano used to say in rhetorical tones; he had been a refugee for many years, for although he was very strong in mathematics and played the cello with taste and sensitivity, he had always been ignored in the city of his birth. But he obstinately refused to believe it. The Sargasso Sea! This vision (he called it a vision but the inhabitants of the coast, poor devils wrinkled and baked by the sun, claimed on the contrary that it was not a vision but a reality), this vision tormented him for several days at the same hour: a few moments before noon, when the surface of the sea lost that shiny look of a burnished mirror which it had in the first light of dawn.

There was one inhabitant in particular who persisted in contradicting him, an old fisherman, the oldest one of all: "Yes, sir," he would repeat in a loud voice, "*it is a reality*; a metaphysical reality if you wish, but a reality. *Dura lex sed lex.*" This, however, was a true fact: This surgeon, already old but still with muscles of steel (and he proved it to you when he shook your hand), this surgeon was actually the only man in the region capable of standing up to the one-eyed buccaneer, a formidable corsair who was not to be trifled with; and this was obvious since he avoided all discussion with him; but sometimes, however, in order to put up a good front and satisfy his self-esteem a little, he would pointedly turn his back on the customers of that filthy tavern and gaze out at the angry sea through the only window, at which a pair of fly-specked curtains dangled forlornly. "A reality," he would repeat automatically to himself, for in fact he was thinking of far other things, a reality, the sublime scene of the pelican! A scene such as Homer could never have imagined or described! This miraculous pelican, with its drunkard's squint, generously rending its breast with great stabs of its beak on the slippery deck of that stranded vessel, and for whom, in fact, I wonder? "His children," you will say, but the poor beggar didn't have any, he had never had any.

Yes, one can after all accept it, but then what of all those sublime and stupid resolutions of going back to the land, of folk art, of sincerity, of abnegation, of honesty, of probity, of simplicity, of bowing down before nature, of the cult of the beautiful, of health in art, of good work done in the morning after rising early, of the Mediterranean spirit, of victory over oneself? Twaddle and utopia? Utopian fancies of a hysterical monk dreaming of ideal platonic republics in which the clergy, authorized by the law, may couple regularly and hygienically each night with women as beautiful as statues? Pure utopias! And of all that, nothing now remains; nothing but a handful of ashes, not even smoking, and a few tiny scraps of white paper, negative reply to the supplanted lover, torn and thrown to the wind, distracted flight of tropical butterflies as the centenarian elephant passes by.

And he took up once more the eternal refrain of a Jules Verne writing for children and predicting modern discoveries in his books. As though everyone didn't know that experiments in submarine navigation had been made long before the appearance of *Twenty Thousand Leagues under the Sea*, and that in general the books of Jules Verne were not for children but their elders, for their *elders and betters*. And here again was that old error of thinking that all those sublime navigators who sacrificed their lives to an ideal were possessed by the demon of travel like those Anglo-Saxons with cast-iron stomachs, pacing across the globe with an obstinacy worthy of a better cause. And he would affirm this. But he was surely not being entirely honest, for he knew that according to the latest discoveries already announced in the last number of the *Monatliche Zeitschrift der Metaphysischen Weltanschauung,* all that was required was the longitude of the floor and ceiling for the famous Cape Matapan to be there, in that disquieting corner of his room, littered with ruins bathed by the yellow wave of the Alpheus.

In the next room the ghost of Pausanias was wandering, his traveler's stick in hand, while the other ghost, that of the brother killed at the beginning of the war at the head of his machine-gun unit, remained sunken in the pink armchair like an English prime minister passing away at the age of ninety-two. Don't talk to me of ruins strewn over the floor and divans drawn up before the permanent spectacle of Thermopylae! The doors ajar on the night of the corridor constitute a danger, you say! Perhaps, but from now on all that is nothing but the palest of memories. In any case, if the lock is missing from the door or you have lost the key, you need only push a heavy dresser against your door, having first taken the precaution of cramming the drawer with books and flatirons; you will see that the ghosts can no longer slip into your room in that sly manner and with that embarrassed look so characteristic of them, smiling at your questions as they gaze absentmindedly at you. Like the one who answered me in almost fraternal tones, in spite of the great difference in age that separated us: "But why do you suppose that we know any more about it than all of you?" Than all of you! A fine way of expressing oneself! And a few moments later he added in a low voice, although there was no one else but us in the room: "And besides, why do you think that there is *something to know?*"

But if he claimed to believe that it was not himself, far from it, for if it had been but for him he would have renounced it long ago, accustomed as he was to seeing the inhabitants of the coast join battle with the mountaineers, who often limited themselves to defending their villages except during the periods of great emigrations from the north, for then, driven by the irresistible mass, they moved down toward the sea and the massacre became inevitable. But it was not their fault, they pushed because they were being pushed, that was all.

So as to spare their passengers a painful if grandiose spectacle, the captains of the liners would weigh anchor and flee those regions of destruction and death. Once the cape had been passed the ships would sail along beside calm and smiling shores. From the top of great rocks yellowed by sulfureous emanations, cascades of boiling water plunged into the sea so that here and there the bottom of the cliffs disappeared amid vapors. Sometimes at night fires would blaze on the shore, and plaintive songs, disturbing chants would reach the decks of the ships where the passengers were enjoying a nap under the stars, after the evening meal. It was the young cohorts who had not yet entered the fray who were singing a despairing farewell to life.

"Poor ephebes," the women would say in tones of deep emotion, "at their age, to be already obliged to take leave of life!" But their husbands, whom these reflections irritated, tried to change the subject.

A complete stranger to these events, trusting only his zebra, to whom he spoke as to a fellow man, as he indicated with a wide sweep of his hand that vast expanse of land whose monotony was broken only by a few outcroppings of the ground, covered by bushes on the side exposed to the sun, and which were situated toward the northwest, he said in his grave and modulated voice: "The plain requested, Colonel."

Too late, he answered nothing this time; his thoughts were far, far away; a memory among a thousand others rose slowly from the twilight of his past: He saw an orphanage built among eucalyptuses at the foot of the acropolis and the friend with the Michelangelesque face who took him by the shoulders and, looking into the whites of his eyes, said to him on that memorable afternoon in his distant childhood: *"Someday you will be someone!"*

EPODE

I have always loved thee, dark forest
   Of my life.
   Forest darker
   Than dark night
   At the dark pole . . .
Vault of the sky, at the pole, *one night* . . .
   Night without veils
   But without stars
   Or northern lights . . .
Vault of the sky, at the pole, *that night.*
In my joy and my intoxication,
In my fatigue and my humiliation,
My wild hopes, my wise discretion,

My great courage, my lassitude,
My cowardice, my turpitude,
My long return, my latitude,
My muffled echoes, my promptitude,
My transparent waking, my solitude,
My good renown, my quintessence,
My mad replies, my fine license,
My futile calls, my heavy confidence,
   In all the voices
   Which sing in me
   The numberless,
   Tremendous agitations . . .
I have always loved thee, dark forest
   Of my life.

Hebdomeros: With Monsieur Dudron's Adventure and Other Metaphysical Writing
(Cambridge, Mass.: Exact Change, 1992). First published in *Art and Literature* 11
(Winter 1967).

SELECTION ONE FROM
HEBDOMEROS

... And so began the visit to that strange building, situated in an austere yet distinguished and not gloomy street. Viewed from the street, the building suggested a German consulate in Melbourne. Large shops occupied the entire ground floor. Although it was neither Sunday nor a holiday, the shops were closed, conferring on this section of the street an aspect of melancholy boredom, a certain desolation, that special atmosphere characteristic of Anglo-Saxon cities on Sunday. A faint odor of dockyards floated in the air, the indefinable and highly evocative odor given off by goods warehouses near the wharves in seaports. The aspect of a German consulate in Melbourne was a purely personal impression on Hebdomeros's part; when he mentioned it to his friends they smiled and found the comparison *amusing*, but they didn't labor the point and immediately changed the subject, from which Hebdomeros concluded that they hadn't really understood what he was saying. And he reflected on the difficulty one has making oneself understood when one begins to operate at a certain altitude or depth.

"It's strange," Hebdomeros repeated to himself. "In my case, the idea that something had eluded my understanding would prevent me from sleeping, while most people can see, hear, or read things that are totally obscure to them without worrying in the least." They began to mount the stairway, which was very wide and entirely made of varnished wood; there was a carpet in the center; at the foot of the stairway, the banister ended in a slender Doric column carved in oak which supported a polychrome statue, also in wood, depicting a Californian Negro holding above his head a gas lamp whose burner was sheathed in an asbestos sleeve. Hebdomeros felt he was climbing toward the office of a dentist or a doctor specializing in venereal diseases; he experienced a slight agitation and something like the beginning of a minor stomachache; he tried to surmount this trouble by reflecting that he was not alone, that two friends were with him, able-bodied, athletic fellows, carrying automatic pistols with spare loading clips in the revolver pocket of their trousers. Seeing that they were getting closer to the floor that had been mentioned to them as being the most rich in strange apparitions, they began climbing more slowly and on tiptoe; their gaze became more attentive. They moved apart somewhat while still keeping abreast, so as to be able to descend the stairway freely and as rapidly as possible in case some apparition of a particular kind forced them to do so. Hebdomeros thought at that moment of the dreams of his childhood; when he would climb anxiously and in a vague light wide stairways of varnished wood in the middle of which a thick carpet muffled the noise of his steps—(all the same his shoes, even outside his dreams, rarely squeaked, for he had them made to order by a shoemaker named Perpignani, who was known throughout the town for the fine quality of his leathers; Hebdomeros's father, on the other hand, had no talent for buying shoes; his made an atrocious noise as though he were crushing bags of hazelnuts at every step).

Then it was the apparition of the bear, the disturbing and obstinate bear, who follows you in stairways and across corridors, with lowered head and the air of thinking of something else; the frantic flight across bedrooms with complicated egresses, the leap through the window into emptiness (suicide in a dream), and the gliding descent, like those condor men whom Leonardo would amuse himself by sketching among the catapults and the anatomical fragments. It was a dream that always foretold unpleasant occurrences, illnesses in particular.

"Here we are!" exclaimed Hebdomeros, stretching out his arms in the classic pose of the temporizing captain who restrains the impetus of his soldiers. They had reached the threshold of a vast and lofty chamber decorated in the style of 1880; completely empty of furniture, this room, through its lighting and general tone, made one think of the gaming rooms of Monte Carlo; in a corner, two gladiators with diver's masks were practicing without conviction under the bored gaze of a master, an ex-gladiator in retirement with the eye of a vulture and a body covered with scars. "*Gladiators!* That word contains an enigma," said Hebdomeros, addressing the youngest of his companions in a lowered voice. And he thought of music halls whose illuminated ceilings evoke Dantean paradise; he thought also of those Roman afternoons, at the end of the spectacle, when the sun is waning and the immense velarium deepens the shade of the arena from which rises an odor of sawdust and blood-soaked sand . . .

Roman vision, ancient coolness
Anxious evening, nautical song.

Still more padded doors and short, empty corridors, then suddenly: *Society! Move in fashionable circles!* Lead *a fashionable life.* The *rules* of high society. *Learn how to live. Notices announcing a family event.* P. P. C. (to take leave). E. M. P. (deliver in person). T. S. V. P. (please turn over). In a corner of the salon an enormous grand piano, its lid raised; without standing on tiptoe one could see its complicated entrails and the clear anatomy of its interior; but one could easily imagine the catastrophe that would result if one of those candelabra laden with pink and blue wax candles were to fall into the piano with all its candles lit. What a disaster in the melogenous abyss! Wax running the length of the metal cords, stretched like the bow of Ulysses, and hindering the precise striking of the little felt-clad hammers.

Beginning pages of *Hebdomeros.* Unpublished.

SELECTION TWO FROM
HEBDOMEROS

Then one could return? The carriage would drive swiftly away, drawn by its five trotting horses and closely followed by a cavalry detachment; all day long under the sun and at night on the great black mountain like a stranded whale that huge man, that hero stretched out on the summit would lie awake watching the stars. Where are you, children? Hebdomeros is in love with Louise, the maid in the house across the way; he has put on his new suit; the bells are ringing in the steeples of the parish churches and springtime smiles in the kitchen gardens. Springtime, springtime! Funeral procession, macabre vision. Corpses in dinner jackets laid out in their open coffins are lined up on the beaches of the south; one can catch the haunting smell of lemon which, like garlic and onion, renders dishes indigestible; here are the oranges with the unavowable symbols of their obscene flowers. Where are you going, man whose coat is trimmed with an astrakhan collar? Prototype of the great traveler, ready to defend the sick child threatened by the bandits' rapacious hands in the train stinking of wet cattle in the August shower? Where are you going, helmeted warrior with shifty eyes? Heart of steel at the windows open on towns that cling like vultures' nests to the rocks, where the innkeeper, thirsty for lucre, points out for you with a sweep of his red hand the vast panorama of the valley, crossed at its center by the river, sometimes opaque, sometimes gleaming, like the life of man. Must one for all that renounce one's seat and, when one has paid for a first-class ticket, obstinately remain in second despite the conductor's gentle insistence? But it is a lake as vast as the sea and which, like the sea, has its dangerous fits of temper; beware of drowning then, and when the motorboats hasten to your rescue you will know, then, what it means to be reborn in that summer afternoon where the sidewalks, bathed by the shower, reflect the lights in the shop windows so faithfully that you would think yourself in Venice; and that charming city built in tiers around the lake? Oh!, but another lake this time, a peaceful lake, a lake nothing ever ruffles, a consoling lake. And when the weather is sultry and the big drops of the beginning storm fall on the water, then it's by dozens you bring them in at the end of your silk-gut line, the great black fish! You call that "The Massacre of the Innocents"? But at this point Hebdomeros would protest; paying no attention to the passengers who were making fun of him as they crossed the gangway, poking their wives in the ribs and gasping with laughter; he confessed his aversion to biblical scenes which he termed immoral and lascivious; he asserted that the idea of Christ depicted in the form of a lamb concealed a sensuous tendency of a very special kind, and he concluded by pronouncing an exaggerated eulogy of cafés which have red velvet divans and whose ceilings are decorated in the style of 1880.

"There," Hebdomeros would say in a voice made slightly hollow by emotion, "you feel yourself safe from the dangers that come from outside; that the rabid enemy sends his élite troops up to the very gates of the city; that comets with deleterious tails appear on the horizon; that pairs of lions vomiting flames stalk the streets in the center of town; that iron-beaked birds infest the trees in the municipal squares; that lightning-swift insects buzz in the fecal matter of cholera patients; all is one and the same to you once you are inside that café. Once inside you are safe, and standing on tiptoe you can look through the fanlight at the enemy ships dropping anchor off the deserted coast and the launches jammed with warriors approaching the shore with great strokes of the oars. Then among these refugees a kind of bond of solidarity forms; the women and children are given shelter in the rear of the shop, behind trunks and cases of canned goods. It is here that all these creatures unfit for dangerous and tiring activities spend their time preparing the rations which consist of preserved *caballo* meat, biscuits, honey, and coffee which is always drunk very hot and flavored with spices; they also busy themselves with carefully cleaning the firearms and mending shoes and clothing; the youngest go out looking for game, for one must think about provisions for the winter; already the stormy season proclaims itself; continual rains have waterlogged the ground and the paths are slippery; puddles form beneath the grass which is quite tall in places where the daisy and the cornflower put in a timid appearance, just enough to make this bit of road look more cheerful and add a note of poetry to the passing of the zealous schoolboys who work with joy and steadfastness in severe-looking classrooms where all is but promise; the polar bear floundering among blocks of ice or disputing a torn remnant of fish with the walrus, and the ostrich fleeing madly before the Arab horseman; and then the bridges and the castles with their innumerable turrets and the ruins where thousands of crows have made their nests. Hebdomeros thought himself safe in this hut for he had seen no trace of a human being in the surrounding countryside; but he was wary despite these reassuring appearances; he was no man to put his faith in appearances; he remembered how many times in his early youth appearances had deceived him; that was why he remained on his guard and why, at night, he slept with one eye open, keeping his loaded walking stick and automatic pistol within easy reach; often he didn't even remove his shoes and went to bed half-dressed so as to be able to cope with any disagreeable surprise if need be. But the winter passed without anything extraordinary happening. Already the air was becoming warmer and plants in the meadow were getting green; the goatherds had come down from the neighboring mountains playing gay tunes on their long copper flutes; everywhere spring announced itself; in this Nordic country it arrived suddenly, it surprised you like a stage set appearing behind a rising curtain; an air of symbolism floated over nature; innumerable little waterfalls, fed by the melting snow, skipped down the mountains; angels with enormous wings like those of eagles but woven of feathers that were white and delicate like those of geese were sitting beside the paths, with one hand resting on the great milestones carved with the image of bicephalous Janus, surmounted by a virile sexual organ; the angels looked mournfully at the lovers moving away under the flowering almond trees. Everywhere there were placards with gaudy lettering; toward the east the volcanic and mountainous country was roamed by bands of hunters who, surrounded by their hounds, were ardently hunting down the few survivors of that almost extinct race of pachyderms. High in the sky vultures described great circles; sometimes they flew lower, sometimes higher, afraid of some evil envoy from the earth, but never losing sight of the hunters. Their intentions were clear: to wait until a pachyderm had been shot down and dismembered so as to be able to feast on the remains later when the last hunter and the last hound had disappeared behind the rocks. In spite of the presence of the vultures and the bones of animals which glistened white here and there in the grisaille of the rocks, there was nothing particularly savage or desertlike about the land; vast mining installations animated it on every side; the chimneys smoked; the tip trucks were running on tiny rails; bearded engineers, their faces flushed from the heat, were bustling everywhere and taking advantage of their rare moments of leisure by angling for fish or target-shooting at empty bottles. The sole diversion was to go in the evening to the Punch-and-Judy. The idea had occurred to a sculptor with a head like that of an Assyrian king who boasted of having been the pupil of a currently fashionable teacher, and who was much admired in his social circle because he played the flute, which as a matter of fact he did quite badly. These Punch-and-Judys did not happen quite so calmly or ingenuously as one might have supposed; sometimes the puppeteer, a hysterical individual who was subject to epileptic fits, would start to manipulate his cardboard-cutout figures with their Cretan eyes, at the same time uttering such screams that the foremen, waking with a start, would bound out of bed and rush for the sirens. Then the hyenas would abandon the partly disinterred corpses and flee toward the nearby mountains. The drivers who had been dozing in their carts, only half-opening one eye at every bump, would send their whips whistling through the air and set their horses galloping at top speed; seen in the night that way, these swiftly fleeing carts had something apocalyptic about them. Leaving the gigantic station of that metropolis where almost eight million men agitated restlessly from morning to night without rhyme or reason, Hebdomeros proceeded toward the quarter of nocturnal fêtes which, at the very heart of the city, constituted a separate world. It had in fact its boundaries and frontiers, its laws, its statutes, and it would have come as no surprise if zealous customs officials were waiting at its gates to ask you if you had anything to declare. At the edge of this ineffable region the traffic of the great city came to a halt; it was there that the convulsive movement of vehicles and the coming and going of busy pedestrians expired as a wave expires on a beach. *Happiness Has Its Rights*, that is what one saw in glowing letters over the principal gate constructed in the center of a vast arch of triumph on which women, carved out of the wood and painted in brilliant pastel colors, blew like obstinate tritons into the long bugles of renown. The fortresses which had been built near by, the almshouses for those whom fortune neglects but whom the gratitude and kindness of men does not forget, kept watch alone in the shadows, their solemn domes silent with the deep peace that repose exacts; the dark night was well along; the world slept, sunk in an immense tranquility, and like it, the storm which had agitated Hebdomeros's heart seemed finally to have subsided. The glory of the past, the vanity of human heroism, and those pyramids which the fear of oblivion incites the administrators of the common weal to command of indifferent hirelings who are thinking of something else as they build, of the fiancée or the wife who awaits them back there, far from the smoke and din, in the peaceful home, close to the window open on the coolness of the garden where thousands of glowworms streak the shadows with phosphorescent lines. Then it is in vain that the processions of kings advance along the regional highways; seen from a distance their solemn aspect looks sadly diminished, alas! Were it not for the flashing of the weapons brandished by the horsemen of the escort one would think them a troop of ragged gypsies going out to beg their bread beneath an implacable sun and the constant menace of mastiffs with mud-caked coats whom the cruel peasants set at their heels. If one believes that love can be born out of pity, then it was a whole promise of unutterable feeling that appeared on the vast horizon of Hebdomeros's life. Infinite nostalgias and impulses which, in his imagination disturbed by sleepless nights in the trains of the state railway system, took the hieroglyphic shape of an immense greyhound with an inadmissibly long body, passing like a meteor over the many-colored diagrams of cities, over the tame forests where each tree has its name and its history, over those fields whose huge basin is fecundated by more than one seed which the farseeing husbandman drops there at the opportune moment; and Hebdomeros's pity went out to all of humanity: toward the talkative man and the taciturn, toward the rich man who suffers and toward the indigent, but the profoundest pity of all he felt for the men who eat alone in restaurants, especially when they are sitting near the window in such a way that the passersby, cruel and disrespectful, true phantoms living in another atmosphere, can soil with their immodest gaze the virginal purity, the tender chastity, the infinite tenderness, the ineffable melancholy of this moment they are living, of all moments the most solitary, covering them with a shame so gentle and so poignant that one cannot understand how the entire staff of the place, from the manager to the cashier, with the furniture, the tablecloths, the carafes and all the crockery, down to the saltcellars and the tiniest objects, don't dissolve in an infinite torrent of tears.

The great hypostases which accompanied these telluric upheavals were followed by unforgettable spectacles at which Hebdomeros never failed to be present. Millions and millions of warriors were invading the country, moving across the vineyards; one would have thought they were oozing through cracks in the rocks, across those mountains carved in the round, ordnance survey maps of a hypothetical general staff riddled with caves, and which the even light from the ceiling rendered all the more convincing. *Myrmidons! Myrmidons!* . . . from echo to echo this cry resounded along the deserted beaches, as during the Tertiary period. Above the peristyle the sky was pure and deep blue; in the offices the barometers were fixed at fair weather, despair of the navigator on his galleon immobilized in the middle of the ocean. At other points of the globe, there where those sinister lakes whose motionless black waters it had never been possible to fathom opened a disquieting eye toward the sky, like the eye of the uranoscopus which the naive fisherman calls so charmingly the vicar-fish, clouds heavy as cliffs and black as night opened out amid the capricious flight and acute angles of the lightning; then the rain in long, close-packed strands, in perpendicular bundles, fell and fell endlessly on the surface of the lake which began to seethe, water into water; dropsical philosophers, demigods become poseurs by dint of wanting to appear simple and open, began to act clever, and after hanging their clothes on the quicklime-spattered branches of a stunted fig tree on the shore, went into the water *so as not to get wet*, as they said, and sometimes they would wait entire days for these singular storms to break so as to have an opportunity to make this excellent joke. Hebdomeros was revolted, but at the same time he was thinking of something else. "Eloquence of the past," he said, addressing his friends, "as I gazed on those indiscreet displays, those sumptuous still lifes wherein bananas and pineapples tumble in an avalanche along the flanks of disemboweled roebucks and polychrome pheasants, that overweening conceit of provocative well-being, that gigantic insult, that fantastic slap in the face of want and sobriety, I saw vengeance snickering in the shadows. Then, amid the overturned stools and the shards of bottles, the tablecloths strewn over the floor twisted themselves like elephant traps around the feet of the hurrying waiters laden with dishes, causing veritable disasters; the bustling domestics topple headlong, producing a tremendous breakage accompanied by an inundation of sauces of all colors on which float like derelicts the roasted and shriveled carcasses of chickens." Hebdomeros could stand no more; he rose like those shadows that rise on the damp walls of cells when a lantern is placed on the floor; he rose and spoke in a solemn voice which nevertheless had something strange about it as though he were not seeing the 2,675 faces of the men come to listen to him, who kept their eyes fixed on him. But at last he once again seized hold of reality and then he evoked September mornings on the sacred heights that dominated the city: At once voices arose: "The Acropolis! The Acropolis!" "No," he replied with a sly smile, "there is no question, this time, of *a crow* or of *Paulus*; and although there is in fact a Pericles, it is not the one of whom you all instinctively think, he whom the relentless plague laid low at the end of a hot summer day and who was the gentle friend of painters, sculptors, architects, and poets; the Pericles I present to you is one-eyed and, to hide this infirmity, wears his helmet pushed down on his head as far as the middle of his nose; but he has style and a certain elegance nevertheless, especially when with a careless gesture he tosses his chlamys over his left shoulder; his long, knock-kneed legs, far from making him look ridiculous, recall, anachronisms apart, those old picadors whom age has banished from the arena but who remain nostalgic for the arena; in his left hand he holds a coin and for a long time contemplates in silence, his head tilted back somewhat, with a fond eye (and no mistake, since he has only one), the profile of a woman engraved on one of its sides." Among the tambours of the fallen columns, where in the evening, when the square was deserted, huge dysenteric mares came to browse avidly on the tender chamomile which blossoms in the shade of glorious ruins, the faithful, those whom fright, selfishness, and shameful cowardice have not managed to conquer, those who preferred to defy fear and look death in the face rather than undergo the shame of disguising themselves as women, as pregnant peasant girls or nurses, and mingle with that flock of two-legged sheep in order to flee on jammed and overloaded vessels that threaten to sink at each stroke of the oars, were all at their posts. At present they stayed lying on the ground, in idle, magnificent poses, listening to him talk, like pirates listening to their chief tell frightful tales of boarding vessels and of combats in the night. When evening descended, the long beams from the searchlights the rebels had installed on the nearby heights darted in all directions, greatly disturbing that noble society of ascetic warriors and disillusioned men of gentle birth; those fortunate enough to be near a heap of ruins, which the hazards of its fall had arranged so as to form a kind of grotto, were less bothered by the flashing of the reflectors; but the others, whose only resource was to rest their stiff backs against the cold and hard tambour of a column, ran the risk of spending a sleepless night. It sometimes happened that several among them would turn their backs to the sea, for the spectacle of the beach interested them not at all. It was after all their milieu, their world, and these fishermen accustomed to nautical mythology were not in the least impressed by what went on around them, rather they were intrigued by the presence of the great luxury hotels lit from top to bottom and shining like lighthouses on the high, sheer cliffs at whose base the waves came to die noiselessly. The windows were open; the rich guests in evening clothes had stepped out onto the balconies and terraces, attracted by the whispering of all those marine gods stranded down below on the dark beach.

Hebdomeros and his companions, leaving behind these places where there was nothing further for them to do, entered the suburbs which were to the city what wings are to a stage. It was there, in fact, that all those personages whose actions attracted everyone's attention so forcibly went to apply makeup, prepare themselves, rehearse their roles like actors waiting for their cue to go on stage and recite with all the art their teachers have instilled into them that which they know by heart, or almost, so as to repeat it on the dusty boards, on those boards which, despite new ideas and the evolution of tastes and customs, still have something dirty and shameful about them. More than once, meditating on many an undeciphered enigma, Hebdomeros had asked himself the question "Why is there always something shameful about the theater?" He never succeeded in giving a satisfactory answer. Now it would happen sometimes that when he was all alone in his room, plunged in his meditations, twilight would slowly fall; his three friends always left him around six o'clock in the evening; they went away lighthearted and singing, their steps quickened by the steep slope that led down to the marketplace. Hebdomeros remained alone up there in that house where, ten years previously, he had rented a small, miserably furnished room. Later, thanks to the money that he had saved up, thrifty in all things, sustained by that will which beneath an appearance of lassitude and weakness had always dominated his life, he had succeeded in renting the entire house and expulsing the former tenants, not to revenge himself for the ill treatment he had on many occasions received at their hands, but to punish them for their unkindness; he considered this a just deed. "Justice before all," he would say, sitting down at table to consume the modest meal he had prepared for himself; this meal usually consisted of a skinny bird (a kind of undernourished lark) which an octogenarian hunter who was also his next-door neighbor brought him every day. This aged man worshipped the hunt with a fervor bordering on mysticism and obsession. Up at dawn, he would whistle to an old dog who followed him yawning after having first stretched itself almost out of joint. Thus each evening Hebdomeros bought from him a bird which he ate only the following evening, because he liked in leisure moments to paint still lifes of game. He would then place the dead bird on a table with a napkin; sometimes too, he would arrange cotton wool around it, as though it were snow, which made him think of hunting in winter and fine hunting parties at inns, with the hunters sitting near the fireplace where the logs flamed, gaily drinking and puffing on long pipes. When the dinner hour had struck, he would pluck the bird and put it to cook in a small pot with some goat's-milk butter and a little salt; while it cooked he would turn it, pricking it with a fork and repeating aloud always the same phrase: "It must feel the heat. It must feel the heat." When someone knocked on his door at the moment he was about to sit down at table, he still had the heart to ask these people to share his meal which, besides the little roasted bird, consisted of a crust of rye bread and a spoonful of blueberry jam; as a beverage he drank barm of fresh beer which he dissolved in a little filtered water with some sugar. On the question of culinary preparations and food in general he professed a morality of his own which earned him the antipathy and often the irritated sarcasms of a large number of his contemporaries. The spectacle of certain restaurants where finicky gourmets go to satisfy the abject concupiscence of their gastrointestinal apparatuses revolted him to the point of disgust and raised a just and saintly anger in his soul. People eating lobster and sucking with bestial voluptuousness on the legs and claws of these hideous armored monsters, having first cracked them open with a nutcracker, made him flee like an Orestes pursued by the Furies. But what troubled him especially was to see, at the beginning of a meal, the oyster fancier swallow this disgusting mollusk with an elaborate ritual of carefully buttered slices of black bread, little glasses of some special white wine, slices of lemon, etc., the whole washed down with theories about the effect that the lemon has on the mollusk, which contracts when it is still alive, or ridiculous tirades about the aroma of oysters which makes you think of the sea, of cliffs lashed by the waves, and other twaddle which only a creature deprived of all modesty and all self-control could find amusing. He also considered very immoral the custom of eating ice cream in cafés, and, in general, that of putting pieces of ice in drinks. Beaten egg white and whipped cream were also for him deleterious and impure substances. He also found most immoral and worthy of the severest repression the exaggerated and instinctive taste, often verging on voracity, that women in particular have for raw vegetables: pickles, cucumbers, artichokes preserved in vinegar, etc. He considered the strawberry and the fig the most immoral of fruits. Having fresh figs heaped with crushed ice served to oneself in the morning for breakfast was for Hebdomeros an act so serious that, according to his code, it would have merited a punishment varying from ten to fifteen years' imprisonment. Very blamable also according to him was the act of eating strawberries covered with cream; he could never manage to understand how reasonable people could commit deeds so ignoble and how they could have the courage to do them in public, before their fellow men, instead of hiding the shame of their unavowable acts deep within pitch-dark rooms after having first double-locked themselves in, as though for a rape or an act of incest. He attributed all that to human imbecility which he considered immense and eternal as the universe and in which he had an unshakable faith. Unshakable faith! He would have very much liked to have a doctor treat it, this time, that faith* swollen with daily examples; he would have liked to have it medically treated as one treats the hepatic patient with hot cholalogical springs; *acquae calidae*; amorous and dyspeptic Caesar, surrounded by his legions in the conquered valley. No one ever read the hymn he wrote that evening, neither his most faithful friends nor even that virgin with the ardent gaze and royal bearing to whom it was dedicated; he was afraid of what people might say; he had a horror of those equally indiscreet and uncomprehending milieux. Now the trees which had invaded the rooms and corridors of his dwelling were slowly departing southward; they emigrated by groups, by families, by tribes; they were already far away and with them left the thousand voices of the forest and its haunting odor. An aged and taciturn chambermaid, whom Hebdomeros called the Eumenide, was sweeping up the ruins that still littered the floor, and faced with this new life, faced with this grandiose and global spectacle, he suddenly *saw* the Oceans. Like the Colossus of Rhodes, like a Colossus of Rhodes infinitely magnified in a dream, his feet at the extremities of his straddling legs touched different regions; between the toes of his left foot, Mexican bandits pursued each other like famished wild beasts around rocks bak-

---

*The author here plays untranslatably on the words *foi* (faith), *foie* (liver) and *fois* (time). (Trans.)

ing in the heat of the dog days, while farther up his right foot trampled immaculate regions: among polar bears and obese elders with ferret-like profiles, wagging their heads at the jagged, notched, sawtoothed glaciers, like the remains of illustrious cathedrals ruined by cannon fire, and where, on the threshold of stinking huts made of sealskins stitched together, Eskimos swaddled in furs politely offered their wives to the excited explorers. Once more the distant rockets climbed silently into the vast somber night; compact groups of philosophers and warriors, veritable polycephalous blocks in delicate, shining colors, were holding mysterious conclaves in the corners of the rooms under the low ceiling, where the molding that joins the walls to the ceiling forms a right angle. "Those heads bode no good," one of Hebdomeros's youngest disciples exclaimed suddenly. "So be it," replied the latter; "I understand or rather I divine your thought; you would have preferred the well-behaved phantoms of the legislated and puritanical society that shuns treatises in which microbes and surgical instruments are mentioned and blanches with fright when boors use expressions like *son of the first bed* in conversation or discuss the techniques of obstetricians and midwives; you would have preferred the company of those phantoms in a closed veranda, when long silent flashes of lightning, like a rapid and repeated batting of the eyelids, announce the distant approaching storm. In fact the rumble of thunder, at first hollow and scarcely perceptible, soon becomes more serious; gusts of wind sweep through the garden, swirling the dried leaves and the illustrated newspapers left on the wicker chairs; then the big hot drops begin to fall in the dust of the walks with the noise of a smart tap of the fingers against a piece of heavy, taut material. 'Shut the windows! Shut the windows!' screams the mistress of the house, flinging herself madly through the rooms like a Niobe obsessed by the spectacle of her children bristling with darts; then, young man, this inexplicable scene takes place: Strange chickens, plucked of all their feathers, run crazily around the dining room table, like tiny ostriches; funereal violinists hastily replace their instruments in cases resembling coffins for newborn children; portraits stir in their frames and pictures crash to the floor; phantom cooks, the prototypes of assassins, creep stealthily upstairs toward the bedrooms of those distinguished and balding elders who, armed with their ivory-handled canes, are preparing to die with dignity so that their nephews will not have to blush when their names are mentioned. You would have preferred that, imprudent youth," added Hebdomeros—still addressing his young disciple with a smile full of unstated implications. "But think rather of those beautiful light days on the edge of beaches, think of those Immortals blessing those who love them, helmeted in gold and armored in silver, they are leaving on ships to go and die on that opposite shore, for they know that it is the best way of coming back afterward to their loved ones and living among them without spleen and without remorse; it is true that they come back only as phantoms but, as the proverb says, 'Better to return as a phantom than not at all'; think of all that and don't trust appearances, and then you will never be so ill-inspired as to utter the phrase I have just heard." Toward the rivers with cement banks, toward the decrepit palaces that raise their domes and weathervanes under the continual flight of the clouds, Hebdomeros still bent his steps. This severe place whose solemn door was closed at the moment ought to have saddened him, but the memory of what he had seen there in those moments spent amid a sparse and indifferent audience more than sufficed to console him. He saw, rising slowly out of the chiaroscuro of his memory and little by little growing distinct in his mind, the shapes of those plaster temples and sanctuaries built at the foot of hospitable mountains and cliffs whose narrow passes give a presentiment of near and unknown worlds as well as of those distant horizons, heavy with adventures, which ever since his unhappy childhood Hebdomeros had always loved. A magic word shone in space like the cross of Constantine and was repeated down to the horizon, like an advertisement for toothpaste: *Delphoi! Delphoi!* A gentle swishing sound as of laurel trees bent by the autumn wind passed through the tepid air and, on the other shore, opposite the sacred spot where the golden columns of the temple of Immortality shone in the rays of a sun nailed to the ceiling so that it could not set, the very sad paintings of vanished epochs appeared on the wall. "It's to keep the balance," said the guide, "for too much happiness is a bad thing." Thus Hebdomeros saw Christ insulted by the mob and then dragged by the legionaries before Pilate; he also saw the Deluge: masses of water unfurling in the plains, and women muscular as Titans clinging to the last rocks while elephants, silhouetted in black against livid bursts of lightning, raised terrified trunks before the storm. But was it really worthwhile evoking all that? Insomnia in the suffocating night and the tiger's eyes gleaming in the bedroom near the closed mosquito netting. The moonlight was so soft that the mountains looked very near, the divinities of night whispered on the outskirts of the city, there where the last sidewalks are like quays facing the sea of fields and meadows; one could embark there, leave, float on the yellow waves of ripe wheat or the green waves of the tender grass; those who remain at the farthest café, over there, at the end of this quarter of the city which advances like a promontory into the area of the fields, those who remain wave their handkerchiefs and raise their hands in a sign of farewell: Be happy! *Lebe wohl!* May fortune smile on you! Good luck! But behind the polychrome waves of that sea blossoming with the red poppy and the blue cornflower, the ship disappears slowly as though it were sinking in a very calm sea; the sails, swollen by the breath of springtime, are still visible, then they too disappear and peace settles once again over the countryside, and the birds who had momentarily left off singing at this unexpected sight, resume their joyful chirping. Now the thousand sounds of nature are born anew, like the sound of life halted for a moment by the passing of a funeral procession; the countryside is again full of life and gaiety and it flaunts it without shame and without remorse; before the arms whose doors are wreathed in flowers, peasant men and girls, flushed from the absorption of fermented beverages, dance in a ring around maypoles and with shrill cries toss their beribboned hats into the air. Hebdomeros, his arms folded on his chest, like a severe tribune witnessing an orgy, gazed thoughtfully at these noisy manifestations of innocent joy; he thought: "These men are happy, or at least they seem to be, for actually a great deal remains to be said on that subject; but, happy or unhappy, or merely tranquil, one fact is certain: that is, that the famous *demon tempter* of the rest of us, men of heart and mind, has never come to sit either at their table or their bedside; he has never followed them when, at daybreak, they go off to work, scythe over shoulder, their eyes following the lark that climbs the sky like the white ball at the top of the jet of water in a shooting gallery; still less does he follow them when at evening they return to their thatched cottages while the crows, in regular couples, after feasting on rotting carrion in the dried-up beds of torrents, regain the neighboring mountains in slow and regular flight, uttering from time to time that gentle cawing that I have ever loved. And we know what that means, that demon who is constantly snickering beside us; you are far from the city, you believe yourself as calm and free as the truant schoolboy; you are sitting on a bench by a deserted road shaded by trees whose dense foliage halts the ardent rays of the sun and forces them to pass through filtered and inoffensive and to sketch on the road the perforated notes of the disk of an aerophone; you believe yourself calm and free and you lose yourself in dreams and memories of the past when suddenly you realize that you are not alone; *someone* is still sitting on the bench; yes, that gentleman dressed with an outmoded elegance and whose face vaguely recalls certain photographs of Napoleon III and also of Anatole France at the time of *Le Lys rouge*: That gentleman who looks at you and chuckles in his beard, it is he again, the *demon tempter.* When you arise a little while from now, long after he has disappeared, you will again be walking along the dusty road and he will emerge from behind a bush, giving a very realistic imitation of a barking dog; if, your patience at an end, you begin to stone him with all your might, he will dash across the fields like a madman, bawling and accusing you to the villagers of the blackest misdeeds, even of raping little girls and setting farms on fire." This long soliloquy had tired and saddened Hebdomeros a little; the weather was still very fine; on the sunny heights green trees spread out their ranks, mingling the tints of their foliage; the clearings were carpeted with a very fine, very green grass on which children played, uttering joyous cries; modest yet clean, gay and hospitable-looking houses thrust their peaked roofs through the trees; everything basked in the light. And yet, close by, events of an unparalleled solemnity succeeded each other with the fatality that the goddess History, a book open on her thighs, had imposed on their sequence; paunchy ministers squeezed the hands and gazed into the eyes of monarchs whose torsos were covered with a mosaic of decorations and ribbons, while down below in the harbor, armor-plated battleships sounded their cannon and hoisted their flags and banners atop their flagpoles and masts; Mercury, who was flying over the spot at that moment, looked down, and when the cannonade awoke echoes in the valley, he made joyous signs and waved his caduceus in his hand.

Where to return? To the mines; Hebdomeros mistrusted those unhealthy terrains where fever reigned supreme all year long and where the innkeepers place quinine sulfate on the table for you the way they give you salt and pepper elsewhere. Rather the boredom of a life regulated by the hands of the chronometer, but fundamentally logical and not devoid of poetry, full of inner tears; life on that high road flanked with villas from which, every morning, issued the rippling plaint of pianos worried by adolescents practicing their daily exercises. All that would after all have been very normal and Hebdomeros as well as his companions and disciples would not have been in the least sorry to taste a few days of repose in this bored and restful spot, but a curious fact drew their attention and made them realize that all did not happen so normally there as they had at first supposed. In front of each villa was a little garden with wicker benches and chaises longues; in each garden, stretched out on a chaise longue, was a gigantic old man made entirely of stone; Hebdomeros was amazed that the chairs could bear up under such a weight, and he imparted his amazement to his companions, but, on drawing near, they saw that the chairs, which they had thought to be wicker, were made entirely of steel and that the intertwining of steel rods, painted straw color, had been so well calculated that they could have resisted much greater pressures. These old men were *alive*, yes, they were alive, but only a little; there was a tiny bit of life in the head and in the upper part of the body; sometimes the eyes stirred but the head did not move; one would have thought that, suffering from an eternal stiff neck, they were afraid to make the slightest movement for fear of provoking the pain. Sometimes their cheeks were slightly tinted with pink, and in the evening, when the sun had set behind the wooded mountains close by, they chatted from one garden to another and recounted memories of yesteryear. They evoked the times when they hunted the roebuck and the grouse in forests that were dark and dank even at noon; they told about how many times they had rushed at each other, holding their gun by the barrel and brandishing it like a club or clenching their hunting knives in their fists. The eternal cause of these fights was an animal which had been shot down and which two hunters claimed to have hit. One evening however the great stone elders spoke no more; specialists summoned in haste to examine them ascertained that the little life that stirred in them had vanished; even the tops of their skulls were cold and their eyes were closed; it was decided then to have them removed so that they would no longer encumber needlessly the tiny gardens of the villas; an individual who called himself a sculptor was called in; he was a horribly cross-eyed man with alarming manners; his conversation was full of stupid puns and his breath stank of eau-de-vie from three feet away. He arrived with a suitcase full of mallets of different sizes and immediately set to work; one after another the great stone elders were broken up and their pieces thrown into a valley which soon took on the appearance of a battlefield after a combat. The waves washed up as far as this sad debris; over behind the black cliffs with their profiles of gothic apostles the moon rose; a moon of boreal pallor; it fled against the clouds and Hebdomeros and his companions, like castaways standing on a raft, gazed toward the south; they knew that there from where the storm was blowing, behind that raging sea that tumbled mountains of foam on the shore, was Africa; yes, those scorched cities under an implacable sun, thirst and dysentery, but also cool oases where one no longer wishes for anything, where a strange, sweet wisdom falls from the top of the palm trees with the ripe dates in the chaste hours of early dawn; nevertheless this was not to be considered; Hebdomeros looked at the clouds which, from the south, were fleeing toward the north, where the sky was still clear; soon this part too of the celestial vault was covered with clouds, at first thin and widely spaced, like great black veils which an invisible hand might have trailed across the sky, then thicker, more compact; in a short while the sky was black everywhere. "It is nevertheless toward the north that we must move," said Hebdomeros to his companions, who approved of this idea. "In fact, my friends," he resumed, "the north is a little like the west, on the other hand the south is a little like the east; I advise you to be wary of the south and the east for they are deleterious and corrosive countries. To the north lie life and happiness, beauty and light, the joy of work and of rest without remorse; if you have something to say or to reveal, say it or reveal it in the north or in the west, you will have more of a chance than elsewhere of being understood and re-warded for your pains. This does not mean, however, my friends, that you must never go toward the south or the east; a day will come when not only shall we go there but we shall remain there; still, it is by return-ing from up above that we must proceed there; those are fortified places which must be taken by ruse; frontal attacks end only in failure and in loss of men and materiel; in this vast world the things which are hostile to you are more numerous than those which are favorable to you; be sure then that you have good tactics and good strategy and that you know how to combat them not only with courage, but also with knowledge and intelligence: Courage is not enough. That your friends, your par-ents, or even people whom you do not know but who know you and who follow with interest and sympathy your acts and deeds may one day be able to say of you: 'He fell with the brave'—this is not enough; in these words you will see all the regrets of your wild youth, wasted away on easy pleasures up until the moment when maturity, awakening in you the deepest levels of reason, forced you toward discipline and work and pushed you toward those ever fairer and greater conquests which henceforth shall light up your life with the immortal flames of glory. That civil engineers toil in shirtsleeves over trenches and drainage sys-tems in the heat of those canicular days should not be for you a cause of remorse and desire of emulation; if the faucets of your house yield a warm and dubious water; if the flies are relentless around your food and if the sauces and buttermilk curdle in your cupboards, think of the hunting expeditions in polar regions, think of the sea lions sinking their fangs into the wood of the ship's boats which are pitching alarmingly; think also of the great pine forests on the slopes of tall mountains at the hour when the sun disappears slowly in the clarified air behind the rocky peaks, and by declining opens the door to cool winds which revive plants and flowers and coax the animals out of the burrows and lairs where the heat of noon had banished them. Think also of those blessed cities where the fog and mist spread out their beneficial veils eternally, where the albino children can stare at the sun's disk at midday, where men are light-skinned and blue-eyed, and where the painters work a long time over portraits and marine scenes which, once they are finished, can be examined with a magnifying glass." Hebdomeros's friends and disciples listened to him, leaning on the balustrades or lying on the floor; after the period of homes they now found themselves on these inner rampart walks, protected by thick fortress walls; around them the pillars were sometimes alternated and the ogival arches raised their harmonious curves on all sides. When he had finished his long speech they applauded and then got up to look down at that little harbor where, at daybreak, two frigates flying unknown colors had dropped anchor. Now the sailors were mending the sails, building lifeboats to replace those the storm had destroyed, and salting their meats, while long-haired and jabbering experts were quarreling noisily as they installed scientific instruments on the blocks of the breakwater under construction. The site of this city which Hebdomeros called the most happily situated in the universe, at the mouth of a river which passed through it, fertilized its countryside, and was easily navigable up to the lake, teeming with fish, from which it flowed, filled with awe these perspicacious young men who were prone to indulge in lyric fancies. Meanwhile night had fallen and the setting had changed. As sometimes happens in a dream, all the charm of this gentle panorama faded away little by little to give way to the hideous silhouette of the inhospitable crags looming out of the twilight, which during the day were hidden by the fog and the smoke from the factories. The crater of a volcano began to belch whirlwinds of short yellow and bluish flames; the luxuriant vegetation of the valleys disappeared in the gloom. The lake occupied a basin bordered by sheer cliffs; the local inhabitants maintained that at its center men had tried in vain to sound its bottom; probably it disappeared into the bowels of the

Earth; strange rumors circulated; people reputed for their seriousness claimed to have seen monsters of the Tertiary period wandering on its surface in the dead of night. The fact was that no one dared venture into the center of the lake; in addition a line of little buoys painted vermilion marked the edge of the area where the sounding line no longer touched bottom. Hebdomeros was more than ever determined to leave this country where, behind a deceptive appearance of peace and fertility, terrors and strange traps were lurking. As long as the sun shone, everything went well, but once night had come you saw the other side of the coin; yet the inhabitants were by no means uncivilized and even had quite refined tastes, as may be judged from this menu which was served to Hebdomeros and his friends in a restaurant where they had gone to dine:

Potage Crécy
Artichauts
Gigot de Mouton
Purée de Pommes
Gâteau de Semoule
Compote de Pruneaux

All the same, one couldn't spend one's nights in the dread of meeting an ichthyosaurus or of being wakened out of a sound sleep by the volcano erupting. Hebdomeros would have preferred to put up with the opposite: to live in anxiety during the day but once night had come, once the bolt had been fastened, the curtains pulled and the doors locked, to be able to repose in safety and tranquility. He considered sleep as something very sacred and sweet, and he would not allow his calm to be disturbed by anyone or anything. He professed the same cult for the sons of sleep, dreams, which is why he had had carved on the foot of his bed a picture of Mercury oneiropomp, that is, the guide of dreams, for, as everyone knows, Mercury was entrusted by Jupiter not only with exercising the profession of psychopomp, that is, of guiding and leading the souls of the dead into the other world, but also that of guiding dreams into the sleep of the living. Over his bed, Hebdomeros had hung a very curious picture which had been painted by one of his friends, an artist of great talent who had unfortunately died very young. He was an intrepid swimmer and once, wishing to swim across a flooded river, he had been swept away by the current, and despite the efforts of those who had tried to rescue him, he was dragged away by the current and disappeared in the eddies. The picture he had painted showed Mercury as a shepherd holding a crook instead of the caduceus; he was driving a flock of dreams before him into the night of sleep. The picture was very well composed; for, in the distance, behind Mercury and his flock, a sunlit land could be seen: cities, harbors, men going about their business, peasants working their fields; life, in a word; while around Mercury and his strange flock all was darkness and solitude as though they had entered an immense tunnel. Still on account of dreams, Hebdomeros abstained from eating beans at the evening meal; he was in agreement on that score with Pythagoras, who claims that beans produce obscurity and confusion in dreams. Hebdomeros sincerely regretted the young painter's death; he owned a photograph of him taken a few days before the rash attempt that was to cost him his life; this photograph showed the painter in full face, with a black beard that contrasted with the almost childish expression of his features. "It was his passion, that beard," Hebdomeros used to say when his friends would ask him for details of the life of the young painter. "He loved something of the past, of that not too distant past we find in the portraits of our parents when they were young. All the same he used to shave, but to have his picture taken he had let his beard grow, as film actors sometimes do so as to appear more convincing in roles where that ornament of the virile visage is indispensable; but they are wrong, they are gravely mistaken, for a false beard is always more real on the screen than a real beard, just as a wooden and cardboard set is always more real than a natural setting. But try telling that to your film directors, avid for beautiful locations and picturesque views; they won't know what you are talking about, alas!" And Hebdomeros fell silent, gazing thoughtfully at the tender arabesques in the oriental rug he had just bought. Sometimes, in the midst of his reveries, he would pass his hand across his forehead as though to push away sad thoughts and troublesome images, and raising his head, he would say: "Let's speak about him again, let's speak some more of that young artist, victim of his temerity. Certainly if he had been fully conscious of his own worth he would never have exposed his life that way, out of bravado, for an athletic stunt which others better trained and more resistant than he would have surely carried off; he would have worked quietly and prudently warded off dangers and risks. In the matter of perfumes, he cared only for eau de Lubin, sometimes for eau de Cologne as well; but he maintained that eau de Lubin, from certain points of view, is more evocative."

Just at the moment that Hebdomeros finished pronouncing these last words a cannon resounded in the harbor; at once a number of pigeons, frightened by the detonation, rushed past the window like a whirlwind; instinctively everyone reached for his watch thinking it was noon, but Hebdomeros stopped them with a wave of his hand: "No, my friends," he said, "we have not yet reached the middle of our day; that cannon shot you just heard by no means signifies that the sun in space, that the hands on clocks and the shadows on sundials have attained that fatal point which, according to certain people, indicates the hour of phantoms far more interesting and singular than those that ordinarily appear at the stroke of midnight in abandoned cemeteries or beneath the wan light of a moon breaking through storm clouds, amid the solitary ruins of an accursed castle, phantoms which all of you, and myself as well, are familiar with for having always seen them from earliest childhood. The cannon shot you have just heard, my friends, merely announced the arrival in our port of the steamship *Argolide*; this event would not be of the slightest interest did I not know from neighborhood gossip that it is precisely on this steamship that young Lecourt is returning to his natal city; yes, Thomas Lecourt, who five years ago left the paternal roof to roam the world and live his life, and whom every country in the world now calls the prodigal son. You know his father, that aged man with the stern profile who recently underwent a liver operation; you know too that he lives not far from here, in a villa hidden among eucalyptuses; from our balcony we can see the park of the villa. This old man, long a widower, hardly ever goes out; he attributes great importance to butter and has made long studies of its making throughout the ages; his friends sometimes jokingly call him the butterologist but he never loses his temper, in fact he scarcely ever loses his temper at all and always smiles sadly behind his white mustache; often he gazes in front of him into space, yet there are moments when his features contract, his hands clench the arms of his chair, and then in a trembling voice he utters these three words: 'Ah! The scoundrel!' His gaze has fallen on the portrait of Clotilde, of his daughter Clotilde, Clotilde the hunchback, abandoned when pregnant a few months after their marriage by her husband, a handsome man with a blond mustache. But to return to the point: The Lecourt boy is coming home to the paternal roof; if at this moment we go out on the balcony we shall not have long to wait before he appears; nothing is more moving, my dear friends, than such a return, especially without the stage business of the fatted calf that is killed and the old man with a white beard stretching out his pardoning arms." On Hebdomeros's invitation his friends stepped out on the balcony, others leaned on their elbows at the windows, and all looked at the white road which went down to the harbor; soon at the end of that road appeared a man who advanced with weary steps, his back heavily laden with a sack and a rolled-up coat tied with strings. The sky was covered with a thin layer of clouds, a slight and very gentle wind blew imperceptibly in the dry weeds and the telegraph wires; a great calm reigned everywhere; one felt however that this would not last and it was Hebdomeros's friends who first gave the signal; no sooner did they catch sight of the stranger than they shouted in unison: "Long live he who returns to us! Long live the returning one! Long live the prodigal son! Long live the return of the prodigal son!" Their cries and acclamations spread from house to house, arousing the entire countryside, and soon flags appeared at the windows, men left their work to come and see what was happening, bands of urchins began to march in front of the escorting soldiers, copying their parade step and making all kinds of unavowable noises with their mouths to imitate the rolling of the drum. The swallows in long black lines clove the air, uttering piercing cries. At the end of the eucalyptus park the father's house withdrew into the muteness of its closed shutters. It remained silent, the father's house, and soon everything began little by little to fall silent with it. The noise died away; the wind held its breath, the curtains which had billowed romantically at the open windows fell back like flags that the wind no longer lifts. Men in shirtsleeves, who had been playing billiards, suddenly stopped playing as though a great weariness had overtaken them, a weariness for their past life, for their present life, and for the years that still awaited them, with their procession of sad or smiling hours, or simply neutral ones, neither sad nor smiling, just hours, in a word! Silence and meditation were everywhere. A crier, caring little about mystery and hardly aware of metaphysical refinements, began to announce at the top of his lungs the next steamship sailings and which ones among them accepted, in addition to merchandise, passengers as well. He was careful to precede each announcement with a violent roll of his drum. A gendarme emerging from a dim, narrow alley put an end to this sacrilege by pouncing on the crier and dragging him back from where he had come, as a lion reenters a thicket with the antelope whom he has surprised at the moment she was slaking her thirst at the edge of a pond. It was the moment that Hebdomeros cherished above all others; immediately he developed an appetite and thought with joy of the midday meal; not that he was a glutton, far from that, but he was something of a gourmand, only with tact and intelligence; he loved the taste of bread; of grilled lamb fat; of fresh, limpid water; and of strong tobacco. He also loved the Jews and everything connected with them; in the company of Jews he abandoned himself to a sweet and strange torpor which was like the emotion that traveling produces, for when he was traveling he always had a slight sensation of dreaming; when he was with the sons of Israel he also left on a journey, a journey to the depths of the dark night of time and of races.

To celebrate the return of the prodigal son, the father gave a large reception a few days later to which Hebdomeros and his friends were invited. The garden of the villa was lit by Venetian lanterns hung on the trunks of the eucalyptuses, and in the veranda, from which all the plants and flowerpots had been cleared for the occasion, a buffet, devoid of idle sumptuousness, but where the guests could find an abundance of wholesome and appetizing delicacies, had been set up. The sky was still light in the west, for in this occidental country the summer days continued until very late and night was extremely slow in falling. High in the sky, little purple clouds, tinted a delicate pink on one side by the rays of the setting sun, were arranged in tiers; but the countryside all around the city began to be invaded by darkness; the shapes of trees grew dark and the whiteness of the houses faded more and more; from far off one heard the sound of a train, moving away somewhere, toward the north. Soon the clocks of the town hall struck nine; the first guests began to arrive. Hebdomeros arrived too, surrounded by his friends, but contrary to what he had hoped and wished, his arrival and presence were not particularly noticed. Out of respect for the mental suffering of the master of the house, suffering which the recent return of his son had certainly palliated but had unfortunately not suppressed, the guests abstained from dancing. Having foreseen this delicate consideration on their part, and in order to divert them, the elder Lecourt had had the idea of setting up a little stage in the main salon of the villa, in front of which were placed several rows of chairs rented from a nearby café. On this stage, amateur actors performed short comedies which were warmly applauded. The elder Lecourt, with his daughter Clotilde on his left and his son Thomas on his right, was sitting in the first row and it was he who always gave the signal for the applause. Everything went perfectly; a delightful cordiality and charming simplicity reigned over the party despite several couples who tried to act smart by moving slowly out toward the shadows of the park, in a silence pregnant with reveries. One would have sworn that this agreeable evening would end as calmly as it began, when a most unfortunate incident occurred; two actors who were performing in the third and last comedy were the cause; in this one-act comedy the scene was a school classroom; while the schoolmaster was lecturing the pupils played all kinds of pranks on him; but one schoolboy in particular proved especially mischievous, and his specialty was pinning the figure of a buffoon cut from a page of notepaper on the schoolmaster's frock coat whenever the latter turned away from the class to write on the blackboard. The actor playing the role of the schoolmaster was a short man of about fifty with a little gray turned-up mustache. He had a particularly irascible and touchy character; he was an old acquaintance of the master of the house; it was said of him that he had been for a time consul in the Orient and that he was very fond of snipe-hunting. At the moment when the actor playing the role of the scapegrace was pinning for the tenth time the buffoon on the tail of his frock coat, he turned suddenly around and no doubt finding that the other put too much zeal in the operation, said sharply to him: "Sir, in my opinion you go too far." To which the other replied in no less vexed tones: "And you, sir, are forgetting that we are actors here, on a stage, and that what we are performing is only a fiction; besides, having had the honor of knowing you for some time, I am convinced that you have no sense of humor." This retort, actually quite a reasonable one, was the last straw for the ex-consul; losing all self-control he stepped forward and slapped his interlocutor in the face. The other actors, joined by the spectators who had hastily climbed onto the stage, immediately intervened, but nothing less than the venerable presence of the master of the house, supported by the shoulders of his children, was necessary in order to calm these over-excited tempers. The comedy was called off. The spectators, deeply perturbed, moved toward the buffet, commenting vehemently on this disagreeable episode, while the ex-consul's wife, leading her husband, still pale with fury, toward the eucalyptuses of the park, said in a voice loud enough for all to hear: "I am proud to have a husband like that!"

The evening was coming to an end; the last guests, and Hebdomeros with them, paid their respects to the master of the house and his children and left the villa, whose park was already plunged in darkness. Outside, the sky offered an unforgettable spectacle: The constellations were laid out so perfectly that they formed real figures drawn with dotted lines, as in illustrated dictionaries. Hebdomeros, delighted, stopped and began to point them out, which was in fact quite simple for him since they were easily recognizable and someone completely void of astronomical learning would have recognized them without difficulty. One could see the Twins, leaning on each other in a classic pose of tranquility; one could see the Great Bear, obese and touching, dragging his pelt against the darkness of the profound ether; farther on the Fish were slowly revolving, always at the same distance from each other, as though attached to the same axis; and Orion, solitary Orion was moving off into the depths of the sky, his club on his shoulder, followed by his faithful Dog. The Virgin with her precise and opulent curves was reclining on a cloud, gracefully turning her head so as to look down at the world, still asleep in the last hours of night which was drawing to a close; farther on to the left was the Scales, the Scales with its pans empty and motionless in their perfect horizontality; there was something there for everyone and even for the most exaggerated requirements. No one felt like going home. Hebdomeros, who felt all emotions more violently than the others and was always ready to go into raptures about something, neglecting all self-control, proposed then and there that they settle down at a table in a little café that stayed open until morning because workmen and engineers repairing the railroad came there to refresh themselves and rest.

Down in the port the fishing boats were casting their moorings; a sound of cars came from the highway and lights began to appear at the windows of the houses; one felt that day was not far off; life was slowly waking up all around. Fresh gusts from the sea passed through the air like a mute call; in the east, the sky was growing lighter. "Insomnia," thought Hebdomeros, and his back felt a little cold, for he knew what that meant ... He knew them well, those mornings after wakeful nights, those mornings after summer nights peopled with the great sculpture of antiquity and during which famous temples, vanished centuries ago, profile their profound lines against the ridge of the dark mountains; he knew them well, those hot days that follow nights of great visions, and the sun as relentless as the obstinate song of the sacred and invisible cicadas, and the impossible coolness sought at noon at the edge of a muddy river.

"But in that case," thought Hebdomeros, "what is the meaning of that dream of combat on the seashore, those dugout canoes pulled up on the beach and those trenches hastily dug in the sand, and over there behind the trenches, tiny hospitals, the trim little hospitals where even the zebras, yes, the poor injured zebras, are cared for with skill and tenderness, and go away bandaged, bound up, stitched up, patched up, disinfected, put into shape again, in a word made good as new! Could it be that life was only an immense lie? Could it be that it was only the shadow of a fleeting dream? Could it be that it was only the echo of the mysterious blows struck against the flank of the rocky mountain whose opposite slope had apparently never been seen by anyone and at whose summit one could perceive during the day dark masses with irregular profiles which were no doubt forests, but from which, at night, came stifled sighs and groans as though a chained giant were suffering without hope up there under the great sky quivering with stars?" Thus spoke Hebdomeros to himself while yet again night fell on the metropolis. People passed him, regularly, continually, as though riveted to a chain moved by perpetual motion. These people looked at him without seeing him and saw him without looking at him; they all had the same face; sometimes a few would detach themselves from their invisible chain to stop in front of the jewelers' blinding shop windows. Cameo, Luxus, Irradio were the sonorous names of the diamonds henceforth renowned which formerly had ornamented the crowns of monarchs assassinated on moonlight nights in palaces hidden in the depths of dark parks. Now these inestimable stones darted in all directions their iridescent sparkles and miniature aurora borealises; on little pedestals made of a cube covered with red velvet they gleamed in the center of the window, as in the depths of the sky on a tranquil summer night gleams the star which through the centuries has seen wars, cataclysms, and scourges sweep down upon the world and destroy what men have built. Sometimes a precise, rapacious hand, like the razor-sharp claw of the full-grown vulture, would slip through the heavy draperies which served as the backcloth of this obscene, brilliantly lighted little theater where luxury, hypocritically masking lust, shamelessly flaunted its maleficent flares. And then revolts would arise as storms arise in the sultry sky of a summer day. Fierce, resolute men, led by a kind of colossus with the beard of a god of antiquity, hurled enormous beams snatched from construction yards at the armored doors of the luxury hotels. The most prudent had already fled; others had fallen at the first blows and it was precisely the ones who had never wanted to believe in the revolt and who had claimed that all those rumors that were circulating were utterly groundless, that they had been started by grasping bankers to provoke a drop in the stock market, so as to be able to speculate afterward on the rise which would follow the denial of these alarming reports. They were the same persons who always ended their optimistic speeches with phrases like: *Our people have too much good sense . . . etc., etc.*

Art and Literature 4 (Spring 1965).

THAT EVENING MONSIEUR DUDRON . . .

That evening, M. Dudron returned home feeling a bit tired, since he had run several errands in the center of the city and seen some people; also the weather was oppressive and charged with electricity; gusts of wind swept the streets and M. Dudron remembered the malicious mirth of passersby confronted with the spectacle of uncoiffed women madly pursuing their hats which a powerful blast from Aeolus had snatched from their heads and pushed ever farther on the sidewalk and sometimes even into the middle of the street, where the vehicular traffic was most intense, which complicated the misadventure and made it even slightly dangerous and almost dramatic. He remembered too the soiled papers and the newspapers carried away and floating upward as high as the fifth story. But what wearied him most was the people he had met; starting with the enthusiasts and the admirers; on the other hand, those in whose presence he felt mistrust, hostility, and ill-will tired him less, first of all because he curtailed the conversation as much as possible, and then also because he had long trained himself to be on guard against their attacks, to ward them off and skillfully give as good as he got. A canny psychologist, he guessed immediately the reason and the first cause of their hostility, and with a flick of the tongue, so to speak, was able to turn the tables on them by revealing what he had guessed; generally speaking, men don't like that, and those armed with malice are particularly afraid of being judged. But what fatigued him most was his admirers, for there he felt himself totally disarmed. The flattery they dispensed moved him not at all, for he knew that it in no way corresponded to the intrinsic value of his work. All those enthusiastic cries ended up not only boring him profoundly but also irritating him. Certain questions put him beside himself, for instance: *"But wherever did you get the idea of painting horses?"* Another thing which caused him profound horror was when they spoke of dreams and mystery regarding his pictures. *"You paint the sky of dreams! . . ."* M. Dudron knew perfectly well that the sky of dreams *doesn't exist*; he had never dreamed of skies either in his sleep or in daydreams. He studied the sky as it was in nature, his eyes wide open, observing the real sky and also the skies in the paintings of the old masters, and trained himself to remember the different aspects the celestial vault assumes according to the times of day, the seasons, and atmospheric conditions. But all was useless; M. Dudron understood that his friends and admirers *enjoyed* expressing themselves in that way and that the wisest course was to let them, all the more since each time he had tried to explain to them the true state of things, he had noticed on their faces such an expression of disappointment, of discouraged hope, that his enormous sensitivity prevented him from proceeding further. So it was that M. Dudron returned home somewhat weary that evening; he undressed and went to bed after inspecting carefully to see that the indispensable chamber pot was in its niche in the night table and that those objects he was accustomed to see within his reach when he prepared himself to leave on a voyage to the mysterious kingdom of Morpheus were laid out on the night table, to wit: a glass of water, a pillbox containing remedies for a possible headache or toothache; a fountain pen duly filled with ink; two pencils, one soft, the other harder, a rubber eraser, a notebook for sketches, writing paper, a book or a newspaper, his carefully wound-up watch, his tobacco pouch filled with his favorite mixture, his pipe, an ashtray, a box of wooden matches, and a penknife. He also habitually placed beside his bed, so as to be able to examine it closely, the painting or drawing on which he was working at the moment. That evening M. Dudron placed on the floor, leaning it against an armoire, a canvas which he had roughed out the night before; even though it was scarcely begun, one could already distinguish a figure with a severe profile, draped in a long cloak, a fold of which encircled his neck; he was astride a little black horse, lean and nervous, whose very lively eye glowed red in the shadows like a live coal; around the horseman and his steed unfolded an alpine landscape of tragic cliffs and profound ravines; M. Dudron had already baptized his painting: *Hannibal*. He contemplated it, all the while smoking his pipe and thinking of the work that still remained to be done. At the same time that name, Hannibal, came back to him. Hannibal, that was the name of a young barber who worked in a shop where M. Dudron customarily went once a month to have his hair cut. M. Dudron had trained Hannibal to cut his hair according to his wishes and not according to the barber's whim; he wanted his hair cut very short on the nape; in front and on the sides, he wanted it merely *trimmed*. Above all he had trained Hannibal not to make at the end of the session the fatal suggestion of a scalp massage, a suggestion which terrified him. M. Dudron was in the habit of going to the barber on Tuesdays, immediately after lunch, since he knew that at that time the shop was almost empty of customers; as he entered, the lads would be dozing in their chairs, and, on catching sight of him, the one named Hannibal would get up and invite M. Dudron to sit down in the barber's chair. This scene, which was repeated regularly every month, reminded M. Dudron of another, almost the equivalent of it. It was when he went to a certain brothel that he was also in the habit of visiting at such and such a day and hour which he knew to be particularly favorable for not running into other clients. There too, on his arrival, the pensioners were yawning, standing or stretched out on divans, or quietly knitting in a corner; upon his arrival, the one with whom M. Dudron was accustomed to *go upstairs* would stand up and, without a word, wearily precede M. Dudron on the stairway which led to the floor above. The similarity between the two scenes had finally produced a strange feeling in M. Dudron's sensitive soul, and when he entered the barber's shop he felt disturbed; he had the impression that Hannibal might have begun wearily to climb the stairs to the floor above and that he, M. Dudron, might be following him—Hannibal! The fog of sleep arose in M. Dudron's mind. It grew as thick as that produced by the smoke from his pipe, which now extended its floating veils around his bed . . . ; and now, slowly through this fog with its strong scent of tobacco, a scene loomed slowly and then grew distinct against the shadowy backdrop of the bedroom. An alpine landscape . . . ; a long caterpillar of men and quadrupeds unfurled and crawled painfully up the steep paths. The men had piled their arms and gear and also the wounded on the backs of their steeds, which bent under the weight. One heard cries, commands, the icy wind whistling through the branches of pine trees, sounds of waterfalls, prolonged whinnying of the horses; rocks detached themselves and rolled down the slopes as the marching horde passed by, bouncing and knocking against the tree trunks whose bark, rotted by the damp, displayed a livid wound after the shock; while, now and again, awaking echoes in those wild and solitary sites, the long braying of elephants resounded in the darkened valleys. Doubled over in the teeth of the gale, a captain, a chief, rode alone at the head of the savage horde; sometimes he would stop to encourage those who were weary or whom fear had begun to overtake, sometimes too, he would draw to one side, urging his mount toward a retired spot where he found himself alone, and there he would gaze for a long time, interrogating them, one might say, at those high summits clad in snow, standing motionless and mysterious like unknown deities, above a frantic sea of vast white clouds . . . ; and then a night fell, like a lowered curtain, on the background of M. Dudron's bedroom; another night than that which weighed on the roof of his sleeping house. Bivouac fires tinted the darkness with large red spots. The chief had now lain down, surrounded by his harried staff. He listened to the thousand sounds, often inexplicable, of the mountain plunged in shadow. He listened to the continuous roar of torrents which, with the odor of dampness, issued from the bottom of those ravines one could no longer see; he listened also, with a vague disquiet, to the poignant singsong of the young mercenaries hastily recruited from the other side of the mountains, in those savage settlements of the Iberian Peninsula, whose plaintive chants rose, like an evil omen, into the great night.

Hebdomeros: With Monsieur Dudron's Adventure and Other Metaphysical Writings (Cambridge, Mass.: Exact Change, 1992).

IT WAS SOMETHING LIKE . . .

It was something like the fear of leaving on summer vacation, the fear of girls' taunts and that of military service. So joy too might have been of a different quality: mingled with surprise, as for example, finding fish in an underground river, or else settling down, with one's family, as a professor of drawing in a small town isolated among high mountains. M. Dudron had often thought fondly of this project, but his friends advised him against it, for, they said, it was a project unworthy of him . . . And yet he would have liked to settle in one of those little-known and seldom visited towns, which are like those small islands situated far from the routes taken by ships of the major navigation lines. He saw himself there, living in a house with many bedrooms and with terraces and verandas perched above torrents whose bed was littered with large stones and whose edges were ornamented with ferns. In the morning, he would get up early and take his café au lait on the veranda while looking out over the romantic landscape of the wooded, shadowy valley and the sinuous course of the streams; then he would go out and walk to school to give himself a bit of exercise. During his course in drawing he would survey the pupils and give them practical advice on how to draw a face by simplifying its planes and giving them geometrical forms, on measuring with the plumb line and wire that was straight and rigid and on modeling by making shadows using the technique of crosshatched parallel lines. He would circulate in the studio, going from student to student, among the plaster casts and lithographs representing Belisarius and Antinous, Alexander the Great and Cicero, as well as hands of men and women in all the positions; hands of warriors clasping swords or lances, hands of orators, making in front of invisible crowds the sign that accompanies and emphasizes speech, hands of mothers holding gently against their breast, in a gesture filled with tenderness, the large curly heads of their children, or hands of virgins lifting a veil with a movement of chaste gracefulness. When the clock struck noon, thus announcing the end of the class, M. Dudron, who ordinarily didn't have lunch until one, would take his cane and hat and go for a stroll through the port; there he would interest himself in the departure and arrival of ships, in the life of those classic sailboats which seem eternally moored at the docks and in which entire families live soberly, drying their laundry in the sun and cooking their meals on the deck in the midst of coiled cables and buckets of tar, and the eternal mongrel dog with intelligent and docile eyes and short tail curled in a spiral. M. Dudron would also go and look at the mermaids who habitually emerge from the water at the stroke of noon, covered with seaweed, and hoist themselves with difficulty on the stone blocks of the pier under construction. There they stay for a long time, elbows resting on the cold, rough stone, with their chins in the palms of their hands, gazing with a nostalgic air at the town with its factory chimneys, its houses, its palaces, its white, straight streets, its squares surrounded by trees and ornamented at the center with a monument in stone or bronze depicting a hero, a politician, a poet, an artist, or a scientist; they listen, sad and dreamily, to the thousand sounds of that life in which they will never be able to share. And toward the most beautiful of the mermaids the thoughts of M. Dudron went and went again, ceaselessly. In a voice cracked with emotion, she told him of her son, that Alfred, whom she romantically called Alfredo, and whom she had left behind up there, toward the north, in that city as it were lost in the cold mists of Septentrion. M. Dudron knew that this Alfred had, though still very young, shown remarkable aptness at drawing and painting. "Besides," M. Dudron said to himself, "it's not for nothing that he's the son of a mermaid; one peculiarity of the sons of mermaids is that they never run the risk of falling in love with a woman, for they are always in love with their mothers, and I remember very well having known the son of a mermaid once, a captain in the merchant marine, who, even at the age of sixty, had a mother who was still desirable. This captain attributed that to the effect of salt water, which preserves the fresh aspect of the flesh for a long time; he claimed that lake and river mermaids, and freshwater mermaids in general, stay young for a much shorter time. One of his colleagues to whom he had spoken about the virtues of salt water made his wife take saltwater baths every day, summer and winter, baths which his servant, a former sailor, went every day to draw in buckets from the harbor; but the captain, fearing that if it were taken near the quays it might, because of the sewers, be contaminated with typhoid fever bacteria, obliged the ex-sailor to go and draw the water at the far end of the pier, which was quite fatiguing, especially in hot weather, and provoked, on the part of the servant, complaints and protests and even threats of leaving the house." To return to Alfred, the child was considered by many to be a child prodigy. M. Dudron was wary of child prodigies, but he thought that in Alfred's case things might be different, that it was by no means a matter of one of those cases of violent precociousness which end like soap bubbles, but that the child was, quite simply, gifted. Having received a box of watercolors as a gift one Christmas, Alfred had painted on a page of one of his school notebooks a tiger's head that was really impressive in its ferocity; this tiny masterpiece had excited the admiration of all who had seen it. Another time, Alfred had rescued an uncle of his, who had one Sunday invited him to lunch in a restaurant, from an embarrassing position. Alfred's uncle had found himself in serious difficulties after unwise speculations on the stock exchange; nevertheless, generous and carefree as he was, he had invited his young nephew to a restaurant known throughout the city for its elevated prices. When at the end of a copious repast the waiter brought the bill, the uncle perceived with terror that the sum of the latter was higher than the amount of money he had on him. But Alfred, perspicacious, had guessed everything in the blink of an eye. He asked his uncle to give him a large stickpin in the shape of a riding crop that he wore on his shirtfront, then, using several matches, he blackened the reverse side of a plate and, with the point of the pin, drew on the blackened surface a horse's head with dilated nostrils and flowing mane. He accomplished this with so much bravura and talent that the people having lunch drew closer to watch the little artist at work, and when he had finished and signed his handiwork they applauded him enthusiastically just as one applauds a tenor at the end of an aria. The restaurant owner hastened to carry away the plate with a delighted air, declaring himself most satisfied to be paid with such a handsome drawing.

Hebdomeros: With Monsieur Dudron's Adventure and Other Metaphysical Writings (Cambridge, Mass.: Exact Change, 1992).

MONSIEUR DUDRON'S ADVENTURE

Around two in the afternoon on April 17, 1939, M. Dudron, comfortably ensconced in his folding deck chair, was taking a siesta in his office-studio. As often happened when he wasn't working, his thoughts turned to painting. "Painters," he said to himself, "today and even for some time past, no longer make painting; *they do not paint*; they lay out pigment on the canvas to dry. Now, a beautiful painting is never dried pigment but *beautiful colored substance*. I understand very well how it is that no one understands. It's been ages (two or three quarters of a century) since that precious thread of Ariadne was lost. Is it my task to find it again and present it to the painters, my contemporaries, who yawn over their palettes until their jaws are dislocated and try to save face by a pretentious and skeptical attitude which, nonetheless, is basically nothing more than dissatisfaction and annoyance? For that matter there is enough to be dissatisfied and annoyed with," M. Dudron continued to himself. "Painters today *no longer enjoy themselves when they paint*. They all feel, most confusedly it's true, but they feel it anyway, that *it's no use*, that *it's no longer any use*. A few, out of despair, dive into the swamp of so-called invention or so-called spirituality; they try to entertain themselves and also to entertain others by talking of inspiration, lyricism, astonishment, strangeness, mystery, oh yes, mystery most of all, but these, alas, are nothing but minor subterfuges which, if they can furnish a few results from the practical point of view, ease their consciences only up to a certain point, while basically, in their heart of hearts, they all yearn with infinite nostalgia for that distant land, that paradise lost, of beautiful, of very beautiful painting."

He had reached this point in his meditations when the tremendous roar of a motor caused him to get up and go over to the window. Down below, before his front door, he saw a magnificent automobile, long and gleaming as a terrestrial torpedo boat. A female acquaintance of his got out. She was a woman with passionate tresses, dressed with an elegance both severe and athletic that suggested a cross between Athena and a modern Valkyrie, but more Valkyrie than Athena. Bursting into M. Dudron's room, she began without sitting down or even greeting him to speak to him very quickly and breathlessly, meanwhile pacing up and down the room. "Be ready this evening at seven o'clock sharp, *Maître*, when I shall come by in the car to pick you up." Then, still striding back and forth, she proceeded to explain that she had arranged to meet several friends at an inn about fifty kilometers away, on a hill above a small town situated on a lake. It was there, close to the inn, that an acquaintance of hers, a superrich industrialist whose specialty was the manufacture of bushings for hunting rifles, had created a *snail farm*. Hence it was a matter of going out there to dine at the inn, eat the snails, and afterward visit the famous *breeding grounds*. "It seems, *Maître*," she informed M. Dudron, who was listening with a benevolent and resigned air, "it seems they have immense fields there full of cabbages and salad greens of every sort. There are also peach trees, lots of peach trees, for snails are very fond of peaches. In the fields and under the peach trees, by tens, by hundreds of thousands, by tens and hundreds of millions, live the snails. When an overripe peach falls from a tree, the snails direct their ocular antennae toward the fallen fruit, as the cannons of a fleet would take aim at the fort on the enemy's coastline. Slowly, but surely, they begin the offensive; they cling like leeches to the unfortunate peach, and in a few moments nothing remains but the pit, as dry as if it had been exposed to the desert sun for a week. Then, sated, the voracious mollusks move off, even more slowly than they came, leaving behind them that trail that everyone recognizes. Before snails are eaten they must be purged; to purge them one lets them fast for a period of from five to eight days." All these vivid descriptions were scarcely what was needed to encourage M. Dudron to eat snails, especially since he had a horror of mollusks in general and snails in particular. He had an innate aversion to all flabby substances lacking an internal armature. This was one reason why he disliked the painting of his contemporaries. Yet it would be wrong to deduce from this that he liked hard substances; thus, he felt no empathy for certain materials such as cast iron and steel. In painting as well he disliked hardness and stiffness; he liked neither the Primitives nor certain painters like Mantegna and Botticelli. He made an exception for Dürer. "But Dürer *n'est pas dur*," he had the habit of saying with a secret smile, "even though Vasari in his *Lives* calls him *il Duro*." For M. Dudron an ideal substance ought to be soft and fluid, but at the same time firm and solid; consequently his favorite painters were Veronese, Tintoretto, Velázquez, and Rubens. M. Dudron would have liked to explain all this to the lady who was trying to drag him off to the snail breeding grounds, but, whether he feared lest she understand not a word of what he was saying and even think him subject to attacks of lunacy, or whether on the other hand his atavistic politeness forbade him to contradict his interlocutrice, he pretended to accept enthusiastically the idea of going to eat snails that evening.

Precisely at seven the same roar he had heard that afternoon informed M. Dudron that the hour of departure had struck. The modern Valkyrie pushed her car to incredible speeds, but drove with such assurance and mastery that the vehicle was completely transformed; it was no longer an automobile made of metal and wood, but something tremendously elastic; it lengthened or shortened itself as the case required; it passed between two obstacles, grazing them with its metallic flanks, and emerged from them like an enormous flow of paste, with the movements of a gigantic and ultraswift caterpillar, only to plunge between two more obstacles even closer together than the first ones. They passed through the suburbs of the city. It was the hour when crowds of workers, having finished work, were bicycling home. They were returning home pedaling patiently and obstructing the whole street. They were pedaling patiently toward hearth and home, where their wives, their children, their parents, all those they loved, whom they cherished above all others, despite the quarrels that often broke out, and the misunderstandings, even though sometimes on Sundays, to amuse themselves and escape the boredom of family life and enjoy a few hours of liberty, they might abandon the house for nearby inns so as to meet their fellow workers, with whom they would empty bottles of wine and cider and stoppered bottles of beer, meanwhile playing cards and billiards and, when the weather was fine, at skittles behind the inns, in courtyards surrounded by fences among whose pickets stems of sunflowers were entwined.

Despite the vehicles of every sort which encumbered the street, the modern Valkyrie, with an assurance and ease which amazed and enchanted M. Dudron, transformed her car into a sort of reptile, a moray eel, slithering between one cyclist and another, between a car and a pe-

destrian, between two pedestrians, with a litheness that was wondrous
to behold. Once the city's suburbs were left behind the car turned onto
the highway. Meanwhile, night had fallen. To the north, near the heights
they were approaching, storm clouds had piled up. The livid glow of
lightning flashes picked out the black crests of mountains, of which one,
very distinctive because its crenelated summit bristled with enormous
teeth, like the jaw of a vanquished dragon, had been nicknamed the
Great Saw. Finding herself alone on the highway, the driver accelerated.
M. Dudron began to feel slightly ill. With a worried eye he followed the
movements of the speedometer's needle: 65, 70, 75, 80, 85, 100, 105, 115,
120, 125, 130. A hundred and thirty kilometers an hour in total darkness
far from the city, and it was the seventeenth of the month, an ill-omened
day. A few drops of rain began to fall, making the road terribly slippery.
M. Dudron was afraid. The night was complete; inside the car too,
darkness reigned, except for a few dials in front of the driver that were
faintly lit by a bluish, cold, wan, lunar, disturbing light, which made one
think of clinics where seriously ill patients dozed, patients who had re-
cently undergone surgery, and also of the laboratories of future centu-
ries, where strange and infernal inventions would have been perfected
by ingenious scientists with hydrocephalic heads like monstrous fetuses
preserved in alcohol. Against the windows and sides of the car one heard
the continuous murmuring of the riven air at an always increasing speed.
They passed through a small town already half-asleep; in the dim light
at the end of a park M. Dudron perceived for a moment the monument
erected by the inhabitants to the memory of the monarch who, at that
spot several decades previous, had been struck down by the regicide's
dagger. This fleeting vision transported M. Dudron back to the remote
time of his childhood; like scenery at the back of a stage which is gradu-
ally lit up, images defined themselves in his mind. He saw himself in his
father's house; it was also a stormy evening; his father had come in hold-
ing a newspaper on which was printed, in huge letters, news of the king's
assassination. M. Dudron remembered his father's anxious and saddened
face. On the walls of the study, amid photographs of various models of
locomotives, were two large portraits of the king and queen in black
carved-wood frames. M. Dudron was seated at his desk on which was
placed a small kerosene lamp with a conical glass shade that was the
green of a baize-covered billiard table. M. Dudron remembered that,
while his father was speaking, he himself was seated on the corner of a
divan, looking at the portrait of the king on the wall as it melted into

darkness and seemed to slide, to sink into the immense night of history and of time. From outside one could hear the lugubrious howling of the tempest that descended from the nearby mountains. Shaken by the wind, the branches of the eucalyptus trees in the garden tapped against the shuttered windows.

The violent glare of a lightning flash revealed the presence of a hill, a lake, and a small town. This brought M. Dudron back to reality. He rejoiced to think that the end of the mad race was approaching and that his fears and discomfort would soon be over. Having traversed the lacustrine town, the car began to climb a slope. The lady behind the steering wheel pointed out to him a villa in a garden; in that villa had lived and worked a famous novelist, whose monument stood in the town square, facing the lake; in the novelist's study everything had been left as it was: the table at which he wrote, his inkwell and pens, his armchair, his library, and even bits of bric-a-brac that happened to be there at the moment of his death. He died while working; one spring morning the old maidservant who tended him had, on entering the study, found him with his head on the table, as though asleep; outside the birds were twittering and the flowering trees shed their perfume; it has been claimed that the old servant had, in talking to her neighbors, recounted that on the eve of her master's death she had dreamed she saw him asleep, seated in his armchair, his head resting on the table, just as she had found him the next day. It was said also that on the day he died, despite the fact that no fire had been lit in the house, a very white puff of smoke had emerged from the chimney on the roof, climbed into the blue sky, and disappeared. The local citizenry believe it to have been the soul of the novelist flying off up into the depths of the sky.

As they climbed the slope, the speed of the car noticeably decreased. That made M. Dudron feel more optimistic. Finally they stopped in front of a vague building which gleamed white in the darkness. Several windows on the ground floor were illuminated. A glance revealed to M. Dudron an inn with a grocery shop and delicatessen beside it; he also had the impression that one could find lodging for the night there. However, this last impression was suggested to him by his subconscious in order to calm him: Nothing, in fact, allowed one to suppose that in this house there were rooms to let to travelers; yet, trusting the impression suggested by his subconscious, M. Dudron imagined that if, when the moment came to take his seat again in the car to return to his lodgings, a sudden discomfort followed by a gastric indisposition, produced by the fear of experiencing anew the fears and the emotions which had already shaken him, were to render his return impossible, he would have found a room there which would perhaps not have offered all the desirable comforts, but in which he might have been able to double-lock himself; a bed which mightn't perhaps have been too good, but in which he would have at last been able to stretch out and rest.

They went in through the grocery shop and immediately a strong odor of laundry soap mingled with an odor of rancid pork fat left M. Dudron with a disagreeable impression. Nonetheless, since the odor of soap reminded him that he had none at home, he immediately purchased a bar of toilet soap which he chose scented with eau de Cologne; he paid a derisory sum for this bar of soap. Despite the modest price and the insignificance of the purchase, the clerk waited on him with such eagerness, wrapped the soap in colored paper with so much care, tied it and offered it to M. Dudron with such deference and respectful courtesy that the latter suddenly experienced immense shame and at the same time enormous pity and great tenderness for the sales clerk; he would have liked to embrace him and weep with him, he would have liked to transform the humble shop into a vast and luxurious department store in which he could have purchased splendid and costly objects for large sums. But this was not possible: It was only a dream, and M. Dudron stopped imagining such unrealizable deeds; he passed on into the dining room of the inn, where a large rectangular table was already laid with a white cloth covered with glasses, plates, knives, and forks. Not far from the large table, like a colt keeping close to a mare, another, smaller table was laden with bottles of various sizes. There were also two-liter bottles containing local wine which, due to their size, dominated the others just as Achilles, son of Peleus, and Ajax, son of Telamon, dominated the other Greek heroes at the siege of Troy. This comforting view reassured M. Dudron; in spite of himself he felt his optimism born again. A new security, a kind of tranquil joy, blossomed within him. However, since fate never sends us happiness unalloyed, untinged with bitterness, M. Dudron suddenly noticed at the moment they were about to sit down at table that they were thirteen, while on a calendar on the wall the ill-omened date 17 was printed in red. It was too much. M. Dudron, having barely sat down, stood up, full of ferocious energy. No, a hundred times no, a thousand times no—amid such signs of calamity he refused categorically to take part in the dinner; he would rather have retraced on foot the fifty kilometers that separated him from his house; yes, he would have gone off alone in the profound night; alone on the rain-soaked highway; alone beneath the threat of the imminent storm; alone . . . but of a sudden a great remorse gripped the heart and the throat of M. Dudron; he had just caught sight, at the other end of the table, of the surprised and worried faces of the lady who had brought him there in her car and of the industrialist snail breeder. This spectacle made him hesitate; he was on the point of sitting down again when a providential servant who was more of a psychologist than he appeared to be saved the situation by bringing another, smaller table, where several place settings were hastily laid and where M. Dudron and two other guests who had joined him out of politeness, lest he assume the ridiculous appearance of someone sent to Coventry, took their places. The dinner was Homerically copious. A kind of small pincers suggesting obstetrical instruments was distributed to the snail fanciers: This produced a detestable sensation in M. Dudron. More than ever he felt doubt increasing within him concerning the intelligence and sensitivity of men in general and his contemporaries in particular. He refused to touch the snails, despite the inducements lavished on him by the other guests, who, not content with praising the extremely delicate flavor of these mollusks, spoke to him also of their valuable therapeutic qualities, especially with regard to respiratory ailments. The servants waiting on table mingled in the conversation, and one of them told how a young girl of the region, a consumptive who had tried all the remedies in vain, had finally been radically cured by eating nothing for two successive months but snails stuffed with chopped onion. But M. Dudron remained unshakable. He ate a leg of roast chicken after an hors d'oeuvre of ham and sardines in oil. Then he had himself served a plate of spinach with butter and, for dessert, an unsalted omelet filled abundantly with strawberry jam, the whole washed down with a glass of local wine. Having eaten, he took from his trouser pocket his pipe, his tobacco pouch, and a box of Swedish matches. He was thus readying himself to digest his meal calmly while savoring a well-deserved repose. But he hadn't reckoned with the wishes and the activity, both untiring and pointless, of the others; all the guests were already on their feet and, led by the industrialist, were preparing to visit the breeding grounds. He had to resign himself: M. Dudron emptied his pipe into an ashtray and pocketed it along with the snuffbox and the matches, buttoned up his jacket, and, seeking to remain steadfast in the face of adversity, followed the other guests. Outdoors it was as dark as the inside of an oven. Lightning flashes streaked the sky and opened up cracks, breaches, and fissures of livid and blinding light. The guests, holding each other's hands, advanced with difficulty, their feet sinking into the soggy ground as they stumbled against stones and tree roots, like the blind people in the famous Brueghel painting. The storm howled as it grew nearer; big tepid drops fell with a dull thud on the ground and on plants. Gusts of wind passed. M. Dudron raised his head and looked up at the clouds, which formed a kind of dark, low ceiling. He saw Aeolus and Boreas flying side by side, holding each other by the waist, like figures of Michelangelo; they puffed out their cheeks like the masks on fountains, to exhale their implacable wrath downward, on the earth and on men.

"Here we are!" cried someone at one end of the human caterpillar.

They had at last arrived at the famous breeding grounds. Some called for flashlights, others contented themselves with rubbing matches; but the matches went out as soon as they were lit, while as for flashlights, no one had any.

"There's one!" cried a guest who had seen or thought he saw a snail.

"There are two!" exclaimed another.

M. Dudron, despite the laudable effort he was making, didn't succeed in catching sight of a single snail.

Meanwhile it had begun to rain in earnest. The retreat was sounded; the chain came apart, each member seeking to reach the inn as fast as possible; they slogged through puddles; it was worse than a retreat, it was a debacle. Suddenly M. Dudron found himself next to the Valkyrie, near the car; the lady climbed in behind the steering wheel; M. Dudron settled himself in the vehicle as well as he could and they took off at top speed. The skies had opened; the wind had fallen; long, luminous cables, perfectly perpendicular, joined sky to earth; the rain fell without ceasing; the ground bubbled up. When they crossed anew the little lakeside town, the streets had been transformed into torrents. The wheels of the car sank into the water up to the axles. Not a single passerby. The lady driver had lost her way; she no longer knew which road to take; in vain did she draw up before houses with blinds hermetically shut, ringing the bell and calling out like a knight-errant demanding hospitality on a stormy night before a castle with a raised drawbridge. No one replied. Only the continuous roar of the storm, the sound of water flowing from all directions. Anxiety again overtook M. Dudron; he thought of catastrophes; memories of terrifying floods in California or China, awesome scenes of which he had seen long ago in illustrated newspapers, came to mind; he imagined the little town carried off by the waters and drowned in the lake; quadrupeds, oxen, horses struggling against the currents; women in nightgowns, their hair undone, gripping a child with one arm and, with the other, clinging to the shutters, the balconies of partly submerged houses; half-naked men on the roofs coming to the rescue, throwing out ropes to the unfortunates struggling in the water, and then the lake overflowing, unfurling on the plain and going to meet, in that other city in the distance, the house in which he jealously sequestered his pictures, his books, his keepsakes, all the things he loved and without which he could not have lived. A real horror, that!

Suddenly the lady uttered a whoop of joy; she had just noticed a directional sign; one must turn left, then right, then left again, and at last one would arrive on the great open road. They left the town behind. The speed increased. M. Dudron noticed with pleasure that as they moved away from the lake and the mountains the intensity of the rain diminished. After a few kilometers he had the impression that it was no longer raining; he looked out and saw the stars overhead. "It's probably the mountains and especially the one they call the Great Saw, which is higher than the others, that give rise to and develop the storms," thought M. Dudron. Now he felt completely reassured; in spite of the speed of the car, everything seemed to breathe security and tranquility; that made him think again of the relativity of all things. They passed again through the small town with the monument commemorating the assassination of the king; but this time it was something else which was to awaken strong, deep, and strange emotions in M. Dudron. As they crossed a square surrounded by porticos topped by houses whose windows were all shut, the car's headlights violently illuminated for a moment a large ornamental pond at whose center a spurting fountain made a large white spot. The appearance of this fountain which, in the middle of the deserted square, in the small town plunged in deep sleep, continued to play, to toss into the air a profusion of watery sheaves, to raise its song in the profound night, awoke in M. Dudron strange and highly metaphysical feelings; he suddenly felt an immense pity for the fountain and also a kind of shame at having to flee and abandon it again to the silence, solitude, and darkness. Yes, the car should be stopped at once; they should run and knock on the doors of houses; awaken everybody; ring the bells; bring torches; light all the lights; hang Venetian lanterns under the porticos, place carpets and festoons on the balconies and the windows; weave garlands; summon musicians with their instruments;

organize dances; open casks of wine; fill the square with rejoicing people; in a word, do something so that the poor fountain wouldn't be left alone to spurt and sing in the midst of the great desert and the silence of the night. But the car passed quickly by and with a pang M. Dudron saw the fountain sink and disappear in darkness.

Soon they had arrived. M. Dudron, most content to find himself back among his lares and penates, bade the lady good night, thanked her, and entered his home. Despite his fatigue, he felt no need of sleep. He opened the window and rested his elbows on the sill. Numerous stars shone in the depths of a sky black as ink. Some shone in groups, some in rows or else alone, at a great distance from the others. M. Dudron thought of the vanity of his sacrifices, of his unpaid debts, of his compromised position. Instead of pitying himself and wallowing in pessimistic reflections on destiny and man, he remembered his youth when the idea had come to him of the means of renewing not only *his painting* but *painting itself.* A formidable pride mingled with memories of the sweetest sort arose within him. He saw again the places of his first experiments and his first works in the new vein. Yes, he saw those places again; the valley stretching into the distance under the soft light of the September sun. Blocks of red sandstone rose up here and there and in the distance larger rocks formed a kind of cliff looming over the open country, which was covered with ripe wheat wherein poppies made red spots. Opposite him, on a hill, the greenery was so abundant and the trees so bushy that they almost hid the houses and villas. To his right, the whole of an estate appeared to be painted on canvas. Tile roofs indicated a farm. The castle, its façade decorated with columns, was situated in the midst of a wood farther on, and a lawn came down as far as the river where a line of poplars was reflected in the water. "Memories!" thought M. Dudron, and completely lost in reveries he continued to gaze at the stars. A zone of luminous dust extending from the Septentrion to the south bifurcated above his head. Among these zones of light were vast empty spaces, and the firmament resembled a great sea of a very deep and dark azure, with archipelagoes, islands, and islets. He remembered what he had read or heard: Behind the Milky Way are the nebulae; beyond the nebulae, stars and more stars without number; the closest is separated from us by three hundred billion myriameters! He turned toward the Great Bear, which he had always loved, looked for the polestar and then Cassiopeia and its constellation. At the same time M. Dudron continued to reflect and talk to himself: "For that," he said "it would be necessary to reevoke a past which, to all evidence, should not have reappeared on memory's stage. It would be necessary, through actions which have already gone on for several years and have allowed the real culprits to indulge in scurrilous operations, to proceed to divers verifications, either in the milieux of the Law, or in the direction of that *other shore* where we seek the reward of an exhausting if not downright dangerous labor."

Suddenly M. Dudron felt a strong shudder penetrate his whole body. "Pneumonia," he thought with anguish; he saw himself laid low by the disease, looked after by indifferent attendants. He was frightened. He came back inside, shut the window, and drew the curtains. He lay down after taking the precaution of placing on his bed, so as to be warmer, all his suits and his overcoat, adding to these an old rug spotted with ink, which happened to be on a table and whereon one could see embroidery depicting Hindu warriors brandishing torches and herding elephants before them. He further added some old newspapers he found at the back of a closet. He stretched out and soon the heat of the bed comforted him. He began to contemplate a picture on an easel that he had finished several days ago, which was faintly lit by the candle he had placed on his bedside table. The sky was an orange-yellow and was reflected in the sea. The horizon was indicated by a flaming red line. In the sky a few small clouds, whose rotundity was modeled by purple shadows, were sailing, scattered like sheep in a pasture. On the top of a cliff overhanging the sea, a sanctuary made a white blur. In front of it, on the shore among some fragments of broken columns which testified to the decrepitude of human constructions, stood a group of people; a young warrior was holding by the bridle a large white horse whose disproportionately large tail trailed on the ground like a solid, curly avalanche. On the other side an athletic old man, a sort of Hercules in repose, was leaning on a boulder, gazing at the distant sea with a pensive air.

"Here," thought M. Dudron, "is what is most pleasing to the people who concern themselves with painting today, to intellectuals and homosexuals. For them, painting is nothing more than a question of images. Our epoch will surely remain celebrated in the history of art for the ignorance of those who will have concerned themselves with painting. They don't understand that the image means nothing at all and that the only thing that saves painting from oblivion, valorizes it, is its *quality*. But let's put aside," he continued, "those thorny questions that time alone will be able to resolve and immerse ourselves anew in metaphysical questions, not to give pleasure to a certain category of our contemporaries, but because that side of painting attracts as much as the other. This picture, is it the memory of a past life which now, in the eternal present, attaches itself to my life? Memories of what was and expectation of what will be; idle or laborious vigils and you, my excellent sleep, who each night cuddles me gently in your arms! You, my excellent sleep, heavy and slow as a great river! The wave where I shall sleep definitively approaches from age to age . . . !"

M. Dudron's eyelids grew heavy; he had to make an effort to keep his eyes open. Then he blew out the candle, stretched out voluptuously under the covers, and, after turning over two or three times on his couch, finally fell into a deep sleep; and he dreamed.

It was still night but the stars had disappeared. M. Dudron found himself in a kind of park or public garden of an unparalleled romanticism and banality. One could see monuments in marble or bronze representing scholars, politicians, and generals who had rendered services to science or to their country. The scholars and the politicians were almost always represented seated in an armchair with a pensive expression, holding in one hand a scroll or a book; the military men were standing, sword in hand, gazing into the distance; at their feet one saw shattered cannons and cannonballs arranged in pyramids. Ivy grew everywhere; one also saw everlastings, ruins, sanctuaries, moss, and grottoes. Here and there tiny rustic bridges had been thrown across brooks which murmured gently among the plants and the pebbles. A kind of Rialto bridge spanned an ornamental pond whose edges were incrusted with mussel shells. Along the dim and deserted walks of this park M. Dudron was strolling slowly as he held by the shoulders a little girl with a melancholy and intelligent expression, pressing her to him. It was the daughter of the woman he loved. "It's her daughter!" thought M. Dudron in his dream, and this thought flooded his heart with infinite sweetness. The landscapes he had loved reappeared in memory, in the dream. Dream or reality, everything was there, everything. Toys taken out of cardboard boxes, varnished and shiny toys spread out on the dining room table on winter evenings, while outside the snow places white hoods everywhere and bells announce the approaching holidays. Warriors of colored lead; tiny houses of unexcelled cleanness; crèches and boats on wheels. All palpable joy, joy one can take home with one, all the guarantees of happiness that even the gods, yes, even those very gentle gods with silky blond beards who squint ineffably, those same gods with distant expressions who smile without understanding anything, those gods who basically know nothing for the simple reason that *there is nothing to know*, yes, even those gods who hesitate to sign and who, before affixing their absolutely illegible signatures at the bottom of the solemn sheets of paper witnessed by Fate and stamped by Eternity, squirm and chew their mustaches and scratch their jaws under their beards with a preoccupied air. But once one has obtained it, that sheet of paper, one can be tranquil, and that for a long time. M. Dudron knew it as he knew that he dreamed. Consequently he was by no means astonished when he perceived that the little girl had disappeared and the décor had changed completely. Box trees whose bitter perfume the heat exacerbated were the sole adornment of a dark and dank gorge where the impetuous water of cold torrents murmured sonorously. And, suddenly, an oasis. The horizon had broadened. Tall trees joined their leafy fronds together and danced in a circle around green lawns where the river, calmed at last, unrolled its silver garlands. Above this unexpected landscape, near a small waterfall which seemed to spring from a rock, an altar, a block of white marble with drapery of a very tender orange-yellow hue thrown on top of it and falling to the ground in classical folds, and, at the base of the altar, roses and branches of laurel. M. Dudron's mother was there, looking as she did when she was young; she was there, seated on the tender sward in a tranquil and resigned pose of prayer and meditation; she was very beautiful; she had the look of a woman in the Bible. In the sky, a brilliant dawn lit up the world with a diffuse light from which the shadows had disappeared. M. Dudron, advancing slowly as though his feet were chained, wanted to approach his mother, but the décor changed once again. It was noon. The sun shone on the countryside, blanketed with yellow wheat. The canvas hood of a wagon slipped away far in the distance. Torpor hung in the air. No bird called, no insect hummed.

"I have returned by tortuous roads," thought M. Dudron in the dream as he looked at the new landscape, "I have returned by roads where sharp pebbles, briars and thorns were not lacking, alas! I have returned to that study of life which I put aside many years ago. I was interested in mountains and coasts, in outlines that define the shores of seas, in the anatomy of branches that differ from tree to tree, in the colors of the sky which change according to the times of day, the weather and the seasons. I believed that all these aspects posed problems of the most numerous, the most complicated, and the most fascinating kind. And yet, well, you have to think of other things too. So that you aren't crushed, or, at any rate, disturbed; so that your thoughts remain natural, you mustn't use too bright a light. Often the demands of life are in direct opposition to those sometimes very numerous ones of the milieu in which you wish to act, work, create, amuse yourself, relax, have fun, and finally live, in a word! One must decoct a very precise and special dosage from the various sources from which one draws one's inspirations. How well I know the joy of discoveries and the bitterness of disappointments. Yes, I remember clearly that pellucid and distant winter day. An immense lassitude weighed on me; the unimaginably pure horizon glittered like a shard of eternity, and at the harborside the shadows of masts and chimneys stretched a long way, as far as the houses, as far as the offices of the great shipping firms, as far as the stores from which issued an odor of leather, tar, and smoked fish."

Thus spoke M. Dudron to himself in a dream, and meanwhile that fear accompanied by the sensation of a slight stomachache which he had felt until now dissipated completely, giving way to a feeling of calm and security. Thus it was without emotion that in his dream he found himself suddenly caught up in a bear hunt, in the depths of a forest: "Be careful," said a voice close by, "the animal is only wounded, he's going to throw himself on the hunter!"

Scarcely had he heard these words when a shot rang out and M. Dudron awoke. He stretched, yawned, looked for his watch, and saw that it was ten o'clock. "It's the neighbor's boy again," M. Dudron exclaimed, "who has wakened me with his shooting at targets in the garden."

In thinking of the neighbor's son, he remembered with sadness that adopted son, that child he had cherished so much and for whom both he and his wife had made so many sacrifices, even in the most difficult times of their lives. They hoped that later on these sacrifices would bear fruit; they hoped that when Bruno (as the child was named) had reached adolescence, they might have guided him toward studies in law or mathematics so as to turn him into a lawyer or an engineer, in sum into an honest man first of all, and then also into a hardworking and serious one. And suddenly, one morning as M. Dudron and his wife entered Bruno's bedroom to bring him his cocoa, they found the little bed empty and his sailor suit on a chair. A letter, prominently placed on the mantelpiece, explained everything: "I'm leaving," the letter said, " because someone down there has offered me more; I'm giving you back your sailor suit whose extremely harsh wool has made me suffer cruelly, as though I were wearing around my neck and wrists a necklace and two bracelets made of nettles. I have no further need of these clothes, for with the money given me I have bought a magnificent lounge suit, with a golfing cap and shoes with triple soles reinforced by one of rubber."

Someone, meaning it was still him, that immensely rich shipping magnate with the long chin and short, knock-kneed legs, who had seduced him and persuaded him to flee, their Bruno, their child! In a *postscriptum* to the letter, the prodigal son had added, *"a villa has been placed at my disposal."*

Yes, he had fled, their turtledove. Like a coward, like a traitor he had fled. The years had passed, more or less sad, as all years pass. Now, down in the vast, solemn white city where the dark and intransigent militarized tribunes stood watch in their severe uniforms, Bruno, mature, successful, bent over beneath the huge vaulted dome to hear the sonorous and polyphonic waves that rose ceaselessly from the melodic caverns, from those caverns which housed, in tight and disciplined rows, formidable orchestras led by long-haired and contorted conductors who, grimacing frightfully and with epileptic gestures, urged ever higher the sublimity of great unfinished symphonies.

M. Dudron reflected thus on the prodigal son, but with neither hatred nor anger. "After all," he told himself, "it's every man for himself: That's the law that rules the world." At the same time he blamed himself for having more than once *missed his chance*. He looked at his bedroom that daylight illuminated and thought of his dreams in the night and his adventures of the evening before. "It's the mysterious life that begins every morning," he said to himself. He knew that on arising he would have to accede to the total assurance of the clean-shaven, well-shod, and smartly dressed man, who touches the buttoned inside pocket of his jacket where he feels the wallet he knows to be supplied with large banknotes and checks to be cashed, with cards of identity and passports that are perfectly in order, and who, moreover, knows that in the other pockets of his suit is everything necessary, nay indispensable, to the far-sighted man, healthy in mind and body, when he leaves his dwelling to hazard himself in that forest, always mysterious and thick with surprises, that a great modern city is, namely: fountain pen, appointment and address book, penknife, small wooden tube containing tincture of iodine, small roll of court plaster, watch and compass, metal box containing at least six pills to combat a possible headache, tobacco pouch duly filled, pipe, matches, piece of rusty iron or coral horn to touch when passing a funeral or an individual reputed to have the evil eye, and, in general, all persons and things likely to cause misfortune.

Having consulted his watch, M. Dudron perceived that it was high time to get dressed and go out. Go out, yes, but where? All that was now no longer sufficient to calm his mind, which had become bucolic and tolerant due to circumstances beyond his control. As far as *excursions in the city* went, he knew henceforth how to proceed. He knew those great centers where the mechanized instincts of millions and millions of his fellow creatures converged and where, night and day, a crowd exasperated by the struggle for life pitched and tossed beneath harmonious groups sculpted in marble tarnished by fog and smoke and which, on their cubical pedestals, represented music, dance, thought, and poetry. "To be satisfied with oneself"—thought M. Dudron—"isn't everything; one must still obtain that series of small victories which assure our position in life and erect around us ramparts indispensable for protecting us from the assaults which our fellow citizens, whoever they may be, launch at us sooner or later. True, there is Nature. Nature!" The sound of this word evoked in M. Dudron's mind images that were far from reassuring. He saw before him deserted beaches and milky, terribly calm seas. On the horizon a sun, a tragically red and solitary disk, descended slowly amid vapors. "Horizon that smokes," thought M. Dudron. A monstrous animal with the head of a parrot, a mass as black and huge as a mountain, emerged slowly from the water and dragged itself along the sand among shellfish, some of which stirred a little, then collapsed and stayed motionless. Next, there were black, tranquil lakes surrounded by dark fir trees. Behind, tall mountains raised their summits whose long crevasses were full of snow, like flows of white lava. From the top of a cliff, a cascade tumbled into the lake. Though it was quite far away, the sound it made reached M. Dudron, so motionless was the air and so complete the silence.

M. Dudron remained thoughtful and undecided. "The fact is," he said to himself, "all that displeases me as much as the spectacle of agitated and mechanized cities. True, there are also men, humanity: the young seamstresses who work until late at night to provide for the needs of a valetudinary father, of an aged mother, of little brothers who must be clothed and fed, whose schooling must be paid for. In the lamplight they ply their needles while their thought flies down toward the fiancé, toward the lover who will drive them on Sunday to the country where they will gather wild strawberries and drink fresh milk at the tenant farm. Yet sometimes there are also treason and dramas. The unwed mother, carrying her child in her arms, hiding behind the pillars of the church like a hunted animal and there, close by, through the chords of the organ playing the wedding march and the odor of the incense, *he* who passes by, in his wedding suit, clean-shaven, with his wife leaning on his arm, *his* wife, all in white and crowned with orange blossoms, and behind them the inevitable cortège of relatives, friends, and guests."

M. Dudron stood up; he slid his feet into his slippers and drew on his dressing gown. His decision was made; it was irrevocable. He sat down at his easel, armed himself with his palette and brushes, and, taking up a picture he had laid out the evening before, began peacefully to paint.

Paris, May 1939

Hebdomeros: With Monsieur Dudron's Adventure and Other Metaphysical Writings (Cambridge, Mass.: Exact Change, 1992).

PIERRE REVERDY

(1889–1960)

HAUNTED HOUSE

Under the rampart of fire, the reassuring details of the bedroom slowly come into focus.

Down below is the rather sinister street, mysterious, with or without passersby, very dark in places, and dimly lit at the corner by strips of light filtering through shutters.

Behind them wealth is being counted, the product of legal plunder. They laugh at how easy larceny is when it's protected by the law. Emaciated men bite each other beneath the dank sky, clouded with heavy blotches of mold of the rotten seasons. Men glare at each other like dogs with hackles bristling as they pass each other on unsafe roads. Men swarm in the choking fog of emptiness, the haunting featherbed of death. They have nightmares and wake up sweating under the heavy covers. When the weight of remorse crushes the conscience of inept workmen, when blood spurts under clothing that is too light for winter, when penury has reduced man to the level of old corks floating in good-natured eddies of the river, blinding flashes of reason seem, to insensitive eyes that judge coldly, like an unbearable enticement. Revolt has placed its white feet on the sill of the passionate personality. Crater in whose depths boils the lava of feelings—one's character. Love has closed its ring around the head and the heart. Hate has outlined the man's back in the night with its needle-sharp stylus. There are tooth marks in the sickly, though firm, flesh of matter. Venomous claws have left suspect swollen traces on the blank screen of the mind. And the man's back, at the corner of the wooden fence, is inscribed forever in the mystery of hatred and of night.

Henceforth no heroic thought will ever come to lean at the ship's rail. No lightning flash of illusion will ever again register on the sensitive plate of desire, and whatever thrusts the crippled being into the gulf that separates him from his ultimate destiny will be only an impulse without a cause. The resources of concrete aspirations having been irreparably spoiled, their foundations destroyed, common sense corroded below the waterline and the asperities of fantasy eroded by the perpetual tonguing of the waves, soiled by foam, the squinting gaze of platitude surfaces prudently to consummate the disaster.

The sordid feet of misfortune will come and swell the ranks of the loathsome gang that sinks deeper into the mud left by these whirlpools of glutinous water. That sinister gang marching complacently toward death. Then if meticulously honed screams begin to rip the night, the sleeping eardrums, the shredded hearts, the wilted souls, the crooked reckonings, the screen of cowardice, the skin of hands without gifts, the veils of palates, the pupils of the eyes, and the dawn of ideas, these troops of shepherds will be rolled like a ball before the storm; along the tracks hewn in the marble of the quays they will be seen running like clouds of smoke caught in the underbrush, transfixed against the parapet of their fragile consciences. And yet it's the beginning of a new life that has been placed on the shelf of daybreak, this morning. A dawn like whipped cream made all the leaves weep for miles around, sorrow streamed along the living timbers, in secret channels and as far as the sluices of the human heart.

On a lattice gate as solid as the lack of mutual understanding that will divide us until death, all the eyes that have been emptied, hollowed out, gnawed by innocent or unhealthy curiosity as though by leprosy, reach out to each other through the bars. Along that trajectory all the signs, predictions, precepts, and prophecies that involve the fate of human-kind rush, pass, and jostle one another.

One waits, one hopes that in a little while the black veil that hides from man the meaning of his own life will be ripped away. The restraints that maintain the limits of reason will be relaxed, the grasp of the iron fist will loosen, fluid matter will overflow a little onto the depilated moorland of madness.

The screw propellers of humankind sometimes trick the hypnotic surveillance of the inner lighthouse to come and beat the ashes of ennui.

Among the numbered chairs, labeled with infinitely dishonored names, the impalpable atmosphere of stormy meetings in Antiquity enters and silently lies down. For old age persists across the carelessly mortared flagstones where beads of sweat break out; weak indestructible roots still conduct a little sap that touches elbows, nets, and joints with a note of green. The switchblade of life is shut in the churches and under the moss of prayers that snakes along the walls, between the disjointed double doors, under the carelessly clasped hearts of penitents ravaged by the rebellious couch grass of doubt, seeking the way out.

At what hour will we be forced to bow our foreheads forever? At what hour will someone come to visit the man condemned to the torture of love without an object and of reasons without hope? At what hour will someone come to change the air of this frightful cell? He stretches his arms out toward landscapes shivering behind glass lashed by the rain, rubbed down by the wind, through the grating and the bars of fire that guard the entrance to a land always promised and always refused. The imagination contracts at the brush with reality like an oyster under the drop of lemon juice that wounds it. Where are you going, miserable wanderer in space?

Poverty hounds you, fatigue hurts you. Stop where you are. Cease to follow in vain this deep highway that cunningly eats away, like scabies, at the greasy epidermis of night. Rest, at last, since your eye perceives the light that filters through curtains of the inn, at the hour when fever diverts its perfidious sparrow hawk toward the world, the hour when forests tremble under the frantic caresses of crystal-fingered delirium.

If you must finally choose to contemplate flight, close the main gate; dogs are barking in the dangerous courtyard and blood beats under the temples like the shutters against the wall.

The sensitive and white man consigned to all the offshore winds, to all the caprices of fortune; he who lacks the motor of shame, the perches of friendship, the breeze from the magnetic crowds. As we were coming down between the black satin cliffs, along paths of unangry sand, on the trail of voices fleeing toward oblivion—missing the goal. As we were crossing deep railways, Despair and I, in the ice and the sea, the hoop of ripe fruits on the cup of the world, our pectoral muscles gnawed by pain, our flesh lacerated from the nape to the lower tendons, the ghosts of the embankment, under the rain of iron dust, told us this story.

When the world had finally renounced forever, in a final burst of sublime heroism, that man without a name, body or face, he went out, unnoticed by the most vigilant reporters, through a basement door of the meanest house in the neighborhood.

Beyond the threshold one steps immediately into a nightmare. The almost weightless pink-and-green sky is attached to the rusted hooks of the gutter by transparent threads of the thaw. It's cold on the slopes of the atmosphere; the buttresses have turned into massive blocks of ice that will never become fissured in the sun as in the past. The foundations are nevertheless unshakable, too deeply sunk in the earth for that. But the road, a straight road, terribly straight, straight enough to make rascals shudder, scores the silence, between window glass and diamond. Trusting in our freedom and only in our freedom, we advance, turning back somewhat frightened toward the left, our backs frozen, no matter how we move, by a crushing void of silence, surprised to see such a distinct line, a light-colored band, yellowish, clean, well tamped down and washed by the weather, the fine weather. Between the hedges of blood we plunge into the underbrush of shame and anguish, leaving behind paths beaten by the rubber-tired wheels of happiness, into the mazes of suffering.

What are you doing there, you, skyscraper without hope or life, empty nest, without satisfaction, amid rectilinear forms, cast shadows, streets without atmosphere, drunken sidewalks, abandoned windows, uninhabited water drops, songs without light, heads with no price on them, hearts without matches, portraits without models, drawn and quartered nudes, advantages of integrity, speculations on the stock market of health, poorly ventilated neighborhoods, and finally migraines of overheated poetry, before a jury of robust men covered with feathers, sharpened into penholders in the form of skeletons, men of letters, actually? What are you doing? Needing to get a little air after a copious repast beneath the chandeliers of glowworms, in the groves of civil war, isn't a sufficient excuse. It's an imprudent act fatal to stronger temperaments to come and glean, without authorization, the trash strewn over the ground when the foam of revolutionary waves has barely finished bubbling in the sawdust of the sidewalk cafés on the boulevard.

It would be wiser to go home now, while lamps are shattering everywhere, and bury your luminous heart deep in your pillows, behind the livid, trembling windowpanes and the partly drawn curtains of fear.

But the half-naked mind contemplates the wild manes of the wind, the barely subjugated mind always awakens facing the morning it will have to penetrate in the throng of human gargoyles.

A mischievous child whose bloodstream ferries blocks of ice, slag, pincushions, was killing time by fervently placing the famous grain of salt on the tails of frivolous philosophers.

Obstinate, however, those birds of ill omen continually fled his approach and eluded his mettle. Later on, what disappointment, what hatred of the fraudulence of which thought is capable when he discovers the true nature of those mechanical toys that for so long tricked him into thinking they were alive.

By sheer force of running his cheeks catch fire, his chest comes alive, and his lungs, transported from one end to the other of the plateau, sponge the air with agile hands and push it to one side.

But soon the anguish of days without bread draws zigzags on his forehead like the sky bleeding on the horizon despite its bandages, that feverish wound of the sky that all the clouds will never succeed in extinguishing.

And yet it is a passenger without fear and without remorse that is resting his elbows now on the balustrade of night. It is not good to be taller than the stem of the ship that plows the ocean of love when that tall white body of a blond woman, blended with her mind like yeast in dough, stands up. At the arrival in port and even closer to the jetty a vigorous wrist constantly planes the sea.

The shavings come and flutter in wild pirouettes on the beach. The inhabitants of the land's open sea, toughened by the heat, have abandoned the countryside broiled to a crisp under summer's grill. They are there to watch the rebellious child gnawing his lessons at the edge of his raft, head cupped in his hands, mind lost in the thickets of the dictionary. He sulks, poking furious fingers into the underbrush of everything he knows. He scorns those ridiculous folk who have assembled to contemplate the sea's profile. He laughs. He laughs. He sprinkles between him and the inquisitive and mean-spirited crowd the powdered laugh that, mingled with the powder of water climbing the reefs, shields him from the sparks of ennui.

But at the bottom of gorges, under the echoing caverns of day, the sound rushes into the depths of the ear like ocean waves through a hole in a rock.

This silence I have kept for thirty years. This vermilion silence swollen in my chest. This blue or black silence like blood trapped under the skin, exploding like a full-blown sun under the thorns, is the death's-head perched on its root. For the sheaves of liberty are soon bound and smothered under the coils of words. And a reflection of that liberty, before everything, against everything, lands smoothly on the wing of the right note.

The cruelties of virtue revolt and join forces to block our path. But we have time. Chain for chain, we shall treat the mind roughly. First of all we shall refuse it that closeted heroism which won't survive the first injection. It's not for nothing that blood coagulates in all the hollows of the dry slopes of the hills. In the cries of the bushes, where shreds of macerated flesh hide themselves, there are also tatters of those fine days that end so badly. Tragic bathing accidents in the hertzian waves and on the sand of coast guard stations where those waves come to die, shuddering through all their moldings. The blond liqueurs of the last fine days of autumn rekindle the veins spread out on the thistles of the light, under pine trees shriveled by the heat. The air is completely inundated with beads of sweat, with the sound of bells.

As for me, I'm shipping out on the triremes of the sun, to earn my living with the robins.

Splendid architecture of negation, tortuous lairs of doubt, tangled subbasements of terror! Where are you going now with that gash in the fabric of reason that renders its impotence so pathetic!

You count the days like gold coins with the contorted gestures of a miser. And its lightning darts between your legs; it is ground down with anguish and stupor. It's cold under the vaults, and the arcades, and the atriums of this circular world, in the countryside with its swelling hips, under the oppressive cloister of the fog.

You think of the undiscoverable nest of those islands that have left it to go and fold their wings again on the surface of the sea.

They will never take flight again, anchored offshore by an inexorable fate. And you, look at you, burning in a sea more desiccated and arid than a desert of salt, your feet bloody, your head on fire, your hands empty, your heart tender as a sun-bud in April. And this heart without reason, this pressure without remission, this blood against the forehead, and finally this life without savor and without pardon. For you issued from a tainted spring and the pleasures of time are no longer accessible except to your desires. Beautiful shop windows, magnificent displays of merchandise, muffled temptations, among which you are marching, I'll explain it to you later, for now it's useless that you know, you'd get confused. You may as well creak with pain, like an old mast, it's all one to me.

Poisoned gold and blood trickle everywhere, incense, derelict songs, temperate visions, all those symbolic adornments and, at the end of this dark corridor, all the darker because it comes after the explosion of luxurious living in the open air, in broad daylight, there is the altar; the impassive hieroglyph of the altar.

When, a little farther on, the puffy and gilded hill, smoking and scented, has just emerged from the oven, wouldn't it be wiser to cast a glance through the first slit in those cracked old walls at inexplicable real life and to forget, in the slight noise of aerial pulsations, the lugubrious antechamber of the tomb?

One cannot, beneath the ashes of boredom and the slabs of stupidity, abolish that flaming vision of love. For behold, in the liquidation of the past, the stimulus of envy, the uneven parquet of dismal fields sown with grain, the dark swollen sea of the passions, salt, the salt of evaporated air, moldy bread, snow hardened in the grooves of winter, time carefully folded and stored in crates, on the docks, next to the new lights, songs permitted and forbidden, the joy of living, unpunished crimes, hearts laden with boredom, distress subdued, peace and prosperity forever compromised, knot-free boards of silence, gaping abysses of fear, delicate zigzags of madness, staccato tenterhooks of murder, icy feet of terror, cold hands of justice, exhausted limbs, head empty of confessions, lassitude that oxidizes reason, alcohol that perforates the flesh and the Earth which is only the rattling bead in an immense silver sleigh bell, across which, still counting the scales of the roof and the gleaming slates of the fish, the convict has slipped back to his penal colony through the crafty slit of the guillotine between the severity and the honesty of the judges where not even a hair could pass through. It's not a question of entering the other world, it's a question of getting out of it. If one may, at the end, succeed in saying what one has to say. Since, as we know well, reading letters backward isn't enough and one must, for the merest trifles, live backward, traveling from death throes back to birth. The flight is accomplished only under the most horrendous circumstances, past the treacherous shoals of liberty, the countless nuisances at street intersections, virgin forests, and the aristocratic outback of the suburbs, close surveillance by the police, prisons of ice, myriad lights of the boulevard, and the steep slope of the emotions that file down his heart from minute to minute.

Here begins the nacreous part of this narrative. At the head of the street that pours headlong into the square like a river into the sea, at the street corner, stands the sinister tavern where the crime occurred. No one could ever find a motive for that atrocious scene of carnage other than madness. Motive? Madness to subjugate, I mean. The cabaret singers could no longer make ends meet. They were considered too happy, too reasonable, and it became necessary to revamp the place and call it

At the Sign of the Dangerous Idiot.[1] What excellent cider you could drink there! There was dancing at all hours of the day and night. Then a few who found that time weighed too heavily on them fell asleep. They were found next morning hanging, like sailors in their hammocks, in the cobwebs of marriage. The others were dead, they were heaved outside, the current dashed them against the pilings of the terrace. And the prospect of wealth finally swept away the last few who had had the patience to wait. For, naturally, the chief ferment in all this rage had its source in the need for glory and gold as it always has.

During this time, on deserted highways licked avidly by an icy wind, we ventured out, Despair and I, to get clear of misfortune by wandering in the marshlands. If, at the exit from an ordinary local road that has already brought us here from quite far away, there is a lugubrious and isolated house that we more than anyone are surprised to find in such a profoundly sinister spot, it must be owned that it was not placed there to reassure us. Indeed, this house, whose literally inconceivable existence was inexplicable in such a cruelly ravaged spot, had an appearance of life more chilling than an appearance of death would have been in different circumstances. As the crow flies, the vertical meanders of the road couldn't be made out, but from our vantage point one could easily see the rows of trees of different species which lined it. There were dwarf trees and giant trees, trees with smooth bark and others with gnarled trunks, svelte ones and scraggly ones. The house was at the center of a vast garden, itself surrounded by an incredibly high wall. It occurred to us to wonder why a wall so high had been built in so deserted a place. From where we stood, still teetering unsteadily on a steep slope, we couldn't see much beyond the green borders of the road, the rather tall hedgerows and the branches of the trees, all of which contributed, along with the wall and the vagrants it was no doubt meant to discourage, to the grisaille of the sky.

For everything there contributed to the grisaille of landscape and sky, especially the branches of the trees lining the road, the hedgerows scoring the landscape, the thickets, the woods, the vagrants, and finally the season and even the hair that is beginning not to flourish on our heads, yet which nevertheless prevents us from seeing the sky as blue as it perhaps is for some.

In a word the wind was gray and, though calm until now and only stirring the tips of the dead leaves, it began to blow violently. It seemed to follow the road naturally, as if it were a corridor. It was traveling at a crazy speed. We were perhaps afraid. A fear penetrated us perhaps at that moment, for our legs gave way, and we turned our backs to the gale, clutching our headgear with our hands. Our clothes, glued to our bodies on one side, were flapping on the other. We felt like stems of grass in a torrent.

I no longer know what feeling seized us at that moment, nor if we were precisely afraid or if we were ready for anything. But suddenly I saw Despair turn toward me with an effort and plunge his deep gaze into my sea-green pupils; then, with a common accord, having said nothing (for the wind would have carried the sound away), we abruptly turned our backs to the storm.

That is, we abandoned all hope of successfully struggling further against the incredible violence of the wind, which thereupon carried us along as easily as it would have pounced on frail and fugitive words.

"We never met one another, kindness and I," said my terrible companion, "in the embrasure of the same oriel window."

You can well imagine the vigor with which I would have settled his hash. From the degree of torpor you found me in when you arrived, you may surmise that I never allowed myself to suffer the slightest humiliation of his breath.

That was what let me control the free movement of my mind.

Since the really terrifying catastrophe during which we had joined our contrary destinies forever, he had never addressed a word to me. But not a single gesture, not a single twitching of his exceedingly sensitive epidermis had, during that protracted period of anguish, left me indifferent.

At that moment we were both shut up in a room devoid of any kind of furniture, with no unnecessary space between the ideally bare walls, that is to say without any obscenity either, and dark because the light from outside was blocked by a dense curtain of moss. I was ensconced in an armchair as deep as my thoughts, in pursuit of which I was squandering all my time. He was lying on his side, couchant on a bed as hard as the life of man and narrower than the ideas of those of their ignoble race who are chained to the pursuit of some ideal or other, or even asleep, between the stone piers—as fatal to the free play of intelligence as they are tall and rigid—of duty.

Soon the visitors entered, not without having first knocked timidly at the door. Then, with infinite precautions, and after having first sought with a gesture my permission to do so, he began to address the group in a forced, artificial manner.

"Be so kind, friend, as to open the window, having first pushed aside that horrid curtain of moss, still wet with tears of the dew. I can barely see you in the dusk, yet I am determined to learn whether you too bear on your wretched face the blemishes common to members of your unworthy species."

The curtain having been pushed aside and the window opened, a magnificent sun stretched an enormous ray into the room.

"What beastly weather," he said. "Never will we be peaceful or happy on this foul planet."

And, addressing the visitors: "From your reserved and courteous manner, from the studied refinement of your dress, from the silence you are not afraid to keep in order to preserve your thoughts like a priceless jewel behind a thick pane of glass, from the timidity and infrequency of your gestures, tallied and tallied again, I understand what has brought you here to satisfy the distressing demands of your shameful profession: It's the accident that happened last night, in which I alone perished."

Despite their open and brazenly flaunted cynicism, the visitors were speechless. There was a fluttering in the leaves, in the hair neatly brushed back, in the branches already laden with buds, of the eyelids. There was a stirring deep within the pupils. The white walls blushed red with the sun and the reflections from their burnished faces. An extravagant light filled the room.

So far my insignificance had protected me; the visitors hadn't seen me.

And suddenly I became so insignificant that I disappeared entirely; I became totally invisible.

"I understand very well why you are here. And you could have done worse than end up in the enchanted disorder of my luxurious hovel. It pleases me to imagine beforehand all the lies, the fantasies, the revenges of self-esteem you'll be able to enjoy once you are far from the firing range of my kindness and my laughter, with pen in hand before the blank paper that lends itself to every collusion.

"But never mind. I savored in one gulp, as others do in tiny sips, the baseness of those strongboxes known as men. This is exactly what happened. We were traveling at top speed on the blade of illusions lost and always found again, night was at first open and pierced by the perforating knives of the headlights—we were joyful as cramps—when suddenly a dark vehicle, its dimensions totally beyond those prescribed by law, barely contained between the two curbs, blocked our way and passed over us. The friends who with me occupied the seats of our car were more or less seriously injured, the car was smashed to smithereens, the driver had given his week's notice, and I was killed on the spot. That is all I have to say to you."

"But," the visitor who seemed to have taken on himself alone the burden of the defense said tremblingly, "we were coming, we were also coming especially, to ask you a question. And please don't think it insidious. Sir, dear sir. What do you think, what do you know. In sum, sir, what are your ideas about God?"

I almost became visible again to the eyes of everyone. He, with an amazingly harmonious motion, had rolled onto his back. In all my life I have not seen, in all my long, interminable, and joyous life it has never been given to me to contemplate a visage as great, a face as completely ignoble as his.

"God?" he said. "What? But he is my father. Then you don't know that in our family we are God from one generation to the next? Come, come; I see you still have much to learn on the subject of God."

Inside, all was calm.

Outside life flowed smoothly, without hope or remorse, like the current of a piddling river. The sun spat everywhere, even on heaps of garbage. The street hoardings flamed around vacant lots for sale on easy terms. Speculation was nearing fever pitch. The level of the franc was falling. Extra precautions were being taken along the flowery banks of the Seine. As for me, I was asleep in my deep armchair. My ideas swarmed over my body like bedbugs voraciously seeking their fodder—everywhere except on my head. I was dreaming with extraordinary vigor, I was in a paroxysm of rage and at the peak of good fortune, but I was dreaming.

Suddenly he seized a Browning that never left his bedside and aimed this ruthless weapon at his inoffensive visitors.

"The villains, coming here to disturb the sleeper swathed in sheets of scorn! Young troublemakers on the trail of all the literary curiosities, all spiritual manna, they should have respected this corpse."

In cemeteries, in the starry attics of the firmament, in cages full of wild beasts who never cease dreaming of the shadowless freedom of the desert, in the amply provided wine cellars of grand hotels, in the salons of high society and the cells of lowbrow society, everywhere a religious silence is kept.

If, in the pastures of the great mountains of Europe and the plowed lands of the plains of every country in the world, rumors fly like a hare hunted relentlessly along the furrows, this is still not a cause for shame.

Silence has been requested of you in this bedroom open to the sky where the deceased is sleeping, glory is half-asleep on a divan, fortune's head is propped against a tub, disease draws her bony hands across the ravines of her bosom. You might at least have walked on tiptoe when approaching this giant billionaire banker who is crushing his twenty-fourth leather club chair to death under him. That is how one wins major battles. No one would dare to express in our presence the slightest doubt concerning the generosity of generals, when it's a question of deeding over the living chattels of the Earth. One's capital. A capital grant without security.

Yet he's there, our man, overflowing, napping in the shadow of an opulent cigar. The reporter has approached him respectfully. Hat in hand, he moves forward, circling that fortress of finance. Not without valor or ruse, without strength or cunning, without talent or an appointment made in advance does one approach a man protected by several layers of walls and salons, guarded by swarms of maids and valets who buzz around his plate—but that doesn't annoy him, he doesn't bother to shoo them away with his napkin—who sleeps sheltered from the bitter cold of the street, at the end of the mysterious galleries of the apartment building, in a secret honeycomb cell, like a worm.

The courageous reporter has approached nonetheless, and is now within earshot; he can hope that his voice, correctly aimed, will manage to pierce the cavity of that august ear. And now, adroitly unfurling his spring-loaded courage, he asks in a firm voice what the man has been waiting for beneath his cigar, forever.

And the latter, lifting without too much effort the less weighty of the two lids of his glowering eyes, answers him placidly.

"I, in this puny land of the chosen few bodies, I await the resurrection of the flesh."

Really, it's hardly worth being awakened first thing in the morning by acids, yielding like stars to that horrible seesawing of love in the turbines of the night, or spending one's time under globes of fire, between the vacillating haloes of pallid faces, running after hot vehicles that drain the fog.

It's hardly worth it, really.

So you, there, you think it's nothing?

You're walking along the highway at night. You have only a vague idea of where you're headed, having received no certain information concerning your itinerary. Where will you sleep tonight, where will you die someday? You don't know exactly what degree of longitude and latitude you are occupying on this gnarled praline that barely tolerates you and that you tolerate even less. But you're beginning to be really tired; the rain that has fallen all day hasn't rendered the going easier; you stumble at each step. No light in the distance, the immense plain surrounds you, solitude, somber thoughts. Abruptly you sense a presence behind you. Little by little the feeling that you are being followed takes shape, you don't dare to turn around. With a dull rumbling sound a very heavy step spatters the puddles, squashes the ruts' smudges. A powerful breath stirs the leaves and begins to make your ears tremble. The poplars groan gently in their mother tongue, the oaks puff out their powerful chests and flex their biceps, the willows, shamefaced old men or squalid philosophers, bow their dented foreheads under their disheveled hair.

You hear voices, voices that whisper to you of good, that preach evil to you, voices of women hoarse with debauchery. They are perhaps not so much voices as pangs that rend your stomach, your heart, your abdomen, they are black veils, heavy silences, inextricable knots of conscience.

Suddenly you realize you are being escorted by a building nine stories tall. You think that's nothing, do you? A metallic fear seizes you like a bale of oats in the terrible hurricane of the threshing machine, madness turns in a heavy spiral around your head and down to the base of your spine.

Finally you arrive at a crossroads; at one corner is a wayside shrine, a cross. The building stops, takes the place of the cross. A door opens. You go in.

There, all the doors are hermetically sealed, hidden behind tapestries. There are no windows and the walls don't form right angles, but an arena whose tiers are lined with seats. It is there that all the spectators of this assembly take their places, all silent actors in this scene. Now a moment of calm allows one to observe certain differences of rank shared by these shadows whom one had at first thought equal in the eyes of the law. But this difference is more the result of traces of manners and customs of the other world that have been conserved and introduced here under the simple trappings of appearance. For on this side of the medal all is but appearance, deliciously unreal. Nonetheless, freed of all earthly obligations and influences, every hierarchical constraint had disappeared, all subordination was extinct. One witnesses in all its simplicity this marvelous spectacle of men whose image retains the air of grandeur or baseness that nature had imposed on them, while the liberated soul no longer conforms to that image. However, on closer inspection one perceives that this soul hasn't totally forgotten its sojourn on Earth either, that it has retained certain minor flaws. Sometimes the shadows quarrel, sometimes a black wave of hatred invades their ideal forms, which then become more opaque, though not so much so that one can't perceive what is going on in their hearts.

Soon one perceives also that the apartments of this strange house are lit by stars, incalculable numbers of which line the ceilings. And this light is so gentle and at the same time so intense that one can tolerate it night and day without being disturbed by it, and one can distinguish perfectly the least details of the anxieties, the hands and the faces of the last spectators seated at the top of the amphitheater, despite its enormous dimensions. However, it is true that here all estimates of distance are altered.

There is no longer any common measure between the one who sees and the one who is seen; between the one who speaks and the one who hears. Confusion and doubt continually guide our steps. Pleasure is king in the vacuum. Soon a marvelous, limpid, and dazzling chime is heard in the distance, marking the hour.

But within this music whose harmonies are so new, it is never possible to take into consideration the concept of number. Time is no longer divisible. Remarks flow along the surface of the ether, and the cruelest witticisms float motionless on their wings for a long time. Without the law of gravity all this gratuitous gossip would vanish into sparks. But here everything becomes luminous; like a brutal shepherd the magic lamp chases away the shadows. The walls are rays, gestures are more luminous in this world where only images live. On the slopes, groups of people mingle among the cliffs and springs of this magnificent landscape.

Memories younger than life blossom in the trees. Others flow along the flowering streams. But beneath the black whirlwind of happiness the magisterial voice resumes, dominating the tumult. I, I too have banged my stricken forehead against the black rafters of hell.

But the safety of nature, which loves us with all its heart, has emerged from behind the wall and again taken up its trowel.

And if it chooses to listen to a purer song, and if it chooses to surpass the swallows?

Far from wishing to weaken that gift of internal crises which lay the groundwork for the future, that heaviness of mysterious disturbances of ideas and feelings, those disconcerting anticipations absolutely dispro-portionate to the struggles of real life, our plan is to cultivate to its fur-thest limit a certain power of penetrating the future, of forgetting the past, of calculating the weight of the secret motives that cause men to act. Whatever may befall at the end of all our deeds, in that nebulous atmosphere that reigns between our hands, between our wrinkles, from the breast to the heart, from the heart to the stomach, and from the stomach to the soul, among our most distant friends, among our tender-est enemies, we shall never abandon the helm that has allowed us to travel as far as the moist and trembling lips of the harbor of love while avoiding death. Still, we shall not lose sight of that extremely fine line that so cruelly slices through transparency.

Isn't it true that between these andirons, against the ashes, one senses a delightful warmth? And this pot of geraniums at the casement win-dow that gave the signal to the sailor who was passing along the road? He came in, the childish voyager whose eyes, on opening, let fall all the images and all the tales of his long sojourns in distant countries. How he sleeps, now, against the ashes! A charming warmth reigns, the curtains are drawn over the casement giving on the harbor. No one else will come, now. The lamp is extinguished. Everyone is asleep.

But outside, calamity will be unleashed. For there is a time that wants uncontrollably to go back, even though the most responsible in-habitants and tenants are unwilling to agree that it's too late. Decidedly, nothing dies, nothing wants to die at one and the same time.

For a trifle one would let one's head, one's heart, one's arm go off in all directions, even though there are still some who want to keep the rest and make do with that.

The old emperors, the old kings, the honorific rosettes, the unexpected windfalls, the noble profiles of those who lack rigor, the brief disgrace, the kepis which would still look so well on certain heads. All that is degraded and dead.

Yet still they battle, they come around walls, they point to airplanes scattered in the olive trees among the cicadas, they drag decapitated bodies into the gutters, they rise up against judges and curb the law like the arch of a bridge for a parade of uniforms of half-mourning, at half price.

Finally time is threadbare, a cast-off coat at the rag merchant's.

Besides, all those old sleeves have their stripes. And henceforth no one will be seen without stripes—whole pagoda sleeves of stripes.

He who cries out with joy tonight, on the jagged ice of the pavement, has a hole in his forehead, but he won't die; farther down he has a red wound under the sun of people's glances—the other one too—but no one looks at him.

Will we be forced to hide someday when, having grown timid and totally ruined, we won't have even the celestial right to utter a word? Prisoners in the glowing circles, we'll have only splinters of that overripe glory, that preference for things that set us apart from the others and fashion us a Venetian frame out of sword blades. The voices are piling up into a storm and roaring at the gate of the courtyard.

Everyone would like to get in so as to find a prey that's easy to strike down without risk, under the heroic rainbow of so many cowards.

At present all those friendly hands, those living profiles, that laughter, those impulsive gestures are entangled in shadows. A fasces of faces laughing and bright as swords clanks in the darkness. Where did I lose you, loving glances? Who stitched your lips together over your teeth, laughing mouths?

Ebony streams are flowing in the ruts, and on either side shapeless birds fly up out of the hedgerows. Their cries mingle with the clamor of the wind and of sheets flapping in the wind, on the wall and against one's face. The air becomes heavy, the sky descends. It's a terrible stretch to travel alone, repelling all the assaults that arise simultaneously from everywhere, from all the countries, all the colors, the facial features that resemble you so strongly. One must pass, certain of receiving no recompense, nowhere and never.

Certainly it's not for lack of a sufficient motive that we have always, in our flight from sorrow, left behind the largest and most valuable pieces of our luggage. Of course nothing is hidden from us, nor, on the other hand, is anything totally revealed to us of what we so urgently needed to know. Yet for better or worse we have, without excessive wincing, lived through the heaviest period of our role.

If a mysterious messenger came to tell you, as you were emerging from sleep, at the moment you were slowly traversing that isthmus of torpor that links the syncope of thought to the lucid vibrations of the evening before, "Don't you want to stay?" wouldn't you experience the long-premeditated impulse to abruptly turn back? Like an expert diver who gently slips into the depths that hide buried treasures, pulling the liquid sheets up to his chin, wouldn't you go back to retrieve the featureless happiness at the bottom of the empty and unlit tabernacle? But if a nightmare grinds down the verdant moss of the reefs behind your eye-lids, if broken lances stain with blood the grooves of your forehead, when the corners of the salty lips of Earth tremble at their juncture with the continents, what slackening breaks the ice that imprisons your hands, the tender hearts of nocturnal lettuce beneath the skidding of steady animals, as dawn the laundress straightens the mortal folds of your frozen curtains?

Outside, due to the market-garden hour, subversive songs are muffled under felt soles, guided through deserted streets between manifestations of bifurcated patriotism that causes the public washhouses to be hung with bunting. Numbers roll under windows overflowing with work when the sun jams its rays into the lock.

It's the awakening of eyelashes, of bayonets twisted in brawls, of knives stabbed into the panels of doors, and the ripping up of the asphalt linings between shop windows still heavy with sleep. But be patient; your hour will come, your eyes will open on the misunderstood hypnosis of faith, the shadows of mouthless winter will dissipate under the warmth of the joyful firebrands of summer's straw torches.

Someday, the mind carefully concealed under erasures will have ceased to believe that its place, like that of nests, is in the bushes. Then along towpaths, the halos, goods on display, horse-drawn carts, we'll discover a thousand reasons to go back to those antiquated and uncomfortable coaches that today we no longer see circulating from stage to stage in Paris at night, and which are no longer used to transport the salad that grows between the paving stones of the city—that's why today they are called baskets.[2]

And at the vital turning points of paganism, on the multicolored highways of peace, we'll hear again the lively cracking of whips, the postilions' insults, we'll see again the sudden ambushes in denuded gorges, in the mountain passes of fear. And inspiration, that free wheel of the spirit, will go off to rejoin the secret calculations of chance, glued to the endless study of lists of the chosen and the condemned, pushing back the edges of forests.

For the moment, in basements and attics, numerous prisoners are moaning in pain. They are on fire. With bloody limbs they implore the end of tortures worthy of times hardly more barbaric than these. They demand the glass of water to which they are entitled. They cry out. But no one answers them. No distinct voice leaves their eternal throats and no merciful ear hears them. The conflagration that erupts in that enigmatic house with its sculpted passages, its secret galleries, is a fire of consuming mystery, an internal heat which incubates under the ashes of life, under the beams of the thorax, in the incandescent organs of breath whose rare flashes illuminate all the miseries of egotism; what are you asking of the ground, majestic thought; what do you anticipate from that adding machine, truant intelligence? Whether the sky is less big than the eye. Whether the sun is darker than the lair, how to cut the thread that is now fastened to the walls of the labyrinth, now that it leads to the wonderful current that makes it swell as blood swells the vein and it goes from lamp to lamp, wrapping around the lightning. How to escape from an elemental rivalry that's so cunning, see daylight again, run across bridges, reconnect the floating thongs of the banks?

When he comes down from the clouds, from the needles of the hill where the sun plays in the mirrors of the lighthouse—he will find the house empty. Wind and the water's iron filings will have swept everything away! If he wants to follow in our footsteps, the rain will have effaced them. The last lightning flash to chip the horizon will tell him that we are already too far away—and he will climb the mountain that the tortures of thunderbolts have spared. Who then is that illustrious physician, with a brain of cork shriveled by a too-long sojourn in northern colonies devastated by gunpowder and bullets, back when it was always hunting season, who claimed that a bird can maintain itself in air while resting as inert as a stone? We were then in the good old days of sail flying (which, by the way, nobody mentions anymore). The helixes of pallid pretentiousness congested the pia-matral meninx of that barely unhooped brain. Under the bull's brow of that gigantic mound of soft sand one could watch, unaided by any magnifying apparatus, the germination, though very slow and excessively sparse, of generous ideas, still however only insofar as they related strictly to the needs of its own existence.

Reader, as you read me, don't you experience a fecund joy as you tell yourself that you are one of the rare beings who can still give yourself, with a modicum of pleasure, to that perilous exercise? Be you stretched out on a sordid pallet, in a sunless hovel, swathed in cold and avid only of self-instruction, or languorously reclining on a downy divan in a nook of some elegant and discreetly perfumed salon, if you are alone, and whether it be intrepid electricity which supplies you with light or the vacillating flame of a miserable candle, and with the sole aim of diverting yourself, savor at its true cost the unctuous sip of pride with which this attention may be capable of flattering your finicky palate.

Ruled by the dimensions of the frame of that page and of his complete works, whose limits nothing in the world could persuade him to exceed, the novelist begins to describe a room in that disquieting building wherein a certain number of the peculiar events of our era have taken place. But as he is about to enter he hesitates and takes a step backward, for in that bedroom where the eye of the most penetrating observer would distinguish at first glance nothing more than a shaving brush, an iron pedestal table, a lead mirror, and a chair whose rush seat has caved in, groans a soul eternally condemned to remove from its cheeks with a nicked razor the down of long sentimental considerations that continually comes to tarnish them.

Nothing is simpler for a free man wishing to charm his summer leisure than to transport himself on the stout, canvas-covered wings of his imagination to the center of the Beauce region (those who don't know the Beauce are advised to go there—they won't regret the trip).[3] It's there, under a chilly, starless sky, darker in the night than my mood, amid geometric hectares, that stands the formidable building which has already been referred to somewhere. Vigilant electricity vibrates at all the windows. And the house stands like a bar of flame in the night. Behind the house is a lake—on the shore of the lake a man is asleep. After waiting a long time he fell asleep and when the noise of the orchestra ceased, wakened by the silence, he slowly raised his eyelids. He no longer has any memory of his sojourn at the edge of the pond unless it's, in his eyes, the incessant movement of the waves wriggling in the sun and the burning bruises contracted at the touch of that fascinating sheet of liquid metal. He doesn't understand how one can live outside the limits of that unknown land where the echoless well of unchaste truth is sleeping. But how to get out of the enchanted ring of this fortress and reach the outside world again, and beyond the encircling wall of the mystery that is barely stirred by the innocent flight of doves?

When the boats raised their sails with the firm intention of following, once and for all, the seagulls who dipped laughing among the silky feathers of the azure sky, he shook his arms and his skeleton, his nervous system vibrated like the cords of a ship, but he remained on shore. His legs collapsed under him and he immediately fell asleep again on the sand.

Yet when the day finally dawned for him to leave this odious country of memories and ash, it wasn't toward the sky he departed nor toward the sea, but toward the still unexplored bowels of the Earth. Along these roads, blood irrigates the brambles and the flesh blossoms out in magnificent flowers amid the fiery thorns of the underbrush. All along these trails, bends and turns erupt like the smiles of the loveliest roses of morning self-esteem.

At the bottom of ravines pocked with chasms rumble the torrents of glory, striated with luminous fish. I was in a very high place. I was on the needlelike summits of the light. There, heads were rolling in the capricious turnstile of happiness. A fortunate dilation made the dimensions of one's being identical with those of the Universe. Laughter of the belly and the mind prevailed. An innate brightness bathed everything and rendered all flesh transparent. A beneficial fire cauterized misfortune's deepest and most obstinate wounds. One bathed freely in the running water of diamonds.

I was very high up but I heard nevertheless an agonizing voice issuing from the deepest abysses of the Earth, a terribly agonizing voice whose furious lament arose from the Earth's sterile entrails.

Whence come you, voice of the fox broken in by all the horse-trading of friendship and intrigue, milky voice of poorly understood repopulation, singular voice, voice with two meanings, more suited to great railway catastrophes, inner voice, so hard to identify, voice, sepulchral voice of vaudevilles, why do you come to trouble my portion of eternal bliss?

The torture arrived on raven's wings to jar rudely the serenity of this peaceful sojourn. I wanted to leap over the safety of these aerial balustrades to stifle the importunate lamentations of that sinister voice. But it was not granted me to traverse that space. I could neither climb nor go down. For the one crying from the depths of the abysses of Earth was me. The lugubrious voice which mounted toward us from the inextinguishable braziers of hell was my own.

In mid-ocean, after one of the most frightful maritime disasters of modern times, the position of the shipwrecked survivor whom a narrow spar allows to float just underwater is singularly critical. How will he manage to go and finish the hand of cards begun at a café on one of the smaller boulevards. Perhaps a shark will soon come and shear off his two legs. What will he do? Viewed from above, or simply from a distance, from the bridge of a comfortable battleship or from an even safer position on terra firma, the ocean's waves are imposing, magnificent to behold; their contemplation raises the immortal soul of man who compares them unfavorably to his perishable casing, but at a considerable distance from the coasts, toward one of those places where, from the height of the crow's nest, one perceives that the horizon has suddenly taken on a circular form as precise as though traced by a full-scale compass, they become terrifying—huge and terrifying. Such is the opinion of the castaway who even goes so far as to add that he finds them vertiginous. Vertigo is swallowed up by the swipe of an albatross's or a seagull's wing between the distance that separates the hollows and the crests of those liquid foothills. The castaway has had about all he can stand; his obvious lack of training begins little by little to aggravate his severe handicap in this endurance test that God has deemed equitable and salutary to send his way. But then too, into what risky adventure did he carelessly plunge? Isn't the weather nicer in that café in the capital, ornamented with luxurious mirrors which make it seem larger? All those sounds of voices in the mirrors, all those reflections of glory in the clouds of smoke; that gale of words which drags the motions of hand and hair toward the revolving doors. Those magnificent poses, in which no line is wasted; those audacious phrases that go flying around the lamps and whose wings will never be censured; that sweetness of living, of wallowing in money, of demanding of others what one can't provide oneself, that ease of daydreaming and forgetting, of shouting for no reason, of singing, of inviting a crowd, of talking at night, of sleeping on emptiness, of emptying the mind, of twisting the heart, of losing at poker, of winning at fear, of laughing in the eyes and the wrinkles of one's best friends, of racing without danger along the tracks of intrepid cities and, above all, that certificate of existence which provides us with the services of our coevals at too modest a price, why did he leave all that for this precarious solitude on the plains of the Ocean? Look at him now, beginning to reflect and rest his elbows on his spar with an anxious air. How will he ever finish that card game?

At this moment a perpendicular star mounts slowly and noiselessly from the horizon. A rapid glance lets him note quickly what is happening. He won't have to make an enormous effort to save the situation.

And in fact, as the perpendicular star climbs ever higher, one can see an unfurling ladder of silvery rays whose lower extremity brushes the crests of the waves.

The castaway summons his last remaining forces and uses them to place first a hand, then a foot on the first rung of this supple ladder. Now he is climbing slowly like a man exhausted by illness, the starvation of the shipwreck, and the mortifications of avarice. And it's not a feebly moving spectacle to watch, across the night's billows, in this muffled solitude far from animals and men alike, far from the sparkling glances and the futile noise of the world, a creature, half-dead with exhaustion, slowly and joylessly mounting the sharp-edged stairs of the path of resurrection.

The entranceways of this mysterious house are congested with the comings and goings of the men and women who go in and go out. Men who enter and who will never leave, women who leave and will never go back in. The men penetrate it at that time of day that is called dusk, the women escape it at that time of day which ought to be called blond. To say nothing of those who throw themselves, like money, out the windows, or who climb and descend, in perpetual motion, that dizzying stairway which drills the core of the building from top to bottom, as far as infinity. For what we are dealing with here is nothing less than infinity, in this system that has nothing in common with our regime except the close relations between the outer surface of the fabric and its lining.

In a hallucinatory nightmare, two men whose moral temperament is as unlike as their physical complexion find themselves face to face in one of the innumerable halls which it is absolutely essential not to describe here, and whose general aspect is that of a totally deserted private bar.

One of them, a great comedian of the bourgeoisie of the twentieth century, is always, prompted by impulsive remorse, on the verge of recounting the tragic details of a crime he once committed.

Once upon a time he killed, doubtless from fairly base motives, someone he loved too much to suffer the slightest abuse from him. The most indiscreet liberating words teem at his lips. The coils of his conscience alternately distend and contract, twist in painful convulsions, the agonies of grief can be fully decoded in the altered features of his masculine face.

The other, a braggart of sorts, full of stupid intuitions, grasping at all the words buzzing around his ears, reassembles them as best he can into swarms even noisier than the ice of marshlands at the all too impatiently awaited moment of its breaking up in spring.

Without realizing it, he ends up attributing to himself all the ideas and acts of his interlocutor. The traits that demarcate them in space are temporarily blurred.

And so it is that after the complete confession of the first, who has unloaded his galling remorse, it's the other one, the idiot, who ends up believing himself guilty. He's boasting naively, he's radiant, for an hour he's been talking like an idling engine, for an hour he's been condemning himself while the discreet men moving along the wall, numbered like the doors that pierce the wall, lay hold of him and drag him off to shelter him from blows of the too-lively air which was recently crimping the river with its curling iron. It would be wrong to suppose that the transient interest of this anecdote was used to deflect attention from the principal figure in this dramatic action that deploys its stirring phases with the serene amplitude of fatality. When the wheels congeal in the chilly air of morning, one may tell oneself, without excessive fear of falling into the dreaded lair of judicial error, that it's the wheels of the milk carts climbing the street again, but if snub-nosed vice sticks its blue face through the chink of the partly opened window, the passersby, coming home late and made to feel unwelcome in this neighborhood totally transformed by the epidemic, complain about not finding their shoes. After committing his crime, the assassin hung the customary sign on the removable metal handle of the shop door: *Closed on account of death*. He went off without leaving the least fingerprint or the least suspicion. And besides, that same day there was such an uproar in the avenues decked with bunting, in the gold nuggets of the dust and the invectives of the women peddling fruit and vegetables, and the glass laughter of the wicker-clad bottle women displayed in the market stalls, that at first no one noticed what had happened in the house set back from the street where no one ever went in. But certainly there was here sufficient incentive to cause the psychologist searching for pleasant lakes in the sands of the unconscious, constantly sifted by the sieves of light, to fall into a chasm of reflections. Taking no notice of the heaviness of this style, borrowed momentarily from a department foreign to the matters under discussion here, let the reader take heed instead of the depths in which swim the passions of the characters in this book. While one may find elsewhere minute research on all the tics, all the words trampled and suppressed in wagons of hay spoiled by the rain, here nothing but that which is truly impenetrable concerns us. Psychology is moving ahead at full speed and psychoanalysis is making excellent progress. But what still greater charm lies in the overthrow of the method of investigation we have adopted from the beginning. One believes, without due reflection, that it is enough to look at a man in order to see him, that it is enough to listen to him in order to hear him, and that the moment he says yes, he is very naively thinking no. We didn't stay long in this pathway of error under the flowering hawthorn bushes. There are better ways, certainly, to know men and to learn what is happening in their souls—we have only not to look at them. So it was that the office boy at the clandestine newspaper of this obscure city, after changing his jacket, found a large acacia thorn under his left armpit and, in the inside pocket, a key. The drawer he had found was full of multicolored papers, notices, censored letters, of which he took possession. Then he disappeared for a while, hiding in a stable at the other end of the village. But illness forced him out to take the air and he wandered at night among the trees of the courtyard. Yet his health only worsened. By the time he decided to seek the help of some doctor or lawyer or professional center at the university, it was too late. The malady had done its work. Besides which, the doctor recognized him by his enormous white beard. And as it was snowing that evening, the doctor, prudent, blew on it. And the wind carried him away.

It's certainly not the moment, you'll agree, to betray the secret of that closed society that lives lavishly in the so superbly illuminated apartments of that frivolous house that our eyes can make out in the vista. Luxury, on bronzed wings, risks its flight in the trees of the wood where fields join each other, shoulder to shoulder. Among the branches the lamp keeps watch, a signal for the heroes of contraband who meet there in the evening to taste the fruits of anxiety, juicy as the carob. But thanks to them I emerged at last from my period of despair. I cured my head, bathed my spirit. I maintained a little light behind my eyes and I can look straight ahead without sliding into the immense void where roils the wind that drags us away. Everything has become flat and glowing and a beautiful blue color in the atmosphere. Even I can see myself in the mirror conveniently placed in the air. Immortal man, man of dust. I am no longer afraid to touch the earth, nor to see it end abruptly ahead of me, and I can walk without fear of meeting that immutable wall.

Always that wall, that immense wall that has been placed before me so as to harm me.

Scarcely deadened by work I was obliged, once evening arrived, to scrub away the fulgurating inscription that rendered intolerable the idea of death that each one of us carries like a too-hard pillow against his temple. Loitering with velvet tread on the damp sidewalks, when evening prowls in the wet streets of poor districts like a rag for mopping the pavement, the gangs have set to work. And all the flattened caps, all the spit curls of weathervanes in the night, on joyful roofs, the unfolded slopes that don't count in articulating cities of rotted teeth. It's with this accoutrement and during these dangerous tasks that the worth of men affirms itself under the crushing commands of their cruel destiny.

Heavy crates, too well nailed together, arrive on steamships whose duty it is to stir up the Ocean.

But what are we supposed to do with those contraband arms against our enemies, touchy as earwigs?

Nocturnal dog-days leaning toward the occident, don't wait for the hail of more or less somber bullets, more or less crackled, striped with revelatory tumefactions—this bruised and so well beloved flesh, rebellious, harassed by fatigue under the lamps of livid streets, of sordid neighborhoods, of nights of orgy when I drag you nauseated along the ground, don't expect me to follow the walls to escape the heat of rays put back into their cases, nor that the fear of the clearly outlined shadow will push me to look at the silvered column which trembles according to the whims of the temperature. In the morning, I am with the disintegrating ranks of revolt; disorganized, overwhelmed, overloaded, in the open sea, weighed down with the flotsam that riddles the abyss that separates me from dry land.

Every evening I stroll with a man chained to a wall, to an idée fixe. We go betwixt and betwixt against the wall. Sometimes we turn, but without ever going far from each other, in a sort of calm whirlpool that stops the movement of the stars.

And as long as I remain in contact with that man, I too am chained to the wall—what could we have to say to each other in that jail, since nothing can supplant that idée fixe, since no other hypothesis can come to supplant the Roman cement of that wall, wall that's so smooth, so hard, so thick, so high, so calm. That wall so patina'd and polished by the rubbing of so many centuries—that horrible wall. But the attacks of saltpeter. But the threats of refined tortures that rip out confessions from the innocent? All that struggle against ghost ships refloated by conspiracies. Yet we have nothing to do with it, or with anybody. Once the door is boarded up, the windows aimed at the beach, we must await the return of the tides toward the stretchers of the cliffs.

An insect, not born yesterday, begins courageously climbing the trunk of a sapling. Once arrived at the top, he summons his last strength to shout—the sea! the sea!—like a sailor in the clouds, in the crow's nest, and the others on the ground listen to him, gaping. When he climbs down they all embrace each other, cheering him on and setting out for that at last discovered distant beach.

No sooner do they arrive than they all rise up in rebellion and scatter in different directions; and boredom activates in alarming fashion the movements of the compass needles of mortality. Each one thinks of his precious apartment in the city that the moths are now devouring—for the intensity of men's desires is not in direct proportion to the pleasure felt when they are satisfied.

And when sinister events from the past begin to well up violently from the crust of goodwill and resignation under which it had been decided to bury them, piercing it everywhere, you should see those bubbles bursting, those features spurting, that heart leaping in its gilded cage. As for the head, it quite simply loses its shape. As the powers of darkness are infinitely superior to those of light, if one looks a little higher than the level of mediocrity where we are all more or less obliged to crawl, it is incontestable that tornadoes of misfortune have an infinitely more efficacious grip on the propeller blades of our mechanism than the intermittent and always belated cascades of success and happiness. The happiness of man is devoid of chlorophyll no doubt because its specific condition is to evolve in the darkest and dankest caves of the heart. Hence it would be singularly unjust and regrettable if one were to condemn an author, with his multiparous entrails, for the superhuman efforts he has been able to make to sustain with sangfroid a dignified attitude before the endless reproaches made to him by his style, and who, confronted by so many insults and offenses, finds himself in the position of a penguin that has been buckled into a straitjacket.

As the icebergs drift majestically across the sky, always in the direction of the hands of the watch, the passengers, ashamed of their trip being cut short for reasons that are still far from clear, set about throwing their baggage overboard.

That lighthouse which stands so cruelly rigid in the night, that telescope so proud of having brought back a star as a prisoner from the ashes of twilight, that siphon of light, in a word, which causes the Ocean to boil in the night, attracts the attention of this band in distress on the quicksands of infinity.

Deep within him, he who speaks now has also discovered all the treachery of these dangerous regions wherein anyone so imprudent as to venture is engulfed without reprieve. There is no place firm enough to set up a lever strong enough to lift the people, given a certain fulcrum. Footsteps sink in deeper and deeper. A pneumatic force violently sucks the soles of feet down into the morass, and animals are lost in this movement of such perfidious sponginess, which requires such an exhausting effort. He whose spirit is sinking in even further, wears himself out trying to keep his balance on the rickety steps leading to the ultimate platform where later all will be able to gaze—he hopes—at the disconcerting flares of dawn. Nothing counts of the words that circulate from the stairway to the ceiling, from the casements to the tips of the stars, from the roots of trembling lakes to the webbed feet of birds who trace these enigmatic numbers in chalk on the sails.

For, to speak plainly, that magnetized needle, highly sensitive to abrupt deviations in temperature, orients itself toward what is good only from a sense of duty and toward evil only for pleasure. Once violent alcohol has slid down the same slope a number of times, it's more than likely it will be allowed to do so again for a long time to come. There's no danger for him in those humorous posters that illustrate for us in such striking terms the extent of its ravages on our precious organism. Man, who loves his body as a blind person loves the light, will never consent to pause before another picture proclaiming the benefits of soothing herbal teas and of grenadine syrup. One would think that he's afraid of being tempted. One would say that he fears disease, that he is terrified of the disastrous effects on its surroundings of a mucous membrane susceptible to infection from compounds of sugar. And the mind, in the same way, is seen to repulse with uncontrollable convulsions the most arduous advances of kindness.

From the weight of the sadness that periodically invades our limbs and the world, we can measure all the advantage there would be for us to make public appearances and evolve in an even larger arena. But this is the hard kernel, the resistant part of universal thought—no doubt the tastiest in the Universe. All the unhappiness of the intelligence resides in its inability, beyond a certain degree of development, to enjoy the present moment. From this flow formidable displacements of general feelings and particular forces.

From time to time a good and sympathetic man will begin to speak from the top of an improvised pulpit suddenly erected in the air by whirlwinds of dust; at once the heavy perfumes of morality suffocate us. If there is someone among those reading me who isn't absolutely fascinated by the scrupulous narrative I am recounting him, let him put it aside and take up another. He's free to do so. But let him make haste; soon there will be no time left. What the devil, we are often told, everything comes to an end. Why shouldn't our period reach its own? Where we are going, with eyes shut, there is certainly no one who would joyfully consent to follow us.

Never, never will I return to that crossroads, dangerous curve, somersault of destiny. Never will the pink houses in their glass jars of frost, between the afternoons of autumn and the evenings of spring, have finer opportunities to remain silent. The moon has risen, after all. It rests, like a mercury ball, in the hollow of the nocturnal hand that sets out the traps of sleep, and everything happens as though we would never die. The black glove of that hand, once it has wearied itself with equivocal mesmeric passes, finally turns all faces to the wall whose tapestry portrays sunken roads traveled by strange beasts. At the bottom of the roads are coarse sand, small stones, barely ripe fruits that abandoned children seek out for their tartness. What shapes could one assign to the carriages that descend the dried beds of torrents which the tapestry represents? There are no troops in the earthworks of the hill.

Then along what road could one return to that white-hot crossroads where the lethal indecisions of travelers are simmering? It's not the delicate leaves that tremble at the slightest suspicion, nor the foolhardy edifices, which, without a moment's hesitation, fling themselves into the abyss, nor even less the flocks of metallic vehicles that fly away at the slightest sound, that could provide a precise indication on this subject. The petals of health float for a moment in the allées, from puddle to puddle, on the steps of the sun, between two shudders, before finally departing to swell the ranks of the victims of the epidemic that is ravaging the whole countryside and has already reached the insalubrious suburbs of the city.

The gale that tonight besieges the windowpanes of the castle keep introduces elements of discord among the hostile classes of the city. Yes, but that lamp, through which travels all the wind from the straits, why does it render the marble in the factories transparent? When one knows only the members of nature, with joints of tempered steel, the lumber trains, the febrile fields, that immobility of desert highways under the pneumatic clock and the words of love in patois, one can easily prevent oneself from trembling at the approach of winter's jets of flame. But if the gilded ferment of lust dissolves in bursts of laughter, too bad for the faces summed up in a few brief lines in the anthropometric albums of ancient families. The incontestable nobility of those sharp features will fade in the rural character of the site where trains packed with emigrants in distress have always been detained in wartime.

And now, let us lead anger's bunches of keys back to the fold. Where were we? It's a question of not missing the hordes of butterflies that come at the end of each Saturday to pocket their moderate salary.

When there is a secret message to be sent from heaven to Earth, the moon serves as a sealing wafer. Still, this is not a reason to betray our expectations endlessly. How long have we been patiently waiting, huddled in this ditch filled with water that forms the livid horizon of the plain? It's cold in the branchings of light, on the three-dimensional quays drawn in prophetic lines. There are the prophets with their kepis, the republicans with their banners, the heads of political parties with their suitcases, the poets with their curled hair and their field glasses, the better to orient their ships—for they are also pilots, those negroes equipped with mauve wings who lead the dragonflies. Finally whether it's songs that disembark or other merchandise, the stationmaster remains unmoved. Let's go straight to the heart of the matter.

The singular house must still be there, and if we don't yet notice anything, it's because the clouds prevent our doing so with their incessant movement—that inconvenient movement of rock crystal.

It would certainly be more agreeable to lose completely the memory of those sad, long winter evenings spent hulling pearl necklaces in the silent family circle. But how to waste time when in times past we accumulated savings at the price of the harshest privations? How peaceful we would be if we were poorer, dangling feet in the water, bareheaded and hanging on, in the street, to the corner of a window or a door to warn those inside of the prodigious rigors of the temperature. How much happier we'd be, bent double, hands in our pockets.

It's snowing in the belly of the herds. Earth has changed its shirt. The trees are installing curtains that slide along their gray rods, from one end to the other of the posts. On days of eclipse, the moon has finally succeeded in recovering its monstrance, which is why all the storks on their pointed roofs are rejoicing. Now, the thermometers—phosphorescent skate fish on the wall[4]—who walk around all day in long lines, under the gray sky, on the sticky streets of the capital, and who are also called, no one knows why anymore, sandwich men, give us only a feeble idea of what science can still accomplish in improving on the animal species. And, as long as a pari-mutuel system capable of stimulating the ardor of those thoroughbred stallions hasn't been organized, appreciable results will never be obtained. Thus man experiences no shame in recognizing his image in so sinister a mirror. On the contrary he feels an unutterable satisfaction in noting that the strange edifice which is passing and which no longer has any but the vaguest connection to the human form is not his counterpart.

When the sky goes flat and black like a phonograph record; when songs from the walls fan out on the plain like stray locks of the fog's hair; when cries of passion follow the lightning of the rails and animals become excited in the brambles; when seeds of paper germinate in the furrows and the poltergeist inseminates the earth—if, by chance, further from the anxiety of hunger, the circle of vicious reasons closes again; if, by chance, the weather changes direction, one will be able to see terror with its big neck collapse on the lemon of tears.

Nevertheless, with night guiding us, the lassitude of the seasons helped us cross the checkered valleys where the inhabitants of furnaces sprang briskly backward. In the pit of a mine where precious materials, colored earths, and sympathetic vegetables were once extracted, a knot of rivers was heating up in the sun. What zeal for correct behavior could be read in all eyes, along the secret trails of sworn conspiracies! From the significant noise which elevators make in the country, after curfew, we understood very clearly that we were approaching the frontier, that we were nearing our goal. Already a great luminous fan warned us of the alarming intensity of forced labor from hands delivered over to the biting of the light. But now all heads are lost in drafts and drowned in rumors of head colds. A dull opposition arises that will henceforth prevent all the threads of the so cleverly plotted intrigue from being woven in the corners of tunnels of greenery. Where will we go now to spend the lengthening hours, lying down dog-tired after such exhausting hunting parties? Along the wall, withered clothes are drying their weary limbs. The tools of mediocre work in the sensitive flanks of the Earth are leaning at the parapet. The squirrel of the treadmill of dreams has once again taken up his august task. Sleep will still be hemmed for a long time by a firm stitch between the canvas bags of silence and the night's large purses of metallic beads. Beyond the underbrush and those folds in the ground where a foreigner gets lost, what are those two suspicious shadows advancing toward us? Neither the snow which never ceases to fall nor the appeal of intimate memories under the lukewarm glass of the lamps of home slows them down. They push onward, determined to conquer this very evening the distance that separates them from the goal of their expedition. Whoever tried to make the voice of reason heard at this moment would certainly not be listened to. And besides, no one is so imprudent as to be outdoors on such a night when the squall reigns supreme between the puddles and steaming spillways of the valley, when the steeples, cypresses, and aspens bow meekly to let it pass.

Likewise, what could possibly disturb him who henceforth will live only under ashes and embers? He never, so to speak, goes out of the dense matrix of sleep, and a gulf separates him from all the flaming calamities. When the most powerful shards of passion are dormant in the most muffled cavities of one's nature, shards of wood, shards of glass, bursts of laughter, and flashes of diamond, one can still hide one's illness from him who, with the help of a mechanical reaper, peels the earth in spirals as one peels an orange. But when purple traces of pain appear on the skin like bubbles rising for a breath of fresh air from the fetid muddy depths, when the eyes, rolling back in the head, change color and sink like a stone; and when the furious howls of the bellows of fear split the walls, it becomes quite impossible to apply the brakes to the impetuous momentum of this sentence. In any case, numbers never lose any of their value, nor do the wrinkles which facilitate the observation of the grid of various parts of the human face. And of the significance accorded certain shapes of the hand, position of the fingers, of the wrist, of the forearm when it becomes a question of raising the intellectual level of the privileged classes to which illegitimate children growing up outside the zone of good breeding may not lay claim, we shall here excuse ourselves from taking note. They are walking, as we have already said. At the bottom of the sky, heavy knapsacks of precious objects that have crossed the line as contraband are accumulating. One sees lightning flashes that are shoeing the horizon at regular intervals. In the hollows of damp meadows, gashed by sharp-edged streams, there are haystacks enveloped in several layers of night, so that night is darker in those places. On the other hand, and even at the same hour, rows of Venetian lanterns are lit along the regular façades of well-appointed neighborhoods in the large cities. All those festoons of windows help to provide a festive air that reverberates in the obscure minds of the dwellers in those dreary thatched cottages that flicker here and there in the grass like modest fireflies. Hence one may imagine the surprise of the traveler settling at this moment into the dining car of the great European express train, who is regulating with the greatest assurance the complicated question of the rational electrification of the countryside, on glimpsing, at the center of the rays of kilometers hastening toward a highly imprecise ideal perimeter, a cluster of those magnificent lanterns. You will have certainly not forgotten what kind of lanterns we're talking about. It's he, advancing toward that cluster despite all the obstacles of night and foul weather, who notices the two shadows of whom mention was made a short while ago. Despite the vertiginous speed of the train that transports him, he succeeds, from the comfortable seat he is occupying thanks to having most scrupulously paid the purchase price, in distinguishing traces of physical fatigue and moral lassitude in the romantic faces of the two common vagrants. If the sight moves him, it must be admitted that he betrays no sign of this. Who in fact are those two men who slip like scissors through the night; what is that house, so tall and shimmering that one might mistake it for a jet of fire or light rising out of the nearby lake as from the basin of a fountain? It is quite obvious, and immediately so, that he has no intention of getting to the bottom of the matter. There is a sewer pipe of worn-out feelings that crosses the world from the ear to the sea. Beneath the frost, drops of water roll down to the needles of the parasol. On account of the weather the call number of a ship at the end of the harbor wags its semaphore, the impatient steamships strain at their cables. Between the steps of the lost passengers, springs gush forth through every drop of water one looks into, and all the colors slide between the fingers, the lashes, the flying images, the serious laundry of suppressed tears which have come to dry in the sun. That day there will be no more laughter for me and my fellow creatures.

They have placed a medal on a hole in the dead man's chest. Only a short while ago he was carrying his dream, carefully folded, in a sack on his back, and his soul ran on a few steps ahead of him. In the puddle in the distance, not far from the blond shoulders of the ditch, was a dying flower, drowned in blood.

Around the continents which assume the place and shape of pears in maps of the world divided into two hemispheres, in the borders of salt marshes where aquatic gardeners endlessly rake the sea, birds and fish often choose the wrong mirage. The birds get lost underwater; the fish fly. One no longer knows who's coming and who's going. One no longer knows who's living and who's dying in that tropical sphere. Thus, the sun rises little by little while the marshaled troops of completed events are set in motion. In the clearings of forests, shutters were banging; from the sculpted pediment of the Ocean wings were taking flight. And here, on the plain where only a little while ago shadows were stirring at the edges of fields, where mysterious shudders abraded the earth, nothing remains. Emptiness stretches away like flaccid lava and overflows the taut line of the horizon. Everything was naked around the dark man who found himself all alone at the moment he ended his disappointing excursion in the other world.

The house had disappeared. There remained nothing but the stars that had been seen dancing for a moment behind the windows. Then the stars too went away.

What cruel and frightening mystery lay dormant under your roof, haunted house?

What acid grief disaggregated your gold heart and your silver soul, O magnetized poet!

1. "Dangerous idiot," *sot périlleux*, a pun on *saut périlleux*, "dangerous leap." (Trans.)
2. *Panier à salade*, "salad basket," is a slang expression for prison van or Black Maria. (Trans.)
3. The Beauce is an agricultural region southwest of Paris known as "the breadbasket of France"; its capital is Chartres. (Trans.)
4. "Skate fish on the wall," *raie au mur*, pun on Réaumur, the inventor of a thermometric scale that bears his name. (Trans.)

Haunted House (Brooklyn, N.Y.: Black Square Editions and the Brooklyn Rail, 2007).

ANTONIN ARTAUD

(1896–1948)

CORRESPONDENCE WITH JACQUES
RIVIÈRE (1886–1925)

May 1, 1923–March 22, 1924; with the poem "Cry"

JACQUES RIVIÈRE TO ANTONIN ARTAUD

May 1, 1923

Sir,

I regret not being able to publish your poems in the *Nouvelle Revue Française*. But I took enough interest in them to wish to make the acquaintance of their author. If it were possible for you to pass by the review on a Friday, between four and six, I should be happy to see you.

Please accept, sir, the assurance of my sympathetic feelings.

Jacques Rivière

ANTONIN ARTAUD TO JACQUES RIVIÈRE

June 5, 1923

Sir,

Will you, if it isn't too much trouble, allow me to come back to several remarks of our conversation this afternoon.

It is because the question of the admissibility of these poems is a problem which concerns you as much as me. I am speaking, naturally, of their absolute admissibility, of their literary existence.

I suffer from a frightful illness of the mind. My thought abandons me at every level. From the simple fact of thought to the external fact of its materialization into words. Words, forms of phrases, inner directions of the mind, simple reactions of the mind—I am in constant pursuit of my intellectual being. Thus when *I can seize a form*, imperfect though it is, I pin it down in the fear of losing the thought. I do not do

243

myself justice, I know: I suffer from this, but I consent to it in the fear of not dying completely.

All this which is said very badly is in danger of bringing a formidable ambiguity into your judgment of me.

That is why out of respect for the central feeling which dictates these poems to me and for the images or strong figures of speech which I was able to find, I propose these poems for existence in spite of everything. I have felt and accepted these figures, these inopportune expressions for which you reproach me. Remember: I did not contest them. They stem from the profound uncertainty of my thought. Fortunate indeed when this uncertainty is not replaced by the absolute inexistence from which I suffer sometimes.

Here again I am afraid of ambiguity. I would like you really to understand that it is not a question of that more-or-less of existence which emerges from what is commonly called inspiration, but of a total absence, a veritable extinction.

This is also why I told you that I had nothing, no work in progress; the few things I showed you constituting scraps that I was able to wrest from utter nothingness.

It is very important for me that the few manifestations of *spiritual* existence which I was able to give myself be not considered inexistent through the fault of the blots and unacceptable expressions scattered throughout them.

It seemed to me as I showed them to you that their faults, their unevennesses were not so glaring as to destroy the whole impression of each poem.

Please believe, sir, that I have no immediate or selfish end in view, I want only to settle a crucial problem.

For I cannot hope that time or work will remedy these obscurities or these weaknesses; that is why I demand this existence, aborted though it be, with so much insistence and disquiet. And the question to which I would like an answer is: Do you think that one can attribute less literary authenticity and power of action to a poem which is perfect but without much inner reverberation? I admit that a review like the *Nouvelle Revue Française* requires a certain formal level and a great purity of substance, but without this, is the body of my thought so confused and its general beauty rendered so ineffectual by the impurities and indecisions scattered through it, that it doesn't succeed *literarily* in existing? The whole problem of my thought is what is at stake. It is a question for me of nothing less than knowing whether or not I have the right to continue to think, in verse or in prose.

I shall permit myself one of these Fridays to offer you the little pamphlet of poems which Mr. Kahnweiler has just published and which is called *Tric Trac du Ciel*, as well as the little volume in the Contemporaries series: *Les Douze Chansons*. You will then be able to let me know your final opinions of my poems.

Antonin Artaud

JACQUES RIVIÈRE TO ANTONIN ARTAUD

June 23, 1923

Dear Sir,

I have read attentively that which you were kind enough to submit to my judgment and it is in all sincerity that I think I can reassure you about the doubts your letter betrays and which I was so touched that you should choose to confide in me. There are in your poems, as I told you first off, awkwardnesses and above all strangenesses that are disconcerting. But they seem to me to correspond to a certain studied effort on your part rather than to a lack of command of your thought. Obviously (this is what prevents me for the moment from publishing any of your poems in the *Nouvelle Revue Française*) you do not attain in general to a sufficient unity of impression. But I am sufficiently accustomed to reading manuscripts to glimpse that this concentration of your means toward a simple poetic object is not at all ruled out for you by your temperament, and that with a little patience, even if this is to be nothing more than a simple elimination of the divergent images or references, you will succeed in writing perfectly coherent and harmonious poems.

I shall always be delighted to see you, to talk with you, and to read whatever it pleases you to submit to me. Am I to send back the volume you brought me?

I beg you, dear sir, to accept the assurance of my most sympathetic feelings.

Jacques Rivière

Paris, January 29, 1924

Sir,

You may rightly have forgotten me. During the course of last May I made you a little mental confession. And I had asked you a question. Will you allow me to complete this confession today, to resume it, to fathom my own depths. I don't seek to justify myself in your eyes, and it matters little to me whether I seem to exist for anyone at all. I have all the distance which separates me from myself to cure me of the judgment of others. Please do not consider this insolence, but rather the very faithful confession, the painful setting forth of a painful state of thought.

For a long time I held a grudge against you for your reply. I had given myself to you as a mental case, a veritable psychic anomaly, and you answered me with a literary judgment of poems I didn't, and couldn't, care about. I perceive today that I had perhaps not been explicit enough, and for that, pardon me once more.

I had thought to attract your attention if not by the preciosity of my poems, at least by the rarity of certain phenomena of an intellectual kind, which were precisely the reason why these poems were not, could not be other than they are, even though I had within me precisely what was needed to take them to the furthest extreme of perfection. Vain affirmation: I exaggerate, but purposely.

My question was in fact specious, perhaps, but it was of you that I asked it, of you and no other, because of the extreme sensibility, the almost unhealthy penetration of your mind. I flattered myself that I was bringing you a case, a characterized mental case, and, curious as I thought you were of every mental deformation, of all destructive obstacles to thought, I meant simultaneously to draw your attention to the *real* value, the initial value of my thought, and to the productions of my thought.

This scattered condition of my poems, these formal flaws, this constant giving way of my thought, must be attributed not to a lack of exercise, of possession of the instrument I wielded, of *intellectual development*, but to a central collapse of the soul, a kind of erosion, essential and at the same time fleeting, of thought; to the temporary nonpossession of the material benefices of my development; to the abnormal separation of the elements of thought (the impulse to think, at each of the terminal stratifications of thought, passing through all the states, all the bifurcations of thought and form).

There is then something which destroys my thought; a something which does not prevent me from being what I might be, but which leaves me, if I may say so, in suspense. A furtive something which snatches away the words *which I found*, diminishes my mental tension, destroys gradually the mass of my thought in its substance, deprives me of everything down to the turns of phrase with which one expresses oneself and which translate exactly the most inseparable, localized, existing modulations of thought. I do not insist further. I do not have to describe my state.

I would like to say only enough to be at last understood and believed by you.

Then trust me. Admit, I beg of you, the reality of these phenomena, admit their furtiveness, their eternal repetition, admit that I would have written this letter before today if I had not been in this state. And once again here is my question:

You know the subtlety, the fragility of the mind? Haven't I told you enough about it to prove to you that I have a mind which *literarily* exists, as T. exists, or E., or S., or M. Restore to my mind the unity of its forces, the cohesion it lacks, the constancy of its tension, the stability of its own substance. (And objectively all this is so little.) And tell me if what my (early) poems lack might not be all at once restored to them?

Do you believe that penetration, in a well-constituted mind, goes hand in hand with extreme weakness, and that one can amaze and disappoint at the same time? Finally, although I am a good judge of my mind, I cannot judge the productions of my mind very well, I can judge the productions of my mind only insofar as they are confused with it in a kind of happy unconsciousness. This will be my criterion.

I send you then, to terminate, I present you with the latest production of my mind. It is worth little relatively to me, though more than nothingness all the same. It is a makeshift. But the question for me is to know if it is better to write this or to write nothing at all.

You will supply the answer to this in accepting or refusing this little essay. *You* will judge it, from the viewpoint of the absolute. But I will tell you that it would be a fine consolation for me to think that even though I cannot be *all* myself, not as high, as dense, as wide as myself, I can still be something. That, sir, is why you must be truly absolute. Judge this prose beyond all questions of tendency, principle, personal taste, judge it with the charity of your soul, the essential lucidity of your mind, rethink it with your heart.

It probably indicates a brain and a soul which exist, to which a certain place is due. In consideration of the palpable irradiation of this soul, do not brush it aside unless your conscience protests with all its forces, but if you have a doubt, let it be resolved in my favor.

I submit myself to your judgment.

    Antonin Artaud

POSTSCRIPT OF A LETTER IN WHICH CERTAIN LITERARY PRINCIPLES OF JACQUES RIVIÈRE WERE DISCUSSED:

You will tell me that another mental cohesion and another penetration would be necessary to give an opinion on questions like these. Well, then! My own weakness and absurdity are to wish to write at any cost, and to express myself.

I am a man who has suffered much from the mind, and for this reason I have the *right* to speak. I accepted once and for all to submit to my inferiority. And yet I am not stupid. I know that there might be cause to think further than I think and perhaps otherwise. I myself wait only for my intellect to change, for its upper drawers to open. In an hour and tomorrow perhaps I shall have changed thought, but this present thought exists; I shall not let my thought be lost.

    A. A.

CRY

The little celestial poet
Opens the shutters of his heart.
The heavens collide. Oblivion
Uproots the symphony.

Stableboy the insane house
That gave you the wolves to guard
Does not suspect the wrath
Brewing under the great alcove
Of the vault which hangs over us.

Therefore, silence and night,
Muzzle all impurity
The sky with great strides
Proceeds to the crossroads of noise.

The star eats. The oblique sky
Opens its flight toward the summits
Night sweeps away the remains
Of the meal which contented us.

On Earth walks a slug
Whom ten thousand white hands greet
A slug creeps to the place
Where Earth disappeared.

Now angels were returning in peace
Summoned by no obscenity
When the real voice arose
From the mind that summoned them.

The sun lower than the day
Turned all the sea to steam.
A dream strange yet clear
Was born on the wildly fleeing Earth.

The little lost poet
Leaves his celestial position
With an idea of the place beyond the Earth
Pressed to the tresses of his heart.

* * * * *

Two traditions met.
But our padlocked thoughts
Lacked the necessary space,
An experiment to be rebegun.

A. A.

ANTONIN ARTAUD TO JACQUES RIVIÈRE

March 22, 1924

My letter was worth at least a reply. Send back, sir, letters and manuscripts.

I would have liked to find something intelligent to say to you, to mark well what separates us, but it was useless. I am a mind not yet formed, an idiot: Think of me what you will.

    Antonin Artaud

JACQUES RIVIÈRE TO ANTONIN ARTAUD

Paris, March 25, 1924

Dear Sir,

Why of course, I quite agree with you, your letters deserved a reply; I haven't yet been able to give it to you; that's all. Excuse me, I beg you.

One thing strikes me: the contrast between the extraordinary precision of your diagnosis of yourself and the vagueness, or at least the formlessness of the realizations you attempt.

I was wrong, no doubt, in my letter of last year, to want to reassure you at any price: I behaved like those doctors who claim to cure their patients by refusing to listen to them, by denying the strangeness of their case, by forcibly replacing them in normality. It is a bad method. I regret it.

Even if I had no other evidence, your tormented handwriting, staggering, collapsing, as though absorbed here and there by secret maelstroms, would be enough to confirm for me the reality of the phenomena of mental "erosion" of which you complain.

But how do you escape them so well when you try to define your sickness? Is one to believe that anguish gives you that force and that lucidity which you lack when you yourself are not directly concerned? Or is it the nearness of the object that you strive to seize which suddenly allows you so sure a grip? In any case, you obtain, in the analysis of your own mind, complete and remarkable results, which must give you confidence in that very mind, since it is in any case the very instrument which procures them for you.

Other considerations may also help you not perhaps to hope for a cure, but at least to bear your illness with patience. They are of a general nature. You speak in one place in your letter of the "fragility of the mind." It is superabundantly proved by the mental disorders that the psychiatrist studies and catalogues. But they have perhaps not yet demonstrated sufficiently to what extent supposedly normal thought is the product of hazardous mechanisms.

That the mind exists by itself, that it has a tendency to live on its own substance, that it grows on the character with a kind of egoism and without worrying about keeping it in harmony with the world can no longer, it seems, be contested today. Paul Valéry dramatized in a marvelous way this autonomy in us of the thinking function, in his famous *Soirée avec M. Teste.* Caught within its own boundaries, the mind is a sort of canker; it propagates, advances constantly in all directions; you yourself note as one of your torments "the impulse to think"; no idea brings it fatigue and satisfaction; even these temporary appeasements which our bodily functions find in exercise are unknown to it. The man who thinks spends himself totally. Romanticism apart, there is no other outlet to pure thinking than death.

There is a whole literature—I know that it preoccupies you as much as it interests me—which is the product of the immediate and if I may say so the animal functioning of the mind. It has the aspect of a vast field of ruins; the columns which remain standing are held up only by chance. Chance reigns there, in a kind of dismal multiplicity. One may say that it is the exactest and directest expression of that monster which every man carries within him, but usually seeks to enchain in bonds of events and experience.

But, you will tell me, is it really that which must be called "fragility of the mind"? While I complain of a weakness, you paint me another disease which would come from an excess of force, of a surfeit of power.

Here now is my thought pursued a little more closely: The mind is fragile in this: that it needs obstacles—adventitious obstacles. Only, it loses itself, destroys itself. It seems to me that this mental "erosion," these inner thefts, this "destruction" of thought "in its substance" which afflicts your own, have no other cause than the too-great liberty which you allow it. It is the absolute which deranges it. To stretch out, the mind needs a limit and the fortunate opacity of experience blocking its path. The only remedy for madness is the innocence of facts.

As soon as you accept the mental level, you accept all the troubles, and especially all the laxity of the mind. If by thought one understands *creation,* as you seem to most of the time, it must at all costs be relative; one will find security, constancy, force only in committing the mind to something.

I know: There is a kind of intoxication in the instant of its pure emanation, in that moment when its fluid escapes directly from the brain and encounters a quantity of spaces, a quantity of stages and levels in which to unfurl. It is that wholly subjective impression of complete liberty, and even of complete intellectual license, which our "surrealists" have tried to translate by the dogma of a fourth poetical dimension. But the punishment for this soaring is ready and waiting: The universal possible is changed into concrete impossibilities; the captured phantom finds twenty inner phantoms to avenge him which paralyze us, devour our spiritual substance.

Is this to say that the normal functioning of the mind must consist in a servile imitation of given models and that to think is nothing more than to reproduce? I don't think so; one must choose what one wants to "render" and have it always be something not only definite, not only recognizable, but also unknown; for the mind to discover all is power, the concrete must assume the function of the mysterious. Every successful "thought," every language which apprehends, the words by which one afterward recognizes the writer, are always the result of a compromise between a current of intelligence which comes from him, and an ignorance which comes toward him, a surprise, an obstacle. The rightness of an expression always involves a remnant of hypothesis; the word has had to strike against a deaf object, and more promptly than reason would have reached it. But where the object, where the obstacle, is totally lacking, the mind continues, adamant and feeble; and everything disintegrates in an immense contingency.

I judge you, perhaps, both from too-abstract a viewpoint and from too-personal preoccupations: It seems to me however that your case can be explained in a large measure by the observations I have just permitted myself (at a little too much length) and that it enters into the general pattern I have tried to outline. As long as you let your intellectual force pour out into the absolute, it is tormented by eddies, pierced by impotence, a prey to ravening gusts which disorganize it; but as soon as, brought back by anguish to your own mind, you direct it at that near and enigmatic object, it condenses, intensifies, makes itself useful and penetrating, and brings you positive benefits; that is, truths expressed with all the contrast necessary to render them accessible to others, something then which goes beyond your sufferings, your very existence, which increases your stature and consolidates you, gives you the only reality that man can reasonably hope to conquer with his own forces, the reality in others.

I am not systematically an optimist; but I refuse to despair of you. My sympathy for you is very great; I was wrong to leave you so long without hearing from me.

I am keeping your poem. Send me everything you do.

Believe, I beg you, in my warmest sentiments.

Jacques Rivière

Paris, May 7, 1924

Very dear sir,

To return to an argument which is already old, it is enough to imagine a moment that the impossibility of expressing myself applies to the most vital needs of my life, to my most urgent contingencies—and to the suffering which follows: Understand that it is not for lack of desperate eagerness that I renounce myself. I am available to poetry. It is only because of chance external circumstances that I do not realize myself. It is enough for me that people believe I have possibilities of crystallizations of things in me, in forms and with the necessary words.

I had to wait all this time to be in a position to send you this slender note which is clear for want of being well written. You may draw from it the obvious conclusions.

One thing in your letter remains a little obscure to me: that is the use to which you intend to put the poem I sent you. You put your finger on an aspect of myself: Literature as such interests me only a very little, but if by chance you decided to publish it, send me the proofs, I beg of you; it is very important for me to change two or three words.

All my good thoughts.

Antonin Artaud

May 24, 1924

Dear Sir,

An idea has come to me which I resisted for a while, but which decidedly attracts me. Think it over in turn. I hope it pleases you. It must in any case be worked out in detail.

Why shouldn't we publish the letters you have written me? I have just reread again that of January 29 which is utterly remarkable.

There would be only a little effort of transposition to make. I mean that we would give fictitious names to the signer and the addressee. Perhaps I could write a reply along the lines of the one I sent you, but more developed and less personal. Perhaps also we could introduce a fragment of your poems or of your essay on Uccello? The whole would form a little epistolary novel that would be most curious.

Give me your opinion, and meanwhile believe me sincerely yours.

Jacques Rivière

ANTONIN ARTAUD TO JACQUES RIVIÈRE

May 25, 1924

Dear Sir,

Why lie, why seek to place on the literary level a thing which is the very cry of life, why give the appearances of fiction to what is made of the ineradicable substance of the soul, which is like the plaint of reality? Yes, your idea pleases me, it delights me, it overwhelms me, but on condition that we give to whoever reads the book the impression that it isn't a fabricated work. We have the right to lie, but not about the essence of ourselves. I don't insist on signing the letters with my name. But it is absolutely vital that the reader think he has the elements of a lived story in hand. It would be necessary to publish my letters from the first to the last and for that to go back to the month of June 1923. The reader must have all the elements of the debate at his disposal.

A man possesses himself in fitful flashes, and even when he possesses himself, he doesn't completely attain himself. He does not realize that constant cohesion of his forces without which any true creation is impossible. Yet that man exists. I mean that he has a distinct reality which enhances him. Do we mean to condemn him to nothingness on the pretext that he can give only fragments of himself? You yourself do not think so and the proof of this is the importance you attach to these fragments. For a long time I have had the intention of proposing collecting them to you. This, to tell you with what satisfaction I welcome the idea you propose to me.

I am perfectly aware of the halts and jolts in my poems, jolts which touch the very essence of my inspiration and which stem from my indelible powerlessness to concentrate on an object. Through physiological weakness, a weakness which touches the very substance of what is commonly called the soul and which is the emanation of our nervous force coagulated around objects. But the whole era suffers from this weakness.

Examples: Tristan Tzara, André Breton, Pierre Reverdy. But *their* soul is not physiologically stricken, not substantially; it is not wounded at all the points where it joins something else, it is not *outside of thought*; then whence comes this sickness, is it really the air of the times, a miracle floating in the air, a cosmic and evil prodigy, or the discovery of a new world, a real broadening of reality? It is nonetheless true that they do not suffer, and that I do suffer, not only in my mind but in my flesh and in my everyday soul. That want of application to the object which characterizes all literature is in me a want of application to life. I can truly say that I am not in the world, and this is not a mere pose of the mind. My last poems seem to me to show definite progress. Are they really unpublishable as a whole? But no matter, I prefer to show myself as I am, in my nonexistence and my rootlessness. One could in any case publish long extracts from them. I believe that most of the stanzas taken as units are good. You yourself will choose these fragments, you will arrange the letters. *Here I am no longer a judge.* But what I chiefly insist on is that an ambiguity not be introduced concerning the nature of the phenomena which I cite for my defense. The reader must believe in a real sickness which touches the essence of the being and its central possibilities of expression, and which applies to a whole life.

I believe I have said enough to be understood; publish this last letter. I realize as I end it that it can serve as a summing-up and conclusion of the debate for the part which concerns me.

Believe, dear sir, in my feelings of great and affectionate gratitude.

Antonin Artaud

ANTONIN ARTAUD TO JACQUES RIVIÈRE

June 6, 1924

Dear Sir,

[...]

My whole mental life is traversed by petty doubts and peremptory certainties which express themselves in lucid and coherent words. And my weaknesses are of a more tremulous structure, they are themselves immature and badly formulated. They are living roots, roots of anguish which touch the heart of my life; but they do not have the disarray of life, one does not sense the cosmic breath of a soul shaken to its foundations. They are from a mind which has not thought out its weakness; otherwise, it would have translated it into dense and active words. And there, sir, is the whole problem—to have the inseparable reality in oneself, and the material clarity of a feeling, to have it said to a point where it is impossible for it not to express itself, to have a wealth of words, of schooled turns of phrase, which could join in, serve the game; and then, at the moment the soul begins to organize its riches, its discoveries, that revelation; in that unconscious minute when the thing is on the point of emanating, a superior and ill will attacks the soul like vitriol, attacks the mass of word-and-image, attacks the mass of feeling, and leaves *me* gasping at the very threshold of life.

And this will, now—suppose I feel its passing physically, that it shakes me with sudden unforeseen electricity, a repeated electricity. Suppose that each of my instants of thinking is on certain days shaken by these profound tornadoes whose existence cannot be suspected from the outside. And tell me whether any literary work at all is compatible with such states. What brain could hold up under them? What personality would not disintegrate? If only I had the force, I would sometimes treat myself to the luxury of mentally submitting some famous mind, some old or young writer who produces, and whose nascent thought is accepted as authority, to the maceration of so urgent a suffering, in order to see what would be left of him. One must not be in a hurry to judge men, one must give them the benefit of a doubt to the point of absurdity, to the dregs. These hazarded works which often seem to you the product of a mind not yet in possession of itself, which will perhaps never possess itself—who knows what brain they conceal, what power of life, what thinking fever which circumstances alone have reduced. Enough of me and my unborn works, I ask nothing more than to feel my intellect.

Antonin Artaud

JACQUES RIVIÈRE TO ANTONIN ARTAUD

Paris, June 8, 1924

Dear Sir,

Perhaps I substituted myself a little indiscreetly, with my ideas, my prejudices, for your suffering, your singularity. Perhaps I prattled where I should have understood and pitied. I wanted to reassure you, to cure you. That comes no doubt from the kind of rage with which I always react, for my part, toward life. In my struggle to live, I will admit defeat only with my last breath.

Your last letters, in which the word "soul" comes to replace several times the word "mind," waken in me even graver, but more embarrassed, sympathy than the first ones. I feel, I touch a profound and private misery; I remain in suspense before illnesses which I can but glimpse. But perhaps this disconcerted attitude will bring you more aid and encouragement than my previous ratiocinations.

And yet! Have I no means of understanding your torments? You say "a man possesses himself only in fitful flashes, and even when he possesses himself, he does not completely attain himself." This man is you; but I can see that it is also me. I know nothing resembling your "tornadoes," nor that "ill will" which "attacks the soul from outside" and its powers of expression. But for all that it is in general, less painful, the sensation of my own inferiority I sometimes have is nonetheless clear.

Like you, I set aside the convenient symbol of inspiration so as to explain the alternatives through which I pass. It is a question of something more profound, more "substantial" if I may dare divert the word from its meaning, than a fortunate wind which might come to me, or not, from the depths of my mind; it is a question of stages through which I travel in my own reality. Not voluntarily, alas! but in a purely accidental way.

There is this that is remarkable: that the very fact of my existence, as you note in your case, is never for me the object of a serious doubt; something of myself always remains for me, but more often than not it is something poor, awkward, infirm and almost suspect. At these moments I do not lose every idea of my complete reality; but sometimes every hope of ever reconquering it. It is like a roof over me which might stay in the air by a miracle, and which I could see no means of reconstructing myself.

My feelings, my ideas—the same ones as usual—succeed each other with a slight air of fantasy; they are so weakened, so hypothetical that they seem to belong to pure philosophical speculation, they are still there, nevertheless, but they look at me as though to make me admire their absence.

Proust has described the "intermittences of the heart"; someone ought to describe the intermittences of the being.

Obviously there are, for these disappearances of the soul, physiological causes which are often easy enough to determine. You speak of the soul as "the coagulation of our nervous force"; you say that it can be "physiologically stricken." I think like you that it is deeply dependent on our nervous system. Yet its crises are so capricious that at certain moments I understand that one might be tempted to look, as you do, for a mystical explanation of the "ill will" from outside which tries relentlessly to diminish it.

In any case it is a fact, I believe, that a whole category of men is subject to oscillation of their level of being. How many times, placing ourselves mechanically in a familiar psychological attitude, have we discovered that it went beyond us, or rather that we had surreptitiously become insufficient to it! How many times has our usual character suddenly seemed artificial to us, and even fictitious, through the absence of spiritual or "essential" resources which were to nourish it!

Where does our being go, and from whence does it return, that all psychology down to our time has pretended to consider it as a constant? It is a practically insoluble problem, unless one has recourse to a religious dogma, like that of Grace, for example. I admire our age for daring to ask it (I am thinking of Proust and Pirandello, in whom it is implicit) and still leaving in the question mark, restricting itself to anguish.

"A soul physiologically stricken." It is a terrible heritage. Yet I believe that in a certain way, that of penetration, it can also be a privilege. It is also the only means we have in us of understanding ourselves a little, of seeing ourselves at any rate. He who does not know depression, who has never felt his soul broken into by the body, invaded by his weakness, is incapable of perceiving any truth about man; one must go down, see what lies behind; one must be no longer able to move, nor hope, nor believe, in order to realize its truth. How shall we distinguish our intellectual or moral mechanisms, if we are not temporarily deprived of them? It must be the consolation of those who in this way test this slow death that they are the only ones to know a little what life is made of.

And then the "maceration of so urgent a suffering" prevents the ridiculous cloud of vanity from rising up in them. You wrote me: "I have to cure myself of the judgment of others, all the distance which separates me from myself." Such is the utility of that "distance": It "cures one of the judgment of others"; it prevents us from doing anything to attract it, to accommodate ourselves to it; it conserves us pure and despite the variations of our reality, it assures us a superior degree of identity for ourselves.

Naturally, health is the only admissible ideal, the only one to which my conception of a man has a right to aspire; but when it is given all at once in a being, it hides half the world from him.

I have let myself go on again, in spite of myself, in comforting you, trying to show you how much, even in the matter of existence, the "normal state" may be precarious. I wish with all my heart that the stages I have been describing may be accessible to you, as much in the ascending direction as in the other. A moment of plenitude, of being equal to yourself—why, after all, should it be forbidden you, if you already have this courage to desire it. There is absolute peril only for him who lets himself go; there is total death only for him who develops a taste for dying.

I beg you to believe in my absolute sympathy.

Jacques Rivière

Correspondence with Jacques Rivière (1886–1925), May 1, 1923–March 22, 1924; with the poem "Cry." *Art and Literature* 6 (Autumn 1965).

GEORGES BATAILLE

(1897–1962)

FROM *L'ABBÉ C.*

Eponine

What attracts me in a priest is, of course, what he lacks. In a way the universe is a fake: the back door of a house opening on nothing. Like the universe in this respect, the priest, if we are to believe him, might be a trap himself. The ordinary man hides nothing: We can easily walk around him: Behind, his house is badly kept and even smells bad: no black curtain there, held in place by an embarrassed silence.

The irritating thing about a priest is that he really has no suspicious curtain either, but *he lacks one*. With him the fraud is, on the contrary, to let us believe that he opens on nothing, but to counter us quickly, to joke with us. Sometimes he mounts the altar with a lump in his throat, and hearing his voice quaver we begin to hope that he has found access to the beyond, that he is suddenly going to fall lifeless at our feet; but then we would have to help him, armed with that unnamed violence which he calls (or pretends to call) killing him: The Church would then drop the falsity which she ordains and *which she lacks*; infinity would open up.

Of all others, the abbé C. was especially deluded by this curse of urbanity. Seldom has a young priest worked harder to disappoint a desire for silence. I spoke to the abbé C. of this powerlessness: Suavely smiling, he had a joking reply.

"You don't understand, not at all; we think of nothing but that," he said to me. "It's that . . . we fool people. On the outside we are all energy, good humor, even slightly in bad taste, but deep in our hearts there is anguish."

Then his eyes gleamed with mischief.

"The love of God," he added, "is the most deceptive of all. They ought to have kept that vulgar slogan for it, which would then pass imperceptibly from witticism to the most pregnant of silences ..."

And he let these words slip from his lips (he smoked a pipe), with an evasive smile: *"Say it with flowers!"*

I had to pick up a newspaper in order to keep from laughing.

I don't know, even today, what he meant.

A concern for goodwill, for openness, won out over prudence in him: His ardent Catholicism, his intelligence, his agreeable temerity, gave him the power to dare anything. The sense of a mystery he ought to have held back was so lacking in him that one day when he was joking with a secretary (she was asking what kind of drawers were worn by the clergy), he gaily hitched up his robe and displayed his shorts and a pair of elegant black socks fastened to his shanks with elastics. There was no libertinism: At the most he was answering a provocative obsession, which made him say, in an idle, gossiping way, that he, if he made love, would kill himself.

In reality this conspicuous, empty, and agreeable man drew from the priesthood a power of fooling not others but himself: Such delight at being in the world, so much activity, whistling its triumph of virtue in the suburbs, are possible only to confusion. Women excel at these naive excesses, but remain in the background: while a man (a priest) struts and swaggers through this comedy of divine benevolence.

What attracts me in these emissaries of the infinite is that they have so thoroughly reduced their Master to obedience that they no longer have anything to hope or fear. If they speak, they hear His voice, to which their tongue has given suavity. They are suavely deaf.

That Sunday I had spent the afternoon with an incongruous girl, and we had drunk beyond measure. I arranged to meet her at the top of the church tower. First of all I went to the presbytery to ask C. to accompany me.

I took him by the arm, and letting my all-too-evident condition justify me, said to him in a tone which had the gentleness of his own:

"Come with me. I am athirst for infinity this evening."

And, facing him and opening my arms:

"Have you a reason to refuse?"

"You see," I pursued, bowing my head, "my thirst is so great at the moment ..."

Nicely, the abbé burst into gay laughter.

I feigned annoyance, and protested:

"You haven't understood my meaning."

I moaned, playing my role to the utmost.

"You don't understand me: I no longer have the power to restrain myself. This is a cruel sensation. I need you, I need a man of God."

I implored him:

"Don't resist my helplessness. You see, drinking makes me blind. Take me up to the tower, where I have an appointment."

The abbé answered simply:

"I'll go with you."

But he added:

"I too have an appointment on the tower."

I pretended confusion; I raised my head and stammered:

"With whom?"

"With the infinite mercy of the Lord," he answered.

The church in that village where we were born is flanked by a tall rectangular tower. A violent wind was blowing. The wooden staircase you go up is hardly more than a ladder, and it seemed to me that the wind was making the tower sway. Halfway up I clung unsteadily to a rung. I imagined the consequences of slipping: the world snatched away into the void, the bottom open at last, the identity of the cry with a definitive silence. Under me the abbé grasped my leg firmly.

"Don't go killing yourself in the church," he said. "You know how I dislike reading the burial service."

He tried to make his voice resound in the commotion of the wind, but only succeeded in chanting the opening words of the *Dies Irae* in falsetto.

It was so painful that my heart skipped a beat: Why had I gone to get him? He was insipid and laughable.

Suddenly, I saw him, from where I was hanging: lying stretched out on a heap of slag made ugly by grass and wildflowers.

I was hanging over the void on the ladder. I saw the abbé dying, in the hands of sordid executioners: rage mingled with suffocation, an endless immodesty of screams, odor of excrement and pus, the pain magnified tenfold by the expectation of mutilating tortures. But at that moment it was my rage, my pity for the abbé that was hitting: I myself was choking, I lashed out, and my fall in the tower turned the empty space into a hell of cries.

Drunk, I had slipped into the arms of the abbé, who was himself in an unsteady position and held on to me only with great difficulty.

"We almost fell," said the man of the church.

I could have dragged him along in my fall, but I was so forsaken in his arms that I could imagine myself happy. His stupidity was helpful in me: In a world of abysses, of sliding, and of horrors furiously desired, there is nothing that is not canceled out by a simple thought: that of the inevitable outcome. To be hanging, precisely, above the void, to have escaped death only by chance, filled me with a feeling of helplessness that was like gaiety. I abandoned myself completely and my limbs dangled lifelessly, but at the end it was as though a cock crowed. At this moment I heard a cry from the top of the tower: the grave voice of Eponine, at the end of the ladder, enunciating gaily:

"Are you dead?"

"Only be patient, we're getting there!" replied the high-pitched voice of the abbé.

My body, at ease, still dangled, but now it shook with light laughter.

"Now," I said softly, "I will walk up myself."

I remained inert all the same.

Slowly night fell, and outside, in long gusts, the wind blew: The helplessness of such a moment had something open about it and I would have liked it to last.

A few years previously the abbé C. had been like me just another of the young gentlemen of the town: He attracted Eponine, who had done nothing about it except in daydreams (she took a furious delight in imagining scandals in which he would take part; it was sweet, but shameful; so much so that it demented her). Although, halfway up the tower and in the shadows, I was kept from a horrible death only by C.'s arms, the spitefulness of my humor toward him surprised me. But the idea of death, scarcely opposed to the sliding state I was in, represented little more than a painful intimacy for me: I had first to satisfy Eponine's desires. She was drunk like me when, on a cruel whim, I had gone to get the abbé. All afternoon we had drunk and made love, and I had laughed. But now I was so weak that when I thought of the top of the tower, of what it meant, I experienced instead of desire (rather, like desire) a feeling of nausea. Now the priest's face was sweating; his gaze sought mine. It was a heavy, alien look, alive with a cold intent.

I thought: On the contrary, I ought to have grabbed the abbé's inanimate body myself and carried it in my arms to the top of the tower, and in the freedom of the wind offered it to Eponine's demented humors, as to an evil goddess. But my wickedness had no force: As in a dream, it slipped away; I was nothing but craven gentleness, jovial, vaguely promised to oblivion.

I heard (I saw Eponine's lowered head at the top of the ladder) cries of vulgar impatience. I saw the abbé's gaze fill with hate, then shut. Eponine's insults had opened his eyes: He saw the trap into which friendliness had lured him.

"What is the meaning of this farce?" he asked me.

There was more weariness than hostility in his voice.

I answered with studied awkwardness:

"You're afraid of going up there?"

He laughed but he was angry.

"You go too far: You're so dead drunk that you fall, and it's I who haven't the courage to go up!"

Very amused, I teased him:

"You've got a little thread of a voice . . ."

I reacted passively, but in a sense apathy left me free: as though I were going to be unable to keep from laughing any longer. I shouted with all my strength:

"Eponine!"

I heard a howl:

"Cretin!"

And other less decorous names.

Then:

"I'll be there in a moment."

She was beside herself with rage.

"But no," I answered, "we're coming up."

All the same I remained inert.

The abbé had trouble maintaining me with a knee and an arm against the ladder: I cannot think of it today without vertigo, but then a vague feeling of well-being and gaiety deceived me.

Eponine climbed down and said harshly to the abbé when she was near him:

"Enough of this now. Let's go down."

"That's impossible," said C. "I can hold him all right, but I can't carry him down the ladder."

Eponine didn't answer but I saw her suddenly gripping the rungs.

"Call for help," she shouted. "My head is spinning."

The abbé answered faintly, "That's all we can do."

At this moment I realized that we were going back down.

It was all over, we would never go up to the top.

I tensed myself in my inertia, and as paralysis never really immobilizes you except in moments of frantic effort, it seemed to me that only suicide would have the power of answering my irritation, only a voluntary death would be a punishment rigorous enough for my failure. We were all three clinging to the ladder and the silence was all the more annoying because I was waiting for the abbé to cry out. In his falsetto voice, which would break in the darkness, he would try to attract attention: It would be laughable, intolerable, and at that moment, definitively, everything would end. I struggled then: weakly, but I wanted to throw myself into the void where I would have liked to drag him. I could only escape him by going up: He was no doubt gripping the rungs firmly and could not prevent me from going higher.

Frightened, Eponine moaned:

"Hold on to him, he'll kill himself."

"I can't," the abbé said.

He thought that if he caught my leg he would precipitate my fall: He could help me only if he followed me.

"Let me past, I'm going to the top of the tower."

She shrank to one side and I climbed slowly to the top, followed by the abbé and by Eponine.

I came out into the open air, stunned by the wind. A wide light glow where the sun was setting was barred with black clouds. The sky was already dark. Facing me, the abbé C., disheveled, his face convulsed, was talking to me, but in the noise of the wind I heard only unintelligible words. Behind him I saw Eponine smile: She looked enraptured, overcome with gratification.

When, on the ladder, he had recognized Eponine, the shame of the village who never failed to try to provoke his love when he passed by (if she caught sight of him in the streets, she would laugh and, as though whistling gaily at a dog, click her tongue and call, "Virgin!"), the abbé C. had momentarily recoiled, but now he could not go back, and when he arrived at the top of the tower, he wanted to take up a challenge that went so far.

Nevertheless he had a moment's hesitation: In that insane situation, angelic sweetness and a smile lit up by intelligence were of no further use. Catching his breath, he was forced to fall back on his nerves' extraordinary firmness, on a dominating will for spiritual illumination. Facing him, Eponine and I had the vague, grimacing power, both anguished and jeering, of the night. In our confusion we were sure of one thing: *We were monsters!* There was no modesty in us, no limit to our passions:

Under the sooty sky we were black as demons! How sweet, how reassuring in a way, faced with the abbé's angry, inward tension, to feel a dizzying slide as though it were freedom. Eponine and I were dazed, violently drunk: Owing to my faintness on the ladder, the abbé was caught in the trap we had laid for him all the more securely.

Raging and panting, enclosed on a tiny platform in the free space of the heavens, we were arrayed one against the other like dogs that an abrupt spell had frozen in their tracks. The hostility that united us was immobile, frozen; it was like a spasm of absurd laughter in a moment of wild pleasure. To the point, swift as lightning, where I suppose the abbé himself felt it: when the distraught face of Mme Hanusse appeared in the door to the stairs, a hideous smile disfiguring furtively her unusually tense features.

"Eponine! Oh, the bitch!" shrieked Mme Hanusse.

Rendered thoroughly nasty by a rustic flavor, her fishwife's voice shouted down the wind. As she emerged, the wind encumbered her a moment: She stood erect, having trouble holding down her cloak (her appearance had the monochrome austerity of a past of cold sacristies, but she had a foul tongue).

She lunged at her daughter, and it was a fury who shouted:

"The slut, she's drunk and she's naked under her coat!"

Eponine backed toward the balustrade, seemingly mesmerized by her mother, who was going to reveal her disgrace. She did indeed look like a slut, cunning, and already, underneath, she was laughing with fear.

But even more quickly and decisively than the old woman, the abbé C. stepped forward.

His slender voice, born on an intimate current of shame, no longer broke: It burst into a command.

"Mme Hanusse, where do you think you are?"

The old woman was tall; she stopped in amazement, looking at the young abbé.

"You are within the walls of a sanctuary," the voice continued.

The old woman hesitated, not knowing what to do next.

Eponine, a little disappointed, smiled laboriously.

There was in Eponine's daze and affected silliness a kind of uncertainty. Drunk and mute, she was at the summit of a sanctuary, all docility and yet menace personified. Apparently her hands clenched her coat to keep it resolutely shut, but they could also be there just to open it. Thus she was both clothed and naked, modest and immodest. The passionate movements of the old woman and the priest, suddenly canceling each other out, had been able only to render this immobility uncertain. Anger and fright had no other effect, it seemed, than this paralyzed attitude which now made the nudity of Eponine the object of an anxious wait.

In the tense calm, through the fumes of my drunkenness, it seemed to me that the wind was dropping. A long silence emanated from the sky. The abbé slowly kneeled down, motioning to Mme Hanusse who knelt beside him. Bowing his head, he stretched out his arms in the form of a cross. Mme Hanusse saw it; she bowed her head and didn't stretch out her arms. Soon after, he sang in a voice of consternation, slowly, as though to a dead person:

> *Miserere mei Deus,*
> *secundum magnam misericordiam tuam*

This moaning of a voluptuous melody was so suspect! He confessed so strangely his anguish before the joys of nakedness! The abbé had to conquer us by denying himself, and the very attitude by which he sought to efface himself asserted him even more; the beauty of his song in the silence of the sky enclosed him in the loneliness of a devout delectation: This extraordinary beauty at night was nothing more than an homage to vice, the unnamable object of this pantomime.

Impassive, he continued:

> *Et secundum multitudinem miserationum tuarum,*
> *dele iniquitatem meam.*

Mme Hanusse raised her head: Motionless, he kept his arms out, his shrill voice punctuating the melody with admirable method (especially the *misera-ti-o-num* which seemed as though it would never end). Dumbfounded, Mme Hanusse made a face furtively and again bowed her head. Eponine at first ignored the abbé's singular attitude. Her two hands placed on the opening of her coat, her hair in the wind, her lips apart, she was so beautiful and so lewd that in my drunkenness I would have liked to answer the abbé's lament with some joyous catchphrase.

Eponine evoked accordion music, but the misery of the cheap dance hall or the music hall where she used to sing, surrounded by naked chorus girls, seemed ridiculous in proportion to so certain a triumph. A whole church should have resounded with the noise of the organ and the shrill cries of the choir if the glory which haloed her had been celebrated properly. I sneered at the song I had once loved to hear her sing, set to a stupid tune:

> *She's got*
> *A heart of gold*
> *Eléonore*

I imagined instead the clamor of a *Te Deum*! One day, a smile of pleased malice terminated a movement which had the abruptness of death, is its result and its sign. I was borne aloft this way, in my gentleness, by a joyful acclamation, infinite but already close to oblivion. Emerging visibly from the dream which had dazed her, Eponine suddenly caught sight of the abbé and began to laugh so rapidly that she jerked from side to side: Turning her back to us she leaned on the balustrade, like a child shaken by a fit of laughter. She laughed propping her head in her hands, and the abbé, interrupted suddenly by an unrestrained guffaw, raised his head, arms aloft, to the sight of nothing but a bare bottom: The wind had lifted the coat she could no longer hold shut when laughter overcame her.

The abbé confessed to me later, blushing (I interrogated him as a joke, and from honesty he kept silent), that he had had an erection. Eponine had shut her coat so quickly that Mme Hanusse, who looked up more slowly, never understood the meaning of the awestruck face, the abbé's arms aloft, his mouth wide open and gasping for breath. Now that he is dead (in Germany, where the torturers put out his eyes), now that Eponine is dead (raped and tortured by the military, but without saying a word), the church tower in the snowy landscape has the baleful look of a dead tree. I have survived, but as a crow haunts the solitude of winter, and my voice shows well enough how I live out the memories of far-off days.

Art and Literature 3 (Autumn–Winter 1964).

HENRI MICHAUX

(1899–1984)

INTRODUCTION TO
AN EXHIBITION CATALOGUE

Is a statement really necessary? Isn't it obvious that I paint so as to leave words behind, to put an end to the irritating question of how and why? Could it really be that I draw because I see so clearly this thing or that thing? Not at all. Quite the contrary. I do it to be perplexed again. And I am delighted if there are traps. I look for surprises. To know always would bore me. It would upset me. Must I at least be aware of what's been going on? Not even. Others will see it in another way and will perhaps be better placed to do so. Do I have a purpose? It doesn't matter. It is not what I want which must happen to me, but what tries to happen in spite of me . . . and happens incompletely, which is not serious. Once the work were finished I should be afraid that it might finish me too and bury me. Watch out for that. I try to rouse that which is not absolutely static within me and which may thus (who knows?) break out suddenly, a suddenly new and living movement. It is this movement which I insist must take place, this improvised, spontaneous movement. I should like to paint the inner ferment, not just paint with it or thanks to it. Why always be in such a hurry to make use of it then to have done with it? Why so much haste to be done with this agitation, with this sprouting forth? Remain rather in their afflux. Prefer their irruption to everything else. Irruption and Inundation . . . that is what appealed to me, I think, in watercolor. Water, too much water, floods of water will deceive, will upset the object of my attention (if I have one), drown it quickly, wake me up finally, force me, really force me to make sensational *volte-faces*. At this point it seems to me that I will have returned to the sources of myself, miraculously dissolving all the rigidity which has so dangerously installed itself within me.

Now about the blots. I have said too much already. I bet that's what they are waiting for, the blots. Well, I hate them. I love the water, but them—no. They disgust me. I am never rid of them until I have made them jump, run, climb, clamber down again. In themselves they are abhorrent to me and really only blots, which tell me nothing. (I have never been able to see anything at all in a "Rorschach Test.") So I fight them, whip them, I should like to be done at once with their prostrate stupidity, galvanize them, bewilder them, exasperate them, ally them monstrously with everything that moves in the unnamable crowd of beings, of nonbeings with a rage for being, to everything, insatiable desires or knots of force, which are destined never to take form, here or elsewhere. With their troop I busy myself with curing the blots. The blots are a provocation. I meet it. Quickly. One must act quickly with those big limp ones which are apt to go wallowing everywhere. The crucial minute comes quickly. Quickly, before they extend their realm of abjectness and vomiting. Unbearable blots.

If I'm a *tachiste*, I'm one who can't stand *taches*.[1]

Mescaline drawings. About these, yes, I ought to make a statement (again . . .). They do in fact happen differently. Strange, strange experience of mescaline, stranger than any drawing could be, even if it were to cover a whole wall with its pointed lines. When one first becomes conscious of internal images (and of external phenomena as well), it is only with a certain limited quantity of consciousness, a certain restricted speed of consciousnesses succeeding each other and making "contact."

Mescaline multiplies, sharpens, accelerates, intensifies the inward moments of becoming conscious. You watch their extraordinary flood, mesmerized, uncomprehending. With your eyes shut, you are in the presence of an immense world. Nothing has prepared you for this. You don't recognize it. Tremendously present, active, colored, swarming in tiny islands very close together with no empty space (the tiny islands are one of the surest signs of the second stage), teeming, vibrating but stationary, festering with ornaments, saturating the space which still remains immeasurable, which keeps coming to life in seethings, twistings, intertwinings, in unpreventable accumulations. You would swear that you are inside it, rather than the contrary—it is so big, so frightfully, magnificently, stellarly big,[2] all-important, ungovernable, beyond your ability to act. One would swear that it is true, an autonomous world, extragalactic perhaps, attained miraculously, the reverse or rather the obverse of this one.

Some have been converted forever.

Those who have once experienced the visions and the fascinating passivity cannot forget.

Mescaline is not however indispensable. Without it I have several times been able to have visions. The brain is able, and must be able, to reproduce everything which it has experienced. If one tells a patient that a phial of distilled water is morphine, it will make him sleep profoundly. My placebo is attentiveness, and the memory of a certain return which I know intimately: direction: sinking. That infinity is just to sink, to sink, to sink deeper and deeper. Then the vision returns.

That world is another consciousness.

But where then is art, where is what distinguishes one person from another? Everything which you yourself thought was canceled, excluded, is not, not at any rate in the way you thought. The roots of art are deep, and the person who, in his ecstasy, thought himself obliterated remains deeply remarkable. And yet, much as the phenomena of that world differ, they also resemble one another. The most easily recognizable are the drawings of those who have seen, whose inner eye has been taken over, commanded by the hypnotic spectacle. The drawings of mediums, of certain hallucinated persons, of some faith healers (though it is only afterward that they began to practice), drawings of Sunday painters (of the Sunday of the new revelation), of visionaries preaching a gospel of peace.

Temples of monotonous contemplation, with ornaments and columns endlessly repeated by the novices of the perpetual . . . Temples of indigent infinity, revealed incessantly, without progress, in a senile, mechanical serenity, devoid of life (of this life) or the eruptions and grimaces of the great Terrifier with his unheard-of rhythms. Each one unknowingly adds his uneasiness, his banality; simple, uneducated people contribute their poor riches. A strange world, that other one, where each sees in a different way, where only the mad multiplication, the accumulation, the repetition have been perceived by everyone.

As for myself, I have usually (not always) seen the rhythms, the counterrhythms. Much remains for me to do. I need other materials and another technique (especially for the colors). I had first of all to record the rhythms accurately, and the process of infinitization through the infinitesimal . . . I am just beginning.

1. Except in this instance, the word *taches* has been translated as "blots" throughout. (Trans.)
2. Or electronically small. (Michaux)

Henri Michaux (London: Robert Fraser Gallery, 1963), exhibition catalogue of drawings and gouaches by Henri Michaux, February 26–March 23, 1963.

MICHEL LEIRIS

(1901–1990)

CONCEPTION AND REALITY IN THE WORK OF RAYMOND ROUSSEL

On December 16, 1922 (a few days before the premiere of *Locus Solus*, which took place in a tumult, before an almost entirely hostile public), Raymond Roussel sent me the following note:

> Thank you, my dear Michel, for your interesting and curious letter.
>
> I see that, like me, you prefer the domain of Conception to that of Reality.
>
> The interest which you are kind enough to show in my work is a proof to me that in you I meet again with the affection your father lavished on me, and I am deeply touched.
>
> Yours affectionately.

In the fragment of Dr. Pierre Janet's work which Roussel reprints in *Comment j'ai écrit certains de mes livres* ("The Psychological Characteristics of Ecstasy," pp. 175–83) we find this remark concerning "Martial," that is to say Raymond Roussel, whom the famous psychiatrist treated for several years and described under this name (borrowed from the principal character in *Locus Solus*, the inventor Martial Canterel): "Martial has a very interesting conception of literary beauty. The work must contain nothing real, no observations on the world or the mind, nothing but completely imaginary combinations: These are already the ideas of an extrahuman world." In another part of the same work (*De l'angoisse à l'extase*, vol. II, p. 515), Dr. Pierre Janet notes again: "'If there was anything real in those descriptions,' said Martial, 'it would be ugly.'"

Finally, toward the end of the prefatory text to *Comment j'ai écrit*, Roussel notes (after paying homage to the writer whom he considered his master, that is, Jules Verne): "I have traveled a great deal. Notably in 1920–21, I traveled around the world by way of India, Australia, New Zealand, the Pacific archipelagoes, China, Japan, and America . . . I already knew the principal countries of Europe, Egypt, and all of North Africa, and later I visited Constantinople, Asia Minor, and Persia. Now, from all these voyages I never took a single thing for my books. It seemed to me that the circumstance deserves mention; since it proves so well how imagination counts for everything in my work."

Thus, from a letter in which he alludes fleetingly to his aesthetic ideals, from confidences recorded in the medical notes of Dr. Pierre Janet, and, further, from this statement in a text intended to be published only post-humously, as befits a literary testament, it emerges that Roussel relied consistently on the imagination, and that for him there was a clear an-tithesis between the invented world which is that of "conception" and the given world—the human world in which we live our daily lives and which we cover in our travels—which is that of "reality."

As for reality, it is certain that Roussel—conscious nevertheless of having received a lion's share of it in the form of his immense fortune— expected nothing good to come of it.

Physical pain disturbed him, and my mother has told me how one day Roussel questioned her for a long time about the pains of giving birth, amazed that she had allowed it to be repeated since she had told him it was a very painful affair; in view of the period and Roussel's cus-tomary reserve, the subject must have meant a great deal to him for him to feel that he could discuss it thus with a woman still relatively young and little accustomed to mentioning such questions. Mme Charlotte Dufrêne, who was his closest friend and to whom the posthumous work *Comment j'ai écrit* is dedicated, told me in another connection that he had asked her never to speak to him of her fear of the dentist (nor of that she had of serpents) because he was afraid that she might, through con-tagion, infect him with her fears. Mme Dufrêne also declared to me that he was unable to bear the sight of tears.

Marcel Jean and Arpad Mezei (*Genèse de la pensée moderne*, p. 192) have noted that, in his works, Roussel seems to picture only objects shel-tered from dust, and Pierre Schneider ("La Fenêtre ou piège à Roussel," *Les Cahiers du Sud*, nos. 306–307) defines his art as "a poetry of high noon, in which objects cast no shadow around them," this in symbolic fashion since, in fact, night and shadow are far from absent in Roussel's work, just as scatology, or the bringing into play of disgusting elements among others, plays a role in it also. These remarks on certain general traits of his work seem to be confirmed in his life, as well, by that kind of dirt phobia which Mme Charlotte Dufrêne—to whom I am indebted for much of my information—noticed in Raymond Roussel: Before the first World War, it was his rule to wear his detachable collars only once (since he had a horror of laundered articles), his shirts a few times only; a suit, an overcoat, suspenders fifteen times; a necktie three times; and when he was clothed entirely in new clothes, he used to say: "I am walking on eggs—everything is new today."

Daily contact with a reality which to him seemed strewn with pitfalls obliged Roussel to take a number of precautions. During a certain period of his life when he suffered anguish whenever he happened to be in a tunnel, and was anxious to know at all times where he was, he avoided traveling at night; the idea that the act of eating is harmful to one's "serenity" also led him, during one period, to fast for days on end, after which he would break his fast by going to Rumpelmeyer's and devouring a vast quantity of cakes (corresponding to his taste for childish foods: marshmallows, milk, bread pudding, racahout); certain places to which he was attached by particularly happy childhood memories were taboo for him: Aix-les-Bains, Luchon, Saint-Moritz, and the Hotel Beaurivage at Ouchy; also, afraid of being injured or causing injury in conversations, he used to say that in order to avoid all dangerous talk with people, he proceeded by asking them questions.

In his investigation of the case of Martial, Dr. Pierre Janet mentions a phobia of disparagement and reproduces (*De l'angoisse à l'extase*, vol. II, p. 146 ff.) this declaration which shows how painful for Roussel must have been the almost total incomprehension which, for his part, he met with: "It's horrible that people don't respect acquired glory; a single detractor is stronger in my eyes than three million admirers; I must have unanimity for my mind to be at rest." Roussel, according to the same author, was prey to a kind of "phobia of cheapening, linked to what he called 'the loss of the inaccessible'": Over and above any puritanical point of view, he disapproved, for instance, of bare breasts being displayed in the music halls (as a cheapening of what, in order to keep its charm, should remain a "forbidden fruit"), and he deplored mechanical progress which devalued travel by bringing it within everyone's range: "One only gambles when one is sure of breaking the bank; the happiness of others makes one suffer." Finally, Roussel's misoneism (*ibid.*, p. 230) had as a corollary his cult of precedents: "Everything that is new disturbs me," he would say, and so profound was his horror of change that, according to Charlotte Dufrêne, it would happen that having once performed a certain act, he would perform it again because the precedent thus formed had the force of an obligation.

From this strategy, which he was forced to use in dealing with reality so as to adapt himself to it as best he could, resulted what Roussel himself called his "rule-omania" (*ibid.*, p. 200), that is, a need to arrange everything according to rules devoid of any ethical character, rules in their pure state, just as the rules to which he conformed in his writing seem exempt from any actual aesthetic intention. "His life was constructed like his books," Dr. Janet told me in the course of a conversation I had with him, several months after the death of the man from whom the celebrated psychiatrist had received many confidences, but whom he considered (in his own words) as a "poor, sick little fellow," completely failing to recognize his genius.

In the course of a trip he made through Persia in the year 1346 of the Hegira (according to the date on a postcard sent from Isfahan), Roussel sent Charlotte Dufrêne from Baghdad a postcard on which could be seen, moving along a wall apparently made of baked mud, three donkeys with packs led by a man in a white tunic and turban, with, on the left, a few trees including some palm trees: "Here I am in Baghdad in the land of the Thousand and One Nights and Ali Baba, which reminds me of Lecocq; the people wear costumes more extraordinary than those of the chorus at the Gaîté." Roussel seems to have paid no attention whatever to the reality of Baghdad; all that counted for him was the city of his imagination: scarcely even that of the folktales of the Thousand and One Nights—rather, the one he had glimpsed at the Gaîté-Lyrique theater, when he saw Lecocq's operetta based on the tale of Ali Baba.

Literarily, it seems that Roussel always proceeds as though it were necessary for there to be the maximum number of screens between nature and himself, so that one might in this case compare him with great aesthetes like Baudelaire and Wilde, for whom art was categorically opposed to nature; but, with Roussel, everything unspools as though one should retain of art only its inventiveness, that is, the share of pure conception by which art distinguishes itself from nature. In all his work, one notes that the plot (the structure of the work or its point of departure) is of an artificial, not a natural character; as Pierre Schneider has pointed out (*op. cit.*), the poem "Mon Âme" which subsequently became "L'Âme de Victor Hugo," written by Roussel at the age of seventeen and published in the *Gaulois* of July 12, 1897, a poem built on the line "My soul is a strange factory," is nothing more than the development of a banal metaphor of the type "My soul is an Infanta in her court dress . . ." and has as its subject poetic creation itself likened to the stratagems of a creating god; the novel in verse *La Doublure*—during the writing of which Roussel experienced that sensation of "universal glory" he described to Pierre Janet—is the story of an actor and consists primarily of descriptions of the maskers and floats at the Carnival in Nice; the three poems "La Vue," "La Source," and "Le Concert" describe, not actual spectacles, but three pictures: a photograph set in a penholder, the label on a bottle of mineral water, a vignette in the letterhead of a sheet of stationery; far from referring to the Africa of travelers, *Impressions d'Afrique* hinges on a fête of a theatrical character given on the occasion of a coronation; *Locus Solus* is the account of a walk through a park full of bizarre inventions; in the play *L'Étoile au front*, a collection of curios forms the pretext for a string of anecdotes, and in *La Poussière de soleils* it is a question of a chain of enigmas which lead to the discovery of a treasure; *Nouvelles Impressions d'Afrique* is nothing more than meditations on four tourist attractions of modern Egypt; finally, of the texts collected in *Comment j'ai écrit*, some are given as illustrations of the eminently artificial method of creation explained in the prologue, the others refer to the Carnival at Nice, with the exception of the six *Documents pour servir de canevas*, which are of the story-within-a-story type so abundantly represented in Roussel's work and which—like the composition with more or less indefinitely prolonged parentheses peculiar to *Nouvelles Impressions d'Afrique*—seems to have served in the most literal way his need to multiply the screens.

In the preamble to *Comment j'ai écrit*, Roussel sets forth the completely arbitrary process which he used for writing his prose works, including the plays; he tried nothing similar for the writings in verse, perhaps because the separation, the distance, the departure from reality was provided by the very fact of expressing himself in verse, without its thus being necessary to resort to additional artifice. "This process is, in short, related to rhyme. In both cases, there is unforeseen creation due to phonic combinations." And reading these lines of Roussel, one thinks of what Racan wrote in his *Life of Malherbe*: "The reason he gave for the necessity of rhyming widely differing words rather than the customary ones was that one happened on more beautiful verses by bringing the former together, rather than by rhyming those whose meaning was almost similar; and he made a point of seeking out rare and sterile rhymes, believing as he did that they engendered new ideas, not to mention the fact that it was a mark of the great poet to attempt difficult rhymes which had never been rhymed before." In reality, it seems that Roussel's assertion is merely a theoretical justification, and that (except perhaps in regard to "Mon Âme," the first and most "inspired" of his poems, and which he regarded as his fundamental work), rhyme never played for him the role of catalyst the way puns did, for, in examining the texture of his verse works, one does not see how rhyme could have served him as a propelling force; one would say, on the contrary, that he put into verse works which might well have been written in prose.

However that may be, the following is the process, in its various forms, which provided Roussel with the elements he used in his prose tales:

1. First, two phrases, identical except for one word, with a play on the double meanings of other substantives in both phrases. "Once the two phrases had been found," Roussel indicates, "it was a question of writing a story which could begin with the first and end with the second."

Example: *Les vers* ("The lines of verse") *de la doublure* ("of the understudy") *dans la pièce* ("in the play") *du Forban Talon Rouge* ("of Red-Heel the Buccaneer") and *Les vers* ("The worms") *de la doublure* ("in the lining") *de la pièce* ("of the patch") *du fort pantalon rouge* ("of the heavy red trousers")—which forms the basis of the story "Chiquenaude," published in 1900, the first work the author considered satisfactory after the profound nervous depression that followed the failure of the novel *La Doublure*.

2. A word with two meanings joined to another word with two meanings by the preposition *à*, "with" (which becomes the instrument of association of two absolutely dissimilar elements, just as the conjunction "as" is used to associate two more or less similar elements in the classical metaphor by analogy).

Example: *Palmier* (a kind of cake, or a palm tree) *à restauration* (a restaurant where cakes are served or the restoration of a dynasty on a throne), a pair of words which, in *Impressions d'Afrique*, produces the palm tree of the Square of Trophies consecrated to the restoration of the Talou dynasty.

3. A random phrase "from which I drew images by distorting it, a little as though it were a matter of deriving them from the drawings of a rebus."

Example: *Hellstern, 5 Place Vendôme*, the address of Roussel's shoemaker, deformed into *hélice tourne zinc plat se rend dôme* ("propeller turns zinc flat goes dome") which furnished the elements of an apparatus manipulated by the emperor Talou's eldest son (*ibid.*).

In the works of Raymond Roussel elaborated according to this method, literary creation thus includes a first stage which consists in establishing a sentence or expression with a double meaning, or else in "dislocating" a phrase which already exists; the elements to be confronted with each other and brought into play are thus engendered by these fortuitous formal aspects. After the intermediate stage which is constituted by a logical plot joining these elements together, no matter how disparate they may be, comes the formulation of these relationships on as realistic a level as possible, in a text written with the utmost rigor, with no other attempt at style than the strictest application of the conventional rules, with concision and the absence of repetitions of terms coming at the head of the list of objectives pursued. This concern for extreme rigor in the production of works of which the least one can say is that they are far removed indeed from any kind of naturalism is reminiscent of an epigram of Juan Gris, the most rationalistic and at the same time one of the greatest of the Cubist painters: "One must be inexact but precise." The deferential obedience to the rules of correct language such as they are taught in a lycée confirms in another connection the accuracy of a remark by Marcel Duchamp, who, speaking to me of Roussel and his special erudition, said that he was a "secondary" the way that others are "elementary."

It should be noted that this abstention from any strictly stylistic effects led Roussel to an extraordinary transparency of style.

In *Nouvelles Impressions d'Afrique*, the detachment from the real which Roussel seems to have aimed at is obtained in quite another way: the dislocation of the phrase by means of parentheses introducing a practically infinite series of "false bottoms," breaking up, parceling out, disarticulating the thread of the meaning until one loses it. In his analysis of the second canto of *Nouvelles Impressions*, a work destined to become a classic among Rousselian studies, Jean Ferry justly writes that "even more than the famous Japanese box whose cubes fit exactly one into the other down to the tiniest of them all, the composition evokes two or three large concentric spheres, between whose surfaces, unequally distant, might float other spheres themselves having several layers," an image taken up in a recent article by Renato Mucci, for whom there is no Rousselian work in which the end and the beginning do not join each other as is the case in those poems whose single sentence is cut up by multiple parentheses to which footnotes have been grafted, each of these works appearing as a differentiated unity which, throughout the series of elements peculiar to it, takes on a value of concrete universality in turning back upon itself.

Not only does the process employed by Roussel for the composition of his prose works have the immense interest of adding up to a deliberate promotion of language to the rank of creative agent, instead of settling for using it as an agent of execution, but it seems that subjugation to a specious and arbitrary law (obliging a concentration on the difficult resolution of a problem whose given facts are as *independent* as possible of each other) has as a consequence a distraction whose liberating power appears much more efficacious than the abandon, pure and simple, implied by the use of a process like automatic writing. Aiming at an almost total detachment from everything that is nature, feeling, and humanity, and working laboriously over materials apparently so gratuitous that they were not suspect to him, Roussel arrived by this paradoxical method at the creation of *authentic* myths, in which his affectivity is reflected in a more or less direct or symbolic way, as is shown by the frequency of certain themes which constitute the leitmotifs of his work and of which the omnipotence of science, the close relation between microcosm and macrocosm, ecstasy, Eden, the treasure to be discovered or the riddle to be solved, artificial survival and postmortem states, masks and costumes, as well as many themes which could be interpreted as stemming from fetishism or sadomasochism, constitute examples (here enumerated without any attempt at a methodical inventory). It is not an exaggeration to say that the establishing of a thematic index of Roussel's work might allow one to discover a psychological content equivalent to those of most of the great Western mythologies; this, because the products of Roussel's imagination are, in a way, *quintessential commonplaces*: Disconcerting and singular as it may be for the public, he drew from the same sources of popular imagination and childish imagination; and, in addition, his culture was essentially popular and childish (melodramas, serials, operettas, vaudeville, fairy tales, stories in pictures, etc.), as are his processes (stories within stories, verbal formulas used as the structure for a tale, and down to his method of creation by dramatized puns—the literary equivalent of the mechanism used in certain social pastimes: charades, for example). No doubt the almost unanimous incomprehension that Roussel unfortunately encountered resulted less from an inability to attain universality than from this bizarre combination of the "simple as ABC" with the quintessential.

Using childish and popular forms to express his own profundity, Roussel reaches down into a common storehouse, and it is thus not surprising that the personal myths he elaborated are liable to converge (as Michel Carrouges maintains) on certain great occult sequences in Western thought; so that it is, to say the least, superfluous to explain (as does André Breton in his preface to Jean Ferry) why the scenario of *La Poussière de soleils* can seem to be based on the traditional evolution of the alchemists' search for the Philosopher's Stone by suggesting that Roussel might have been an adept of hermetic philosophy. In view of the rules of secrecy which the initiates observe (a rule to which Roussel as an initiate would have been by definition subjected, confining himself, in accordance with the custom, to revealing it in an occult way), such a hypothesis escapes refutation and one can only argue, in order to reject it, the absence of any profession of faith of this kind, in his conversation as well as in his writings; still, the fact remains that in spite of certain aspects of Roussel's work (the important role played by techniques of divination, the frequent use of legendary and marvelous elements), this work utterly lacking in effects of shading has an essentially positivist coloring and that nothing we know of this writer of genius—not even the phrase in which he was illumined by a sensation of "universal glory"—inclines one to attribute to him aspirations of a mystical nature.

When Roussel had a kind of skylight built into his mother's coffin so as to be able to observe her face to the last moment, and when he imagined the refrigerator in *Locus Solus* in which corpses, thanks to scientific processes, relive the crowning incident of their lives, he was recording, no doubt, his refusal to accept death, but recording it as an unbeliever for whom nothing exists after our corporeal existence is finished. Evidence of a deep attachment to his own physical person is provided both by his taste for elegant clothing (an elegance which, in its sobriety, was literally all-important for him) and by the troublesome treatment which he underwent, even during his trip to Persia, when he began to be obsessed by the fear that his hair was getting white. If, when conversing with the late Eugène Vallée (the chief typesetter of the Lemerre printing house who worked on the composition of all his books and who, like almost all those who had any contact with Roussel, spoke of him as the simplest and most charming of beings), he frequently indulged in estimates of the probable time that each of them still had to live, it was to statistical data that he referred for these calculations and, deep as his obsession was, it was a scientific point of view that he adopted. Such a scientific approach allied to a passionate desire to expand, not on a mystical but on the material level, the limits which are imposed on man, is found again in his admiration for Camille Flammarion (to the point where he had a tiny transparent box in the shape of a star specially constructed to conserve a little cake of the same shape brought home from a lunch at which, on July 29, 1923, he was a guest of the illustrious astronomer at the Observatory of Juvisy), in his identification with the inventor Martial Canterel, in his interest in Einstein's theory of relativity, and in his certitude—which he confided to his friend Charlotte Dufrêne—that a day would come when men would discover a means of travel by reascending the course of time. As for the pleasure he took in visiting crèches at Christmastime and altars on Good Friday, and in attending High Mass at Easter, this is probably nothing more than the expression of his fondness for folklore and, perhaps, that of his attachment to a childhood of which he wrote that he had a "delightful memory." Similarly, the edifying and marvelous tales which abound in his work are always presented between ethnographic or historiographic quotation marks. Finally, that very sensation of "universal glory" which he declares having experienced while writing *La Doublure* (and which he was anxious to know whether certain well-known writers had experienced also) is not a spiritual state but something felt physically, an intoxication, a "euphoria" (which he sought in drugs after having sought it momentarily in alcohol, after becoming certain of not finding it while writing), a satisfaction which seems quite close to that "serenity" in whose name he paid his chess instructor's debts: Thus, if it is in card games he found serenity . . .

It seems in short that if Roussel declared that he preferred "the domain of Conception to that of Reality," the world which he thus contrasted with that of everyday life had no belief in the supernatural at its base. In *Comment j'ai écrit*, Roussel prides himself on being a logician, and one must admit that his essential ambition of a man pursuing "euphoria" in the almost demigodlike exercise of his intellect was to be the champion of the imagination: a Victor Hugo, a Jules Verne, a phenomenal chess player, an Oedipus solving riddles (leading one to wonder whether the riddles which perhaps still remain to be deciphered in his work are not perhaps of the same order as those he solved with enormous pride at the Théâtre du Petit Monde, which he used to attend with his friend Charlotte Dufrêne, taking along a little girl of their acquaintance to serve as a pretext). His effort tends toward the creation of a fictive world, entirely fabricated, having nothing in common with reality, as he succeeds in creating truth by the force of his genius alone, with no recourse to some further reality. Logically, this supremely negative effort—to cut the bonds which might be able to attach his conceptual world to reality—was to lead Raymond Roussel, who was no idealist, to the definitive disengagement which is voluntary death. This seems to be what he had always dimly felt, as is borne out by this addition "from earliest youth" to a poem by Victor Hugo (*Comment j'ai écrit*, p. 38):

> Comment, disaient-ils
> Nous sentant des ailes
> Quitter ces corps vils?
> —Mourez, disaient-elles.

> How, they asked,
> Feeling that we have wings
> Shall we leave these vile bodies?
> Die, they replied.

In 1932 Raymond Roussel had stopped writing. He had taken up chess and was drugging himself with soporifics (barbiturates).

On April 16 he gave the printer the main part of his "secret and posthumous" work dedicated to Charlotte Dufrêne.

At that time he had ceased to live in his sister's private mansion in the rue Quentin-Bauchart, and had taken up residence at 75 rue Pigalle in a residential hotel frequented by homosexuals and drug addicts, that is, by people who shared the exclusive taste he had always had, and his more recent passion for drugs.

On December 24 he attended Midnight Mass at Notre-Dame-de-Lorette with his companions.

Returning from the African tropics toward the beginning of 1933, I went to call on Roussel, who had been one of the patrons of the scientific mission of which I was a member. He received me, as he had since he had given up his house at Neuilly, at the home of Charlotte Dufrêne in the rue Pierre-Charron. Clad in an extremely dark gray, if not completely black, suit, he was wearing the decoration of the Legion of Honor (this, at least, of his ambitions had been fulfilled, although he had been unable to have his photograph in an album of celebrities published by Mariani Wine, or have a street named after him). He had shaved his mustache; still handsome and elegant, but somewhat heavier and slumping a bit, he seemed to be speaking from very far away. He had not seen me for some two years and asked me successively for news of a large number of my relatives. A melancholy reflection (with a smile) on life: "It goes by faster and faster!" After I said goodbye to him, he accompanied me into the anteroom and we stood talking for a long time (according to his habit—was it shyness? fear of seeming to show me out?—of keeping people with him long after saying goodbye). During the same visit, when I asked him whether he had been writing, he replied: "It's so difficult!"

On May 30, 1933, before leaving for Sicily, he made detailed arrangements for a posthumous volume, in a series of four notes written at the Lemerre printing house.

In Palermo he took up residence at the Grande Albergo e delle Palme, room 226, communicating with number 227 (occupied by Charlotte Dufrêne, his "housekeeper") at the corner of Via Mariano Stabile and Via Riccardo Wagner, the quietest part of the building, in which Richard Wagner had lived on the first floor while writing *Parsifal*, and where Francesco Crispi, the statesman, had also lived, as is mentioned in two plaques.

Roussel used to say that, except during childhood, he had never had an hour of happiness and described his anguish as a kind of suffocation, a gasping for breath. But in Palermo he found complete "euphoria"; he was no longer preoccupied with his "glory" which had not been recognized, nor with his writing; he said that he would give the whole world for a moment of euphoria. "Cut, cut, but give me my drug!" he said one day when he was deprived of drugs, meaning that the amputation of his two arms and legs would have been preferable to such a deprivation.

According to Charlotte Dufrêne, Roussel when drugged had a taste for death, which before had frightened him.

One morning around seven o'clock, he was found bleeding in his bath; he had opened his veins with a razor, and he burst out laughing, saying, "How easy it is to open one's veins . . . It's nothing at all." Later, when the drug had worn off, he wondered how he could have done this.

Several days after arriving in Palermo he had begged Charlotte Dufrêne to return to Paris to dismiss his servants (whom he had amply remunerated) and asked her also to liquidate his apartment, so as to be rid of everything he still possessed in Paris, his intention being to travel and not to return for a long time.

He was at this time so weak that he could scarcely eat. He slept on a mattress placed on the floor, afraid of falling out of bed while under the influence of drugs. The reason he gave for not wanting to eat was that it disturbed his "serenity."

One day he had Charlotte Dufrêne write to his manservant, asking him to send a case with a certain number, and he said that this case contained a revolver which he wanted sent to him because as a foreigner he could not (or so he thought) buy one in Palermo. He told his friend that unfortunately he would not have the courage to press the trigger, and that perhaps she would do it for him. As she tried to thrust aside this idea, he attempted to make her give in by bringing out his checkbook and asked her how much she wished; after each refusal he raised the sum. In the end the letter was not sent.

At Mme Dufrêne's insistence, Roussel finally decided to go to Kreuzlingen in Switzerland to be cured. On the morning of July 13 he had a telegraph sent to this effect. In the evening he told his companion that she could go to sleep in peace, as he was feeling well that day and had taken no soporifics. For several days the connecting door had been shut at night, whereas before it had remained open.

On the morning of the fourteenth, not hearing any noise, Mme Dufrêne knocked on the door between the two rooms. Obtaining no answer, she called a servant. The latter entered by the door from the corridor, which was unlocked. Mme Dufrêne and the servant found Roussel stretched out on his mattress which he had pushed or dragged as far as the connecting door (representing a superhuman effort in view of his weakened condition). His face was calm, restful, and turned toward that door.

In order to bring the body back from Palermo it was necessary to embalm it.

In the theatrical adaption of the novel *Locus Solus*, one of the chief attractions of the spectacle was the "Ballet of Glory": the suicide of a misunderstood poet, whom one subsequently sees enter into immortality—an immortality which is, of course, by no means that of the other world but the purely civic immortality of the world of statues, monuments, and street names. One cannot refrain from emphasizing that it was at the foot of a communicating door—that which led to the room of his friend and confidante—that Roussel had insisted on dying (unless it was that before his privation he had wanted to experience to the utmost the euphoria that the soporifics gave him). Whatever may have been his immediate motive and the reason for which he had chosen such a position—was it to be close to the door or to barricade it?—he died by his own hand on the very threshold of that *communication* which he had recognized as impossible, at least during his life, and with his eyes turned toward the place occupied by the only person, apparently, who had shared a little, but only a little, in his intimacy.

1954

Atlas Anthology 4 (1987). First published in *Art and Literature* 2 (Summer 1964).

SALVADOR DALÍ

(1904–1989)

THE INCENDIARY FIREMEN

Our era has seen the publication of a staggering number of books dealing with contemporary art. Almost none have been devoted to those heroic painters called the *pompiers*.[1] For a period so utterly dominated by information of all kinds, this is a unique phenomenon. We have a fantastic choice of albums of color plates on the work of Picasso, Utrillo, or Dufy, but you will look in vain for anything on Bouguereau, Meissonier, or Detaille. And yet who today can continue to affirm without blushing that Dufy is a more important artist than Meissonier?

The *pompier* painters, especially the glorious Meissonier and Detaille, found in their own time nothing less than the "structure" of the most important subject in the history of civilization: the history of our time itself, at its most complex, dense, tragic, ineluctable, climactic. Detaille in particular discovered in the structure of the most important subject (I repeat: the historical subject) what is most rigorous, hierarchical, physical, biological, nuclear, cellular, atomic; i.e.: *"the infrastructure, the military structure and superstructure, the most explosive of all that exist."* To the point where Detaille, despite all the accepted notions (which are the result of contemporary aesthetic myopia), will soon be ranked as the supreme painter of the *living structures* of the future, just as Cézanne will be known as the supreme painter of the *withered structures* of the past.

The great explosion of the sublime period of 1900, still known today as the *Style Nouille* ["noodle style"], was preceded by the music of Richard Wagner (*Tristan and Isolde,* 1857–59); the philosophy of Friedrich Nietzsche (1844–1900); the genius of Barbizon, François Millet, whose erotic cannibalism radiated into "the tragic myth of Millet's *Angelus*" (1858–59), which broods over the *pompiers* Meissonier and Detaille, themselves destined to accomplish the historic mission of perpetuating the genetic code of the fatherland through the flesh and the spirit of Karl Marx (*Das Kapital*, 1867), Max Planck, Friedrich Hegel, Albert Einstein, Sigmund Freud, Antonio Gaudí, Cézanne, Marcel Proust, Raymond Roussel, Mariano Fortuny, Pablo Picasso (b. 1881), and his contemporary Norbert Wiener (1894–1964), who came out of Raymundo Lulio; and the monarchical domes of Buckminster Fuller, which in turn came out of Louis XVI's architect, Ledoux. Since 1900 there has been *nothing, absolutely nothing new*: We have been living on the debris and the rubble of more and more minimal explosions, down to the tiny helpings of the minimal art of today.

Summary list of explosions:

Millet exploded into Seurat and Dalí, driving van Gogh mad in passing. Detaille, with his microstructures, explodes into Cézanne, Cubism, and anecdotal Surrealism. Gustave Moreau with his swarming mythology explodes not only through the work of his most notorious students, Matisse and Rouault, but also into the LSD of oneiric and automatic Surrealism. Boldini's whiplash graphism explodes into Mathieu's calligraphy; Gaudí and Fortuny explode into Picasso and Miró; and so on and so forth. Picasso's *Guernica* is a delayed-action explosion of Carolus-Duran's *Murdered Woman*. The *pompier* Cormon is an unexpected prehistoric explosion of Millet and, to top it all, Gérome explodes in the hands of Marcel Duchamp: The optician has a hot seat, the heat of a Minim. Because, in Gala's proverbial phrase, it is always those who are against who are the last ones to understand. Conclusion: Fortuny, the most inspired of all, explodes into Willem de Kooning, who is the most inspired of them all.

Finally, Mr. J.-P. Crespelle in his book *Les Peintres de la Belle Époque* proves totally and apotheosisistically the utter misunderstanding of *pompier* art that exists intact down to this day. He writes:

"Suppressed during several decades, the taste for Salon painting from before 1914 now reappears, thanks to the excesses, the pirouettes, the absurdities of the avant-garde; whether it be *informel*, gestural, miserabilist, or neo-Dadaist. Disconcerted, disgusted collectors have by a kind of boomerang reflex turned their attention back to descriptive painting and 'well-made' work, which takes on the supplementary prestige of a period with the nostalgic charm of a paradise lost. To the point where we can no longer really make fun of those artists who often joined love of their profession to a professional conscience that is disdained today. The smile they provoke is tinged with regrets."

Dalí says no, no, no! No boomerang! On the contrary: Everything in the avant-garde happens necessarily and ineluctably, like the deadly or invigorating debris of the explosion of 1900. After the flushed toilet of microphysics, after Pop, Op, and the minimalism consequences, we shall see *pompier* art once again very much alive, fresh as a rose and quantified by everything that will have taken place meanwhile in our contemporary aesthetic drama, one of the most grandiose and tragic in history.

Captions of Illustrations

[The paintings noted in the following captions were reproduced in black and white, along with Dalí's comments, in the original article, "The Incendiary Fireman," when it was first published in *ARTnews Annual* 33 (October 1967). Most of these paintings can be viewed on the web. —Eds.]

Ernest Meissonier, *The Sergeant's Portrait*, 1874. Collection of Baron Schroeder.
Dalí comments: "This picture is an illustration of microphysics. The instantaneity of the glances forms an antigravitational structure, like that which may be suggested in painting by the trajectories of flies or of pi mesons. The painter is looking at the sergeant. Three people are looking at the painter's drawing. One is looking at the dog. The sergeant and the smoker look at nothing. The whole permits an antiproton explosion."

Edouard Detaille, *The Dream*, 1888.
Dalí remarks: "Chain structures of the discontinuity (and, for the same price) of the ondulatory and corpuscular light of the prescientific dream. *Olé!*"

Detaille, *Saluting the French Wounded*.
Detaille, *Saluting the German Wounded*.
Dalí: "At first glance these two paintings of Detaille seem

merely to be faithfully transcribed anecdotes, photographs of reality. On an intuition of Mr. Salvador Dalí, a study of their structure was undertaken which reveals the following. Suppose that an arrow on a black circle indicates a cavalryman in black, and an arrow on a white circle one in white, and that the black triangles represent the foot soldiers in black. The graphs are practically identical—the same number of arcs and the same trajectories, with the following exceptions. The direction of the black horsemen is inverted within the logarithmic spiral indicated by the arrows. The white horsemen and the foot soldiers remain unchanged. The stationary foot soldiers mark the axis of the spiral."

Gérome, Optician's sign in rebus form, 1902.
Duchamp, *Mona Lisa: L. H. O. O. Q. Rasé*, 1964. Cordier and Ekstrom, New York.
Dalí: "The Oedipal-anal complex in Gérome's work would be evident to any psychoanalyst, as it was to Duchamp."

Boldini, *Portrait of Réjane*.
Mathieu, *For Elizabeth of Austria*.
Dalí: "Boldini's whiplash graphism explodes into Mathieu's calligraphy."

Horace Vernet, *Horace Vernet's Studio*.
Dalí points out: "All the elements of a contemporary Happening are here, down to the marijuana smoker with a long pipe for the kif of the period." Identifiable among others are the painters Eugène Lami, with trumpet, and Vernet, the duelist in profile.

Meissonier, *Napoleon III at Solferino*, Detail, 1863. Louvre, Paris.
Dalí: "Self-explanatory detail."

Pablo Picasso, *Science and Charity*, 1896–97. Private collection, Barcelona.
Dalí says: "This picture was shown in the autumn of 1966 to four hundred brains of polytechnicians in excellent con-

dition, not one of which was able to identify it as a Picasso. Yet no one could deny that it contains all the 'bits' of information in his future work: the watch, the limp hand, the sisters of mercy protecting the progeny. Every July I send a telegram to Picasso, which reads, 'For July, neither women nor snails.'"

Meissonier, *The Deathbed*, 1838. Fodor Museum, Amsterdam.
Dalí: "Neither watch, nor woman, nor child, nor snails."

1. *Pompier*—literally, a fireman. Various origins are given for the adjectival use of this word to describe a style that is "banal and emphatic" (Larousse). One argument supposes that it comes from the resemblance of the neo-Greek helmets favored by members of the Academy in their Neo-Classical battle scenes to the brass helmets of French firemen. Another places it in a remark by Degas about Academic painters: *"C'est les pompiers qui se mettent en jeu"* ("The firemen are setting fire to themselves."). (*ARTnews Annual* Ed.)

ARTnews Annual 33 (October 1967).

DE KOONING'S 300,000,000TH BIRTHDAY

There is not the slightest shadow of a doubt that the sublimest moment in the history of our planet occurred several hundreds of millions of years ago when the Bay of Biscay opened up and the Pyrenees held fast, thus protecting the divine immutability of the Sals-Narbonne passage, which is really and basically the only thing that interests us. For if one had had to wait for the Indians (who incidentally are deserving of my entire respect and merited a better fate; they were creatures who wore a vertical black or colored feather on their heads; some still wear it); if, I repeat, one had had to wait for the Indians to discover the microscope, which was one day to be the privilege of the city of Delft and the glory of Leeuwenhoek, then it is almost certain that those Indians, despite the fact that they spend most of their lives observing things, would have been incapable of inventing a single pair of spectacles, for the very simple reason that in order to follow the progress of their own reveries with half-closed eyes they had absolutely no need of such inventions. If we pass from the Americas to Africa in search of the first microscope we again find nothing, since even the geography of that continent, which strikes our eyes first because of its mountains and our feet, next because of its seas which one cannot cross on foot, was domesticated and hung up like bunches of raisins on the walls of Dutch interiors, while at the same time in African exteriors the only terrestrial globes observable were those which the rhinoceros wears engraved on its backside, which, before maps of the world existed, resembled charts of the sky, especially the rhinoceros of India which Dürer engraved, which brings us from Africa to Asia, where once again we shall not discover the first microscope, for the wisest Asiatics are like raving maniacs despite the fact that maniacs of this sort sometimes succeed violently, like those two Chinese scientists, Tsung Dao Lee and Chen Ning Yang, who recently robbed us of the famous law of parity which is a lot to violate and might well be enough to make us lose all sense of direction if the Asians themselves had not created a Corneillian situation by inventing the compass, thus favorizing from a distance the one transcendental thing which matters for man, that is, the geodesic triangulation of the Sals-Narbonne air base where, for the first time in the midst of the French Revolution, by dividing the ten millionth part of the terrestrial meridian, physicists established the standard meter which, scientifically and fortunately for all, is since May 3, 1961, the equivalent of 1,650,763.73 wavelengths, in a vacuum, of the radiation corresponding to the transition between the levels $2p10$ and $5d5$ of the krypton 86 atom. And now we have almost totally eliminated America, Africa, Asia, and Oceania (since the latter liquidates itself because of the great quantity of liquid which it contains and which dissolves it), and the few kangaroos who inhabit Australia, aborted parachutists who instead of falling like semen from the sky jump on the earth like fleas, without for all that being able to help us at all with the monarchical unity of Europe which is presently being formed. And now be assured we are finally reaching the conclusion, for my readers might begin to grow impatient and rightly wonder what this geological preamble is leading up to, a most justifiable expectation which, far from displeasing me, delights me since it allows me at once and in the most dazzlingly veracious way to shout from the housetops that *Willem de Kooning* is the greatest, the most gifted, and the most authentic finial point of modern painting, and the initial point of the *pompier* art of the future.

Let us recapitulate without recapitulating and observe that it was ineluctably necessary, several hundred million years ago, for America and Europe to break away from each other, so to speak, parting company, so to speak, at the supreme moment of the opening of the Bay of Biscay (we are back at our point of departure) in order that one day Willem de Kooning, born in Amsterdam, might cross the ocean to New Amsterdam, now New York, in which city the phenomenon of Abstract Expressionism and Action Painting was to take place, thus allowing the most gifted modern Dutch painter to become the greatest painter of America. And now let us observe de Kooning with his prematurely white hair making his great sleepwalker's gestures, as though he waited in a dream to open Bays of Biscay, to explode islands like orange sections or Parma violets, to tear up cerulean-blue continents split by Naples yellow oceans, the whole with happenings of virtuosity worthy of Velázquez, superposing cataclysms like earthquakes of burnt sienna, Venetian red, and ocher on the geological delirium of the winged and subtle *bravura di tocco* of his violent squalls of brushwork—and if, by chance or misfortune in these gesticulations of a dionysiac demiurge of reality, amid the collapse of mountains and the formation of volcanic seas, the image of the "eternal feminine" were to appear, above all if it were to be personified in a contemporary woman, the least which could happen to her would be to emerge (from all that chaos) wearing only a little makeup and depersonalized to the point of being transformed into a woman-landscape or a landscape-woman, thus verifying the hypothesis about dreams of Theophrastus Bombastus von Hohenheim called Paracelsus, who, going far beyond Prof. Freud, said that if one dreams of a fish which swims in a straight line and it suddenly swerves to the right or the left, this deviation may be verified in the past or in the future, and thus one will find it also in a deviation or accident in a mineral or a metal in the process of formation, which in journalistic language (so that all may understand), means that de Kooning in each of his gestural dreams registers nothing less than the geological "happenings" which took place on our planet Earth tens of thousands of millions of years ago, which is already saying a lot since today there are few painters sufficiently great to stand up straight, gesticulating, dreaming, and painting with feet wide apart like a new Colossus of Rhodes that, instead of letting boats pass between its shanks, would bestride the entire ocean—one foot in New York and the other in Amsterdam. And now that I think of it, my friend Malcolm Morley painted a great painting called *The Rotterdam* [a boat] *before Rotterdam*, which recalls Amsterdam, so I shall seize the occasion to excuse myself for not having attended his opening the other day; but I wish to tell him that I have already written an article about him, which, like all that I write, will be magnificent, since I make clear as day that his serious and anguished Neo-Dadaism is not only the culmination of Pop Art but also of Minimal Art, for no one can deny that, in his work, art is minimal, and even the commencement of the imminent *pompier* art, which is already many things together for the price of one.

ARTnews 68, no. 2 (April 1969).

JEAN HÉLION

(1904–1987)

FIGURE

We do not know whether the prehistoric artist sketched his first bison in a single spontaneous outburst, in a first flash of understanding.

But today, to draw a head is to suppress on the one hand the automatic scribbling that tempts everybody, and on the other, the previously formed images which influence us. Especially the paintings of others.

In order for this choice to assume its full meaning, it must be fully recognized that the painter has the right to do anything.

Surrealism breaks down barriers and causes unexpected constellations of images to flower. A new kind of abstraction gives structures to light. Cubism and constructivist abstraction, in which my painting began, raise monuments to space.

Today there are messes of paint, smashed tubes, accumulations of debris, combinations of all kinds. Why not?

I hear something in this uproar; I feel at ease in it. In the midst of these contradictions I build up my figures.

How lucky I am, really, to be defied on all sides.

•

The rubbish which has been written about figuration! The usual stuff about "photography." Or else, "seen already, finished, old-fashioned," etc.

Efface everything.

What is figuration, then?

It is looking for and keeping your path between proud, obvious Creation and the Void whose dizziness affects us all.

The painter works on horseback, the reins of color in his hand, his head in the wind of ideas, his eyes wide open on the world. Without knowing what his goal is to be.

Is it anything but life? The most different kinds of artists are occupied with nothing else. Some give it color, others madness; a few give it meaning. To figure is to try to grasp it in its entirety.

Everything must constantly be thought out again, reformulated, redone. You feel that there is an ideal central point from which the image would radiate through colors as well as through things.

Throughout your life you grope blindly for this point, with sometimes the magnificent illusion of reaching it.

And then you are left saddened by so much physics and metaphysics and you try, humbly, to make on a scrap of canvas something that is good to look at, good to keep.

•

I have painted pictures of shop fronts, stacked-up cellos, gangs of fishermen, the serious faces of my friends. Candidly. Looking at nothing but them. Freely, with my paraphernalia of experience with different techniques, trying to decipher them. Driving away every other idea with blows of the brush. Yet nothing can be done. The question is always elsewhere. You speak of what is far away in the language of what is near.

Each thing, for the painter, is both what it seems to be and, at the same time, something unknown.

•

Reality has no limits. Searching for it, I have several times passed from one side to the other of the mirror in which we recognize things.

The surface of the mirror is Realism. The thing takes refuge in its appearance.

You cross over and it is as though, in a way, the thing became identified with the visual elements which make it up. It is the realm of the Plastic. Everything becomes a cone or a cube, tension, quality.

The other side of the mirror flows into Dreams. The object transformed by the idea. You search for its meaning. You surrender to intuition.

To figure is to define by means of an image the oneness of these three domains.

We would like, of course, to paint *complete* works, in the style of Carpaccio, Masaccio, Velázquez, Géricault. Technically, it is not utterly impossible. Spiritually, it is refused us.

Something fundamental has gone wrong. Each time a painting moves in this direction we must rub it out, return to plans that are both simpler and more complex; to firmer notions of space, to a tenser and less explicit degree of representation, the only one our senses can bear today.

Finally we must break off all relations with nostalgia. The canvas is not an open window giving onto the room in which the still life sits. It is a bare wall, or a public square in which the image will be built like a monument.

Keep your distance from the inspiring object, that distance which allows liberty without depriving it of its force.

•

From Nature

A side of beef hung up by the shank.

A fat, full cone; the hollow trunk underneath.

Recognize and define the tension between what is broad and what is sharp; between what is flesh and what is symbol.

The leg of beef crowning the nave of its sliced-off chest.

Underneath, in a white smock, precise as a high priest, the Porter lifts up this architecture, takes it over, jolts it onto his shoulder and goes off.

A white touch, under the yellows of the skin, the scarlets of the meat.

The man carries the animal. The corpse is a sign of life. It's dramatic and joyous. It makes you want to paint.

Art: when an intuition weds color. Or rather, when an intuition sleeps with an idea on a bed of right colors.

But beware of the hollow dream.

You must dream with the brush in hand.

The flayed flesh bursts onto the canvas.

Underneath, the white apron constructs itself in columns to support the animal.

In the street it is the concealed muscles of the butcher that do this.

FIGURE   309

•

Working with the pear tree at Bigeonnette is to apply to it the notions about space I have collected, so as to seize it.

The branches grasp the sky in fistfuls.

All of it is balanced on a trunk, a handsome cylinder slightly twisted by what it holds up.

•

When I think of Poussin's splendid wash drawings of trees, I can get nothing at all from his method. It doesn't seize the polyhedric aspect of things so dear to us since Cézanne, or the space the Cubists opened up.

Yet Cézanne and the Cubists don't satisfy my need for completeness and natural movement. I must question this pear tree. Everything is there.

Its richness is made up of simple but crossed angles, balanced by an internal movement whose unity I can feel but of which I can see only the complexity. For the latter I must invent a means of access, a ladder to climb up on.

Pear tree. Suite of pear trees. Until I grow disgusted at my helplessness and despair at ever succeeding. And now, this morning, a panel cut into the very surface of this despair has perhaps succeeded.

How can I ever be proud of my work, after so many failures, in such a climate of panic? And yet, what euphoria just because of six square inches of paint that sings a little!

I have really learned to swallow my pride since the thirties when I constructed big abstract paintings. The world at that time seemed a safe place; painting meant peaceful, strong harmonies.

But it began to develop cracks and it collapsed in 1940. As for me, I found myself once more at the base of things, the elemental.

Now I work facing the earth and the sky. There is the tree, still vaster and deeper than the image I get from it.

Each confrontation with nature is a rude humiliation for our concepts.

Yet only the concept is transmittable.

The pear tree in my orchard knows everything and says nothing. It must be given a voice; that is, I must get to work on it, start endlessly all over again. I gorge myself on this subject.

Beyond the pleasure of placing contrasting colors, of establishing values, of inventing new rhythms, something which is always on the watch inside us will know how to project the sign, the strong image suddenly seized, into consciousness. That's that. And you have gone on a little further.

Further on there will be more difficulties. You will stumble, because the solidity of reality escapes all bounds. To imagine that solidity, to profile the shadow of that unknown quantity, to make people feel a little of the richness of the pear tree—that, as I see it, is all my ambition.

Nature is what is most continuous in every direction. Indicate this continuity. A brushstroke, a line, must be laden with fullness as well as emptiness. A simple rhythm has to enliven the canvas, swelling up here, tightening in there, sensitive, down to the leaf which trembles at the edge of the sky.

•

Technique

I have spent much time trying to define a durable way of painting. But the ways wear out under the weight of the fingers, of the eyes. It is understanding that must be attained.

Sometimes I amuse myself with patting the light tones together at the top of my palette and then crushing the dark ones together at the bottom. With broad strokes of a flat brush. With the point of a brush as slender as a fencing foil. Games that brighten your work, revive the artist when he's exhausted, keep the spectator alert. But it is not in them that meaning is to be found.

You can trace an essential symbol with one finger in the dust.

No matter how you go about it, the important thing is to prolong drawing beyond your fingers onto the palette, beyond the palette onto the canvas. And, in the mass shaken by the dance of brushstrokes, to find again, *in extremis*, the simplicity of the first idea.

Light the picture according to its meaning. Let the light be straightforward, flowing toward the mind and coming from it. The object off which it rebounds gives it form and at the same time constructs the image and the way to read it.

I should very much have liked, this morning, to paint a blue sky, blue roofs, a blue sea. I started to. I had the necessary tubes of paint. But I found no blue in me, this miserable me I am equipped with.

FIGURE 311

So I made roofs, a sky, and boats, as best I could, with the stormy colors of my being.

But it is of roofs and boats that I wanted to talk to you. If they speak of me, it is unimportant and superfluous.

In a composition, in this picture which you invent with the usual elements, or which you forge, each detail is a personification of the subject, or rather of the action which the picture unfolds.

The role of the detail is not to act itself, but to construct, to give meaning to that action.

That is the danger, the stumbling block. The detail has to participate in this major action by offering up whatever constitutes it, by putting its own reality at the service of the whole, yet without contradicting itself.

There is submission of the detail to the whole but there is also differentiation.

In a perfect painting, the secondary characters sustain the main character without merging with him. They act in the same way toward each other.

In a less good painting the secondary characters resemble each other. Limpness. Loss of interest.

Carefully prepared, based on careful drawings, long dreamed of and begun on the right day, the picture is going well. Very well. My friends find it excellent; they wish I wouldn't touch it again.

A certain brilliance in the result—that is the trap.

Avoid it. Smear the painting. Mess it up with an inexorable brush, until nothing remains but a magma in which a spectral image floats.

Then, without regrets and singing as loud as you can, work inside it, with broad, precise strokes, until a real work of art is born, no longer seductive, but with everything enunciated on the highest level of your mind.

And you emerge feeling dead tired but happy.

Art and Literature 1 (March 1964).

PIERRE MARTORY

(1920–1998)

INTRODUCTION TO *WASHINGTON SQUARE* BY HENRY JAMES

One could scarcely call *Washington Square* a youthful work or a beginning: In 1881 James was thirty-eight years old; his first novel had appeared five years earlier. In 1879 *Daisy Miller* had achieved a solid success with the English reading public, while numerous articles in American reviews had already established this scion of one of the Union's wealthiest families as an informed critic of the European literature of his day. Yet at first glance, there seems nothing in *Washington Square* that anticipates James's great novels, the ones best known in France, wherein we discover a genuine temperament, along with an inimitable way of telling a story. These masterworks (which one could recognize from a single sentence, so vastly does his "manner" differ from that of any other writer) have earned James a reputation as a difficult and even boring writer among lazy readers, and, among admirers of literary dexterity, that of a subtle splitter of hairs; in any case, they are real monuments; the fictional donnée always has something imprecise that empowers all the developments, all the feats of composition; the main characters being thus placed in a state of compromised equilibrium which renders plausible their consideration of the several paths of conduct they might follow; these take place in a world where the good and the wicked, while perhaps not clearly depicted as such, nevertheless form opposing parties whose conflict— with all the nuances that good breeding provides—assumes the proportions of tragedy; the intolerable atmosphere in which they unfold is made up of an infinity of small details whose importance appears only in their juxtaposition. They are, as James himself said, like a tapestry whose figures have an imperious tendency to fill up as much as possible the tiny perforations prepared for the needle in the canvas background. One can say of these novels that they pave the way for a whole series of works in a new tone, which will come into being in France and England at the beginning of the century, and in which the very procedures of intense psychological analysis will become essential.

Washington Square, on the other hand, is constructed along the traditional lines of the French or English novel of the mid-nineteenth century; it tells a familiar tale of literary fiction: the opposition between a lovesick daughter and the father who disapproves of her suitor; both for its dramatic situation and the manner in which the subject is conceived, it has sometimes been compared with *Eugénie Grandet*.

James had a highly informed admiration for Balzac, having studied his work closely. He also had a clear awareness of his own talent, and the thought of remaking *Eugénie Grandet* in his own manner would have struck him as unworthy. The subject of *Washington Square* was furnished him by a Mrs. Kemble. In telling James this story, Mrs. Kemble is certainly responsible for having alerted him to its similarities to *Eugénie Grandet*, but more than the anecdote in itself, it was the suggestions it wakened in him that appealed to the writer. And here the conscientious critic has no choice but to seize the occasion for a comparison between the genius of Balzac and that of James, judging each according to the evidence.

In Balzac, there is a liveliness of the first draft which is lacking in James; in James, a concern for artistic composition and unity that seems to have seldom bothered Balzac. Balzac aims to get beyond circumstances and their psychological prolongations so as to attain the universal. His characters tend to become types. He supplies the reader with a mass of documentation wherein each can make his own choice. James creates a world of less breadth, but which gains in density what it loses in generality. The omnipotent author, having laid out the previous history and the foundations of his story, moves forward unerringly into the logical development implied by his characters' temperament, up to the moment when the final curtain falls, so to speak, once the drama has ended.

The setting and the secondary characters lack, in *Washington Square*, the importance which Balzac accords them. While, in order to appreciate the respective relations of Eugénie Grandet and her father, we have to wade through a veritable monograph on the small city of Saumur, James barely suggests what the fact of residing in 1850 in one of New York's most opulent neighborhoods might mean for Catherine Sloper or the doctor. Whereas old Grandet grabs all the attention and assumes the position of principal character, Dr. Sloper makes an appearance only insofar as he plays a role in the marriage plans of his daughter; beyond that, we know almost nothing of him. Such remarks can illustrate how James, more than Balzac, addresses himself to the intelligence and imagination of his reader; how he confides in him, with a sort of refined politeness. To this trust, the reader must respond with equal goodwill; he must supply a truly active collaboration, unleash his imagination, and lend all his intellect toward helping create the beings that words and phrases have depicted for him.

"A novel," wrote James, "is in its broadest definition a personal impression of life; that, to begin with, constitutes its value, which is greater or less according to the intensity of the impression . . . The characters, the situation, which strike one as real will be those that touch and interest one most, but the measure of reality is very difficult to fix . . . Humanity is immense and reality has a myriad forms . . . It is equally excellent and inconclusive to say that one must write from experience . . . Experience is never limited, and it is never complete; it is an immense sensibility, a kind of huge spider-web, of the finest silken threads, suspended in the chamber of consciousness and catching every air-borne particle in its tissue. It is the very atmosphere of the mind; and when the mind is imaginative—much more when it happens to be that of a man of genius—it takes to itself the faintest hints of life, it converts the very pulses of the air into revelations."*

The implementing of relationships which a given situation engenders, the deepening of the protagonists' reciprocal reactions in a dramatic action, the kind of poetic power the novelist lays claim to, constitute one of the most exciting adventures of the mind. They also entail countless risks, which are sometimes difficult to avoid. One of these consists in wanting to tell everything when it's a question only of not suppressing the essential. It's silly to claim that characters force themselves on the novelist and impose their own determination on him. In reality, they derive everything from him, even as he eludes them. Not for an instant does he cease to exert the most rigorous control over their words and deeds. But, like a painter, he must play with light and shade so as to give his creatures the three-dimensionality without which they would be little more than anatomical engravings. He must leave them the sometimes

---

*Henry James, "The Art of Fiction," in *The Art of Criticism: Henry James on the Theory and the Practice of Fiction*, ed. William Veeder and Susan M. Griffin (Chicago: University of Chicago Press, 1986), 170–72. (Eds.)

dark, sometimes glittering dazzling aureole that for each of us surrounds the person who confronts us and whose mind we try to penetrate. The author of a novel has to acknowledge that there are aspects of his characters' personae he is ignorant of, while still not seeming to mute them because of a too-forceful and too-visible concern for artful composition. He must reach the point where these obscurities seem legitimately justified.

The characters in James's novels are, more than types, cases in point. Their story is conveyed to us in the terms of their inner lives, and this method, in 1881, is highly original.

Children always have two opinions of their parents, one biased, stemming from the restrictions which parental authority has placed on the demands of their youth and character, and another, less often acknowledged by them, more detached from immediate contingencies, which will be the stronger one if they manage to arrive at a degree of independence in their judgment. Catherine Sloper isn't immune to this rule. One phase of her drama consists precisely in her awareness of the rightness of her father's reasoning, in remorse for the harm she has caused him. Dr. Sloper, on the other hand, if he exerts a rigorous tyranny over his daughter that stifles the most natural paternal feelings, to the point where we see him as "the perfect incarnation of old New York respectability," strikes us as less rigid and more explicable. One can't help but sympathize much more wholeheartedly with him than with old Grandet, for example, since his motives are more noble. The impression that he is the "villain" in the drama weakens if we take into account that his experience of men, the diagnostic art that his profession confers on him, the sense of responsibility toward his daughter—to whom local society would be closed if she were one day to separate from her husband—amply justify his attitude. He is as blinded by his reasons as Catherine is by her love. His humor and irony, which link him to Henry James himself, render him sympathetic at least during the first part of the novel. And if we can believe up to a point that his daughter is his victim, the end of the book amply demonstrates how Catherine, after her father's death, behaves exactly as he would have wished her to.

Once we have closed the book, however, we have the feeling of not having understood the imperious reasons that have made the characters act as they do. The explanation our mind has supplied in the course of reading isn't enough for us. It seems that the author hasn't dared dig too deeply into the hearts of his protagonists, that he has respected their most important secret. Our intelligence and curiosity require that the last veils be lifted. And just as, in a discussion that fascinates us, we have no way to succeed in understanding our interlocutor other than by putting ourselves in his place, so, to stifle the flame of interest kindled in us by the novel, we force ourselves to reconstitute the entire psychological evolution that has been described for us, adding the resources of our own sensibility and experience to the indications provided by the novelist. "The true inner language," wrote Edmond Jaloux, precisely in a discussion of a work of James, "is incommunicable." The novelist's task consists in transcending the barrier that separates the characters in a novel from each other, and from the author or the reader. His talent can be gauged by the delicacy with which he opens doors, scrapes away varnish, lightens shadows, without depriving the reader of his greatest pleasure, that of reflecting on what he tells us.

It's here that James excels, and from this vantage point that *Washington Square* is linked to the great novels on which James's fame rests. The same year, 1881, will in fact see the publication of a work which many consider his most fully realized, *The Portrait of a Lady*, in which the ambiguous game between the novelist and his characters, on the one hand, and with his readers on the other, attains a perfection that isn't gratuitous since it helps to create that "impression of life" which is the raison d'être of every novel. *The Portrait of a Lady* initiates what has been called James's second period; *Washington Square* closes the first. There is no gap between the two. There are no abrupt fractures in James's career. If, later on, he himself judged *Washington Square* rather harshly, it's doubtless because he felt he had transcended whatever that traditional conception of the novel had been able to provide him with. But the work marks a stage, with its references to two currents of literary fiction and the clear trace it bears of the writer's personality. No one knew better than James what he wished to accomplish and to what public he addressed himself. The great critical prefaces he composed in 1904 for the monumental edition of his principal novels (the New York Edition) reveal him as a meticulous craftsman who leaves nothing to chance. In writing *Washington Square* he knew what he owed his masters and his models, but he also knew what his own genius contributed to their teaching. Thus the work takes on the charm of the first paintings of a great artist. And if James could never be mistaken for a beginner, if he was never among those writers whose position vis-à-vis their art establishes itself gradually as they create their works, one can see in *Washington*

Square the freshness of his talent at its dawning, one can admire there a realism which James will later abandon somewhat to devote himself only to subtler variations. Reading this novel will help in reading the later ones. The pleasure it provides increases with the aid it offers to understanding the true James, that of *The Ambassadors* or *The Golden Bowl*, whose place is alongside that of the greatest analysts of the human spirit, such as Proust, Joyce, or Virginia Woolf.

Introduction to *Washington Square* by Henry James, translated into French by Camille Dutaud (Paris: Denoël/Club du livre du mois, 1954). *PN Review* 40, no. 3 (January–February 2014).

RAYMOND MASON

(1922–2010)

WHERE HAVE ALL
THE EGGPLANTS GONE?

Raymond Mason was born in 1922 in the English Midlands. After studies at the Birmingham College of Arts and Crafts which were interrupted by the war, he returned to work at the Royal College of Art, the Slade, and the Ruskin School of Fine Arts, Oxford. In 1946 he made his first trip to Paris and immediately fell in love with the city; the asthma from which he had always suffered suddenly vanished; he has lived in Paris ever since. From paintings and drawing he went on to sculpted landscapes and tableaux of such subjects as the Barcelona tramway and the Boulevard Saint-Germain, and a striking life-size sculpted impression of an urban crowd (La Foule) exhibited at the Pierre Matisse Gallery in 1968. Inspired by the "example" rather than the actual work of his friends Giacometti and Balthus, he has elaborated an art which aims to "include everything," and of which the Les Halles sculpture is the most ambitious example to date. It is at the Matisse Gallery until November 23 [1971], along with a large group of preliminary drawings.

Les Halles, the fruit and vegetable market of Paris, held at night, under the stars, at the historic center of the most beautiful city in the world, was much more than a commercial phenomenon.

It was a place of happiness. Powerful and vast because it made an infinite number of persons happy. The news of its condemnation caused a general sadness.

The work in Les Halles was hard. The rain and the cold were hard to bear. Among the men and women who worked there, many were hard, crude human beings. Nevertheless, the enchantment was such that this hardness was transmuted into a strange sweetness and the toughest characters became gentle. Of course this was partly because of the pleasure of working together, but the work was also subtly ennobled by the fresh beauty of the country produce. Actually, the market of the Halles Centrales was the last image of the Natural in the City. It is now a Paradise Lost.

I have attempted in the present sculpture to reconstitute, to the best of my ability, this superb vision. My work will obviously be a poor substitute for the emotion that this magnificent display caused in me. But I hope that at least it will speak quite clearly to the spectator who reads its title, *The Departure of the Fruit and Vegetables from the Heart of Paris*, reminding him also of that other and no less definitive departure of the men and women mentioned above who are symbolized in my cortege. A moment of silence. It is the man of the Middle Ages who is leaving. The "little vegetable" of our species, who emerged out of the earth and assumed any old shape. But he was a natural man and he always sprouted. We shall never again see a head like that, and we shall never see his like again.

And then there is a church, one of the most remarkable in the world, the only witness of the centuries that have now come full circle. Witness? An actor itself, and no doubt the principal actor. Towering over the market, it supervises all the thousand activities and wares, giving them a grandiose scale, the essential and spiritual dimension—and this was felt however obscurely by each member of the chaotic, teeming congregation at its feet.

In case you don't believe me, there still remains a fruit and vegetable lady with her back to the wall of a corner of Saint Eustache. Ask her whether she would have preferred something other than those huge stones during all the years of cold nights. In Les Halles, one was much closer to Hugo's *Notre-Dame de Paris* than to Zola's *Belly of Paris*.

Such a long association of ideas and things had produced an interpenetration of forms and styles which I discovered little by little as I developed my sculpture. The main stem of the cabbage leaf which I had suspended at the center of my composition was supposed to follow the serpentine "line of grace." Yet soon, the leaf with its veins began to suggest the late Gothic of the church. The bristling stone finials were echoed in the artichokes. And this prolix architecture multiplied in mounds of fruits and vegetables: In its windows, triangular spandrels are filled with circles, and in its upper stories, stone crates are displayed to the sky, in equilibrium, forever.

The acquired certitude of a vast web of related forms held for me the subject that I wanted to make live again, and made me decide to sculpt and paint not only the heart of Paris but everything that is to be found there—including the heart. I would detach each tuft of cauliflower, each artichoke leaf, just as I would also enumerate the windows of the rue Montmartre and the rue Montorgueil. Night would flow everywhere like a reservoir of ink, emphasizing the drawing.

There were moments at the end of the day when I would say to myself, "Look—there goes a potato nose." And there were even better noses, the color of eggplants. The cauliflower returned, in the form of an ear this time, and even the Adam's apple (it is behind the cabbage leaf). And I was delighted to be able to place an embracing couple in the middle distance and to say to myself: "Here is a suggestion of the forbidden fruit." A sympathetic spectator will perhaps find other crosscurrents of ideas, more serious ones, I hope—which would only be normal given the fact that the work occupied my thoughts continually for two years.

A work of art. Does one ever know what to put in it? In this hour of simplification, the answer seems to be: As little as possible. For me the answer comes to be an embarrassment: Everything. Certain people have explained to me in a friendly way that I am going against the current.

Yes, I am against the current. I always hear of movements and tendencies in art, of men who have made breakthroughs in painting and sculpture, of an avant-garde which has already reached the year 2000. The perpetual "movement" that artists are supposed to follow.

As for me, art on the contrary should be the means of intercepting thought in its flight, of confounding it with matter, giving it body and weight so that it might halt time, resist the centuries.

I really don't want my little parade from Les Halles ever to start.

ARTnews 70, no. 7 (November 1971).

IANNIS XENAKIS

(1922–2001)

THE COSMIC CITY

Faced with the drastic urban and architectural situation of today, we are obliged to lay down axiomatic foundations and to attempt a formalization of the two "sciences." This is why the first question is that of urban decentralization.

It has been customary for a number of years to speak of the decentralization of the major urban centers, of the dispersal of the industrial centers over the whole of the nation's territory insofar as possible. This tendency has been transformed into governmental policies that favor economically the transferring of industries and the construction of housing, and not only of large and small industries but also administrative centers and universities. The obsession with decentralization is, one may say, universal, in France as well as in Japan, in the United States, etc. That is to say, in all the countries whose urban concentrations are gigantic. Moreover, in a few generations the "demographic thrust" will render the situation of the cities of the future impossible and deadly, if the urbanists and the governments do not change their traditional mentalities and points of view, rooted in the past and henceforth ineffectual. The solution given to the question of decentralization will determine the shape of any urbanism as well as of architecture.

Must one then decide in favor of decentralization or on the contrary accept centralization?

First of all, if we place ourselves in the role of observers of contemporary history, it is clear that we are witnessing the development of a powerful force, blind and irreversible, which creates urban concentrations despite all the joint efforts of governments, a force which augments the density and the area of cities. It even seems that a simple but terrible law might be deduced from this observation: The major centers grow faster than the small ones, in a logarithmic curve.

Next, if we place ourselves in the sociocultural perspective of exchanges as well as in that of technology and economy, we see that the large centers favor expansion and "progress" of all kinds. It is a historical conclusion that has been arrived at for thousands of years but continually forgotten, whose equivalent could be found in other domains, for example in complex biological cultures or merely in the abstraction of phenomena of masses, which, in following the law of high numbers, render possible the advent of exceptional and rare events which would be highly improbable (= impossible) in smaller populations. On the other hand, decentralization leads to a dispersal of centers, to an augmentation of the length of routes and of the duration of exchanges, to an airtight specialization of collectivities and to sociocultural stagnation. The university cities prove this, as do the workers' cities and all kinds of "cities" within a country, thus invalidating the theories of *linear cities* and similar naive notions.

These reasons and conclusions are in the air and simple to observe even for those who do not have the leisure to consult or learn to read the statistics of specialized services.

But in that case, why decentralize?

In reality this policy stems from two principal tendencies:

a. the suffocation of present-day cities beneath the mass of anarchical communications and the poor distribution of activities over the national territory;
b. a tradition and mental inhibition of geometrization and planning of urban entities which, having sprung up again with new vigor in the nineteenth century, became fixed and rooted during the 1920s under the influence of cubism and constructivism.

This second tendency has already shown that it was powerless to resolve the simplest problems, such as the construction of new cities, even when the urbanists have the total cooperation of governments as was the case with Le Havre, Brasilia, and Chandigarh, which for the moment are stillborn cities. In fact it is impossible under the present educational conditions of urbanists and architects (a conservative, oversimple education) for these individuals to resolve *a priori* on paper the birth, composition, and development of a city which is one thousand times more complex than the problem of a dwelling or a housing unit, problems which are themselves solved haphazardly. This deficiency results in urbanist situations on paper being limited to barren combinations of straight lines and rectangles corrected by incongruously curved spaces (= "green areas"). It is in fact this same deficiency which causes those who have the responsibility of parceling out the territory to be led astray by the biological complexity of a city emerging from the centuries, such as Paris, and who, weary of breathing gasoline fumes and of endlessly waiting in all kinds of lines, preach the explosion of this living complex encroaching on the green desert, rather than attacking, for example, the real problems of the automotive industry, to say nothing of the solutions given by the so-called avant-garde urbanist architects which are in fact nothing but short-sighted and cringing naiveties, since the impossible decentralization-panacea-for-all-urban-ills has not been for them a point of conscience.

Thus, under the tyrannical yoke of these two forces, one real, the other mental, we proceed to decentralize on paper, creating satellite cities (= modern slum cities), dormitory cities, or specialized cities equipped with an absurd architecture (shoe boxes or rabbit warrens), standardized sometimes with a grotesque decorative affectation (Stockholm, for example), or sometimes without (Paris or Berlin).

It is also true that the algorithm of the plane, the right angle, and the straight line, issuing directly from the depths of the millenniums and which is the basis of contemporary architecture and urbanism, has been strongly consolidated by the "new" materials: concrete (because of wooden molds), steel, and glass, as well as by the relatively simple theory of plane and especially linear elements.

But if concentration is a vital necessity for humanity, the present ideas of urbanism and architecture must be changed completely and replaced by others.

I shall outline a group of ideas which lead to the conception of the vertical Cosmic City.

Here is a list of axiomatic and implied propositions which will perhaps help us to imagine its face and formalize its structure:

1. The absolute necessity of promoting vast concentrations of population for the general reasons listed above.
2. The high concentration and the enormous technical effort needed imply total independence with regard to the surface of the

Earth and the landscape. This leads to the conception of the vertical city which can attain heights of several thousand meters. This independence leads in turn to a giant standardization in which the formalizations of theoretical conceptions and their putting into practice will be necessary and alone effective.

3. The shape which the city is to take will have to eliminate the stresses of anti-economic flexion and torsion from its structure.

4. Daylight and a direct view of and over space are to penetrate everywhere. Hence a relatively negligible thickness in the vertical city.

5. Since the city will be vertical, its occupation of the ground will be minimal.[1] The liberation of the ground and the technical advances of such a city will result in the recovery of vast stretches of land and an automatic and scientific cultivation of the soil utilizing electronic means of management and decision, for the classic peasant with his manual toil is destined to disappear.

6. At the outset, the distribution of collectivities will have to constitute a statistically perfect mélange contrary to every present conception of urbanism. There will be no specialized subcity of any kind. The mixing process will have to be total and calculated stochastically by specialized bureaus of the population. Young people and workers will live in the same sector as old people or government officials, for the mutual good of all categories. The living heterogenization of the city will happen by itself later on.

7. Consequently, the internal architecture of the Cosmic City will have to be oriented toward conceptions of interchangeable locales (cf. traditional Japanese architecture), adapting itself to the most varied uses, with internal nomadism (movements of populations) becoming more widespread after a certain level of progress. *Mobile architecture* will thus be the fundamental characteristic of this city.

8. Since this city will be fashioned by universal technology, it will be suited to lodging the populations of the far north (or south) as well as those of the tropics or the deserts. Climatic conditioners will thus equip certain of its sections so as to render hundreds of millions of human beings independent of climatic and meteorological contingencies, so that they may attain temperate living and working conditions at any latitude. Thus, its entirely industrialized and formalized technology will transform it into the

veritable biological *collective garment, receptacle, and tool* of its population.

9. Communication will be effected by means of cylindrical co-ordinates with the advantage of great vertical speeds of from 100 to 200 kilometers per hour.

10. Communications through the transport of materials (men or goods) are to be accomplished by new techniques—for example, moving sidewalks or streets at slow, medium, or high speeds; vertical or horizontal pneumatic express travel for passengers, etc. Hence, suppression of all types of individual locomotion on wheels.[2]

11. Three-dimensional transportation (by air) will be favorized by airfields at the summit of the Cosmic Cities (hence a consider-able saving in fuel). The lost time between city and airport will be eliminated.

12. The great height of the city will have the advantage (in addi-tion to the very high density it will be able to achieve—from 2,500 to 3,000 inhabitants per hectare) of rising above the most frequent clouds, those moving between 2,000 and 3,000 meters, and of put-ting the populations in contact with the vast spaces of the sky and the stars, for the planetary and cosmic era has begun and the city must no longer be earthbound but oriented toward the cosmos and its human colonies.

13. The transformation of industrial and domestic waste in a closed circuit will take on vast proportions to the benefit of health and the economy.

14. By definition, the Cosmic City will not fear the devastations of war since disarmament will have been accomplished on Earth, and outlets and other expansions will be sought in cosmic space, the present nations having transformed themselves into provinces of a giant World State.

Rapid summary of technical data of the Cosmic City:

The preceding fourteen points require technical solutions that utilize shell structures and in particular warped surfaces such as hyperbolic paraboloids or revolving hyperboloids which avoid ef-forts of flexion and torsion and (except at the margins) allow only for cutting stresses of compression.

The form and structure of the city will thus be a hollow shell with a double partition, crisscrossed because of the ruled surfaces employed, having the additional advantage of using linear elements which will always be cheaper.

The 5,000-meter altitude is at the limit of normal pressure and oxygenation which a man can endure without any special apparatus and without previous adaptation. Which is to say that the Cosmic City can "leap" this barrier and grow taller than 5,000 meters on condition that artificial pressurization, humidification, and oxygenation are provided.

If we admit of a diameter at the base equal to five kilometers, the surface of the dome will be approximately 60 km^2. This approximate calculation is based on a cone truncated at a height of five kilometers and of bases of 0.5 and 2.5 km. Since the thickness of the shell supporting the city is 50 meters, the volume of the shell will be approximately 3 km^3. Now, a city like Paris (which serves as our model), with a density of 500 inhabitants per hectare, forms a layer of a thickness of 22 m^2, and 5,000,000 inhabitants occupy on the average, with their houses, their public buildings, their industries, and their parks and traffic areas, a volume of 2.2 km^3 or a total of 10,000 hectares.

That is to say an average weight of 400 kilograms per square meter of floor (= ultralight materials, plastic or metal, of very slight volume, thanks to the spatial industries which will thus find outlets on Earth); seven stories. 400 kg/m^2 = 2800 kg/m^2 for the three-quarters of the city's hectares, the remaining fourth being formed by streets and green areas. Consequently the total weight of the city will be of (3/4) 10,000 hectares 2800 kg/m^2 = 210,000,000 metric tons to be distributed over a circular ring on the ground 250 meters wide and with a perimeter of 16 kilometers, with a pressure on the ground of 5 kg/mm^2.

Here then is an aspect of an agglomeration, like the one stretching from Washington to Boston, with several tens of millions of inhabitants lodged in the shells of the cosmic cities, situated on a plain between the sea and mountains.

1. In fact, for a density of 500 inhabitants per hectare (2.47 acres), a city of five million inhabitants like Paris covers around 10,000 hectares. The city we propose

will cover around eight hectares of ground, or less than a thousandth of this space. (Xenakis)

2. The curse of modern cities, inflicted by the complex and multiple automotive industries. This is one of the examples of pointless economic and social cancerization, difficult to stamp out in free-enterprise nations. (Xenakis)

Art and Literature 10 (Autumn 1966).

JACQUES DUPIN

(1927–2012)

TEXTS FOR AN APPROACH

I

Each work by Giacometti is the looming of a separate presence which reveals itself as a totality, or rather as the movement and the demands of a totality that awaits only our consent in order to be finished, accomplished—and called into question again. It may initiate us, but it also deprives us at the same time of our instruments of analysis and investigation, our questionnaire and our references. It discourages and ruins any gradual accession to knowledge of itself. It subjugates us at once by a kind of silent commotion which keeps us, but at a distance, in the grip of a gaze whose intensity is almost unbearable. If we can bear this look, if we accept the fascination it exerts, we ourselves become the locus of an acute questioning which obtains no other reply than the same interrogative, fascinated space opening up inside us. Through this movement of our being, this unconditional acceptance, we supply a meaning, but an absolute one, to the sculptor's activity; an outlet, but a fictive one, for his torment; a new object for his thirst to destroy. Through this act we accept to be changed into Giacometti's people, that is, figures of petrified incompletion; and we reopen for him the space which he again closes around us. From this work which renders such a transmutation not only necessary but possible, I can speak only as a stranger, or at most as an accomplice with a faulty memory, a victim determined to keep up the misunderstanding.

And in fact the written word, condemned to deviousness, tries desperately to find the sudden approach again and is tormented by nostalgia for it. It tries to re-create the strangely active space of that work by attacking it from several sides, as one reconstitutes illusively the unity of a sculpture by multiplying one's vantage points. In its fragmentary pursuit it takes the same path a dozen times, while certain areas remain inexplicably barred to it. Too close to its object, it petrifies and consumes it; too far away, it loses its way and disintegrates in a maze of expectancy that has no beginning. Entangled in lacunae and contradictions, it leaves behind nothing but the muddled traces of an approach, scattered fragments, the least significant debris, spared by the flames, of an imaginary edifice which had to be abandoned.

2

It begins with the painful awareness of solitude, a desire to communicate with others, with the world, and anguish before the recognized impossibility of that communication. No matter how near he may be, how affectionate, how understanding, that other person can do nothing for me and I can do nothing for him: We speak but do not hear each other; we touch without knowing each other. Or *almost*. But that almost is not enough, or is just enough to enrage the man who refuses to give up. A gulf separates us, a vacuum we secrete, a distance which our lucidity and our efforts to narrow it only make more painful. This distance, this vacuum which turns Diego into a stranger, which turns a chair into an incomprehensible, uncertain, dangerous object . . . Face to face with this vertigo and this fear, Giacometti seizes a pencil, a brush, a handful of clay . . . By *copying* what he sees, as his father taught him when he was a boy, he hopes to give consistency to the reality which eludes him, to see it, hold on to it, and hence to affirm himself in its presence. And as he copies it he advances toward the most exact portrayal of what he sees, but also toward awareness of the absolute impossibility of this attempt. The affective ordeal becomes identified with his experience of the perception which objectifies the inner drama. His procedure turns into a stubborn, furious pursuit of a prey which escapes him or of a shadow which he rejects. The closer he comes to the *truth* of the object, the more he deepens the gulf which separates him from it, the more he feels and communicates the acute feelings of his difference and his separation.

Have others succeeded in finding what he searches for in vain? In museums Giacometti hunts that truth, which is not realism but *likeness*, with the same avidity. By turns he imagines that he has captured it in Venice with Tintoretto, in Padua with Giotto, in the Cimabues of Assisi, in Corot, in Cézanne. As he draws he falls in love; he copies "almost everything that has been created since the beginning of time." In Chaldea, Fayum, Byzantium, the Egyptians—especially the Egyptians—he imagines he has really found that unexpected likeness. But no matter how promising the trail is, the reality of a tree or of three girls walking ahead of him dissolves what was once again only the marvelous illusion of art. It is impossible to render, hence to know, reality; but the impossibility is fascinating and its temptation irresistible. Solitude closes in once more on man, but man's fate is to strive without respite and without hope, to open a breach in the wall of his prison. Through series of trials, failures, leaps ahead which are but the varied moments of a single experience, Giacometti approaches the inaccessible goal he assigned himself, and at the same time expresses the lyric investigation of a conscience tortured by the impossibility of communication. This expression of a private drama, determining an aesthetic style, insures his success with the public, while the advance of his art on the level on which he himself places it, that of realistic representation, leaves his admirers indifferent. Yet these two aspects of his experience are inseparable, and the fertile ambiguity of his work is the direct result of his fierce attachment to the subject.

From this standpoint, Giacometti is today as far removed from abstract painters as from figurative artists. For the latter, with rare exceptions, reality is only a point of departure, a springboard. They use it and play upon it; it presents them with no problem; still less does it confront them with its refusal. Giacometti, on the other hand, does not interpret reality deliberately; instead he strives to copy what he sees, simply, "stupidly," desperately. He plants himself in front of the model and works from life; he copies in a way that no one dares to. His attitude is in absolute contradiction to all the tendencies and experiments of his time and the theories which justify them. He is alone in his century and against everyone, clinging to his obsession, against the current in spite of himself. He opposes everyone and yet no one is indignant at this intransigent, insolent behavior. In museums and private collections his works are placed near paintings and sculptures whose meaning and basis they contradict, whose very meaning as works of art they contest. How is it that the scandal has not yet broken out? Why has no one rid our cities of these men who walk against time, of this woman who stands like a silent challenge, of the many insistent, haunted faces who emerge from the walls like proof of those depths whose name we no longer have the right to pronounce? How is it that we tolerate this single, inexorable question, we who open the door only to answers?

3

In his studio, Giacometti seizes a handful of earth, mounts it on an armature, and kneads it for a few seconds. A standing woman has emerged, living and indomitable, fortifying and satisfying my expectation. But the moment I dream of taking her away with me, Giacometti's work begins, that work which has no beginning continues. Abrupt and infinite birth, dizzying spectacle in whose presence I can hardly banish the strange feeling of being personally involved. Agility and sureness of those hands, running from the top to the base and from the base to the top, as though over a wild keyboard. Each isolated gesture here seems meaningless. Yet their rapid succession and the ease of their sequence gives the impression of a mysterious necessity. And this stratagem, this ballet, this struggle goes on for nights and for months on end. Furious and futile activity, necessary and tedious, in which the positive act and the destructive act join and become indistinguishable, weaving the same creative duration without beginning or end, from which the standing woman draws her authority, her grace, and her separateness.

Abrupt and infinite birth, and, rather than a finished work, a continual work. The essential purpose of the sculptor's gestures seems to be to keep up a dialogue between the figure and himself, to perpetuate a living exchange, to unite them both in an intimacy and an expectation which little by little would take the place of that communication whose impossibility fascinates him. As I look at them, the figure and the hand begin to form a single being, at once self-contained and in perpetual gestation, a being which never ceases to live and yet is always beginning to live, to perpetuate itself and to become visible.

With any other artist it would be theoretically possible to determine exactly what a single touch of color or a stroke of the chisel brings to the work in progress, for each gesture adds itself to the preceding one, modifying the part and the whole, causing the work to advance toward its end (the end proposed or supposed from the beginning). Giacometti's gesture is of another sort. His repeating, his reexamining contradict the deforming brutality of each particular intervention. To make and unmake incessantly is to diminish, to deaden each gesture, to drown it gently in sequence and number, as the sea absorbs its waves. Thus the figure I am watching him model seems to me at first indifferent to the cruel attentions the sculptor inflicts on her. Kneaded with an imperious, violent touch, so fragile an apparition must, it would seem, inevitably return to the chaos from which it came. Yet it resists. The destructive assaults it endures modify it only imperceptibly. Their repetition immunizes and protects it, allowing it to live its life on the sidelines. It accepts them and grows accustomed to them; soon it can no longer do without this rough, rude caress. In fact its autonomy and its identity spring out of this torture, *on condition that it be limitless*. From the exact distance which it needs in order to subjugate us, it calls with its desire for this punishment which fashions it and strips it bare, which detaches it and strengthens it, to surge at each moment out of the void. Immediately this standing woman erects before my eyes her fierce, mysterious presence. With the promptness of lightning she strikes me without giving herself. But at the same time, because she yields nothing of herself—nothing but her totality—she does not drain my desire and her refusals paradoxically develop an enduring power of attraction. I obtain all of her at first glance—that is, her distant, separate being—and losing her so quickly makes her newly desirable to me, with a desire no sooner fulfilled than renewed. Simultaneously she attracts me, pinions me, and keeps me at a distance. Because she is both the looming of a presence and the inexhaustible possibility of communication by default, she advances on me and recoils at the same moment, or rather outside of time. There is in her structure as well as in her unfurled power a resolved conflict which remains conflict. That is, a tension which submits and does not destroy itself. An integrity which reestablishes itself incessantly in the perpetual motion of the opening and the destruction which it provokes. Every work of Giacometti, like this figure, draws its sovereign affirmation from the interrogative space which it renders visible, from its refusal, its withdrawal, from that menacing and nourishing lived period of time which makes and unmakes it.

4

There is, or at least there was, an instinct of cruelty in Giacometti, a need for destruction which closely conditioned his creative activity. From earliest childhood the obsession of a sexual murder provoked and directed certain imaginary performances, like the cruel, darkly romantic reverie he recounts in *Hier, sables mouvants*. He was fascinated by accounts of battles. The spectacle of violence intrigued and terrified him. Formerly, with chance acquaintances or friends, especially women, he could not refrain from imagining how he might kill them. Many of his early drawings are illustrations for the bloodiest episodes in the tragedies of Aeschylus and Sophocles, which were his preferred reading. Certain of the sculpture objects from his Surrealist period stem directly from his attraction to scenes of horror linked with erotic obsessions, torture, and madness. *Man and Woman* of 1928–29 is an almost abstract portrayal of a sexual murder or rape. The man is slender, bent like a blade for the terrible pickaxe blow he is leveling at the round, concave, half-inverted form of the woman's body, which is surmounted by a broken line, like a scream or a flash of lightning. In *The Cage* of 1931, the forms tear and devour each other in a climate of convulsiveness. Another sculpture is *Woman with Her Throat Cut*. In *Point with Eye* of 1931, a kind of long, sharp point, held in equilibrium by a nail which pierces it, menaces the eye of a tiny skull-like head fastened to a stem. The suggestion of a destructive act, halted at the fatal moment of its accomplishment, appears again in *Taut Thread*, in which a kind of flower-woman, graceful and delicate, is about to be crushed by a curved rod, like a spring which only a very thin thread holds in check.

And if Giacometti admires Callot's engravings to the point of devoting a text to them, it is because he finds striking similarities with his own obsessions in them. "There is nothing but scenes of massacre and destruction, torture and rape, fire and shipwreck," he writes. But at the same time, in Callot as in Goya, the scenes of horror and the figures of monsters or madmen are strangely linked to the same insistent evocation of emptiness, the same treatment with incisive lines which seem to rend space.

The sensation of the void which separates beings, isolates them from the world, and plants an obstacle to communication is at the origins of Giacometti's instinct of cruelty. One does not violate the creature who consents but the one who refuses. The recourse to violence is nothing but an extreme, desperate means of provoking the impossible encounter. Giacometti's relation to reality, and his relation to his sculpture or his canvas are tinged with violence in proportion to the dissatisfaction to which they drive him. It is not compensation for defeat but an instrument designed to combat the fatality of failure, reverse situations, penetrate the fortress. Giacometti cares little about caressing things, playing with their external appearance, the light which enfolds them, the color which diversifies them. He never shows us matter at rest, a smooth structure, a polished surface. He does not linger over appearances, but he destroys them, breaks into them by force. Hence the grinding motion when he sculpts: He kneads the earth in a rage, as though to question it incessantly and grasp its secrets through torture. In his painting he never works over all the parts of the canvas equally. The manner of a tranquil promenader in a garden is utterly foreign to him. He creates a sensitive zone on the surface (determined by the subject), focuses desperately on it and devotes all his energies to it, attacking a single point as though he wished to open a breach in a wall. He must penetrate, force his way into things, into beings, and into himself, and violence should enable him to enter by surprise, overturning the barriers in a single stroke. But whatever the depth holds, it also withholds and defends the access to it with ferocity. It does not surrender after a single assault. And each refusal provokes a new violation. One must repeat the attempt continually, endlessly keep up an act of murderous interrogation and dispute. Giacometti advances only through a havoc of canvases, a hecatomb of statues. He seems to raise destruction to the level of a method. At certain times not a single work finds favor with him. And he mistreats his life as fiercely as he does his work. In his studio a rubble of broken plaster, naked armatures, abandoned or mutilated sculptures are so many vestiges of massacres, fêtes of exasperated fury.

5

In the center of the tiny, cluttered studio, lit by a skylight, Diego poses, sitting immobile and resigned on a stool: He is used to it. But Alberto, in spite of having examined his brother's face for almost fifty years, is not yet used to it. He is just as astonished as he was on the very first day before this unknown, immeasurable head, which defies and refuses him, which offers only its refusal. If he approaches his brother, the latter's head grows out of all proportion, becomes gigantic and threatening, ready to topple on him like a mountain or the angry face of a god. But if he backs away a few paces Diego recedes into infinity: His tiny, dense head seems a planet suspended in the immense void of the studio. In any case, and whatever the distance, it forbids him to approach. It looms abruptly, a separate, irreducible entity. The pure questioning of the eye, purged of all the habits which impede it, transforms Diego's familiar head into something unknown. "We know what a head is," exclaimed André Breton one day, disappointed and irritated that Giacometti preferred reality to the imaginary. We do indeed know what a head is. But the knowledge, precisely, is what Giacometti is struggling against. This false knowledge, the unverified heritage which our laziness accepts and passes on, this pretend knowledge which is the opposite of knowing and the real obstacle to the eye. The mental figuring of reality has expelled true, living perception. We do not know what a head is, and we need only look a little closer to see that we do not.

This is precisely what happened to Giacometti around 1935. At that time he was alternating between sculpture objects with poetic overtones, which leaped fully equipped from his imagination, and flawless plastic constructions whose success, in his eyes, was confined to the merely aesthetic level. The desire to realize compositions with figures prompted him to make several studies from nature. He hired a model for two weeks: The model came to pose every day for five years. "Nothing was as I imagined it," he wrote later on. "A head—I dropped the figure quite soon; it was too much—became for me a totally unknown object without dimensions. Twice a year I would begin two heads, always the same ones, without finishing them, and I put my studies aside."

Once again he had come up against this impossibility of sculpting a head which had made him give up representation in 1925, but this time he was to persist, to force himself with furious stubbornness up a path which seemed to him without a goal but also without an alternative.

This human head of incredible density is not a sum of parts or details, nor their more or less complex organization: It is the manifestation of a whole, indivisible and unanalyzable, which emerges out of the emptiness and night like a fantastic apparition. Giacometti sees it loom for the first time—at each moment for the first time—at that impassable distance which it maintains in order to be and to appear. In his attempt to represent this new head, the unknown quantity that is every head, neither his artistic culture (so many copies made in so many museums) nor his mastery of his own means of expression, nor his practiced sensibility is enough. The purified vision which reveals it demands that the sculptor discover new means and new instruments, that he reinvent them at each moment. That he abandon the hand of former days, the obsolete tool, so as to learn everything all over again, and to approach, correct, prune, destroy, and begin again without respite. Without hope. In order to fix reality as he finally sees it, in its emerging and its brutal withdrawal, all the sculptor can do, paradoxically, is to imprison it in the close-knit mesh of a lived period of time, and to approach it gradually in an alarming and exhausting series of advances and retreats, with the painful knowledge that his work is only an attempt and the finished work only an approximation.

After five years of failures with the model, Giacometti attempted on the eve of the war to do heads from memory. Each time, without his intervening, they became curiously pointed. Then he reacted against this irritating deformation and fell into another trap. His sculptures, heads and figures, grew smaller and smaller. "They were only 'like' when they were small," he writes,

> And yet their dimensions repelled me, and I would begin untiringly all over again, only to arrive after several months at the same place. A large figure was false for me, but a small one intolerable all the same, and then they became so tiny that they often disappeared into dust with a final stroke of the penknife.

From 1942 and the years which followed in Geneva, Giacometti saved only a small number of these tiny figurines, most of which fitted easily into a matchbox. Once back in Paris, he succeeded in realizing larger sculptures, but he could not avoid new deformations: extreme elongation of the figures, threadlike thinness of the bodies and limbs, reduction and flattening of the head, voluminous development of the feet. What happened between the real person and his depiction, since in no case did Giacometti yield to an expressionistic intent, and since he was seeking only the pure equivalence of the work to his vision of the subject? Giacometti elongates his figures and flattens his heads, without ceasing to *copy* the model, because it is the only means of which he disposes, at a given moment of his experience, to render what he sees, to make a *likeness*. The characteristics of his work which seem to remove it from realism are merely manifestations of a superior realism, at once broader and more precise, which no longer has as objects man or the world as they are, but as Giacometti's eye sees them. "Man" of the realists, that abstraction, that mental reconstruction, has given way to the *other*, to the encountered, near, and inaccessible being, who has depths within him and the void outside and around him, without which he would not be alive for us.

6

Face to face with his sculpture, we are scarcely freer than Giacometti in front of his model. For it carries its distance within it and keeps us at a respectful distance. And our relationship re-creates the strictly evaluated space so that its totality, and that alone, may appear. This figure does not allow us to rest our eyes on one or another of its parts; each detail refers us back at once to the whole. It does not develop a rhythm which would gradually conduct us toward an encounter. It does not reveal itself as a series of plastic events leading to a harmony, a chord. It bursts forth in its immediate presence: It is an advent.

If we run the risk of defying the interdict, of crossing the prescribed distance, that is, if we linger over a detail, if we look at the sculpture as a sum of parts, we see it literally disintegrate before our eyes. The human portrayal gives way to that of a monstrous being, a tracked monster, inert as though pinned down between two moments of agony. A monster which has just emerged recently out of a volcano, still dripping and sticky with warm lava. This body which was that of a man or a woman is now nothing but a deformed or clenched mass, swollen and horribly distended. We are witnessing its torture and its disintegration. We slide after it into an infrahuman region. We participate in the dislocation of the human edifice through the upheaval, the insurrection of the very substance of which it is made. We are implicated in this ultimate disintegration. If this flesh is still alive, it has nonetheless been riddled, lacerated, plowed like a field and sown with plague sores. Already it is nothing but the convulsions of disorganized matter in search of a form, the petrified tumult of chaos, that chaos from which the creature came and to which it returns, and to which we would not dare to admit that man is so close.

Let us back up a few paces and once again seize the figure in its totality. The vision of chaos becomes blurred. The fury of matter subsides. The forms organize themselves, become precise, justify one another reciprocally. The mortal collisions between light and shadow are submitted to the laws of a ritual struggle, a strict dance. The volumes become ordered and equilibrated. A tolerant space develops around the figure, who comes to life again under our eyes. If the recaptured form contradicts the formless substance from which it issues and from which it is molded, it still keeps the stigmata of its terrible birth.

The figures keep us at a distance; they carry their remoteness inside them and reveal their profound being. Naked, unmasked, it is now their unknown doubles who come to light. Their hieratic attitude reveals an imperious insensitivity. They elude our understanding, reject our impulsive gestures. They do not distain us; they ignore us and dominate us. One would think them fastened on their pedestals for eternity, rooted to their rock. The gravity of their bearing, the asceticism of their demeanor, and their gaze which traverses time and traverses us too without flinching, without suspecting our opacity and our stupefaction, gives them the appearance of divinities. They seem to await a primitive cult. Disposed in groups in a gallery or a studio, gathered in clusters in *Square*, on a single pedestal, they form an assembly of sacred figures whose distance accentuates their enigmatic likeness and their obsessive questioning. One feels them at grips with a truth which consumes them and makes them spring up out of their pedestals, a truth hardly more terrible than death, perhaps the presentiment of impossible death . . . Giacometti would like to enclose his figures this way between rigorous, but intangible and moving, boundaries, beyond which they could not stray without returning to the chaos from which they issued or be condemned to the torturing lucidity of the gods, to that annulment in a sacred space which gives them the rigidity but not the peace of death.

7

Drawing is for Giacometti another breathing. In order to model or paint one must have earth, canvas, colors. Drawing is possible anywhere, at any time, and Giacometti draws anywhere, at any time. He draws to see and can see nothing without drawing, mentally at any rate: Each thing seen is drawn within him. The drawing eye of Giacometti knows no rest, no fatigue. Nor does our eye, as it contemplates his drawings, have the right to rest. It is forbidden to linger over a detail, a form, an empty space. A strange, perpetual motion, without which it would lose sight of the subject, draws it on. This optical phenomenon results from the very nature of Giacometti's drawing, from its mobility which is the product of the repetition and discontinuity of the line. The form is never immobilized by an outline or held within isolated and sure strokes. It is not detached from the background or separated by a reassuring boundary from the space which surrounds it. It issues from a multitude of overlapping lines which correct and weight down each other, and abolish one another as lines as they increase. Thus the line is never continuous but broken, interrupted, open at every moment on the void but revoking it at once by its renewals, its unforeseen returns. This results in an imprecision of detail and an intentional indefiniteness which repel the eye at each impact, as though by a miniature electric shock, sending it from one detail to the next, and from each to the totality which they produce as they disappear. These goings and comings, this dancing race of our eye, gives us the subject to see at a distance, as Giacometti sees it, in its impassible space, across the ambient void which disturbs and inflects its image.

We may note how much this highly personal manner of drawing is basically calculated on the movement of the eye in normal perception. The eye does not isolate several lines of an object to the detriment of the others; it is incapable of following an outline or dwelling too long on a detail to the exclusion of what surrounds it. All these operations are mental. The eye comes and goes rapidly, moves restlessly from one point to another and from a part to the whole. In its leaping course and its thousand capricious turnings it comes back constantly to the same object but each time in a way that is slightly different. The eye has until now scarcely found a more formidable rival in the speed of its travels than Giacometti's line.

In the majority of his drawings a multiplicity of horizontals and verticals seem to search out a certain space; they define it less than they evoke it—and invoke it—by their insistence and their indecision. This space has the peculiarity of being both immense and enclosed. Thus the modest dimensions of his studio always seem vaster in the drawings. Whatever the place is, it gives us a feeling of confinement, of seclusion, but in immensity. One cannot escape it; at most one is in danger of getting lost or dissolving in it. We are prisoners but the cell is as vast and mysterious as a palace or a temple. This space, which seems to illustrate the title of Irénée Philalèthe's work *Open Entry to the Closed Palace of the King*, proceeds no doubt from extremely precise proportions, from a particular density of emptiness, from a certain vibration of light which is very easily obtained and very easily compromised. For Giacometti there is no question of a formula to be discovered and applied, there is only a pursuit which he must experience intensely and render visible. And the coordinates he traces, separately imprecise, constitute together the surest approach to that privileged space, charged with a secret power.

In contrast with this scheme of straight, slanting lines, the figures and heads are obtained by dense curved lines, fluid and nervous, a mesh of lines which appear subject to a circular, or more precisely, centripetal force. If the drawn form is not marked off from what it is not by an out-line or any other intangible frontier, it still has to affirm and define itself. It succeeds in this by expressing an internal cohesion, an energy folding upon itself, a kind of gravitation which the network of interrupted lines reveals. In its rapid whorls the drawing carves out depth, or rather breathes it in, opens itself to it, and renders it active between the strokes. It is as though a force issuing from within beings or things gushes out like a fluid through the interstices of the drawing and the porousness of the forms. And the lines must reveal this force, that is, both contain it and provoke its escape. This is the reason for their discontinuity. The interruptions and accumulations of line are never felt as superfluous rep-etitions and incongruous stops since they are the equivalent of the eye's mobility. On the contrary they contribute to give the objects this trem-bling, this feeling of truth and life. Thus it may happen that a figure may lack part of his body, and yet one sees him in his entirety. It may happen also that he is made of lines so vague, so far in appearance from the human form that he seems almost a wager or a tour de force: and yet he lives. One cannot examine him, but his living presence imposes itself with force. In extreme cases, as in certain drawings and a well-known poster, Giacometti is attracted by the vertigo of the white page, that is, of limitless space. But one must still draw, for the virgin sheet of paper is nothing—neither white, nor void, nor space. We can experience the white page, the absolute void, only when the drawing is still sufficiently sure, sufficiently present to give us intimations of its imminent suppression.

What Giacometti's drawing gives us, it gives us in a way that is both imponderable and intense. For his line is at the same time light and inci-sive. He grazes the paper and tears space open. He lets vacancy invade the form through innumerable fissures and simultaneously drives it off with the promptness of his repeated interventions, like a sudden swipe of claws. The purposeful indefiniteness which results isolates the objects and figures, expresses my separation from them, leaves them free, that is, in a position to choose among various possibilities. When Matisse draws a leaf with his lively and supple line, he also fixes it in a single one of its appearances and thus immobilizes it tyrannically for eternity. Giacometti cannot or does not care to gather such an image and immolate it accord-ing to his whims. As he multiplies its possibilities of seeming, he leaves the object its uncertain development, its anxious mobility. He does not draw up a single course but opens a multitude of paths among which the object can choose, or at least seem to hesitate continually, drawing from its indecision its quivering autonomy and the trembling of a separate life.

Isn't this multiplying of lines nothing more nor less than the refusal to allot significance and certainty to a single one? Here we come again upon contention as a creative principle. To trace a second line is to call the first into question without erasing it, to formulate a regret, to repent and correct, to start a debate, a quarrel between them which a third line will come to arbitrate and revive. From dispute to dispute, all certitude is withdrawn from the form which can only appear in an interrogative mode. Doubtless we still see this landscape, this bouquet of flowers, this head, but they will not let themselves be seized. They manifest themselves only by moving away, which prompts us to call to them, to question them. Once we have discovered them we must still constantly ask them: "Are you there?" For them, being means to be questioned, invoked, to be the object of our desires. Giacometti does not hand over the world for our embrace, our consummation, but to our desire which is still kept in suspense, to our thirst for the impossible.

And for him, a successive, line-by-line contestation of his drawing is the only way of placing himself in the world without betraying the truth of the excisions and the solitude which his lucidity shows him. Loneliness and the urge to have done with it, the wound and the prostration followed by a new hurtling against the wall—this is also the way we ourselves enter and do not enter the space of communication that Giacometti partially opens for us and from which he is excluded.

8

Except for a few paintings done in Stampa, Giacometti abandoned the model and even all realistic figuration during a ten-year period from about 1925 to 1935, in order to interpret the human figure freely, to make abstract constructions and above all to compose sculpture objects with symbolic or erotic content. And yet at no moment did he deliberately renounce his desire to represent reality: It was reality which abandoned him. In Bourdelle's studio or at the Grande Chaumière, he would vainly strive to copy a figure or a head from a model. If he starts with a detail he cannot succeed in a synthesis of the whole. And how can he render the whole without passing through the parts of which it is made? So he tries to take up the same subjects from memory. This results in the flat sculptures of 1926–28, which, satisfying as they are from the plastic point of view, only allude to a real head or figure. He tries again to model a bust, to paint a portrait. Reality eludes and rejects him. After a final unsuccessful attempt at self-portrait, Giacometti learned a lesson from his failures and turned from reality.

This wholly provisory decision was nonetheless the sign of a soul-searching whose consequences were to prove incalculable. Giacometti had just experienced not only the divorce between classical representation and real perception, but also the absolute impossibility of a total realism. A partial image of reality is false, a total expression humanly impossible. From this observation one can deduce two diametrically opposed alternatives: to cast one's lot with this impossibility, turn one's back on reality and substitute the imaginary as a field of experience (this is what Giacometti, out of spite, was to do for ten years); the other, which he will later adopt definitively, is an absurd and heroic obstinacy in the pursuit of unseizable reality.

The flat sculptures of 1926–28 are the first consequences of his abandoning of the model. These heads and figures which have the aspect of thin, smooth plates touch us through the rightness and the sensitivity of their forms and their proportions, but their very perfection betrays their limitations. And yet they are not the result of a preconceived idea, but of an involuntary deformation, of an organic metamorphosis. Starting with a head or a figure as they appeared to him at the time of his fruitless exercises at the Grande Chaumière, the sculptor sees the structure become flat in his hands, the details disappear, the surface become smooth. The thinning of the volume shows the temptation to abolish the third dimension as much as possible; Giacometti goes as far in this direction as the resistance of his material allows. The thickness of the plates is thus determined by technical and tectonic reasons. A transposition without hitches but also without surprises. The flat head gives the totality of a head, simplified to the extreme by total perception, stripped to its essentials and made thin so as to give the impression of bursting forth, of a sudden presence. The extreme stylization results however in changing the head into an idea of a head, into a beautiful object. Paradoxically it is the allusions to the details of a figure, added by incising or lightly hollowing the surface, which identify the head and convey the meaning of the whole.

Although Giacometti is unable during these years to do what he really wishes, he can do everything else. The basic idleness to which he yielded gives him great technical ease and leaves the way open to imaginary creations. Out of curiosity he accepts and profits by numerous influences— the desire to see and to experience primitive and archaic art and that of the moderns, especially the Cubists, Laurens, and Lipchitz. He participates in the experiments of his contemporaries and generally surpasses them or anticipates their discoveries. Affective stimulations converge with problems of construction and the quest for space, leading to extremely varied realizations. To the primitive fascination of the 1926 *Woman* (known as *The Spoon-Woman*), in which the erotic mechanism of attraction-repulsion is suggested by the opposition of the body, an immense cavity, welcoming and auspicious, to the hard and angular masses of the head and the bust. Or, again, to the *Couple* of 1926, which juxtaposes the trapezoidal volume of the man and the fish-shaped ellipse of the woman in a rough and barbaric contrast. Most of the sculptures are thus transpositions and variations on the human figure, accomplished through vigorous oppositions of round or circular forms and angular masses, analyses and syntheses of structures in space in which it is difficult to locate the realistic point of departure. These assemblages of alternating forms, this rhythmic accentuation of the void lead Giacometti to the idea of the open sculptures of 1928–29 which he purposely calls "clear structures." These are ideas rendered concrete in three dimensions, "forms in space; open, airy constructions, so as to slough off the mud." He banishes closed masses which confront space. Vacancy traverses these sculptures and animates them, and it is by this means that the symbol catches fire, that oppositions and accords spring to life. *The Reclining Woman Dreaming* dreams in horizontal planes which undulate like waves and whose calm cradling motion is emphasized by the supple pilings which support her. In its simple and geometrical construction, *Apollo* rises like a harmonious diagram, a grill traversed by space as a messenger of light.

Vacancy participates in the sculpture; it is visible, alive, sometimes disturbing. It takes over forms, separates and brings them together again, hollows them with its whirlpools or slips dizzily down smooth, profiled structures. It sometimes takes on an oppressive character of dreams and cruelty. *Man and Woman*, unlike the *Couple* of 1926 which juxtaposed two figures with contrasting forms, unites them this time in a rigorous image of murderous love. Almost forming a cage, the *Three Figures Outside* of 1928–29 reduces the men to straight verticals and the woman, who seems to evoke a lascivious dance between the two rivals, to a quadruple broken line.

With the *Cage* of 1931, eroticism takes on a convulsive and agonizing character, as much through the aggressive modeling of the bars which enclose space as by the exasperation of the forms and their furious modeling. Giacometti was haunted by the inside of things, especially of the human figure. This *Cage* is like the inside of a thorax, and what is being torn and devoured there represents the functioning of the human organism in its implacable autonomy. If man cannot be seized on the outside, by interrogating his visible aspect, the temptation is strong to re-create him with the imagination when the imagination is stimulated and oriented by subjectivity's obsessions and passions. The clear transparent structures are to represent organic visibility: They are mentally precise constructions capable of being executed from their imaginary representations.

This same cage becomes, in *Suspended Ball*, a simple and clear geometrical construction and the same obsession expresses itself in an encounter of extreme and suggestive simplicity: a cloven ball, suspended by a thread, which can slide along a crescent shape. A perfect symbolic object, which fascinates by its elementary obviousness, but in which the possibility of an effective motion, an obsessive motion which is a swinging motion, disturbs its deceptive calm.

Several sculpture objects between 1930 and 1932 also avail themselves of real or suggested motion. In *Point with Eye*, a movement which is suspended, halted in its paroxysm, gives the feeling of the lightning-like speed of a point piercing an eye. It is an atrocious mechanism which suggests both a child's toy and a model conceived by a sadistic engineer. Other objects pose enigmas. In *Circuit*, a marble rolls endlessly in a circular track, while its place, its repose, are prepared elsewhere in a tiny cavity inaccessible to it. Motion as the expression of the vanity of all motion reappears in *Man, Woman, Child*, where the elementary forms which represent the figures move without being able to join each other. *Hand Seized by the Finger* is a horrible system of gears which draws the finger and the whole hand into the perpetual motion of its wheels and pulleys. Giacometti, who could no longer bear the illusion of movement in sculpture, reacted by introducing a real motion which could be identified in most cases with the perpetual motion of solitude, with the erotic and cruel mechanism of his profound dreams. He speaks in one text of "pretty, precise mechanisms which have no use." His own, however, serve as vehicles for the mental imaginings he thus rids himself of. Dissatisfaction, revolt, bitter humor lead him to realize works of provocation and anti-sculpture: These are the *Disagreeable Objects, to Be Thrown Away* of 1932. These objects without bases, which one can place in various positions, all equally valid and equally absurd, are pure manifestations of undisguised aggressivity.

More and more the contradiction between work (useless, gratuitous) and life tormented Giacometti, who, from 1932 on, is above all concerned with expressing what he lives and feels, his conflicts, passions, desires, and dreams. Like a chessboard whose squares have been replaced with circular cavities of different diameters, *The Game Is Over* presents a man and woman who gesture to each other from far away; between them is an empty zone comprising three rectangular holes, like tombs with their lids; one is empty, another shut, the third contains a skeleton. We find the same obsession in *The Palace at 4 a.m.*, a kind of complicated cage in which are found a backbone, a bird's skeleton, a phallic form and a female figure in a long skirt; but they are separated and some are shut up in a second, smaller cage. The orientation, placing, and respective heights of these objects seem very precise, as though they were the plotted equation of a nightmare. Here again we find the obsession with the cage and the skeleton, with the clear structure and the hard structure identified as man's truth and the sign of his death. The cruelty and the fascination of terror are even more precisely the inspiration of *Woman with Her Throat Cut* and *Taut Thread*, which represent the temptation of communication through death and destruction. *The Table*, the materialization of a pure hallucination, supports the bust of a partly veiled woman between a severed hand and an enigmatic polyhedron. Giacometti approaches reality without leaving the climate of dreams in three versions of a long, thin, and very disturbing *Walking Woman*, whose proportions, but these alone, announce the future elongated figures. The sculptor was hovering at the time between abstract form, plastically and aesthetically satisfying, and the concrete realization of his dreams and obsessions; between the mysterious seated woman of *The Invisible Object*, predominantly affective, which he wanted to destroy because he found her too sentimental, and the polyhedric sculpture of 1934–35 which, in its limited perfection, is no longer anything but an aesthetic object without content. He strives to reach a synthesis in the *Head-Skull* of the same period. Actually the subject lends itself admirably to this treatment. It is first of all a powerfully suggestive reality to which Giacometti is extremely sensitive. Also, through its very structure, it calls for and facilitates a rigorous plastic interpretation. Concentrating closely on construction and expressing simply one of his deepest fantasies, the sculptor manages to reconcile geometrical construction and hallucinatory magic.

But this contradiction, resolved for a day, returns to torture him. Imaginary and inner reality attract him, but clash with the formal demands of the constructor and the plastic artist. In $1 + 1 = 3$, harshly derisive of woman, he does not escape the dilemma and is almost at the end of his nonrepresentational adventure.

In all the work of this period one hesitates to say who is triumphant: the fantastic poet or the abstract constructor. Giacometti finds relative satisfaction in the creation of plastically rigorous sculptures, in the search for the abstract harmonies and flawless structures. He likes also to be invaded by the flux of images and unconscious imaginings in which, when he succeeds in grasping them, he discovers the profound mechanisms of emotional life and the constants of his being. But what stays with him more than anything else, no doubt, is despair of reality, and his nostalgia shows through the narration of dreams and the plastic experiments. When he evokes the human face, and this is almost always the case, it is to tell passionately again and again his powerlessness to attain it. A defeatist attitude, with which he tries to persuade himself to renounce reality without really breaking with it, all the while preparing unconsciously, deep within him, his return to the visible world.

9

In 1921 during a trip to the Tyrol made in strange circumstances, Giacometti spent a day alone in a hotel room with his traveling companion who was dying.

> I watched the head of Van M. being transformed; the nose became more and more accentuated, the cheeks grew hollow, the open, almost immobile mouth was hardly breathing and, toward evening, trying to draw his profile, I was seized with a sudden panic before his oncoming death.

"This event," Giacometti continues, "was for me a kind of breach in my life. Everything became something else, and this trip obsessed me continually for a whole year." And will obsess him, perhaps, for a whole lifetime, considering that this revelation has not yet exhausted all its consequences. It announced what the sculptor would discover much later, scrutinizing with a scalpel-sharp gaze the appearance of a human face. Before the insistence of such a look, the model is metamorphosed, gives way to the human being in its terrible stony nakedness. The eyes become black excavations. The perfection of the skull, the frightful tongs of the jawbones, and the grooves of the teeth show through the skin. Doubtless the primordial need for a sculptor to discover structures makes him come forth to touch with his hand the mineral hardness of the skeleton and the skull. But this explanation is insufficient. One must also take into account the feverish passion with which Giacometti perseveres in his pursuit of truth, of a likeness, and tracks it down to its final lair. He will remain haunted by the idea of death and overwhelmed by the signs of its manifestation. He will seek to rid himself of the obsessive image of Van M., dying, his mouth open, when he models the hallucinatory *Head on a Stem* of 1947, whose impalement seems to wrest a silent scream from it. It is terrible in a much different way than the *Skull* painted in 1923, which Giacometti finds "in one sense as perfect and as living as anything alive." Again, evoking the sight of a corpse: "I looked at this head become an object, a little box, measurable, insignificant." The head is measurable and an object only when it is dead. We must return to that which lives, to the presence of death in it, to the active presence which sustains it and is its framework, which rears it above things but at the same time rejects it beyond recall from the world and from others and walls it up in its solitude. Thus, in different moments and works, the human face seems stricken with stupor, halted in its drive, wrenched by surprise from the convulsions of death agony, or more often torn from tranquil contemplation, beyond the emptiness which assails it from every side.

This revelation penetrates the sculptor's vision so strongly, around 1946, that he experiences its effects constantly in the most ordinary circumstances of his life. "At that time," he writes,

I began to see heads in the emptiness, in the space which surrounds them. When for the first time I perceived clearly the head I was watching grow rigid and motionless in an instant, forever, I trembled with terror as never before in my life and a cold sweat ran down my back. It was no longer a living head but an object which I looked at like any other object, but no, in another way, unlike any other object, but like something simultaneously alive and dead. I cried out in terror as if I had just crossed the threshold, as if I were entering a world never seen before. All the living were dead, and this vision was repeated often, in the Métro, in the street, in a restaurant, with my friends . . . That waiter at Lipp's who became motionless, leaning over me, mouth open, with no relation to the preceding moment or the next, his mouth open, his eyes fixed in an absolute immobility. But at the same time that men underwent a transformation, so did objects—tables, chairs, suits, the street, even trees and landscapes.

This morning as I woke up I saw my napkin for the first time, that weightless napkin, in an immobility never seen before and as though suspended in a terrifying silence. It no longer had any relation to the bottomless chair or the table, whose legs no longer rested on the floor, barely touched it; there was no longer any relation between these objects separated by immeasurable chasms of emptiness.

The phenomena which affected his seeing brought a complete change to the outer appearance of beings and things. Giacometti discovered only silence and immobility around him. Even in a noisy and bustling scene, the world seemed totally silent, totally immobile. He had an acute sensation of inertia, of silence, of the death of things. Time seemed abolished, reduced to a succession of discontinuous moments, stopped (as sculptures and paintings actually are, silent and immobile in relation to the movement which they express, or to the creative lapse of time from which they issue). This perception of arrested, suspended life was for Giacometti an experience as overwhelming as that of the mystics, but that modestly affected only the appearance of everyday reality. As though death had come down all around him. Or rather as though he had been transported to a place beyond death where the spectacle of life was like a hideous simulacrum. A frightening sensation, as the quoted passage shows, but at other times an exalting dizzying discovery of a reality completely transformed, saved from all erosion, restored to its virginity. One day in 1946, leaving a movie the falsity of whose images had tormented him, Giacometti thought his eyes had opened for the first time. The Boulevard Montparnasse with its café terraces, its trees, its passersby, plunged him in a daze and a wonder of which he had hardly until then anticipated the possibility. Reality appeared to him suddenly of a richness and beauty superior to all dreams, artistic creations, or the imaginary world of poets. He trembled with emotion before a table or a glass, before reality which is "terribly superior to any surreality," as Antonin Artaud remarked. At the same time his work with models, particularly Colonel Rol-Tanguy, provokes in the sculptor analogous sensations, but in fortunate circumstances which allow him to explore them more deeply. Returning to the human head, he does not stop at the hard structure he had laid bare and which displayed the motionless presence of death. Rummaging deeper in the face, penetrating the wall of bone which death had applied to it like a mask, he sees and gives to be seen the living depths which inhabit it. For life is within, walled up in the skull and the bones, filtering through the slits of the eyes, circulating in the vertebrae like that pillar of fire which, according to the science of the pharaohs, sustains and irrigates the human edifice. Life gushes forth from death and takes refuge in it. Through an invisible presence, it attracts and retains the eye by acting on the outer appearances of which it is a prisoner, in changing what I see. The vision, simultaneously purified and enlarged by the revelation of the internal dimensions of beings and things, suffices to change the aspect of the world. The latter, finally seen (and not imagined, interpreted, reinvented), is a prodigious, fantastic spectacle, infinitely rich, since everything in it simultaneously reveals and hides its unknown face. The overwhelming effect which depth has on real appearances at these moments must then be seized and expressed by the painter and sculptor.

10

To build a wall, the mason adjusts his stones one after the other in a logical order, in this case beginning with the bottom and finishing with the top. Similarly the artist's labors are subordinated to finishing the work, each of his movements is directed toward that realization and has its own function as does each of the mason's stones, within the limits of his project. But because his vision of the world and the meaning of his undertaking command it of him, Giacometti must on the contrary immediately seize and express the whole of the object he is depicting. No one can force a head more quickly out of clay or onto canvas. But having made it appear, he must continue indefinitely to seek it, to approach it, since what he has set out to represent is the distance and the refusal of that head, the impossibility of absolute communication which it means to him. From the first moment, the diabolical mechanism is in operation. Giacometti's eye and hand never stop. He smokes, chats, thinks of something else, but at the same time in a kind of hypnosis or second state, the eye and the hand continue to come and go, to do and undo, while on the sidelines the painted face or clay figures rise up with haughty intensity, as though detached from the wild effort, the incessant torture which are creating them. When will Giacometti stop? He cannot stop. When he lets a sculpture leave the studio, it is because of an arbitrary, insignificant decision. He does not stop, he interrupts the work in progress. Throughout all the sculptures, paintings, and drawings, he pursues one and the same attempt to approach reality. The work is single, unfinished, impossible.

His not stopping means that he never stops looking at and depicting what he sees, in any circumstances and at each minute of his life, even if he is not "working." In the café, he draws on his newspaper, and if he has no newspaper, his finger still runs over the marble top of the table. If his hand is occupied, his eye still draws. He draws as he walks in the street, and when he sleeps. His not stopping means too that Giacometti can only present us the rough draft of an unaccomplished, unfinished undertaking. A reflection, an approximation of reality—of that absolute reality which haunts him—and which he pursues in a kind of amorous or homicidal fury. He pursues it and approaches it. That the end is inaccessible does not as a matter of fact exclude the possibility of progress. And Giacometti places himself in a perspective of progress which seems to him even to obey a law of continuous acceleration. According to this Mallarméan arithmetic, a future minute could represent a year of past work. In a month he could go through as many stages as he once did in ten years; and in front of him seems to stretch the perspective of several lifetimes of work. The fantastic acceleration of the time necessary for creation would thus be the equivalent of a slowing down, a progressive spinning out of the actual duration. His optimism is thus as disproportionate with regard to the relative as his pessimism is categorical with regard to the absolute. Yet people readily accuse him of repeating himself, of marking time, especially when he neglects works (such as *The Chariot, Figurine in a Box, The Nose*) whose affective, experimental, sometimes anecdotal nature resulted in a seeming diversity. In returning untiringly to the bust of Diego, the standing woman, the walking man, the portrait of the same model, he may discourage the inattentive spectator, but his austere research allows him to concentrate his ways of approaching. The slower his walk toward his goal appears, the more rapid it actually is. Each acquisition is definitive, each progress irreversible. But progress plays only with imponderable elements. A single line can stop it a whole night and hold up the whole work with the question of the exactness of its inflection. Giacometti's not stopping means also that he does not stop advancing.

II

We walk in the street with our eyes closed. We see only through the deforming prism of contracted habits, of a blinding knowledge: We see those passersby only as we *know* they are. If I call this knowledge in doubt, if I purify my eye of all the mental correctives which dull and estrange it, everything changes. These same passersby issue from a wide lateral opening; the immense space which imprisons them makes them appear small, thin, nibbled by the void, almost undifferentiated and especially elongated, drawn out by the accentuation of their verticality. The eye does not distinguish, *at first*, the butcher boy from the office worker. Its spatial perception retains almost nothing of their peculiar natures, except the indications of their movements: This one walks, that one leans toward the ground, that other one holds out his arm. It is thus that the eye really sees and it is thus that Giacometti represents beings and things: in their distance, in their space, hence by depicting that space, by incorporating into his figures the distance which separates them from him. He represents what he sees and sees what one doesn't dare see, because he has been able to effect a true liberation which is not that of reality but that of the vision. He has thus brought himself to the antipodes of the teaching of the Academy, anatomy, and the classical tradition, which disregard the distance of the subject and demand that one respect reality as it is and not as it appears. That reality, objective and measurable, is an object of science, not the subject of a work of art.

The purified perception of Giacometti is equally opposed to the instantaneous and mechanical objectivity of photography. The lens does not transmit distance and does not know how to sort out and grade the messages it receives. It collects, and transmits to us a mass of information which the eye would in reality gather by repeated forays. It transcribes everything but the essential, our relation to the subject, that is, it sees nothing or it kills what it sees. Also the lens is at best an eye cut off from life, with no connection to the density of existence, to the experience and depth of a human being. The eye on the other hand plunges its root, its optic nerve, into a rich and active interior which intervenes strongly in the phenomenon of perception, projecting inner space into real space to modify its coloring. The visual distance is added and combined with an affective distance which, in Giacometti's case, will move the person or thing looked at ever farther away. Finally the photographic lens operates instantaneously; the artist, in his relation to his model, establishes duration. The new, penetrating look which sees the model for the first time at every moment, with the freshness, intensity, and violence of the first meeting, must paradoxically be attained through the exercise of prolonged contemplation, through insistent questioning. The essential is not granted at first glance. This virginity of the sight, its power to lay bare and deepen a relationship, might even be the inaccessible goal of continual interrogation; one can but dream of it and work at approaching it. Thus the model is not represented the way she is, nor the way anyone might see her, but the way that a unique individual, with his particular memory and affectivity, patiently questions her and questions himself through her. In one sense the artist always creates a self-portrait.

The characteristics of this vision are more clearly highlighted at certain stages in the sculptor's experience. Thus, from 1940 to 1945, Giacometti, without seeking anything but life, the likeness of a head, or a figure, experienced with each try the same phenomenon: The figure's size diminished progressively until it became tiny and often completely disappeared. The figurines which survive are astonishingly true in their distance and in the expression of their separate lives. Reduction obliges one to take a total view of oneself, hence to become strongly aware of all the space around one. They are small in size but big in proportion. For the first time Giacometti dissociates dimension and proportion in expressing size, and this discovery will have the most fertile consequences. As they become tiny, the figures call attention to the enormity of their pedestals, and this disproportion defines their distance. Soon Giacometti will translate the "remoteness" of the personage by playing with the relation of the figure to the pedestal: The larger the pedestal in relation to the sculpture, the farther away the figure appears to be. The precision of this quantitative measure contrasts with the inevitable but highly significant imprecision in the treatment of details. Obviously there can be no question of modeling the ear or the hand of a man no taller than a fingernail. But one sees that this forced imprecision contributes to the rightness and the truth of the ensemble. The impossibility of stopping at the part sends one back to the whole, communicates the sensation of the totality of the figure in space. This discovery too is decisive. It will allow Giacometti, around 1946, to return to sculptures of normal dimensions. The characteristics of the tiny figurines, inherent in their size, will survive in dimensions which no longer oblige them, this time expressing the distant totality of the personage. In addition, we find again in the sculptures of this period the imprecise construction, the disproportion of the volume of the pedestal. The determining of space will also be effectuated simply by boundaries in the form of rods which outline the edges of a cube, as in the *Cages*, or else by placing the figure between two rectangular opaque boxes, as in *Figurine in a Box*. Whatever their dimensions, the figures are large in their proportions; their thinning and lengthening communicate violently the feeling of an immediate presence. The lengthening is in a way the plastic translation of the words "he arises" or "he stands up" which correspond both to the pure perception of a man in space and to the feeling of incommunicability and separation which Giacometti experiences.

The rendering of movement in the sculptures, starting in 1947, is another consequence of distant, spatial perception. The movement, the attitude, the gesture disturb space, cut it up, sculpt it, and the eye records its slightest changes. Giacometti did several versions of the *Walking Man*, the *Capsizing Man*, *The Hand*, *The Man with a Finger*, because he was struck by signs of movement in his vision of space. But inversely he treats such subjects in order to communicate his distant vision and to render visible the space around a figure. To sculpt a walking man is also, in a sense, to depict space agitated and modified by the walker's passing.

Finally, the movement of one figure leads almost inevitably to depicting the movements, conjugated or not, of several figures. An immobile figure surrounds itself with closed space. A figure in motion opens space and attracts other figures there, without however meeting them; in open space, solitude is plural.

From 1948 to 1949 date the *Group of Figures* and the *Square*; the pedestal widens, becomes the very precisely circumscribed place which permits walking men to pass each other by in mutual ignorance, to avoid without seeing one another. Impenetrable solitudes in motion, but subtly attuned by the unity of place and space which they reveal. A hidden organizer still directs the respective placing and orientation of the figures. The *Square* and *Forest* of 1950 are on the contrary free of this constraint. Looking at the floor of his studio arbitrarily strewn with figurines placed close to one another, Giacometti found that they "worked" just as they were, that they formed a whole as satisfying as the composed groups. And he had them cast. But one should not imagine that this result was a triumph of objective chance. If several isolated figures are right in actual space, the group they form by being brought together—whatever their differences of position, orientation and scale—will be necessarily right as well. Outside in the street, any group of passersby is as "true" as a single individual, because it is situated in actual space. A director is necessary only in conventional space—in the theater or in painting.

12

When I mention the anguish of communication in connection with Giacometti, I mean the impossibility of absolute communication and not the difficulty of being and living with others. For, since childhood, Giacometti always loved to charm, dominate, and fascinate, and his gifts, his intelligence, his charm and physical ascendancy, his cleverness and obstinacy, the force of his singular personality, apparent to everyone, did in fact enable him to charm, dominate, and fascinate in all circumstances. At school in Schiers he was gifted in all branches of learning and passionately fond of literature, science, politics, and, of course, the arts. His precocious intelligence, his amazing memory, and his faculty of assimilation enabled him to take up any new studies and investigate them thoroughly without sacrificing the time necessary for conversation, games, and friendship.

He so pleased his teachers that he was given permission to set up his first studio in an empty loft at the school. His friendships with classmates were as easy as his relationships with his parents and brothers had been; they have remained close, affectionate, understanding, and free. Since then, whether at the Grande Chaumière, among the painters of Montparnasse, or at the center of the Surrealist group, he never had any real difficulty in his relations with others. On the contrary, he attracts and charms the people he meets or seeks out, for he seeks contact with others with a passion and an avidity which one day caused him to remark: "I would give all my works for a conversation."

And yet . . . And yet an obscure and profound dissatisfaction subsists which he is all the more compelled to project into the absolute since he can scarcely nourish it with failures in ordinary human relations. Fully gratified, Giacometti remains essentially destitute. Surrounded, admired, he only experiences his solitude the more, and with it, the temptation of a total communication through murder or love but even more by an annihilation in love, or through the work of art, but in that case in the infinite pursuit of an impossible work of art. What he retains from childhood, what he writes of in any case, is not the games or rambles in the countryside but the memory of certain objects or certain places, "trees and stones more than anything," in which he recognized a friendly, protecting presence. A shelter dug in the snow, for instance, or

a golden-colored monolith with the mouth of a cave at its base: Water had completely hollowed it out inside. The entrance was long and low, barely as tall as we were at that time. Inside, certain places were deeper than others, and at the very back it seemed as if there were another tiny cave. It was my father who showed us this monolith one day. What a tremendous discovery. I at once felt this rock as a friend; it called to us, smiled at us, like someone you used to know and love and whom you discover again with infinite surprise and joy.

He adds: "All the rest was vague and insubstantial, air which catches hold of nothing."

All the rest, that is, the outside, the distance from the others, that immeasurable and foreign space for which Giacometti tried to substitute an enclosed, auspicious place, the monolith, the studio, and above all the often-pursued space of the work itself. At this price, proportion becomes real, entrenchment fertile, and the approach to another, to the unknown, a fantastic adventure to be undertaken. But the privileged space is obtained only for an instant, to vanish and spark the pursuit once again. The interior is as threatening and as fleeting as the exterior. The studio is only a fragile transparent prison suspended in the void and enclosing it. At each moment one must lay its foundations, rebuild it again. Four walls, or any other boundary, against the dispersal, loss, or change of something essential whose growth and chances must be safeguarded against external aggression and internal disintegration. But above all to prepare oneself to face under less precarious circumstances that aggression and disintegration which inevitably occur. Thus Giacometti leaves the studio and himself only the better to return to them; he does not leave. He is the opposite of an escaped prisoner; he is a recluse. Is he immobile, halted? Quite the contrary, but he has chosen once and for all to do without the illusory aid of open space and so to travel more freely, that is with extreme difficulty, in the only dimension in which he hopes to advance: depth.

Giacometti shuts himself up, concentrates. He remains faithful to his friends, his passions, his obsessions. He has occupied the same studio for thirty-five years, haunts the same neighborhood, the same cafés, and has changed nothing in his way of life, as singular as it is regular and almost ritualistic. In the same way he doesn't attempt to vary his subjects, the attitude of his models, the lighting in his work, the colors of his palette. He is capable of shutting himself up for a hundred nights on end with the same model, of tracking the same face a hundred nights on end. He detests change and disdains travel.

The only journey which Giacometti regularly allows himself is not a journey but a return. Just as, in the studio, he will step back so as to tear himself away from a sculpture, to recapture it and regain control at a distance, so he returns periodically to be with his mother in Stampa, in the mountain valley where his roots are. A high, narrow valley, where the mountains are Swiss but the dialect Italian. This is all I know of the place. Of his mother I know only a few portraits and the almost sacred feeling of admiration and piety her son has for her. Yet it is impossible to come near Giacometti without turning toward her. She personifies the presence and the permanence of that deep-rooted fire which sustains the sculptor's work and his existence, that source and that foundation to which he is attached by an essential bond. A nutritive bond which allowed him to leave home without expatriating himself, to expose himself to the dangers of an extreme adventure without breaking with his beginnings. She is the pole, the fixed center that assures the orientation and the tension of this spiritual experience. A watchful and silent guardian, she seems by her presence alone to nourish a tradition, not a repertory of obsolete forms but an inexhaustible lode of energy. Through her mediation, Giacometti's link with the earth, with the substratum, with depth, is as powerful as it is invisible. One feels behind each of the sculptor's gestures, each of his words, the impulsive force and the subterranean echo of a back country which he does not need to reveal, that is, to verify, so secretly active is it within him. His mother seems by her demeanor alone a proof of this. In addition, her great age, to whose trials she seems immune, gives her an almost mythological dimension. One is tempted to evoke some inaccessible and benevolent mother-goddess, firmly entrenched in her mountain, and, like the monolith, destined to conjure away dangers. Outside of her, of what she personifies, illuminates, and permits, "all the rest is vague and insubstantial, air which catches hold of nothing."

13

It is arbitrary to separate Giacometti's paintings from his sculpture. His first picture, *Apples*, dates from 1913; his first sculpture, a head of Diego, from 1914. Since then the sculptor has always painted, the painter has always sculpted. The two means of expression are nothing for him but the tools of the same research and the same experiment. They complete each other, support each other mutually; the exchanges between them are constant and each advance in one has immediate repercussions on the other. It may happen that color brings a confirmation or an indication to the expression of a modeled figure, and Giacometti has in fact often dreamed of painting all his sculptures. Inversely, the subject of a picture is often a figure on its pedestal or sculptures in the studio. In these cases the remoteness of the figure is increased by this figuration twice removed, which locates it on the inside of a double transparent enclosure. For the problems of distance with which we have seen the sculptor struggling pose themselves in identical terms and with the same intensity to the painter. Only the circumstances differ: Deprived of the faculty of playing with real space, Giacometti has to find in the two dimensions of his canvas other means of creating distance than those he uses in sculpture.

Hence he almost always surrounds his compositions with a false frame of neutral color or rough drawing. This tangible limit traced by hand attenuates first of all the geometric rigidity of the stretcher. Above all it allows us to see the subject through an indefinite and ambiguous opening which at once creates the illusion of remoteness. This false window plays the role of the "cages" in the sculpture, tightening space and increasing its density as one might compress a gas. The painter will still determine the measurement of the distance with precision by effecting the dimensions, the proportions, and the construction of the false window. But he does not resolve this problem in the abstract, through some mental operation; on the contrary he seeks his "distance" on the scene of the action, the canvas, by successive estimates and gropings whose traces remain visible. So that the manifestation of this blind search for a distance at once tactile and metaphysical also has the character of an anxious appeal, a wait, an entreaty as though the favor of the gods would confirm the surveyor's ungrateful task.

Thanks to this calculated remoteness, the relations which we may have with the subject of the painting exclude all familiarity and forestall any ill-timed intervention on our part. This figure, for example, does not suspect that he is being looked at; he is alone in his space, foreign to the things which surround him, lonely and exiled in the midst of the studio which has become immense, imprecise, disturbing. Formerly (around 1946–47) the décor was sometimes rendered with all its details but by a multiplicity of lines which referred one back to its basic indefiniteness. Today it is hardly sketched in, or else treated with utter unconcern. The lack of differentiation of the backgrounds sets off the isolation of the subject and reveals the presence of emptiness around beings and things. The figure occupies, without inhabiting it, a vague, mysterious, dilapidated space; apples graze the table which remains in ignorance of the other furniture, and whose legs scarcely rest on the floor. The background is purposely left to itself; gray and formless, both dirty and luminous, it takes on by turns the aspects of an ocher mist, a cloud of soot, of leaden or silver pools or vapor. Traversed by vague currents whose light and shadow sluggishly oppose or penetrate each other, it gives the sensation of a substantial but neutral and unreal space, whose colors are those of waiting and foreboding. It is a propitious space for apparitions. Seemingly random lines cross it, organize it, detach in passing the outline of an easel or a sofa. Careless indications, but they give this immense uncertain space its exact dimensions, and provide unreal space with its own sensory quality.

The uniformity of the subjects is more striking here than in the sculpture, for the latter means of expression traditionally implies a restriction if not a codification of the subjects. One sculpts a nude, not a woman in her bath. In painting, diversity is the rule; the limitation to two dimensions paradoxically allows one to represent everything. Yet Giacometti hardly varies the subjects of his paintings. The landscape is almost exclusively the houses of the rue d'Alésia or the trees against the background of the mountains of Stampa. The still life is apples, bottles, a bouquet, a few familiar objects on the table. Or else a corner of the studio, the stove and the coal scuttle. The faces are those of the same people from his close-knit circle: his wife, his brother, his mother, his usual model, Caroline, Lotar. The seated person, his hands on his knees, does not change his pose. The nude is standing, her arms hanging close to her body. And all the heads have the same expression, the same bearing, the same fixity. This uniformity of subject in an artist for whom "in every work of art the subject is primordial, whether the artist is conscious of it or not," is most revealing. The explanation, as we have seen, is that the subject of the picture is not Diego or Annette, is not yet Diego or Annette, but for the moment Diego withholding himself, Annette unattainable. If he were to change his model oftener, Giacometti would perhaps experience less vividly the necessity to change himself, that is to advance, to explore each new work a little further. But there is a simpler reason: The more known the model is, the more unknown he is. The insistent, obsessive questioning of a human being (or any other subject) finally strips him of his known part and uncovers the unknown which is all in depth within him. The model lends himself all the more submissively to this laying bare when the painter ceases to linger over superficial details and particularities which might distract him in a person chosen at random. An occasional model might give a portrait that would be more like, would resemble the model more and Giacometti less. The longer the sittings last and the oftener they are repeated, the more the model will resemble Giacometti, to the detriment not of the profound personality of the model but of its surface particularities. One evening at a café, Giacometti looked at Annette with insistence.

She was surprised. "Why are you looking at me like that?" "Because I didn't see you today." Annette had just posed the whole afternoon for him. He had not seen Annette, but the unknown stranger, the model. The creature close to us becomes a stranger, the unknown par excellence, revealing man and the world as unknown, revealing him, Giacometti, to himself as an unknown being.

Giacometti's paintings are painted less with colors than with lines, and his palette is as restricted as his subjects. A range of grays and ochers; black, white, and gray lines are apparently sufficient. But within this dominant tone, where all the nuances and transparencies of gray echo each other, appear colors, rare and scarcely exuberant ones, discreet and refined, drawing a sure power from their very restraint, from the rightness of their pitch or their place. The abuse and exasperation of pure or mixed colors to which painters have habituated us have ended by blunting our sensibility and smothering color in its own excesses, leaving us with an insipid impression of grisaille. Starting with gray and using it as an alembic, Giacometti resensitizes colors, gives them back their subtlety and their acuteness. They emerge from gray but remain suspended in it. They no longer act on their own, but are strictly subjected to the necessities of a pictorial language, itself dominated by the subject. That is, they obey that gradation in expressive intensity which mounts from distances and inanimate things to the human face, passing through familiar objects and places. As one draws near the face the intensity increases and the difficulties of portrayal increase. The light fails, the color becomes dimmer. Thus the still lifes are generally more colored than the portraits and less so than the landscapes. In the latter, despite the alliance with gray, the color sings, the greens of the foliage respond to the blue of the sky and the red of the bricks. The grays of the still lifes are already denser and more encroaching, and in the figure paintings they are the very color of that unfathomable and hallucinated space of which the figure is captive. They create obsessions, dull the light, and sometimes make it well up behind the head which then seems surrounded by a mysterious halo.

Giacometti's paintings are painted less with colors than with lines, because color is the quality of surfaces and parts, and, as we have seen, Giacometti precisely refuses to give expressiveness to surfaces and parts. The eyes are blue and the lips red, but Giacometti does not paint eyes or lips, but the distant totality of the face and the depths which it reveals. The vacuum which exudes the vague and dense skein of lines of a face cannot be anything but gray, the canceling out of the colors of the spectrum, the color of refusal and the impossible.

The circular arrangement of the picture around a central point also indicates the character of the line, which, as I have already indicated, plays the chief role in it. We again come upon Giacometti's so-characteristic line—rapid, discontinuous, indefinitely repeated. Preferably black, white, or gray (but it may happen that a thread of color intrudes in its meshes), it defines forms less than it calls on them to reveal themselves by multiplying within the outlines. Its frequency and its insistence increase as it nears the center. Thus, in a portrait, Giacometti treats the background hastily, lingers but little over the body and the arms, to apply all his care and effort to the head. Although often barely sketched in, it is the décor which is located and fixed. The head is all the more vague and fleeting for being worked over, weighted with color, and loaded down with line. For the looming of its totality, that is, the condition of its truth and its likeness, depends on the indefiniteness of its parts and the eruption of its surface. The face appears like the arena of a fierce combat; it is there that the match is played, that the frenzied interrogation of the eye takes place, that the most precise of all instruments, the eye and brush together, must operate with patience as well as cruelty. The immediate presence demands rapidity, violence of attack and penetration, but the definition of distance implies minute care in the approach. Without moderating its fury, this contradictory instrument pursues sometimes for nights on end a single undiscoverable line. The struggle has its ups and downs, its successes and reversals. From one day to the next the portrait can vanish, reappear, disappear again, revive again; and nothing allows one to foresee the outcome. A constant pursuit in the form of successive contentions. A line is added to another line, obliterates it, and advances. Innumerable lines which outline nothing, define nothing but which cause something to appear. More than in the drawings, the line explodes, crumbles, scatters into segments which mingle with the brushstrokes. Multiplying and dividing, the lines seem to cancel each other out and vanish in the totality of a head which bursts spontaneously out of the void, the excess of work effacing the traces of work. We no longer see how it has come nor from where it has come. The familiar face of Annette is still present, more present than ever, but detached, transfigured, so that it seems to us that we recognize the unknown which she is, that we sense without distinguishing it. A solitary apparition of an unknown Annette, that seems created by the sole power of a silent injunction.

Giacometti goes from known to unknown by stripping down, by progressive asceticism. He flays appearances and digs into reality until he renders visible the essence of their relationship, that is, the presence of something sacred. That sacredness whose nostalgia is expressed in all modern art, whose lack gives rise to undertakings as poignant as they are sterile. Giacometti drives it out of hiding and wakens it where it is hidden, in the depths of each new thing and each being. It is useless to dissociate the nymph from the forest and the siren from the wave. There is a sacredness only in the excess relationship between man and reality, in the impossible communication of the one with the whole, laceration of oneself and lacerating of the other, sole threshold and lightning flash, which the totalizing power of the creative act establishes.

"Texts for an Approach," trans. John Ashbery, *Giacometti: Three Essays*, by Jacques Dupin (New York: Black Square Editions–Hammer Books, 2003). First published in *Alberto Giacometti* (Maeght Éditeur, 1962; Fourbis, 1991).

MARCELIN PLEYNET

(1933)

THE IMAGE OF MEANING

We have heard much talk about novelists in the past few years and we have heard much talk from novelists . . . and more often than not we listened with great interest. Since then these novelists have become famous and they now talk a little less. What I should like to say here is that, despite the fact that the title of this evening's discussion is "The New Poetry,"[1] I do not in the least intend to present myself as a poet, I do not in the least intend to take the floor in the name of any kind of poetry, modern or anachronistic. There is no question of letting it be supposed that after the novelists it will be the poets who will try to get themselves talked about, then, after the poets, the painters, the musicians . . . in short, the corporations. None of that has any interest. Perhaps there is nevertheless a lesson to be deduced from the fact that the novelists, once they became famous, stopped talking . . . There certainly *is* a lesson to be deduced for the novelists, the poets, and the others. One is inclined to wonder, for instance, whether these novelists weren't more interested in communicating the problems that their craft imposed on them, the problems they encountered in writing, than in having their work assimilated to a kind of literature recognizable by the reader . . . Once the label appears on the merchandise, everyone feels reassured. As for me, I must say that I am no more interested by the sonnet than I am by the novel, nor by anything which could come under the heading of entertainment or the art of staging what is by common consent called the world, reality . . . all things which I don't really have much knowledge of, if indeed I have any knowledge of them at all. If I knew what it is that is by common consent called the world, I would no doubt write novels and poems, or perhaps in that case I wouldn't write at all. What I mean is that I haven't the vaguest notion of what happens when a man feels exalted, when he is in love, or when he is cuckolded. Not only do I have no ready-made answers to these questions but furthermore I don't think it will ever be possible to answer them. Besides, these questions are badly chosen; to wonder what happens when a man feels exalted is already to presuppose a number of certainties which may be relied on . . . Actually, all these certainties seem to me highly contestable. And in this light, the question to which I would be most willing to accord its due is: *"What is happening?"* It is because I don't know *what is happening* that I write. In the same way, it is because I don't know *what is happening* here at this moment that I believe myself authorized to speak. Nevertheless, let there be no mistake, I do not plead for a happy ignorance, or a painful one. By refusing to recognize literary categories I claim the right to find the place in which I may look for myself and recognize myself. The structures and forms proposed to me (whether they be novelistic, poetic, pictorial, musical, social, etc.) have this in common: They presuppose that I might recognize myself in an order whose meaning would then become apparent, on condition that I grant it its authority, that I justify myself. For example, one can suppose that certain works have a temporary success because they confer authority on a meaning which criticism and the public recognize (at which point we have illustration: The work has no function beyond ornamenting what has been lived) . . . Let such an enterprise become dogmatic and we have academicism. Now, as far as I am concerned, in my ignorance of what is happening, how could I accept one form rather than another, how could I accept to confer authority on a form which doesn't take ambiguity into account, but speaks in terms of what is happening; which ignores the multiplicity of answers, no doubt contradictory, to the question "What is happening?" This multiplicity of answers may nevertheless be resolved . . . I would resolve it for the moment by saying that what speaks in what is happening is thought—the thought of what is happening.[2] That is, the formulation of the proposition which Jakobson attributes to Peirce: "The meaning of a sign is another sign by which it may be translated." What speaks out in this passing from one sign to another is nothing more than the thought that a sign must be translated. By this I mean that what speaks—elicits speech from what we may call the text and the translation, the apprehended sign and the translated sign—is the thought that there can be no text without a translation and hence, with all the more reason, no translation without a text. Certainly a table has no meaning beyond the word "table," and yet we live neither in the table nor in the word "table," we live in the exchange. It is this that I would like to write: the meaning that alights on the table.

Thus, in the title we have chosen, "The New Poetry," what seems to me particularly interesting is not the accent placed on poetry, but the accent placed on newness. In my opinion we haven't sufficiently examined this newness which is as old as the world and which never stops being new. And today, when fashions, novelties, and dubious originalities succeed each other at an ever faster pace, I am sure that we have a great deal to gain, if we want to find our bearings, by asking ourselves what is the perennial character of newness. What the newness of Baudelaire, Lautréamont, Mallarmé, Cézanne consisted of for their contemporaries . . . What the reader confronts in an essentially new work. Let us, to be brief, say it is a shift which situates the reader not in the unreadable but facing the unreadable. If as Peirce says, "the meaning of a sign is another sign by which it may be translated," it is enough that the reader, or what is read, or the artist's translation (his vision) use another set of rules than the one agreed on, or transform the rules agreed on (Baudelaire, Mallarmé) for the eyesight to cloud over behind a disappointed convention (in the case of Baudelaire and Mallarmé, the convention would be that of nineteenth-century bourgeois morality and syntax), a convention disappointed by a new meaning, purer or more ambitious. It remains to be seen what this set of rules is, and how it is created. Why does Hugo abandon classical verse, why does Mallarmé see verse breaking up, why is Rimbaud not satisfied with subjective poetry, if not because the agreed-on set of rules plunged *them* into unreadability. Example: General Aupic found it utterly meaningless for the young Baudelaire to be interested in poetry, while for Baudelaire poetry was meaning itself. Thus a new set of rules and new worlds were created. Because the rules (or the syntax if you will) no longer allow what has been lived to be read (General Aupic's rules don't allow Baudelaire to understand what he lives), the rules (or the syntax) of this experience (to understand what he experiences Baudelaire discovers a new set of rules), the rules (or the syntax) of this experience involve a reconversion of such a kind that the rules, which we may call anachronistic, will not succeed in deciphering anything of the new code but faults, when they ought to be deciphering their own shortcomings with regard to a meaning which they are unable to satisfy.

What has happened to this novelty today? What is one to understand when Francis Ponge writes: "One must work onward from the discovery made by Rimbaud and Lautréamont of the necessity of a new rhetoric"? If we can no longer persuade the table to be a table except in the very act of its disappearing, if words continue to evoke what we are losing hold of, if, as Roland Barthes says, "Language has become simultaneously a problem and a model," what can our speech resemble in this distribution of meaning among signs, in this abrupt multiplicity of meaning which is made up of nothing but questions? Doesn't everything point to the fact that man is today facing for the first time something which is no longer the vocabulary of the identity of appearances (the vocabulary as catalogue), the dogmatic grammar of the unity of a meaning, but, at the heart of a language which is inexhaustible and which cannot be resolved, multiplicity where the image of meaning occurs? An image which cannot be pinned down and which language does not exhaust. What does this mean? No doubt nothing more than that we must accept the consequences of Jean Paulhan's statement in *Clefs pour la poésie*: "The elements of mystery are those of any expression: sign and meaning" . . . and that this mystery is perhaps not so mysterious since not only does it understand us but we understand it. These consequences (the thought of everything that makes a sign in meaning) are those of a new rhetoric or of new rhetorics which will allow us to write everything that we write—that is, to perceive and to live everything that we live. How can we develop this into a discursive language? An anecdote quoted by Jakobson may provide an answer: "In Africa a missionary criticized his faithful for not wearing clothes. And you, replied the natives, pointing to his face, aren't you naked somewhere? Of course, said the missionary, but that is my face! Well, they answered, with us the face is everywhere." How can we write everything we write? First of all, perhaps, by not following the example of the missionary who clothed his nakedness with the word "face." Perhaps by consenting to see that words don't clothe it, but that they thrust into the world the image we have of our nakedness, and they will not fail someday to transport us to some Africa where the face is worn everywhere, since the body (and, like the body, the word) is not clothed . . . Where, at the center of the multiplicity of appearances, the familiar solidity of meaning, undergone today but not experienced, will speak (where what today appears as madness, derangement, will reveal itself as liberty). One can think, or hope, that today for the first time works tend more and more to claim this multiplicity and to comprehend it—that is, to think it. Today for the first time the works which claim this meaning try to think its multiplicity.

One may illustrate this by walking. When we walk in the street, what presents itself to us, the multiplicity of signs which offer themselves to us (the car sign, the black sign, the black-car sign, the four-door sign, the black four-door-car sign, the yellow sign, the wheel sign, the black four-door-car-with-yellow-wheels sign, etc.) and among which we move, ourselves a sign, is practically infinite. And what brings it about that we are walking in the street is not the single vision of each sign considered separately, or in a discursive mode, what brings it about that we are walking in the street is the fact that we are living what we see . . . that we are thrusting ourselves forward with each sign, that we are compromising ourselves in a meaning for which walking, the fact of walking, is itself only a sign. When we walk, or, to drop the metaphor, when we live, the world is not a spectacle, it is a meaning, the meaning which we compromise, in which we are compromised and of course overwhelmed . . . If we agree on that, we may then ask ourselves what happens when, as with the majority of works with which we are familiar and which are proposed to us as models, the world is offered as a spectacle, as a well-known reality which unrolls before our eyes (or as a mysterious reality but mysterious with relation to a well-known reality) . . . What then is given to us to experience in that *fiction* which *truth*, as we all know, is stranger than? What is then given to us to experience is, as a certain school of journalism says, *real-life experiences*; the fixed image of a reality which would be outside us and which we are asked to approve . . . the image of a reality which we can very easily understand and refuse. It is the same with all conventional literature, with any conventional work of art, whether it be artificial or, to use a once-fashionable word, committed. Why are "committed" works, even those of talented artists, ineffectual? Simply because in these works *real-life experiences* refer back to a thought which must be recognizable, which each of us must be able to adapt for himself . . . and that this recognition instead of committing and compromising within meaning liberates a meaning (that of experience) which is then lost in the continually rebegun reality which meaning gives to be experienced. That is, because they are not "to be experienced" but are rather "experienced," these experiences distract us much more than they instruct. As with emotions, as with tears, as with all thought of a reality which offers itself as already experienced, they erase what they teach. Artaud sums this up admirably when he speaks of "that faculty we have of deducing thoughts from our acts rather than identifying our acts without our thoughts."

The newness on which I have here attempted to cast some light forces us in fact to completely reconsider the notion of a work. The work as we know it often presents itself as the final outcome of the thought of our civilization and claims to cover over all those that preceded it (Mallarmé as well as Joyce) . . . On the contrary, the newness which preoccupies us places the work in interdependence, or, as Michel Foucault says, in a network, with all works of the past and future . . . A network into which history falls and disappears. "Committed" only in the sense that it is compromising, it finds its justification only in writing . . . not the image of a thought-up experience, but the thought of the image of meaning . . . considering, of course, that this meaning whose image is thought can only be compromised and compromising, that it cannot be discovered without immersing oneself in a thinking experience, without thought's being able to create itself in its image, continually duplicating it, as it were. Now the question is important enough to be dwelt on: This meaning can in no way have what we call a precedent, a duplicate: It is what is being made, it ceases to be what is made. To be more precise we should say that the work as image of meaning offers itself as the thought of the work as image of meaning.

To return to a previous point, my reading of the signs I perceive (walking in the street, for example) is viable only if I don't exhaust it, if I don't reduce these signs, if I take them with those I don't perceive. Consequently, if I want the work I am creating to appear to the reader as *to be lived* and not as *lived*, this work will have to present the same margin of ambiguity with which I was able to perceive and read it myself . . . This supposes of course that there are only two kinds of perception: that of reading and that of writing; it presupposes a reader for every writer, a writer for every reader. To develop this point: When we are about to be faced with a given work, the ambiguity of the meaning of the reading to be proposed to us, the choice of a certain number of meanings left at our disposal (either by the juxtaposition of words seemingly foreign to one another, or by a typographical layout allowing the text to be read vertically)—this choice of one reading among others, the attention it requires and the subjectivities it brings into play, will make of us no more the absentminded and drowsy author who lulls his intellectual comfort with the droning of a fable, but the author committed to the core of a revealing reality wherein choice supposes exclusions which reveal and compromise as much as the choice.

When I raised a little while ago the question of the myth of committed literature, I wanted not only to arouse its partisans and to contrast two literary genres, but to accentuate one of the aspects of this new notion of a work which is especially close to me. It is in fact impossible to separate the writing which tries today to illuminate this fundamental experience from that crucial commitment within meaning . . . toward which we are drawn by the works which place writers and readers on the same footing and which, showing that liberty consists in knowing that we choose our derangements, introduce a thought which for each sign evokes the totality of the languages with which we act on language. To commit the world (reading) to this reality (writing) is to understand that one does not cure the illness by striving to make its symptoms disappear (whether this method of striving to make the symptoms of noncommunication disappear be classical or avant-garde: whether it take the form of psychological conventions, the convention of serial music, or the farce of Lettrism). To understand what speaking means, and that misunderstandings involve what joins as much as what separates, that noncommunication remains alive at the heart of the message, that it is its dynamics; to refuse the set of rules agreed on . . . is to be what is written (what is read), the pole which furtively fixes the thought of an image already assailed by everything that can contest it and that justifies it, is to be this sign which thrusts mystery aside and speaks what is written; it is to be what is written, it is to be what happens.

Nothing more than this preoccupies me today. Is poetry involved? No doubt, if poetry is linked to what preoccupies us.

1. The third meeting organized by the review *Tel Quel* on June 11, 1964, in Paris, in the course of which this text was read aloud. (Trans.)
2. I attach the greatest importance to this formulation; it has in fact the advantage of illuminating the question without diminishing it. (Pleynet)

Art and Literature 4 (Spring 1965).

APPENDIX: CHRONOLOGY OF FIRST PUBLICATION DATES OF TRANSLATIONS

1955

Jacob, Max. "Literature and Poetry." *Le Cornet à dés. Semi-Colon* 1, no. 1 (ca. 1955).

1956

Unpublished selections from Fulbright Project:

Blanchard, Maurice. "The cloud distributes its rain impartially . . ."

Char, René. "Play and Sleep," "The Lords of Maussane," "Forehead of the Rose," and "The Room in Space."

Daumal, René. "Always in Vain."

Éluard, Paul. "The Evil," "Universe–Solitude," "The Covered Forehead," and "The Broken Bridge."

Follain, Jean. "The Accidents," "The Handyman's Indifference," "Metaphysics," and "The Portraits."

Ganzo, Robert. "Caught in the high branches . . ."

Lubin, Armen. "Temporary Lodgings."

Supervielle, Jules. "47, Boulevard Lannes," "To Lautréamont," "The Lane," "Beautiful monster of the night . . . ," and "In the Forgetfulness of My Body."

1960

Reverdy, Pierre. "The Route" and "Surprise." In "A Note on Pierre Reverdy," by John Ashbery. *Evergreen Review* 4, no. 11 (January/February 1960).

———. "That Memory," "Clear Winter," "A Lot of People," "Endless Journeys," "Love Again," and "The Invasion." *Evergreen Review* 4, no. 11 (January/February 1960).

1961

Breton, André, and Paul Éluard. "Intra-Uterine Life," "An Attempt to Stimulate the Delirium of Interpretation," "There Is Nothing Incomprehensible," and "The Original Judgment." From *L'Immaculée Conception. Locus Solus* 2 (1961).

Char, René, and Paul Éluard. "New" and "Landings." *Locus Solus* 2 (1961).

Pleynet, Marcelin. "of coal," "the new republic," and "Black." *Locus Solus* 3–4 (1961).

Roche, Denis. "As a matter of fact . . . ," "Tears allowing one to think that there are . . . ," and "The sensory organs watered . . ." *Locus Solus* 3–4 (1961).

1962

Ashbery, John. Preface to "Un Inédit de Raymond Roussel." *L'Arc* 19 (Summer 1962). French text of "In Havana." This preface was translated from Ashbery's English to French by Michel Thurlotte. See 1987 entry for Ashbery's translation of this preface back into English as "Introduction to 'In Havana' by John Ashbery" to accompany his first translation of Roussel's "À la Havane" in *Atlas Anthology* 4 (1987).

Dupin, Jacques. "Texts for an Approach." *Alberto Giacometti*. Paris: Maeght Éditeur, 1962.

Roussel, Raymond. Chapter 1 from *Impressions of Africa*. *Portfolio and ARTnews Annual* 6 (Autumn 1962).

1963

Michaux, Henri. Introduction to an Exhibition Catalogue. *Henri Michaux*. London: Robert Fraser Gallery, 1963.

1964

Bataille, Georges. "Eponine." *L'Abbé C*. *Art and Literature* 3 (Autumn–Winter 1964).

Hélion, Jean. "Figure." *Art and Literature* 1 (March 1964).

Jacob, Max. "The Spy's Memoirs," "Poem in a Style Which Is Not Mine," "Poem," "The Italian Straw Hat," "The Rue Ravignan," "Translated from the German or the Bosnian," "Untitled," "Literary Manners," "Time and Tide Wait for No Man," "The Aunt, the Tart, and the Hat," "Adventure Novel," "The Situation of Maidservants in Mexico," "Mutual Contempt of the Castes," "Another Point of Law," "The Beggar Woman of Naples," "In the Hill Country," "The Name," "The Centaur," "A Great Man Needs No Valet," "Errors of Pity," "They Won't Come Back Again," "Certain Disdains and Not the Others," "Life and Tide," "The Bibliophile," "The Poet's House," "Modern Family," "Maecenases," "Picture," and "Charlie Chaplin at the Seashore." Selections from *Le Cornet à dés*. *Art and Literature* 3 (Autumn–Winter 1964).

Leiris, Michel. "Conception and Reality in the Work of Raymond Roussel." *Art and Literature* 2 (Summer 1964).

1965

Artaud, Antonin. "Correspondence with Jacques Rivière." *Art and Literature* 6 (Autumn 1965).

de Chirico, Giorgio. Selection Two from *Hebdomeros*. *Art and Literature* 4 (Spring 1965).

Pleynet, Marcelin. "Reread What Is Written" and "The Image of Meaning." *Art and Literature* 4 (Spring 1965).

Redon, Odilon. From *To Oneself*. *Art and Literature* 6 (Autumn 1965).

Roche, Denis. "Eros Gone Wild." *Art and Literature* 4 (Spring 1965).

1966

Xenakis, Iannis. "The Cosmic City." *Art and Literature* 10 (Autumn 1966).

1967

Dalí, Salvador. "The Incendiary Firemen." *ARTnews Annual* 33 (October 1967).

de Chirico, Giorgio. "Courbet," "The Engineer's Son," and "The Survivor of Navarino." *Art and Literature* 11 (Winter 1967).

1969

Dalí, Salvador. "DeKooning's 300,000,000th Birthday." *ARTnews* 68, no. 2 (April 1969).

Cravan, Arthur. "Some Words." *World* 17 (November / December 1969).

1972

Cravan, Arthur. "Elephant Languor." *Juillard* 9 (Spring 1972).

1973

Chassignet, Jean-Baptiste. Six Sonnets from *Le Méspris de la vie et consolation contre la mort*. *The World* 27 (April 4, 1973).

Jarry, Alfred. "Fear Visits Love." *Fiction* 2, no. 1 (1973).

1975

de Chirico, Giorgio. "On Silence." *Big Sky* 9 (August 1975).

1984

Baudelaire, Charles. "Landscape." *A Wave*, by John Ashbery. New York: Viking, 1984.

1987

Ashbery, John. "Introduction to 'In Havana' by John Ashbery." First appeared in French, as a preface to "Un Inédit de Raymond Roussel," *L'Arc* 19 (Summer 1962), the first publication in French of Roussel's "In Havana." It was translated from Ashbery's English into French for *L'Arc* by Michel Thurlotte. Ashbery then translated it back into English as "Introduction to Raymond Roussel's 'In Havana,'" to accompany his translation of "À la Havane," in *Atlas Anthology* 4 (1987).

Roussel, Raymond. "In Havana." *Atlas Anthology* 4 (1987).

Roussel, Raymond. "An Unpublished Note." With Ashbery's notes. *Atlas Anthology* 4 (1987).

1990

Martory, Pierre. "Ganymede." *O-blēk* 8 (Fall 1990). "Prose des Buttes-Chaumont," "Return of the Birds," and "Toten Insel." *Every Question but One*. New York: Intuflo Editions, Groundwater Press, 1990.

1991

Martory, Pierre. "Black Diamond." *The New Yorker* (June 10, 1991).

Monnier, Pascalle. "In the spacious and flower-decked salons . . . ," "Luck is now sent to you . . . ," and "The Murphy Bed." In *Violence of the White Page: Contemporary French Poetry*. Edited by Stacy Doris, Phillip Foss, and Emmanuel Hocquard. Special issue of *Tyuonyi* 9/10 (1991).

Reverdy, Pierre. "Tip of the Wing," "Messenger of Tyranny," "Heavier," "That," ". . . Is Ajar," "The Crystal Cobblestone," and "From Another Shore." *Selected Poems*. Selected by Mary Ann Caws. Edited by Timothy Bent. Winston-Salem, N.C.: Wake Forest University Press, 1991.

Roussel, Raymond. *Documents to Serve as an Outline. Atlas Anthology* 7 (1991). With Ashbery's introduction and notes. First English publication of Documents 1–6.

1992

de Chirico, Giorgio. "That Evening Monsieur Dudron . . . ," "It Was Something Like . . . ," and "Monsieur Dudron's Adventure." *Hebdomeros: With Monsieur Dudron's Adventure and Other Metaphysical Writings*. Cambridge, Mass.: Exact Change, 1992.

1993

Martory, Pierre. "Red and Black Lake." *The World* 46 (February 1993). "From Here On . . . ," "Ma Chandelle est morte," "The Landscape Is Behind the Door," "The Landscapist," and "American Nocturne." *American Poetry Review* 22, no. 5 (September/October 1993).

1994

d'Aulnoy, Marie-Catherine. "The White Cat." In *Wonder Tales: Six French Stories of Enchantment*. Edited by Marina Warner. London: Chatto and Windus, 1994; New York: Farrar, Straus and Giroux, 1996; New York: Vintage, 1996.

Martory, Pierre. "At the Bottom of the Steps," "Under the Elm," "A Sunday in Montfort l'Amaury," "Blues," and "Recitative and Aria of the Tears." *The Landscape Is Behind the Door*. New York: Sheep Meadow Press, 1994.

Monnier, Pascalle. "Para siempre Teresita? Para Siempre Rodrigo" and "Locations." *Conjunctions* 23 (Fall 1994).

1995

Martory, Pierre. "Oh, Lake . . ." *Trafika* 5 (Autumn 1995).

2000

Martory, Pierre. "Bastille" and "Wine." *Poetry* 177, no. 1 (October–November 2000).

2002

Fauchereau, Serge. Selections from *Déplacements* (1996) and *Expositions et affabulations* (1992). "Displacements" and "Demonstrations and Fabulations," in *Complete Fiction*. Translated by John Ashbery and Ron Padgett. New York: Black Square Editions, 2002.

2003

Jamme, Franck André. *The Recitation of Forgetting*. New York: Black Square Editions, 2003.

2005

Mallarmé, Stéphane. Selections from *Recueil de "Nursery Rhymes."* *Conjunctions* 45 (Fall 2005).

2007

Reverdy, Pierre. *Haunted House*. Brooklyn: Black Square Editions and the Brooklyn Rail, 2007.

2008

Martory, Pierre. "Pygmalion." *Oh, lac / Oh, Lake*. With monotypes by Francis Wishart. Edited by Olivier Brossard and Eugene Richie. Hove, East Sussex, U.K.: Artery Editions, 2008.

2011

Rimbaud, Arthur. "After the Flood," "Sideshow," "Cities [I]," "Promontory," and "Genie." Selections from *Illuminations*. New York: Norton, 2011.

2013

Bonnefoy, Yves. From "Théâtre": "XIV I see Douve stretched out . . ." and "XVII The ravine penetrates the mouth now . . ." From "Real Location": "The Real Location of the Stag." *The Massachusetts Review* 54, no. 4 (Winter 2013).

Monnier, Pascalle. "I will look at . . ." *The Massachusetts Review* 54, no. 4 (Winter 2013).

Ponge, Francis. "The Insignificant" and "The Candle." *Jacket2* (Fall 2013). http://jacket2.org.

2014

Martory, Pierre. Introduction to *Washington Square* by Henry James. *PN Review* 40, no. 3 (January–February 2014).

UNPUBLISHED PROSE TRANSLATION

de Chirico, Giorgio. Selection One from *Hebdomeros*.

BIBLIOGRAPHY

Ashbery, John. "Appearing on Belgische Radio en Televisie, Brussels (date unknown)." Interview. *Pennsound*. http://writing.upenn.edu/pennsound/x/Ashbery.php.

———. *Collected Poems 1956–1987*. Edited by Mark Ford. New York: The Library of America, 2008.

———. "Contributor's Statement." Special issue, "Poetry and Translation: Interchanges." *Mantis* 2 (2001). 45.

———. "Growing Up Surreal." *ARTnews* 67, no. 3 (May 1968). 40–44, 65.

———. "John Ashbery." *Bookworm*. KCRW. Interview by Michael Silverblatt. May 21, 2009. www.kcrw.com/etc/programs/bw/bw090521john_ashbery.

———. "John Ashbery: An Interview." Interview by David Remnick. *Bennington Review* 8 (September 1980). 14–21.

———. "John Ashbery Interviewing Harry Mathews." *The Review of Contemporary Fiction* 7, no. 3 (Fall 1987). 36–48.

———. *Notes from the Air: Selected Later Poems*. New York: Ecco, 2007.

———. *Selected Prose*. Edited by Eugene Richie. Ann Arbor: University of Michigan Press, 2004; Manchester, U.K.: Carcanet Press, 2004.

———. *Where Shall I Wander*. New York: Ecco, 2005.

Ashbery, John, and Mark Ford. *John Ashbery in Conversation with Mark Ford*. London: Between the Lines, 2003.

Bennett, Guy, and Béatrice Mousli, eds. *Charting the Here of There: French and American Poetry in Translation in Literary Magazines, 1850–2002*. New York: New York Public Library/Granary Books, in association with the Book Office of the Cultural Service of the French Embassy in the United States, 2002.

Crase, Douglas. "The Prophetic Ashbery." *John Ashbery*. Modern Critical Views. Edited by Harold Bloom. New York: Chelsea House, 1985. 127–43.

Englert, John. "John Ashbery: Bard's 'Literalist of the Imagination.'" *The Bard Observer*, May 17, 1991. http://inside.bard.edu/campus/publications/archive/pdfs/OB91_05_17.pdf.

Flood, Alison. "Nobel Judge Attacks 'Ignorant' US Literature." *The Guardian*, October 1, 2008. www.guardian.co.uk/books/2008/oct/01/us.literature.insular.nobel.

Hickman, Ben. *John Ashbery and English Poetry*. Edinburgh: Edinburgh University Press, 2012. 27–53.

Kermani, David K. *John Ashbery: A Comprehensive Bibliography*. New York: Garland Publishing, 1976.

Lehman, David. *The Last Avant-Garde: The Making of the New York School of Poets*. New York: Doubleday, 1998.

Mathews, Harry. "Introduction to a Reading by John Ashbery and Pierre Martory." Dia Center for the Arts, New York. October 5, 1993. Unpublished typescript. Flow Chart Foundation, Hudson, N.Y.

Reverdy, Pierre. *Haunted House*. Translated by John Ashbery. Brooklyn, N.Y.: Black Square Editions and the Brooklyn Rail, 2007.

Roffman, Karin. "The Art of Self-Education in John Ashbery's Childhood Diaries." *Raritan: A Quarterly Review* 30, no. 4 (Spring 2011). 94–116.

Shapiro, David. *John Ashbery: An Introduction to the Poetry*. New York: Columbia University Press, 1979.

Sweet, David LeHardy. *Savage Sight/Constructed Noise: Poetic Adaptations of Painterly Techniques in the French and American Avant-Gardes*. North Carolina Studies in the Romance Languages and Literatures no. 276. Chapel Hill: University of North Carolina Press, 2003.

Towery, Micah. "Google Translates Poetry." *THEthe poetry* (blog). December 5, 2011. www.thethepoetry.com/2011/12/google-translates-poetry/.

Warner, Marina, ed. *Wonder Tales: Six French Stories of Enchantment*. Translated by Gilbert Adair, John Ashbery, Ranjit Bolt, A. S. Byatt, and Terence Cave. New York: Farrar, Straus and Giroux, 1996.

ACKNOWLEDGMENTS

As editors, we have received help in gathering and selecting the works in this book from many sources. Foremost, of course, are John Ashbery and David Kermani, whose invaluable *Comprehensive Bibliography* of works as early as 1943 and up to 1975 saved us years of searching through archives. Both of these dear friends read drafts of the introduction and provided us with insightful suggestions in our revisions. They guided and encouraged us as we worked on this book. The online Ashbery Resource Center of the Flow Chart Foundation, which they conceived of initially as an extension of Kermani's bibliography, is essential for any study of Ashbery's life and work.

Many other poets, writers, artists, and scholars in New York and in Paris have worked over this decade with Ashbery, Kermani, and us, often in various capacities at Flow Chart. We wish to thank all who gave time and energy to this project. Micaela Morrissette initially located in the Flow Chart Archives many of the texts that appear in this book. Olivier Brossard and Claire Guillot hosted us in France, and Olivier co-organized the Ashbery in Paris conference and helped us contact French poets whom Ashbery had translated. Olivier also co-edited the Artery edition of Martory's *Oh, lac / Oh, Lake*. Karin Roffman read a draft of the introduction and shared with us her detailed research into Ashbery's childhood. We are also grateful for help over the years from many of Ashbery's friends and assistants, especially Ava Lehrer, Marcella Durand, Adam Fitzgerald, Jonathan Boyd, Emily Skillings, and Timothy O'Connor.

Our research at the Bibliothèque Nationale in Paris was made sweeter by the hospitality of Denis Demonpion and Amy Roarke; the archives at Harvard's Houghton Library were graciously made available to us by

Leslie Morris. Librarians at the Bibliothèque Nationale were immensely cooperative, both with helping us to access the collections and with operating necessary machinery. The poet and publisher Stanley Moss was instrumental in bringing Pierre Martory's two poetry collections *The Landscape Is Behind the Door* and *The Landscapist*, with Ashbery's translations, to the wider public; John Yau and the editors at Black Square Press brought out not only a beautiful edition of Ashbery's translation of Reverdy's *Haunted House*, but also Serge Fauchereau's *Complete Fiction*, translated by both Ashbery and Ron Padgett; and Ashbery's translations of *The Recitation of Forgetting* by Franck André Jamme, as well as Jacques Dupin's essay on Giacometti. In Britain, Patricia Scanlon at Artery Press produced Ashbery's translation of Martory's *Oh, lac / Oh, Lake*, with monotypes by Francis Wishart. Anne Talvaz, poet and translator, found the Martory introduction to Henry James's *Washington Square* and assisted John with translation questions. The painter Trevor Winkfield located a Martory poem that appeared long ago in his journal *Juillard*. Robert Weil at Norton gave us Ashbery's version of Rimbaud's *Illuminations*; and all have generously shared selections from those publications for inclusion in this volume. George Silver, the brother of the photographer Walter Silver, gave us permission to print the photograph of young Ashbery in Paris that appears here.

Our colleagues at Pace University and the United States Merchant Marine Academy have also supported the long effort of editing this book: We have been helped immeasurably by support from both institutions for our project and by the librarians' assistance with interlibrary loans. Our gratitude goes especially to Thomas Breidenbach, Martha Driver, Laury Magnus, Josh Smith, Charles North, Steven Goldleaf, and Walter Raubichek, for their encouragement, advice, and friendship. Wai-Wan Lam worked tirelessly typing early drafts of texts from many pale and tiny-fonted copies.

Our work on the manuscript progressed significantly due to our participation in three important conferences over the last decade: the John Ashbery Festival coordinated by David Lehman at the New School for Social Research, New York, in April 2006; later that same April, the Juniper Festival's Ashbery celebration coordinated by Dara Wier, at the University of Massachusetts, Amherst; and "John Ashbery in Paris," an international conference coordinated by Olivier Brossard, Abigail Lang, Vincent Broqua, and Antoine Cazé, at the Université Paris 7 Diderot LARCA (Laboratoire de Recherche sur les Cultures Anglophones), during March 11–13, 2010 (for the conference blog, please see http://johnashberyinparis.blogspot.com/). We are most grateful for being invited to present our work in progress at these gatherings of poets and scholars, whose enthusiasm for John Ashbery's work was truly inspirational.

PERMISSIONS ACKNOWLEDGMENTS

Grateful acknowledgment is made for permission to reprint the following material:

Antonin Artaud, "Correspondence with Jacques Rivière," translated by John Ashbery. Original French from *Préambule. Correspondance avec Jacques Rivière. L'ombilic des limbes. Le Pèse-nerfs. L'art et la mort. Textes et poèmes inédits* in *Œuvres complètes*, Volume 1, Tenth Edition. Copyright © 1960. Reprinted by permission of Éditions Gallimard.

Georges Bataille, "Eponine," translated by John Ashbery. Original French from *L'Abbé C.*, in *Œuvres complètes*, Volume 3. Reprinted by permission of Les Éditions de Minuit S.A.

Giorgio de Chirico, "On Silence," "Courbet," "The Engineer's Son," "The Survivor of Navarino," Selections One and Two from *Hebdomeros*, "That Evening Monsieur Dudron . . . ," "It Was Something Like . . . ," and "Monsieur Dudron's Adventure," translated by John Ashbery. Translated and reprinted by permission of Fondazione Giorgio e Isa de Chirico.

Salvador Dalí, "The Incendiary Fireman," translated by John Ashbery, from *ARTnews Annual* 33 (October 1967) and "De Kooning's 300,000,000th Birthday," translated by John Ashbery, from *ARTnews* 68, no. 2 (April 1969). Both © Salvador Dalí, Fundació Gala–Salvador Dalí, Figueres, 2013.

Jacques Dupin, "Texts for an Approach" from *Giacometti: Three Essays*, translated by John Ashbery and Brian Evenson. Copyright © 2003 by John Ashbery and Brian Evenson. Reprinted with permission.

Jean Hélion, "Figure," translated by John Ashbery, from *Art and Literature* 1 (March 1964). Copyright © 2013 by Artists Rights Society (ARS), NY / ADAGP, Paris.

Michel Leiris, "Conception and Reality in the Work of Raymond Roussel," originally in Raymond Roussel and Michel Leiris, *Épaves, précédé de "Conception et réalité chez Raymond Roussel."* © 2004 Pauvert, département des éditions Fayard 1972, 2000.

Pierre Martory, "Introduction to *Washington Square* by Henry James," translated by John Ashbery. Reprinted by permission of Éditions Denoël.

Raymond Mason, "Where Have All the Eggplants Gone?," translated by John Ashbery, from *ARTnews* 70, no. 7 (1971). Copyright © 1971. Reprinted with permission.

Henri Michaux, "Introduction to an Exhibition Catalogue" (Robert Fraser Gallery, London, 1963), translated by John Ashbery. Original French from *Œuvres complètes*. Copyright © 1990. Reprinted by permission of Éditions Gallimard.

Marcelin Pleynet, "The Image of Meaning," translated by John Ashbery. Original French "L'image du sens" from *Tel Quel*, no. 18, été (Summer) 1964. Reprinted with the permission of the author.

Pierre Reverdy, *The Haunted House*, translated by John Ashbery (Brooklyn: Black Square Editions, 2007). Original French *Risques et périls* (1930) in *Œuvres complètes*, Volume I, edited by Étienne-Alain Hubert. Reprinted by permission of Flammarion, Paris.

Iannis Xenakis, "The Cosmic City," translated by John Ashbery. Original French from *Musique. Architecture*. Reprinted by permission of Editions Parenthèses.

BIOGRAPHIES OF TRANSLATOR AND EDITORS

John Ashbery was born in Rochester, New York, in 1927. He earned degrees from Harvard and Columbia, and went to France as a Fulbright Scholar in 1955, living there for much of the next decade. His many collections of poetry include *Quick Question* (2012); *Planisphere* (2009); and *Notes from the Air: Selected Later Poems* (2007), which was awarded the 2008 International Griffin Poetry Prize. *Self-Portrait in a Convex Mirror* (1975) won the three major American prizes—the Pulitzer, the National Book Award, and the National Book Critics Circle Award—and an early book, *Some Trees* (1956), was selected by W. H. Auden for the Yale Younger Poets Series. The Library of America published the first volume of his collected poems in 2008. Active in various areas of the arts throughout his career, he has served as executive editor of *ARTnews* and as art critic for *New York* magazine and *Newsweek*; he exhibits his collages at the Tibor de Nagy Gallery (New York). He taught for many years at Brooklyn College (CUNY) and Bard College, and in 1989–90 delivered the Charles Eliot Norton lectures at Harvard. He is a member of the American Academy of Arts and Letters (receiving its Gold Medal for Poetry in 1997) and the American Academy of Arts and Sciences, and was a chancellor of the Academy of American Poets from 1988 to 1999. The winner of many prizes and awards, both nationally and internationally, he was awarded two Guggenheim Fellowships and was a MacArthur Fellow from 1985 to 1990; most recently, he received the Medal for Distinguished Contribution to American Letters from the National Book Foundation (2011) and a National Humanities Medal, presented by President Barack Obama at the White House (2012). His work has been translated into more than twenty-five languages. He lives in New York. Additional information is available in the "About John Ashbery" section of the Ashbery Resource Center's website, a project of The Flow Chart Foundation, www.flowchartfoundation.org/arc.

Rosanne Wasserman's poetry books include *Apple Perfume* (1989), *The Lacemakers* (1992), *No Archive on Earth* (1995), and *Other Selves* (1999), as well as *Place du Carousel* (2001) and *Psyche and Amor* (2009), collaborations with Eugene Richie. Both John Ashbery and A. R. Ammons have chosen her work for the series *Best American Poetry*. She has written many articles on New York School poets and other writers, including an interview with Pierre Martory and a memoir of Ruth Stone in *American Poetry Review*, and a feature on Ashbery's home in Hudson, New York, for *Rain Taxi*'s online *A Dream of This Room: A Created Spaces Portfolio of Works on John Ashbery's Textual and Domestic Environments*, edited by Micaela Morrissette (2008). Also with Richie, she edited two collections of Ashbery's translations of Martory's poems: *Every Question but One* (1990) and *The Landscapist: Selected Poems* (2008). Together, they run the Groundwater Press, whose latest publications are Gerrit Henry's posthumous poetry collection, *The Time of the Night* (2011), and Tom Breidenbach's *The Wicked Child / IX XI* (2013). She studied with Stone at Indiana University, and with David Ignatow at Columbia University's School of the Arts. As an editor at the Metropolitan Museum of Art, she helped create many books and exhibition catalogues, including *Metropolitan Cats* and Eliot Porter's *Intimate Landscapes*. Her doctorate in English is from the CUNY Graduate Center, where she also studied Greek. She teaches at the United States Merchant Marine Academy, Kings Point, New York.

EUGENE RICHIE's collections of poems include *Moiré* (1989) and *Island Light* (1998), as well as *Place du Carousel* (2001) and *Psyche and Amor* (2009) with Rosanne Wasserman. With Edith Grossman, he cotranslated Jaime Manrique's *Scarecrow* (1990) and *My Night with Federico García Lorca* (1996, 1997, 2003). He has edited John Ashbery's *Selected Prose* and three collections of Ashbery's translations of Pierre Martory's poems: *Every Question but One* (1990) and *The Landscapist: Selected Poems* (2008), with Wasserman; and *Oh, lac / Oh, Lake* (2008), with Olivier Brossard. He has published articles on New York School poets and co-edited, with F. B. Claire and Stephen Sartarelli, two anthologies of poetry and fiction. He studied at Stanford University with Donald Davie and Al Young, and with Manuel Puig and Mark Strand at Columbia University. He has studied the craft of translation with Gregory Rabassa and Suzanne Jill Levine. At New York University, he earned an MA and a PhD in comparative literature. He is Director of Creative Writing in the Pace University English Department in New York City.